BERKLEE PRESS

UPDATED FOR 2005

FINALE®

An Easy Guide to Music Notation
Second Edition

Thomas E. Rudolph and Vincent A. Leonard, Jr.

Edited by Jonathan Feist

Berklee Media

Vice President: Dave Kusek
Dean of Continuing Education: Debbie Cavalier
Director of Business Affairs: Robert Green
Associate Director of Technology: Mike Serio
Marketing Manager, Berkleemusic: Barry Kelly
Senior Graphic Designer: Robert Heath

Berklee Press

Senior Writer/Editor: Jonathan Feist
Production Manager: Shawn Girsberger
Marketing Manager, Berklee Press: Jennifer D'Angora

Printed in the United States of America by Bradford & Bigelow

12 11 10 09 08 07 06 05   6 5 4 3 2 1

Library of Congress Cataloging-in-Publication Data
Rudolph, Thomas E.
  Finale : an easy guide to music notation / by Thomas E. Rudolph and Vincent A. Leonard, Jr.– 2nd ed.
     p. cm.
  Includes index.
  ISBN 0-87639-068-8
  1. Finale (Computer file) 2. Musical notation–Data processing. I. Leonard, Vincent A. II. Title.

MT39.R83 2005
780'.1'48–dc22

2005005534

1140 Boylston Street
Boston, MA 02215-3693 USA
(617) 747-2146
Visit Berklee Press Online at
www.berkleepress.com

DISTRIBUTED BY

HAL•LEONARD®
CORPORATION
7777 W. BLUEMOUND RD. P.O. BOX 13819
MILWAUKEE, WISCONSIN 53213

Visit Hal Leonard Online at
www.halleonard.com

Dedicated in loving memory of
Virginia Unsinn Rudolph
and
Vincent A. Leonard Sr.

Contents

Acknowledgments vi

Introduction to the Second Edition vii

Section I   Single-Staff Parts 1

Chapter 1   Getting Started 3

Chapter 2   Keyboard Note Entry ("Aura Lee") 17

Chapter 3   Chords ("Amazing Grace") 31

Chapter 4   MIDI Entry, Chords, and Lyrics ("Three Blind Mice") 47

Chapter 5   Articulations and Metatools ("Trumpet Voluntary") 63

Chapter 6   HyperScribe: Real-Time Note Entry ("America") 85

Section II   Grand-Staff and Small-Ensemble Scores 101

Chapter 7   Piano Piece Using HyperScribe ("Musette") 103

Chapter 8   Small Arrangements: Saxophone Quartet ("The Entertainer") 121

Chapter 9   Vocal Score with Percussion ("Simple Gifts") 165

Chapter 10   The Art of the Piano Part (Bach's "Fugue in G Minor") 189

Chapter 11   Jazz Notation: Leadsheets and Guitar Tab ("Blues for a Hiccup") ... 225

Section III   Large-Ensemble Scores 265

Chapter 12   Big-Band Score ("Blues for a Hiccup") 267

Chapter 13   Orchestral Excerpt (*Petrushka*) 291

Section IV   Getting the Most out of Finale 339

Chapter 14   Importing and Exporting 341

Chapter 15   Music Education Applications 351

Chapter 16   Finale Support 359

Appendix   The Finale Book Web Site: File Index 363

About the Authors 367

Index 368

Acknowledgments

The authors, Tom Rudolph and Vince Leonard, would like to thank the following individuals for their help and assistance with this publication:

The editor for the second edition, Jonathan Feist. The editor and beta testers from the first edition, including Lorry Lutter (first edition editor and beta tester), Larry Kerchner, Helen Nick, Ed Schweibacher, and the teachers who attended courses over the past summers with Tom and Vince at Villanova University and Central Connecticut State University.

The authors would also like to thank Tom Johnson, Scott Yoho, Tom Carruth, Debbie Cavalier, David Mash, Jennifer D'Angora, Tiiu Lutter, and Shawn Girsberger for their help and assistance.

Introduction to the Second Edition

This book is not an attempt to replace the *Finale User Manual* that comes with Finale. Rather, it is meant to be a resource and a method book for how to learn and how to use Finale. We have addressed most of the common and not-so-common musical needs of most educators, composers, and arrangers. It is based on Finale 2005.

This text is designed for both the novice and experienced Finale user. Section I, "Getting Started," addresses single-line parts. Section II addresses smaller multiple-part scores and part extraction. Section III addresses larger ensemble scores. Section IV features Finale support and educational applications.

If you are a beginner at using Finale, we suggest you start with chapter 1 and proceed sequentially through the text. If you are already using Finale, peruse the chapters, and look for musical examples that contain information you would like to review. You can skip around to specific topics as needed.

This book assumes that you have a basic knowledge of music theory and are familiar with using the computer's mouse.

Compatibility with Mac OS and Windows

This book is compatible with Finale versions for both Mac OS and Windows. Throughout the book, there are references to both Mac and Windows versions of Finale. Both Mac and Windows screen shots are used and included. When both Mac and Windows screens are used simultaneously, the Mac version is on the left and Windows version on the right.

Finale Support Files and Using the Book with Courses

This book has a companion Web site at www.finalebook.com. This site includes files and templates that can be used with this book. These files can be downloaded and used with Macintosh or Windows versions of Finale.

The files on the Web site correlate to each chapter. For most chapters, there are several versions of each file. Instructors using this book with a course, and experienced Finale users, may want to use these files, from time to time. For example, the chapters that include lyrics have versions of each file, with and without the lyrics. Whenever there is a relevant file on the Web site, we have an icon:

FileReference.mus

The appendix lists the files included on this Web site.

The Goal of Notation Software

Before you read on, be sure you are attempting to learn Finale for the right reasons. Many people struggled to learn Finale, only to realize that they really needed a different type of software. Finale is a notation program or a music-scoring program. There are other programs designed to record music (sequencers), create accompaniment parts, or to learn about music. Finale is a program designed with one specific goal: to produce printed notation.

A music notation program such as Finale is to music what a word processor is to text. Be sure that your goals match the design of the program: to print out scores and parts.

Why Finale?

Finale is one of the most powerful and most popular music notation software programs. Because of its complex capabilities, it can be difficult to master. Finale is designed for the person who wants to have a powerful tool for printing out music notation. With patience and practice, Finale will enable you to create and print music faster and more legibly.

The Latest Version

Co-author Vince Leonard started with Finale version 1.0! With every upgrade, the program has improved and become more powerful. For this reason, it is important to upgrade or purchase the latest version of Finale. If you own an earlier version of Finale, you should upgrade before beginning to use this book. Upgrades are cheaper than buying the program. Check the www.finalemusic.com Web site for the latest versions of the program.

Purchasing and Registering Your Software

You can purchase Finale directly from MakeMusic or from just about any music dealer or software vendor. If you are an educator, or work for a nonprofit institution such as a religious institution, MakeMusic offers a special discount. Contact MakeMusic for details.

MakeMusic usually announces an update every year for Finale. In order for you to be on the mailing list, you must register your software. Also, even with this book, you will have questions and problems that need to be answered. Once you are a registered user, you will be able to contact MakeMusic with your questions. It is important to write down your Finale key number that is printed on the back of the installation manual. MakeMusic will request this number when you call or write for support.

We welcome your feedback. Please feel free to contact Berklee Press (info@berkleepress. com) or us with your comments: Tom Rudolph (terudolph@aol.com) and Vince Leonard (VincentL10@comcast.net).

SECTION I
Single-Staff Parts

1

Getting Started

A notation program such as Finale can be an extremely timesaving tool, after you learn to use the program properly. Be gentle and kind to yourself! It will take time to become comfortable using this program.

Also, you will need to be open to new ideas and suggestions for entering music notation, especially if you have only prepared handwritten manuscripts. Using Finale, we will give you specific recommendations for how and when to enter the notes and other markings in your score. These recommendations have come after years of experimentation. This is not to say that our way is the only way. Just like any method book for learning a musical instrument, this book contains our best recommendations for how to use the program. Hopefully, by entering the examples that follow, you will be able to learn to use Finale to suit your own needs.

Keyboard Terminology

Before you begin using this book, familiarize yourself with the key commands that are used in Finale. There is a brief explanation in the *Finale Installation & Tutorials* guide, and you should take a few moments to familiarize yourself with these commands.

Mac OS	Windows
• The Command key is next to the Space Bar and looks like ⌘. • ⌘-A (or any letter): Hold the ⌘ key down, and press the letter A. • ⌘-click: Hold the ⌘ key, and click the mouse button. • Shift-click: Hold the Shift key, and click the mouse. • Option-Shift-click: Hold the Option and Shift keys, and click the mouse. • Double-click/drag: Click the mouse button twice, but hold the mouse down on the second click. • Control-click (CTRL-click): Hold down the Control key, and click the mouse. This can also be accomplished with a 2-button mouse available for Macintosh computers.	• Control-A (CTRL-A): Hold the Control key down, and press the letter A. • Control-click: Hold the Control key, and click the mouse. • Shift-click: Hold the Shift key, and click the mouse. • Alt-Shift-click: Hold the Alt key and shift key and click the mouse. • Right-click: Click the right mouse button. • Click: Click the left mouse button.

4

 If you are a Mac user, you are not used to a 2-button mouse. However, I have found that a 2-button mouse on a Mac saves me time using Finale. You can purchase a 2-button mouse from any Macintosh store or dealer, and I think you will be glad you did.

Selecting Menus and Submenus

Menus, along the top of the Finale window, are indicated with the menu name in bold, and each submenu or choice indicated with a > . Throughout this book you will see references such as: "**File** > New > Default Document." This means to go to the File menu, select the New submenu, and release the mouse on the menu choice "Default Document."

Installing Finale

The first step is to install Finale. Follow the instructions in the installation manual. Be sure to review the "Before You Begin" chapter of the *Finale Installation & Tutorials* manual. The purpose of this chapter is to familiarize you with the look of Finale and how to navigate around a piece of music. We won't be entering any notation in this chapter, just viewing Finale from different perspectives. If you are already familiar with Finale, move on to chapter 2.

Start Your Engines

The next step is to Launch Finale.

Mac OS	Windows
If you put an icon on the Dock when you installed Finale, simply click on the Dock's Finale 2005 icon. If not, open the Finale folder on the hard drive, and double-click on the Finale icon.	From the Start menu, select the Finale 2005 folder and then Finale 2005.

Finale Launch Window

In Finale 2005, the Launch Window was introduced. The Launch Window appears when you open Finale for the first time. If you already have Finale open, you can access the Launch Window from the File menu. We will start our tour of Finale using the Default Document.

• Click the Default Document option in the Launch Window.

(If you are using a Finale version prior to 2005, close the Wizard, and from the File menu, choose New and then Default Document. Note that many of the techniques described in this book are new in Finale 2005.)

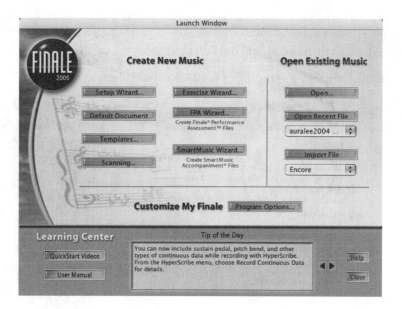

The Finale Main Tool Palette

The first item to become familiar with in Finale is the Main Tool Palette. Some software programs can place all of their commands within the menus at the top of the screen. However, since Finale has so many commands, the screen would have to be twice as large to include all of the menus. To solve this problem, Finale uses several tool palettes. Think of each tool as a subset of Finale. In order to access the specific area of Finale, you must first select the proper tool. This takes some getting used to, especially if you haven't worked with a program that uses this concept.

By default, Finale displays the Main Tool Palette whenever any document is opened.

- Macintosh tools are displayed on the top left of the screen, and the palette is movable.
- In Windows, tools are in straight lines at the top of the screen.

There are several menus in Finale that always display, no matter what tool you have selected. These include the File, Edit, View, Options, MIDI, Tools, Window, Plug-ins 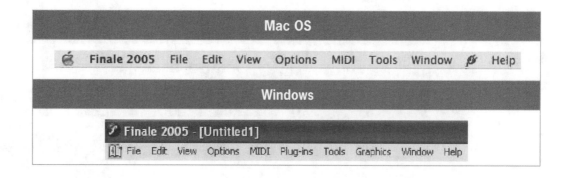, and Help menus.

You may want to hide the Main Tool Palette so you can use 100% of the screen to view the page layout. To turn the Main Tool Palette display on or off:

• From the Window menu, select the Main Tool Palette.

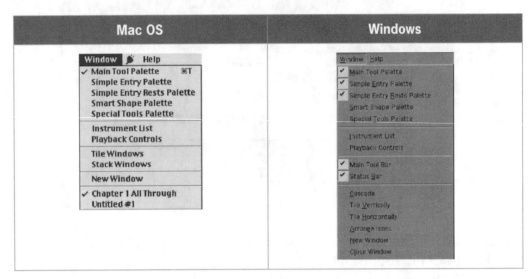

With any menu item, a check mark indicates that the item is selected. The check boxes work like on-off switches. So, if a tool palette is missing, you can usually get it back by selecting its name in the Window menu.

The Tools

Be certain that the Main Tool Palette is displayed on the screen. There are quite a few tools to choose from on this palette. This is the most difficult part of Finale to learn. It will take some time to become familiar with all of the tools. Keep in mind that you don't have to use all of the Finale tools, or even know what they do, until you need them. Some are highly specialized.

To explore how Finale tools function:

• Click on the Staff Tool .

Notice that when you select the Staff tool, a new menu appears in the Menu Bar: the Staff menu. Many tools have unique menus of options that only appear when the tool is selected.

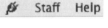

Finale displays a Message Bar with the name and description of the selected tool. This Message Bar is located at the top of the window in Mac OS and the bottom of the window in Windows.

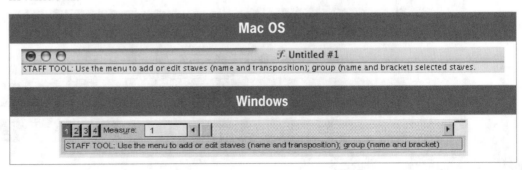

Try selecting various tools. As you select them, read their names in the Message Bar, and notice that new menus appear in the Menu Bar. Some tools do not have a corresponding menu.

Don't try to memorize the names of the tools. The only objective at this point is to learn how to select a tool and to see its name. Think of tools as subsets of Finale functions. There are so many commands that they can't all fit on the screen at the same time. As you are perusing the tools, avoid the temptation to experiment with them, for now. We'll cover most of them in the chapters that follow.

The Selection Tool

If you have used an older version of Finale, the Selection tool is a new addition that can be very helpful. For example, it can be used to drag text and edit information without requiring you to click on a tool.

1. Choose the Selection tool ⊕, or press the ESC (escape) key.
2. Move the cursor to the top of the page, and click and hold the mouse button on the word "[Title]."
3. Drag the text to a new location.

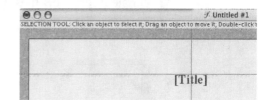

The Selection tool can also be used to edit text and other markings on the page.

1. With the Selection tool selected (see step 1 above), double-click on an object such as the treble clef symbol.
2. Choose a new clef from the Change Clef dialog box.

Contextual Menus (Right-click and Control-click)

Another way to edit and change items is using contextual menus.

Mac OS	Windows
(Tradional 1-button mouse only)	**(And Macs with a 2-button mouse)**
1. Press ESC to choose the Selection tool ⊕.	1. Press ESC to choose the Selection tool .
2. Control-click on an object, such as the clef or a text element, to display the contextual menus. Remember to press ESC each time before choosing a contextual menu.	2. Right-click on an object, such as the time signature, clef, or text to display the contextual menus.

The View Menu

Finale can display music in two ways: Scroll View and Page View. Scroll View is a linear view. Think of it as an endless staff to the right. This is the view recommended for entering music into Finale. Page View is often used for preparing the page layout before printing. One way to select or change the view for a piece is via the View menu.

- From the View menu, select Page View.

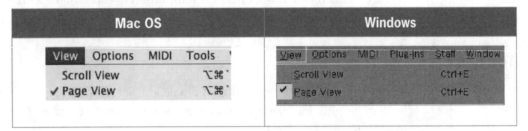

Finale opens new files in Page View. Page View displays documents as they would be printed.

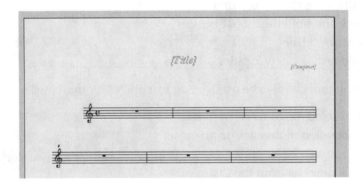

I prefer to enter notation and staff markings in Scroll View—the endless staff. To change from Page View to Scroll View:

- From the View menu, select Scroll View.

Shortcut Commands

One way to increase your notation entry speed is to use Finale's built-in shortcut commands. It is possible to switch back and forth between Scroll View (designed for the entry of notes and other markings) and Page View (where the page layout and formatting are done). These shortcut commands require that you hold down one or two keys and then press another. Specific shortcuts are listed in the menus, to the right of each menu option.

For example, look in the View menu. You will notice the shortcut commands to switch back and forth between Scroll View and Page View. These key combinations are different for Mac and Windows.

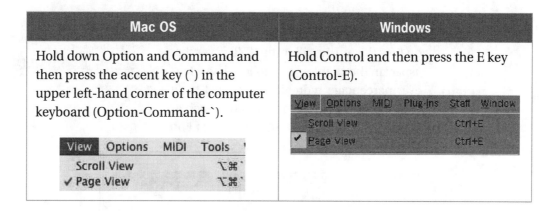

Mac OS	Windows
Hold down Option and Command and then press the accent key (`) in the upper left-hand corner of the computer keyboard (Option-Command-`).	Hold Control and then press the E key (Control-E).

Try it now. Finale will switch between Scroll View and Page View. Again, it is not necessary to memorize all of the shortcut commands. You will remember the ones you use most frequently and apply them to save time.

Scaling the View Percentage

There are several helpful options available in the View menu. One that you will use frequently is the View command. This allows Finale to change the view percentage of the music on screen. This is very helpful when you want to preview the entire screen before printing. To use this command:

- Switch to Page View (from the View menu, select Page View, or use the shortcut command).

The example that follows shows the default document in Page View at 100%. Since monitors are of different sizes (15-inch, 17-inch, 19-inch, and so forth), not all of the score will be visible at all view percentages.

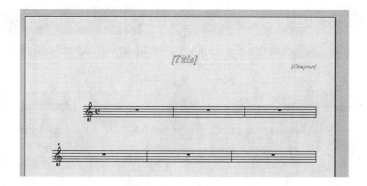

To view the score at a smaller size, in this case 50% reduced:

- From the View menu, select Scale View to 50%.

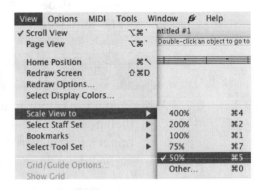

The score will appear on the screen reduced to 50% of its original size. This has no effect on how the music will print. We'll cover that aspect in the chapters that follow. Use whatever percentage reduction you need to fit your monitor. With some monitors, such as 17-inch and larger, the entire page can fit on the screen with little or no reduction.

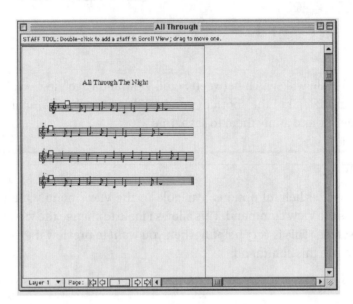

Scaling the view is one of the shortcut commands that I frequently use. To go back to 100%, use the following shortcut commands:

Mac OS	Windows
Hold down ⌘ and press the number 1.	Hold down Control and press the number 1.

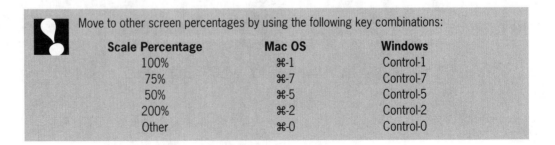

Move to other screen percentages by using the following key combinations:

Scale Percentage	Mac OS	Windows
100%	⌘-1	Control-1
75%	⌘-7	Control-7
50%	⌘-5	Control-5
200%	⌘-2	Control-2
Other	⌘-0	Control-0

When the "Other" option is selected from the Scale View submenu, any percentage increase or decrease can be entered.

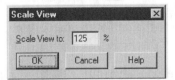

Centering Music for Viewing

Oftentimes, the page will not be centered on the screen. Finale offers two ways to center the music for viewing on the page.

- From the View menu, select Scale View at 50% (or use the shortcut command, above).
- Use the vertical and horizontal scroll bars to center the music.

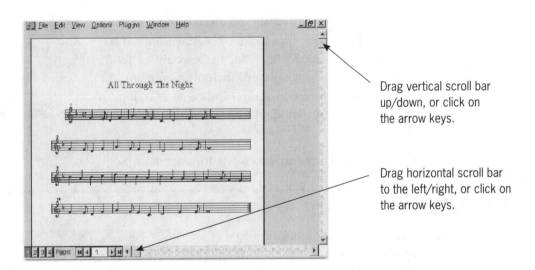

Drag vertical scroll bar up/down, or click on the arrow keys.

Drag horizontal scroll bar to the left/right, or click on the arrow keys.

Using the scroll bars is a two-step process. A quicker way to center music on the page for viewing is by using the Hand Grabber tool. The Hand Grabber tool is the quickest way to move notation on the screen for viewing.

- Choose the Hand Grabber tool .
- Click the mouse anywhere on the screen, and then drag so all of the music is visible.

Moving Around the Score in Scroll View

In Scroll View, the horizontal control at the bottom of the window can be used to skip to any position in the piece.

1. From the View menu, choose Scroll View (or use the shortcut command).
2. Use the horizontal scroll bar to move to different positions in the piece.

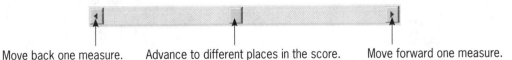

Move back one measure.   Advance to different places in the score.   Move forward one measure.

It is possible to jump to a specific measure.

3. Double-click in the Measure box at the bottom of the screen.

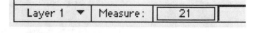

4. Type in a measure number. To jump to the end of the piece, type in the number "21," and press Return/Enter.

To return to the first measure of the piece, you have four options:

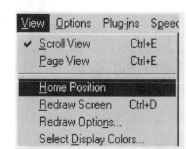

1. Enter the number one in the Measure box, and press Return/Enter.
2. Drag the horizontal scroll bar to the far left.
3. From the View menu, choose Home Position.
4. Press the Home key on the computer keyboard.

Redrawing the Screen

Every once in a while, Finale will display a note or character on the screen that looks strange. Perhaps it has partially disappeared. This is due to the complex nature of all that must be displayed, including notes on the staff, titles, lyrics, articulations, and other markings. If the screen display ever looks a bit strange, try redrawing the screen.

*   From the View menu, choose Redraw Screen.

Automatic Spacing

Finale will automatically space the music, lyrics, and other markings, so long as the Automatic Music Spacing option is activated in the Edit menu. This is checked when a new file is created in Finale.

The Options Menu

Most of the selections in the Options menu will be discussed in the chapters that follow.

The MIDI Menu

If you are using a MIDI keyboard, be sure to check the setup before continuing to the following chapters. Refer to the *Finale Installation & Tutorials* manual for details.

The Plug-ins Menu

The plug-ins feature adds more power and options to Finale. Plug-ins will be covered in the chapters that follow. In the Mac OS version, the menu icon looks like a plug 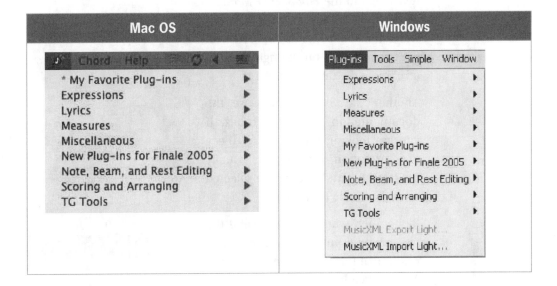.

The Tools Menu

There are two direct ways to select a tool in Finale: click on the tool icon, or choose it from the Tools menu. If you find it difficult remembering the icons, use the Tools menu.

The Finale Help Menu (User Manual)

Early versions of Finale (older than Finale 97) included a box full of manuals. In 1997, the printed documentation was converted into a menu-driven format from within Finale. Now, when you install Finale, the user manual also installs and can be accessed from the Help menu.

When you install Finale, another program called Acrobat Reader is installed. This program displays the pages contained in the user manual. When you choose an option from the Finale Help menu, Acrobat Reader launches, and you are able to select areas from the *Finale User Manual*. Acrobat Reader is a free program distributed by Adobe Systems, Inc. The Finale manual is extensive. Several hundred pages of documentation are included.

If you are not familiar with Acrobat Reader, take time to review the *Reader Online Guide*, available from the Finale Help menu. This guide will show you how to use the Acrobat Reader program. If you have ever used a Web browser, you will find Acrobat Reader easy to understand. To learn how to navigate around Acrobat Reader:

- From the Help menu, select How To Use the User Manual.

The *Acrobat Reader Guide* will provide you with instructions on how to use Acrobat Reader. It is important to remember that you are running a separate program to view the *Finale User Manual*. It takes some time to become familiar with navigating around the Help options.

After you have some facility with Acrobat Reader, go to the *Finale User Manual*, via **Help** > Table of Contents. From within the *Finale User Manual*, click on the letters "TOC" on the right edge to take you to the Table of Contents.

TOC = Table of Contents

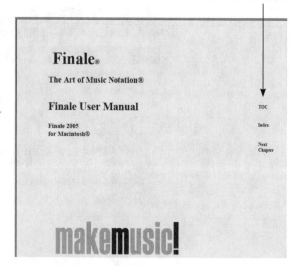

Another way I frequently use the documentation is via the Index. If you are looking for a specific piece of information, the Index is usually the fastest route that can be selected from the Finale Help menu.

Remember, when you are using the *User Manual*, you have two programs running at the same time: Finale and Acrobat Reader.

To quickly switch between programs that are already loaded in the computer's memory:

Mac OS	Windows
Hold down ⌘ and press the TAB key. Press the TAB key to switch to the desired program.	Hold down Alt and press the TAB key. Press the TAB key to switch to the desired program.

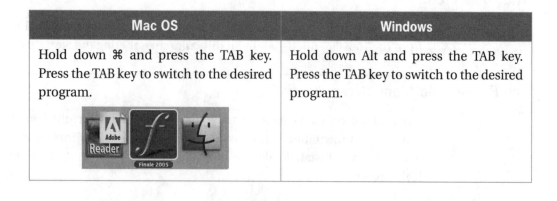

I frequently use Help to solve problems using Finale. Typically, I will go to the Help section and then print the pages related to the area I am studying. The Help section is the first place to turn when you are stuck.

QuickStart Videos

Another excellent resource provided to Finale users is the QuickStart Videos. These videos give a short, informative overview of literally every aspect of Finale. I have found them to be most helpful especially when a new feature is introduced. You can access the videos by:

1. From the Help menu, select QuickStart Videos.
2. From the File menu, select the Launch Window, and then click on the QuickStart Video option at the bottom of the screen.

Summary

This chapter introduced the operation of Finale and included the following:

- suggested order of events
- keyboard terminology
- installing and launching Finale
- exploring the Main Tool Palette
- selecting tools from the Main Tool Palette
- the Selection tool
- contextual menus
- the View menu
- using the Hand Grabber tool to center music on the page
- moving around the score in Scroll View
- redrawing the screen
- the Options and Plug-ins menu
- using the Finale Help menu
- operating the *Finale User Manual* via the Help menu
- viewing the Finale QuickStart Videos

2

Keyboard Note Entry ("Aura Lee")

Each chapter will introduce a specific set of notation skills. The first piece of music to enter into Finale is a single-line melody, "Aura Lee." First, look at the final version of "Aura Lee" below. The goal is to reproduce this using Finale.

Aura Lee

entered by [your name]

The skills to be covered in this example include:

- using the Setup Wizard to enter the title, composer, and time and key signature
- entering the notation using Simple Entry by typing the letters on the computer keyboard
- entering a tie
- deleting extra measures
- playing back to check for mistakes
- preparing the page layout
- saving to disk
- printing the example

Setting Up the Score

If Finale is not already open, launch it.

1. When Finale 2005 launches, the Launch Window appears.
2. If Finale is already open, choose New from the File menu, and then Launch Window.
3. Click the Setup Wizard button.

The Setup Wizard button

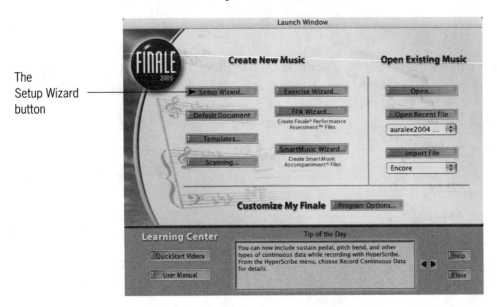

The first window of the Setup Wizard allows you to enter the Title, Composer, Copyright information, Page Size, and Page Orientation.

4. Enter the Title and Composer as shown in the following graphic.

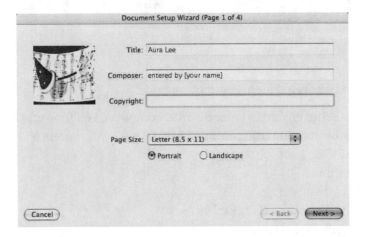

5. Click the Next button.

 To move from one entry area to another in a dialog box, just press the TAB key on the computer keyboard.

6. Choose Empty Staves, Treble Clef Staff, and then click Add. A shortcut is to double-click on the desired instrument or voice, such as Treble Clef Staff, and it will add it to the score.
7. Click Next.

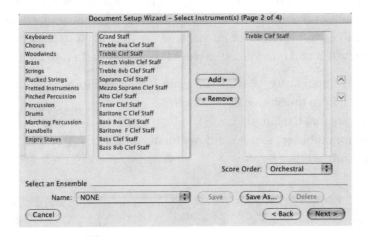

8. Choose **C** for "common time."
9. Change the Key to D major—Up Arrow scrolls through the circle of fifths, Down Arrow scrolls through the circle of fourths.
10. Click Next.
11. "Aura Lee" requires no changes on page 4 of the Setup Wizard.
12. Click Finish.

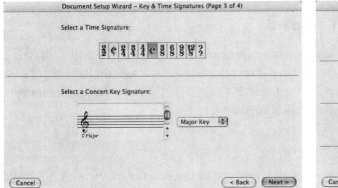
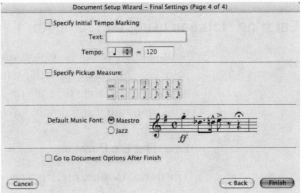

Using the Setup Wizard in Finale 2005, one complete page of music is created. For this particular file, thirty-one measures are created. The additional measures will be deleted after the notation for "Aura Lee" has been entered.

Aura Lee

entered by [your name]

Entering Notation with Simple Entry

Finale offers several ways to enter and edit notation in a score. All of the various methods will be explained and explored in the chapters that follow. The simplest way to enter notation in Finale is using Simple Entry. This method was designed to be easy to use and learn. The tool has been vastly improved over the last several updates to Finale. If you are familiar with earlier versions of Finale, take the time to study Simple Entry, as it now is one of the fastest and most versatile ways to enter notation into Finale.

1. Choose Simple Entry ♪ from the Main Tool Palette or click on the desired note duration from the Simple Entry Palette.
2. Make sure that the Simple Entry Palette is visible. If it is not visible, go to the Windows menu, and select Simple Entry Palette.

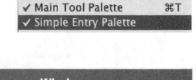

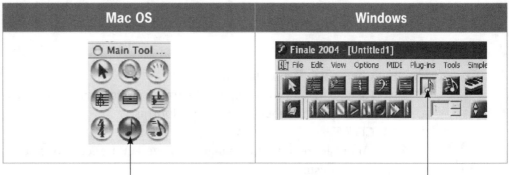

Mac OS	Windows

Entering Notation using the Computer Keyboard

Simple Entry features several ways to enter notation. This chapter will deal with typing into the score using the letter names on the keyboard. The system works like this: choose a duration and then type the desired letter: A, B, C, F, E, F, or G. This is an excellent way to enter notation if you do not have a MIDI keyboard.

Selecting the Duration

The duration must first be selected. This is be done by clicking the mouse on the desired duration from the Simple Entry Palette.

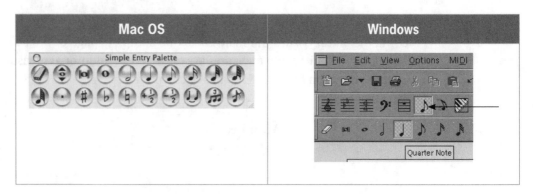

Mac OS	Windows

To save a mouse click, just click on the desired note value in the Simple Entry Palette. When you click an entry, Finale automatically switches to the Simple Entry tool.

A faster way is to use the computer numeric keypad. Press the number 5 for a quarter note, the number 4 for an eighth note, and so forth.

Note that the numbers at the top of the computer keyboard **cannot** be used to enter the duration. These numbers are used to enter intervals above or below the selected note, which will be discussed in detail later in this chapter.

If you have a full sized keyboard with a numeric keypad, place your right hand over the numeric keypad with your middle finger over the number 5. With practice, you will begin to "feel" the different note durations: 5=quarter, 4=eight; 6=half, and so forth.

If you are using a laptop, there are two options. Since most laptops do not include a numeric keypad, you can purchase a keypad that connects to the USB port. The other option is to use the keypad numbers on the keyboard. Press the fn or function key, and press the desired value: I=5, U=4, and so forth.

Entering the Notation

Choose the view that you prefer: Page View or Scroll View. I prefer to enter notation in Scroll View and deal with page layout at the end.

1. From the View menu, select Scroll View. (You can enter notes in Page View; I personally find it easier, in the long run, to enter in Scroll View.)
2. Choose the quarter-note value in the Simple Entry Palette, or press the number 5 on the keypad.

The Finale cursor location is represented by a vertical line. The duration currently selected will be displayed—in this case, a quarter note. This is referred to as the Simple Entry Carat and indicates the beat where the next note entered will appear.

3. Type the letter name of the first note, in this case A.
4. Type in the rest of the quarter notes in the first two measures: D, C, D, E, B.

When using Simple Entry and typing the letter name, you enter only the letter of the note. Finale will assume you want C♯ if C♯ is in the key signature. You can override this by entering a = for a sharp, a – for a flat, or an N for a natural. Refer to the Simple menu for a complete list of options.

5. Select the Half Note duration, or press the number 6 on the numeric keyboard, and enter the E half note in the second measure.

Complete the first eight measures of "Aura Lee." If you are in Scroll View, you can manually scroll to the right to show additional measures. Use the scroll bar at the bottom of the Finale window to advance to the next measure. Click the Right Arrow to advance one measure.

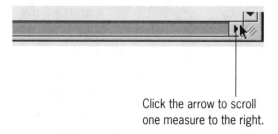

Click the arrow to scroll one measure to the right.

To enter the dotted note in measure 3:

1. Press the number 5 on the numeric keypad to select the quarter-note value.
2. Enter the note D by typing the letter on the computer keyboard.
3. Type the period on the keypad to enter the dot.

Erasing Mistakes

If you type in the incorrect note, the fastest way to delete it is by pressing the Delete key on the computer keyboard. You can press Delete several times to delete more than one note. If you need to delete a note from a previous measure, use the Eraser tool, located on the Simple Entry Palette. This is also a good place to start getting in the habit of using the **Edit** > Undo command. This command is in many software programs, and it lets you undo the last or previous to the last items. You can access it from the Edit menu, but learn the shortcut command, as it will save you time in the long run: ⌘-Z (Mac) and Control-Z (Windows).

To enter a rest using Simple Entry:

1. Type the desired note value (in measure 8, select the number 5 on the numeric keypad for a quarter note).
2. Press zero (0) to enter a rest.

 Finale will automatically enter rests to a measure that is incomplete. When you enter the next note or rest in the following measure, Finale will complete the measure with rests. This can be a timesaving feature. It can also be turned off from the Simple menu, Simple Entry options.

Copying and Pasting

Measures 9 and 10 are identical. Think of Finale as a music processor, similar to a word processor. It is possible to copy and paste similar information to save time.

1. Enter the notation for measure 9.

Since measure 10 is identical to measure 9, use a shortcut to copy and paste the information from measure 9 to measure 10. The proper tool must be selected first.

2. To copy and paste measures 9 to 10, choose the Mass Edit tool .
3. Be sure that measure 9 and 10 are both visible on the screen. Use the scroll bar at the bottom of the window, if necessary.
4. Click in measure 9. The measure will highlight.
5. Drag measure 9 into measure 10 (click and hold the mouse button). As you drag the mouse into measure 10, be sure a box appears around the measure. Then release the mouse button.
6. The "How many times?" dialog box comes up, with the number 1, so no change is needed. Click OK to copy measure 9 to measure 10.

 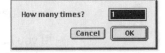

Anytime you are presented with a dialog box, such as the "How many times?" dialog box above, you do not have to delete the number in the box if it is highlighted. Just enter the number you desire, and the default number will be replaced.

Finale can copy a measure or measures from 1 to 999 times. For this example, we only need one. This is a tremendous time saver for music with many repeated measures, such as percussion parts.

Enter the rest of the measures of "Aura Lee" using Simple Entry.

1. Choose the quarter-note value.
2. Use the left and right arrow keys on the computer keyboard to advance from note to note and measure to measure.

To enter a tie in the last measure:

1. Choose the Half Note duration by pressing 6 on the numeric keypad.
2. Type the letter D to enter the D half note.
3. Press T for Tie.
4. Change the note value to a quarter note (press 5).
5. Type the letter D to enter the second note of the tie.

 Be sure to enter all ties when you are entering the notation. Ties are entered from the Simple Entry Palette. Slurs are handled differently and will be covered in chapter 7.

Editing in Simple Entry

If you need to correct or change a note, choose it in Simple Entry and use the Left and Right Arrow keys on the computer keyboard to highlight the note. The note that is highlighted can be edited by moving the up or down keys to change the pitch.

- To select and edit a note, choose Simple Entry.
- To select a note or rest, ⌘-click (Mac) or Control-click (Windows) on the desired notehead.

Use the Up or Down arrows to change the pitch or any of the other key commands to enter ties, sharps, flats, and so forth.

If you have trouble remembering all of the key commands (I never can remember them all), use the Simple menu to help. To access the Simple Entry edit commands via the Simple menu:

1. Choose the Simple Entry Palette .
2. From the Simple menu, select Simple Edit Commands.
3. Drag to any of the submenus, such as Accidentals or Add Pitch.
4. Select the desired edit command from the submenu.

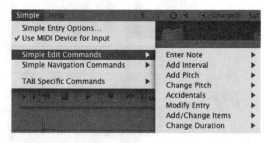

The Simple Entry shortcuts are listed in Help. Go to the Help menu, and select Keyboard Shortcuts. I suggest that you print out the list and paste it next to your computer monitor for reference.

Adjusting the Page Layout

Review the file before printing. First, view the entire document on the screen. Some monitors are too small to display the entire page. If this is the case, then you must adjust the display size.

1. From the View menu, select Page View.
2. From the View menu, select Scale View to 75%, or use the Shortcut command ⌘-7 (Mac) or Control-7 (Windows).

If the entire page does not fit on your monitor, press ⌘-I (Mac) or Control-I (Windows). This will fit the entire score in the window on your computer. Use the Hand Grabber tool to center the music on the page, if necessary.

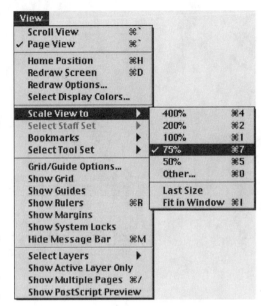

Finale automatically formats the number of measures per line as you enter the notation, so long as Automatic Music Spacing and Automatic Update Layout are both checked in the Edit menu. However, the number of measures per line can be adjusted. To change the number to four measures per line:

1. Choose the Page Layout tool ⭕.
2. Go to the Page Layout menu, and select Fit Music.... (The Fit Music option is also listed in the Mass Edit menu.) Enter the number 4 to group all measures to four measures per line.

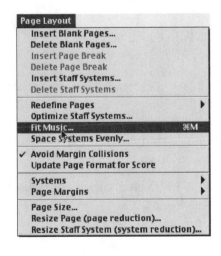

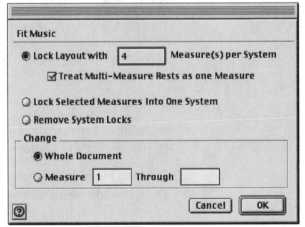

Your file should now look like the following:

Aura Lee

entered by [your name]

To turn off Locked Systems (page layout icons):

When you select Group Measures from the Page Layout menu, Finale locks the systems. Finale displays the locked systems by showing a lock at the end of the system. These locks will not print. They are just for viewing on screen. To turn off the icons:

- From the View menu, choose Hide Page Layout Icons.

Eliminating Extra Measures

Finale automatically creates a new single staff file with thirty-one measures when you use the Setup Wizard. The extra measures must be deleted.

1. To select measures 17 through 31 to be deleted, click the Measure tool ⬤.
2. From the Edit menu, choose Select Region....
3. Set the region from measure 17 through 31.

4. Type the number 17 in the From Measure box; press the tab key; enter the number 31 in the Through Measure box. Then click OK.

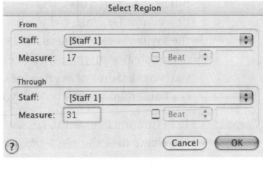

5. From the Measures menu, select Delete.

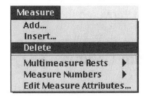

Playback for Proof Listening

Music entered in Finale can be played using either an external MIDI device, using the computer's internal sound source, or by using software synthesis. If you have a MIDI setup, configure it for use with Finale as described in the *Finale Installation & Tutorials* manual.

Check to see if the Playback Controls are already on the screen. If they are not displayed, from the Window menu, select Playback Controls. Click the green Play button for playback.

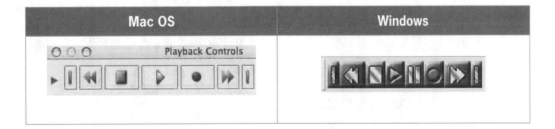

When you click Play, you will see the Human Playback dialog box and then the playback will begin. Human Playback is a comprehensive utility that attempts to interpret every aspect of the piece, such as articulations, dynamic markings, crescendos, and the like. I usually leave Human Playback turned on, during playback. There are times when you may want to alter the standard settings for Human Playback, and these will be discussed in chapter 7.

Saving and Printing

It is important to save your work frequently. If a piece has not been saved to disk, it can be lost due to a power failure or a computer crash (which happens to me often!). I like the saying: when you smile 😊, save. In other words, if you accomplish something you like, save it! Try to save every sixteen measures or every page of music. Frequent saving is a habit that you will be glad you adopted. To save a file:

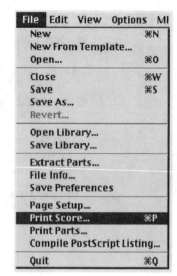

1. From the File menu, choose Save.
2. Name the example "Aura Lee," and save it to your hard drive.
3. To print the file, from the File menu choose Print.

(The Print Parts option is only used for scores; it will be covered in a later chapter.)

Finale Program Options

Finale offers a wide range of options for saving files. Finale can be told to automatically back up at any time interval. Finale can also automatically create a second copy (backup) of the piece you are working on.

1. From the Options menu, select Program Options.
2. Click on Save.
3. Check or uncheck "Make Backups When Saving Files."

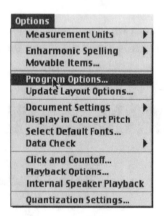
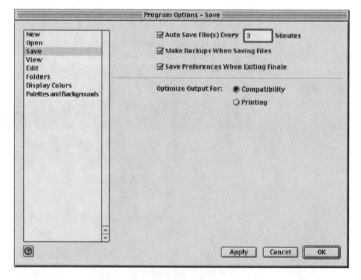

It is not a bad idea to automatically save, especially if you are not in the habit of saving your work frequently. Making backups is also a good idea. Sometimes, the file you are working on will become corrupted, and the backup can then be a real asset. All of these options will be retained after you quit the program.

Congratulations! You have successfully entered and printed your first Finale example. Feel like you've accomplished something? You should! On their own, it takes some users months to learn the skills introduced in this chapter.

 If you need more than two or three copies of a piece of music, use a duplicating machine. It is usually cheaper to print one copy and then take it to a duplicating machine to make additional copies than to print a large number of copies from a computer printer.

Summary

For this "Aura Lee" example, only basic tools were used. We could have used others, to speed things up or to improve the look, but only the tools we covered were truly necessary. Although Finale is a most complex program, it can be learned in stages, focusing only on the necessary tools for your project. These basic steps can be used to enter similar pieces of music.

1. Launch Finale.
2. Select New from the File menu, and use the Setup Wizard.
3. Enter the notation using Simple Entry and typing the letter names on the computer keyboard.
4. Delete the extra measures using the Mass Edit tool.
5. Use Playback to check for errors.
6. View the entire page (at 75% if necessary) using Scale View to from the View Menu.
7. Use the Hand Grabber tool to center music on the screen.
8. Use the Page Layout tool to fit the measures four per line.
9. Save a copy to disk, to protect against Murphy's Law.
10. Print a copy of the score using Print Score from the File menu.

Review

1. Review the list of Finale skills above. To review any or all, go to Finale Help, and search for the specific item.
2. Re-enter "Aura Lee," starting from scratch. Refer only to the list of steps above and relearn the skills.
3. Enter a similar piece of music, using the tools discussed in this chapter.

3

Chords ("Amazing Grace")

The song "Amazing Grace" offers some new challenges in Finale. Review the printout below to see what is in store.

Amazing Grace

entered by [your name]

The new areas include:

- creating a pickup measure
- displaying measure numbers on every bar
- Simple Entry using Return/Enter
- entering dynamic markings
- entering notation with Simple Entry to include triplets and grace notes
- scrolling the music during playback
- reducing the size of the music
- creating different files of the music in different keys

The first step is to prepare the score. See chapter 2 for details on the use of these tools, or refer to Help.

1. From the File menu, select New and choose Document from the Setup Wizard. Or from the File menu, select Launch Window.

 Use the shortcut for creating a new file using the Wizard Setup: ⌘-N (Mac) or Control-N (Windows).

2. Enter the Title "Amazing Grace." On the composer line, you can enter "Traditional," or type: Entered by [your name].
3. Select Empty Staves: Treble Clef Staff as the instrument.
4. Set the meter to 3/4.
5. Set the key to C. (There is no change needed as Finale defaults to the key of C.)

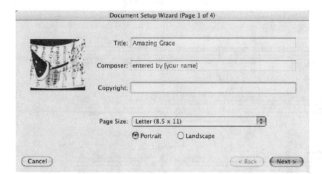

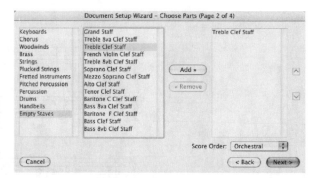

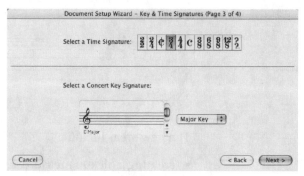

Creating a Pickup Measure

In page 4 of the Setup Wizard, there is an option to "Specify the Pickup Measure."

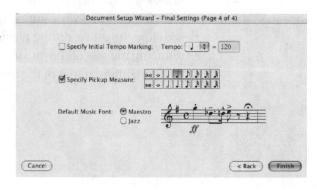

1. Click the box next to Specify Pickup Measure.
2. Select the total value of the pickup measure. In this case, it is the total value of a quarter note.
3. Click Finish.

The score should look like the following. Finale will automatically format the pickup bar after the notation is entered.

Amazing Grace

entered by [your name]

Displaying Measure Numbers

It is frequently desirable to display the measure numbers under every measure of the piece. This is commonly done by publishers and helps the performer by having number clearly displayed. Even if you don't intend to print the measures in your final copy, it is often helpful to have them visible while you are entering the notation. Only a few measures at a time are displayed on the computer screen, and having a visual cue as to which measure you are working on is helpful. Remember, you can remove or change the placement and frequency of the measure numbers at any time.

1. Choose the Measure tool.
2. From the Measure menu, select Measure Numbers and then Edit Regions.
3. To set the measure frequency to 1 (every measure), click the radio button next to "Show Every" (see graphic that follows).
4. Enter the number 1. This will display measure numbers on every measure.
5. Uncheck the box "Hide First Measure in Region."

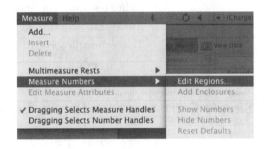

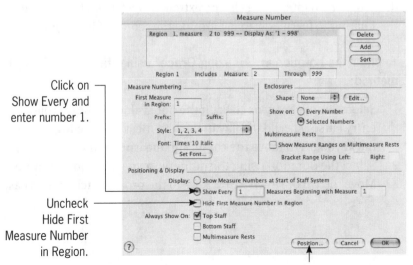

Click on Show Every and enter number 1.

Uncheck Hide First Measure Number in Region.

Click the Position button to move all measure numbers.

Finale automatically displays the measure number above the measure. It is possible to position the measure numbers above or below the staff. To change the position of all measure numbers to below the staff:

6. Click on the Position button at the bottom right of the dialog box.
7. Drag the number position underneath the measure. Most music publishers place the number just to the right of the left barline. Remember, you can change this at any time.

Click and drag the 0 to move the position of the measure numbers for the entire piece.

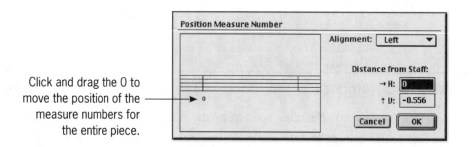

After you click the OK buttons, the measure numbers should appear below every measure at the position you assigned. Note that the handles (little boxes) appear next to every measure number. You probably can't read the numbers at this point. The handle indicates that you can select, or in this case, move individual measure numbers if needed. These handles (boxes) do not print; they are only for editing.

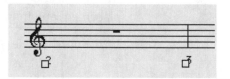

Simple Entry using the Return/Enter Key

The fastest way to enter notation in Finale is by using a MIDI keyboard. This option will be discussed in chapter 4. If you do not have a MIDI keyboard, then I have found the fastest way to enter notes using the computer keyboard is using the Return/Enter key to enter the notation. With very simple melodies, typing the letter keys on the keyboard as described in chapter 2 can also be extremely fast. Even if you have a MIDI keyboard, use this chapter to learn how to get around the score in Simple Entry.

To enter the notation in "Amazing Grace" using the Simple Entry Return/Enter-key method:

1. Select Simple Entry or click on the note value on the Simple Entry Palette. The entry cursor should display in the first measure. Use Right and Left Arrow keys on the keyboard to move the caret from measure to measure.
2. Select the duration using the numeric keypad: 5 = quarter note.
3. Move the Up or Down Arrow keys to the proper pitch, in this case G.

4. Press the Return/Enter key to enter the duration. The cursor will automatically advance to the next entry point or measure.

5. Change the duration by using the numeric keypad. Press the number 6 for a half note.
6. Use the Up Arrow key, and move to C on the third space.
7. Press Return/Enter to enter the note C.

This can be an extremely fast way to enter notation. I find that by placing my right hand over the numeric keypad and my left had over the up and down arrows, I can enter notation extremely fast using this method.

 It is possible to enter a pickup measure if you forgot to select this when you set up the score using the Setup Wizard. The steps include: From the Options menu, select Pickup Measure. Enter the value of the entire pickup measure. In the case of "Amazing Grace," it is a quarter-note pickup.

Entering a Triplet in Measure 1

1. First, enter the half-note C. Then change the note value to an eighth note by entering a 4 from the numeric keypad.
2. Move the Up Arrow key on the keyboard to E on the fourth space.
3. Enter the first eighth note of the triplet by pressing the Enter key.
4. Press the number 9 on the keypad to enter a triplet. Note that you enter the first note of a triplet or tuplet first, and then press 9 to enter a triplet.
5. Move the Down Arrow key to D, and press the Return/Enter key.
6. Move the Down Arrow key to C, and press the Return/Enter key.

 If you have a passage with many triplets in succession, you can use the Triplet tool from the Simple Entry Palette. When you click on this tool, every note will be entered as a triplet. For music with an occasional triplet, I recommend the above steps.

Enter the rest of the notation in measures 1 through 6, using the steps mentioned previously:

Simple Entry Navigation Commands:

1. To move to the previous or next entry, use the arrow keys.
2. To move to the previous or next measure, press:

Mac OS	Windows
⌘-Left or -Right Arrow keys	Control-Left or -Right Arrow keys

3. To select one note to edit: Option-click (Mac) or Control-click (Windows).

To change the octave in Simple Entry:

Frequently, when entering notes using the computer keyboard, there will be a need to shift the entry caret up an octave. To shift the entry caret up an octave before entering a note, hold down the Shift key, and press the Up or Down Arrow key to move the caret up or down an octave.

Entering the Dot and Tie, and Adding Harmony in Measure 7

1. To enter a dotted note, first enter the half note. Then press the period to enter the dot.
2. To enter a tie, press T for Tie on the keyboard (Shift-T will enter a tie to the previous note).
3. Press Return/Enter to place the G in measure 8.

 I often use the Undo command to eliminate the last thing that I did when I make a mistake. The undo selection is in the Edit Menu; select Undo. The shortcut key is a good one to remember: ⌘-Z (Mac) or Control-Z (Windows).

Entering Harmony

Entering harmony is a snap with Finale 2005 or later versions. Harmony can be entered above or below a note using the numbers at the top of the computer keyboard. Each number represents the interval above or below the note entered: 2 = second; 3 = third; 4 = fourth, and so forth. If you press the number alone, the harmony will be entered above the entered note. If you press the Shift key and then the number, the harmony will be entered below the entered pitch.

1. In measure 9, enter an E dotted quarter note.
2. Press the number 3 on the QWERTY keyboard to enter the harmony above the existing note. (Do not use the keypad.)
3. Change the duration to an eighth note (4 on the numeric keypad), and enter E.
4. Hold down Shift and press the number 3 on the QWERTY keyboard to enter the C a third below E.

To enter an accidental:

1. In measure 10, enter the notation. Enter the note G on the last half beat of the measure.
2. Press the equals (=) key on the keyboard. Pressing + (plus) on the keypad also enters a sharp.
3. To enter the harmony below the note entered, hold down Shift and press the number 3 on the QWERTY keyboard. This will enter an E below G♯.

To enter the E♭ grace note in measure 13:

1. Press the number 4 on the keypad to enter the value of an eighth note.
2. Enter an E on the fourth space.
3. Press the minus (–) key to make it an E♭.
4. To turn the note to a grace note: Option-G (Mac) or Alt-G (Windows)
5. Press Return/Enter to enter the first note of the triplet.
6. Press N to make it an E-natural.
7. Press Shift and the number 6 on the QWERTY keyboard to enter the harmony.
8. Press 9 to enter a triplet.
9. Enter the rest of the triplet and harmony.

Adding the tie in measures 15 and 16:

1. Enter the third space C half note.
2. Press period (.) to add the dot.
3. Press the letter T to add a tie.
4. Hold down Shift, and press the number 8 on the QWERTY keyboard to add the octave below.
5. Press T to add a tie to the lower octave.
6. Press the Right Arrow key to move to the next measure.
7. Enter both Cs in the last measure.

Adding the fermata:

1. To add the fermata in measure 16, select the Articulation tool 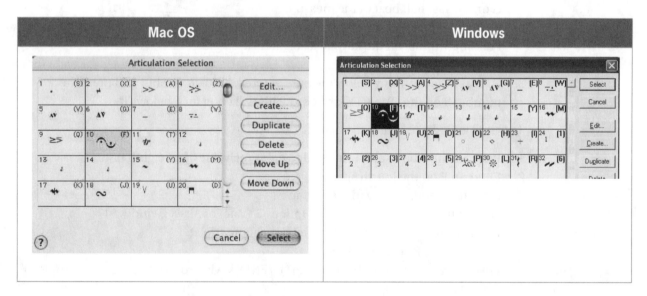, or choose it from the Tools menu.
2. Click on the notehead of the last note in measure 16.

Finale assigns articulations, such as fermatas, to the actual note. When you click on the notehead, a dialog box appears that contains the various articulations available. Select the fermata marking.

Finale displays two fermatas: one upside down and the other right-side up. This indicates that the marking will automatically flip to above or below the notehead according to its stem position on the staff.

- After you enter the fermata, you can move the marking by dragging the handle (little box) with the mouse.

In order to display a handle of any Finale object, press ESC to choose the Selection tool. Then double-click on the object, in this case, the fermata.

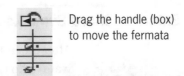

Drag the handle (box) to move the fermata

 Have you saved lately? Try to form the habit of saving your work frequently. Remember, when you enter something that makes you smile, SAVE.

Eliminating Additional Measures using Shift-Click

Since Finale creates a new file with thirty measures, the additional measures must be deleted. (There are actually thirty-one measures, if you count the pick-up measure.) So far, we have used the Select Region option to select a group of measures. Another way to select a group of measures is using the Shift-click command. To delete measures 17 through 30 using Shift-click:

1. From the View menu, select Scroll View. (This can also be done in Page View if you prefer.)
2. Select the Measure tool .
3. Advance to measure 17.
4. Click inside the lines and spaces in measure 17 to highlight it.
5. Advance to measure 30 (measure 30 is the last measure of the piece, including the pickup measure). Be sure *not* to click on the white portion of the screen. If you do, the highlight in measure 17 through 30 will be lost.
6. Hold down the Shift key, and click inside measure 30. Measures 17 through 30 should now be highlighted.
7. To delete the selected measures, press the Delete key on the computer keyboard (or select Delete from the Measure menu).

Be sure to select the correct measures. If you delete more measures than you want, go to the Edit menu and select Undo, or use the shortcut ⌘-Z (Mac) or Control-Z (Windows).

Specifying Five Measures Per Line

In this example, five measure per line works out to be the best overall layout. To change the measure layout, use the Fit Music command. This option is found in both the Mass Edit and the Page Layout tool menus.

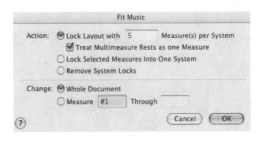

1. Choose the Mass Edit tool (or the Page Layout tool).
2. From the Mass Edit Menu, select Fit Music: shortcut Shift-⌘-M (Mac) or Shift-Control-M (Windows).
3. Lock the layout with five measures for the whole document.

Entering Chord Symbols

After the notation is entered, add the chord symbols. Like most tasks, Finale has several ways to do this. Chords can be entered using a MIDI keyboard, analyzing existing music, or by manually typing into the score. In this chapter, we will use the Type into Score method.

I usually enter chords in Scroll View; however, they can be entered in Page View as well.

1. Go to the first measure of the piece. Finale can quickly go to measure 1 by using the Home Position command. This can be selected in the View menu or by pressing the Home key on the numeric keypad.
2. Choose the Chord tool .
3. Check to be sure that Type into Score is selected from the Chord menu.

When entering chords, it is important to be able to see the left margin of the page. If the Main Tool Palette or any other menu palette is covering the left margin, move it to another position on the screen.

4. Click on the first note in measure 1.
5. Type in G7. Be sure to use a capital G and no space between it and the number 7.
6. Press the Space Bar to enter the chord and move to the next note.

Enter the rest of the chords. See the printout that follows.

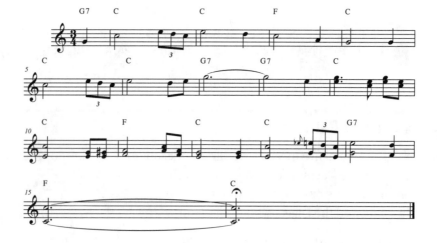

Redrawing the Screen

Every once in a while, Finale will display a chord or other symbol on the screen that looks strange. Perhaps it has partially disappeared. This is due to the complex nature of all that must be displayed, including notes on the staff, titles, chords, articulations, and other markings. If the screen display ever looks a bit strange, try redrawing the screen.

- From the View menu, choose Redraw Screen, or use the shortcut command ⌘-D (Mac) or Control-D (Windows).

To edit an existing chord symbol:

1. Choose the Selection tool (press ESC or escape).
2. Double-click on the chord you want to edit.
3. Type in the correct chord symbol to replace the old.

To edit a chord suffix:

1. After entering the chord symbol, for example C, enter a colon followed by a zero. C:0. (Be sure not to enter any spaces).
2. Press the Return/Enter key.
3. Choose the proper suffix (Maj7, min7, etc.).

> Finale has a preset list of chord suffixes that can be used with any chord symbol. This is referred to as a "chord suffix library." If you want the chords in your piece to play back properly, you must choose the correct suffix from the library. If you enter a suffix that is not in the library, Finale will warn you and ask if you want to add it to the library. If you say yes, it will be added. However, if you don't spent the time to tell Finale how to exactly playback the chord, it will not play back properly. Moral: if you are in a hurry and don't care about exact playback, skip the somewhat tedious steps of telling Finale how to properly playback a chord suffix that you create. Consult Help under Chord Tool Suffix for more information.

☺ Have you saved lately?

Adding Dynamic Markings

This example also includes dynamic markings. They can be attached to individual notes or measures.

1. To enter dynamic markings, choose the Expression tool .
2. Double-click just below measure one to enter the piano marking.
3. Select the dynamic marking from the dialog box. Click Select.
4. When the next screen appears, click Select.

(Measure and Note Expressions and other applications of this tool will be discussed in chapter 8, "Small Arrangements").

42

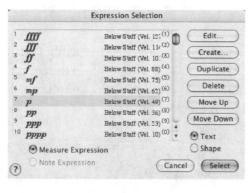

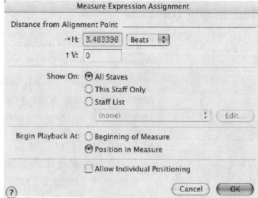

1. Choose *p*, click Select, and the piano marking will be placed into the score.
2. Click on the handle, and drag it slightly to the left of the first note.

Repeat this process to enter the dynamic markings for the rest of the piece. Expressions will enter automatically below the staff.

Amazing Grace

Playback

Before we make the final adjustments to the page layout, take a minute to play back the piece to check for any mistakes in the notes and/or the chord symbols. Move the Playback Controls to the lower portion of the screen so that the music can be seen during playback.

1. To move the Playback Controls, or any window, drag the box with the mouse. Click anywhere inside the gray bar at the top of the box, hold the mouse button down, and drag.
2. Click Play to hear the playback and see the notation scroll across the screen.

The other controls on the Playback Controls window can also be helpful. These include the two double arrows to the left and the right. These are Rewind and Fast-Forward buttons, which can be accessed before starting or during playback.

The two controls to the far left and far right let you to jump instantly to the beginning or to the end of the piece.

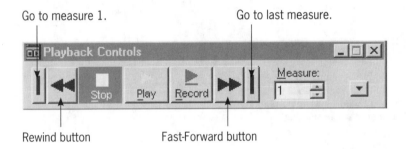

The other double arrows are to move in either direction one measure at a time, either before starting playback or to repeat or skip music during playback. Click the Play button, then click on the Fast-Forward button three times. The playback will skip ahead three measures. This is helpful when listening only to a particular passage.

Adding the Instrument Name (left header)

1. From the View menu, select Page View.
2. To enter the instrument name select the Text tool Ⓐ.
3. Scroll to the top of the page or use the Hand Grabber tool to move the music.
4. Double-click the mouse in the upper left-hand corner of the page.
5. Type in the instrument name: Flute/Oboe.
6. Drag the box of the instrument frame so that it aligns with the composer [your name] frame.

If you are familiar with using a word processor, the Text tool in Finale will be somewhat familiar to you. You may want to change the size of the text for the title and/or credits.

7. From the View menu, choose Page View.
8. Choose the Text tool Ⓐ.

9. Scroll to the top of the page.

10. Double-click on the handle of the Title, in this case, "Amazing Grace."

11. From the Edit menu, choose Select All to highlight the text, or use the shortcut: ⌘-A (Mac) or Control-A (Windows).

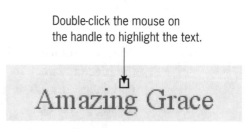

Double-click the mouse on the handle to highlight the text.

12. After selecting (highlighting) the text, go to the Text menu, select Size, slide the mouse to the right, and choose the point size. Higher numbers of point size are for larger text.

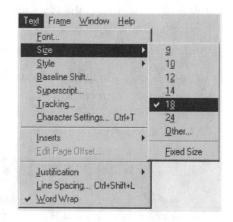

Text elements, such as the text blocks for title and the credits, need to be aligned to the left, right, or center. You can tell where a text block is aligned by looking where the handle appears. If it is in the middle of the word, it is aligned center.

To align the "credits" frame to the right:

1. Be sure the Text tool is still selected.

2. Open the contextual menu Control-click (Mac) or Right-click (Windows).

3. Select Edit Frame Attributes from the contextual menu.

4. Next to Alignment and Position, choose Right.

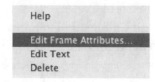
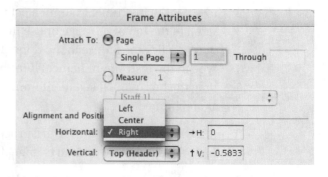

The text should now be aligned to the right. Finale displays handles to indicate which alignment has been selected. Notice the location of the handles below. Each is appropriately aligned: left, center, and right.

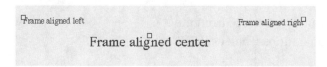

🙂 Have you saved lately?

Adjusting the Position of the Pickup Note

It is possible to manually control any note, such as the pickup note. Finale does a pretty good job of setting the alignment automatically, but if you must tinker with it, here is one way how it is done:

Click top box to move barline.

Click bottom box to move individual beats.

1. Choose the Measure tool .
2. Click on the top of the two boxes. This allows for the adjustment of the barline. Drag it to the left.
3. Click on the bottom box. This allows for the movement of beats within the measure. Drag the bottom handle to the right. This will move the quarter-note pickup closer to the barline.

Printing the Score

The last step is to view the entire page, to check for errors. If everything looks good, then go to the File menu and select Print.

Saving Copies of the File in Different Keys

Now that you have saved the file in the key of C, you may want to save another version in another key, perhaps for a transposing instrument such as a saxophone, or to raise or lower the key for a specific vocal range. One way to accomplish this is to change the key and then use the Save As command to rename and save a second file without erasing the first.

• You have already saved the file with the name "Amazing Grace in C."

Let's raise the key to the key of A. To do this, first change the key of the piece:

1. Choose the Key Signature tool.
2. Double-click in the pickup measure (between the five lines).

3. Change the key to A. (Up Arrow scrolls through the circle of fifths.)
4. Select "Measure 1 Through End of Piece."
5. Select "Transpose notes Up" from the Transposition options. Then click OK.

The piece will be transposed to the key of A.

Now, save the file with a new name. To do this:

6. From the File menu, select Save As. (Save As allows you to save the file with a different name).
7. Name the file something different from the original, such as "Amazing in A."

You will have two files: one in C and one in A. Additional keys and copies of the files can be created this way.

Summary

The steps included in this chapter are:

- use the Setup Wizard to create a new score
- identify the first measure as a pickup
- display measure numbers on every measure
- enter the notation using Simple Entry via the Return/Enter key method
- enter triplets and grace notes using Simple Entry
- enter harmony
- enter the chords
- enter the dynamic markings
- play back the piece to check for errors, setting it to scroll during playback and using the fast-forward and rewind commands
- lay out the page
- save a copy to disk
- save a second copy in another key
- print a copy of the score

Review

1. Reenter the piece using only the printout of the notation. Refer to the chapter pages, if you run into something that you can't remember or solve.
2. Use the Finale Help to review any of the areas included in this chapter.

4

MIDI Entry, Chords, and Lyrics ("Three Blind Mice")

This example will focus on practicing and extending the Finale skills introduced in earlier chapters.

Three Blind Mice

Piano/Vocal

entered by [your name]

The new areas for this example include:

- entering lyrics
- deleting specific entry items
- fitting music to specific numbers of measures per line
- laying out the page and individual systems
- developing a Finale checklist of sequence of events
- entering notation using a MIDI keyboard
- change the page size to Octavo

Setting Up The Score

Set up the score following the same steps covered in previous chapters:

1. To create a new file using the Wizard Setup, use the shortcut keys: ⌘-N (Mac) or Control-N (Windows).
2. Enter Empty Staves > Treble Clef Staff.
3. Set the Time signature to 6/8.
4. Change the key to D major.

Display the Measure Numbers on Every Measure

When entering lyrics into a score, have the measure numbers print above the staff to avoid colliding with the lyrics.

- Use the Measure tool 🔲 to set the measure numbers to print on each measure and position them above the staff. (Refer to chapter 3 or use the Finale Help menu.)

Entering the Notation with Simple Entry and MIDI

There are several ways to enter notation in Finale. Each type of input has its strengths and weaknesses. The last two chapters dealt with using Simple Entry without a MIDI keyboard. Without a doubt, the fastest way to enter notation into Finale is using a MIDI keyboard. This chapter will focus on using a MIDI keyboard to enter notation one step at a time, hence the name Step Entry.

In order to use a MIDI keyboard, you must have it connected to your computer via MIDI. Refer to the *Finale Installation & Tutorials* manual for instructions how to connect the instrument.

> Be sure to spend some time setting up your keyboard location. I like to have the MIDI keyboard to my right so I can play pitches with my right hand and use my left hand to identify the duration using the numeric keypad. If you do not have a MIDI keyboard, use Simple Entry as described in chapter 3.

To use Simple Entry with a MIDI keyboard:

1. Choose the Simple Entry tool .
2. Go to the Simple menu, and be sure Use MIDI Device for Input is checked.

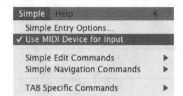

The process to enter notation with a MIDI keyboard, is as follows:

1. Select the note duration (quarter note, eighth note, half note).
2. Play the note on the MIDI keyboard.

To enter the notation for "Three Blind Mice:"

1. Choose the Simple Entry tool .
2. Choose the quarter note value by pressing 5 on the numeric keypad.
3. Press the period to add the dot.
4. Play F♯, E, and D on the MIDI keyboard.
5. Enter zero (0) on the keypad to enter a dotted quarter rest.

Finale will automatically jump to the next measure. Enter the first four measures of the piece, notation only, using Simple Entry with the MIDI keyboard. Remember, it is usually faster to enter the notation for the entire piece and then go back and enter the chords, dynamics, titles, and other information after the notes are entered.

Entering Dotted Notes and Rests

There are two ways to add a dot to a note or a rest. If a note or rest is selected (highlighted) and you press the dot, the dot will be added to the highlighted note or rest only. If no note or rest is highlighted, then the dot will be added to every entry. How can you tell? Look at the Simple Entry Palette. If the dot is selected, it will be added to every note and rest.

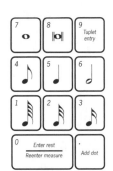

The fastest way to enter values is via the numeric keypad. There is a period next to the zero that can be used for dotted note values.

 When using Simple Entry, if there is an occasional dotted note, as in "Aura Lee," first enter the note and then press the Period key on the computer keyboard. This will add the dot to the entered note only. If there are many notes with dots, as in this example, click the dot key *before* entering notes. This will select the Dot tool in the Simple Entry Palette, and a dot will be added to *every* entry until the tool is turned off. A quick way to turn off (deselect) the Dot tool is to enter a note value twice. In other words, double-click the note value, and the Dot tool will be deselected.

Saving Time with Copy and Paste

In most music, as with the song "Three Blind Mice," similar measures can be copied to save time. Take a moment to look over the score. In the first few lines, the first two measures can be copied and pasted. With music that includes chord symbols, it will save time to enter the notation and the chords **before** copying and pasting the measures.

It can save a lot of time if you analyze the piece and look for ways to incorporate Copy and Paste. Sometimes, I actually mark identical places in the piece on the printed music. This can save time because similar sections can be copied and pasted throughout the document.

Copying and Pasting Measures 1 and 2

1. Show measures 1 and 2 on screen.
2. Choose the Mass Edit tool .
3. Highlight the first two measures with the mouse by dragging a box around them. When you release the mouse button, Finale displays the measures selected as measures highlighted.

4. Click in the highlighted portion of either measure, and drag it into measure 3. Be sure your mouse is positioned inside the staff of measure 3.

5. Finale will ask how many times you want to copy the measures. In this case, answer "1." Continue to use this technique to copy other measures, as you enter other notation.

Enter the rest of the notation for "Three Blind Mice" (see page 51).

1. Choose the Simple Entry tool 🎵, or click on the quarter-note value in the Simple Entry Palette. This will automatically select the Simple Entry tool.

2. If the cursor does not appear in measure 5, use the arrow keys to move the cursor left or right.

The steps for entering the notation in measures 5 and 6 (see page 51):

1. Type 5 on the keypad and the dot key.
2. Play A on the MIDI instrument.
3. Double-click on the number 5 to select just the quarter note.
4. Play the note G on the keyboard.
5. Type 4 on the keypad to select an eighth note.
6. Play the note G on the keyboard.
7. Type 5 on the keypad to select a quarter note.
8. Play F♯ on the MIDI keyboard.
9. Press period to add the dot.

10. Press the Right Arrow key on the keyboard to go to the next measure. Finale will fill in the rests.

Enter the rest of the notation for "Three Blind Mice."

FORMAT FOR SELECTING MENUS

From this point forward, references to menu commands will be shortened as follows:

Menu Name > Submenu(s) > Selection.

"Select **File** > New > Default Document" therefore means "From the File menu, go to the "New" submenu, and select "Default Document.""

Deleting Extra Measures

To delete the extra measures:

1. Choose the Measure tool 🔲.
2. Select **Edit** > Select Region.
3. Enter measure "17" through "31."
4. Select **Measures** > Delete.

Play Back to Check for Mistakes

Before entering the chords, check the piece for mistakes. Use the Playback controls to listen to the piece. Correct any incorrect notes if needed.

Entering Chords via MIDI

This time, we will enter the chords by using the MIDI keyboard. Finale can analyze what is played on the keyboard, and it will attempt to guess the proper chord name.

Be sure to play the chords in their proper inversions; in this example, every chord is in root position, so be sure to play them that way.

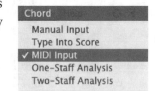

1. Choose the Chord tool .
2. Select **Chord** > MIDI Input.

Using this method, you will click on a note and then play the chord on the MIDI keyboard. Be sure to play in the desired inversion, because Finale will interpret the notes from the bottom to the top.

3. Click on the first note of the piece. An ear icon will appear. Finale is listening.
4. Play a D chord on the keyboard: D, F♯, A. Finale will display the chord over the note.
5. To advance to the next chord, play any single note on the keyboard above middle C.

Continue this process, and enter all of the chords for the piece. Remember to play all chords in root position.

Be sure to watch where you are in the score. For example, you will have to play any single note on the MIDI keyboard above middle C multiple times when there are eighth notes in the measure.

Deleting a Chord

When you enter a second chord on a particular note, Finale does not erase the old chord. It places a second chord on top of the first. So if you make a mistake, first erase the existing chord and then re-enter the correct chord.

1. Press the ESC (escape) key to choose the Selection tool.
2. To select the chord you wish to edit, double-click on the chord symbol.
3. Press Delete (Mac) or Backspace (Windows) on the keyboard to erase the chord.
4. Re-enter the chord using MIDI or Type Into the Score input.

When you use the Selection tool to select a chord, Finale automatically switches back to Type in the Score, one of the Chord menu options. If you want to return to MIDI entry, select it from the Chord menu.

Showing the Guitar Fretboards

It is many times helpful to include guitar fretboards with music. Finale will create appropriate fretboard notation on top of the music. The fretboards will be correct if Finale recognizes the chord that you enter. After entering a chord, if it turns red, Finale has recognized the chord and will print an accurate fretboard. If, however, you enter a chord that Finale does not recognize, the fretboard will not be automatically added. You will have to define the fretboard. See Help for more information on how to define the fretboard.

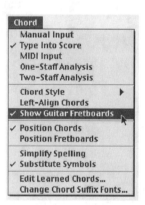

• Select **Chord** > Show Guitar Fretboards.

Making More Room for the Chords and the Guitar Fretboards

When Finale inserts the fretboards, they often collide with the staves above.

To make more room for the guitar fretboards and chord names:

1. Go to Page View.
2. Choose the Staff tool .
3. Click on any handle of any staff, and drag it to make more room. This will increase the space between all staves.

Positioning the Chord Names and Fretboards

The fretboards and the chord names can be independently adjusted.

1. Choose the Chord tool.
2. From the Chord menu, select Position Chords.
3. Be sure the arrows appear on the left of the screen. Mac users may need to move the Main Tool Palette in order to see the arrows.

4. Drag the left arrow to adjust the chord a little closer to the fretboard.

Drag the left-most arrow to move the chord names down for the entire piece.

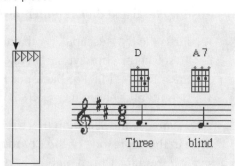

Fretboards can also be moved by choosing Position Chords from the Chord menu and then dragging the leftmost handle up or down, as desired.

Enter the rest of the chords. You could Copy and Paste the measures again, this time with the chords. However, I find it faster to simply type in the chords from beginning to end .

54

Entering Lyrics

Lyrics in Finale are entered using the Lyrics tool . Lyrics, like just about every aspect of Finale, can be entered in a variety of ways. The easiest way to enter lyrics is to type them into the score, one syllable at a time. Lyrics can be entered in scroll or page view. I prefer to enter lyrics in Scroll View.

To enter lyrics:

1. From the View menu, select Scroll View. (Lyrics can also be entered in Page View if you prefer.)
2. To go to the first measure: from the View menu choose Home Position.
3. Choose the Lyrics tool .
4. Select **Lyrics** > Type Into Score. If the option Type in the Score is checked, you do not need to change it.

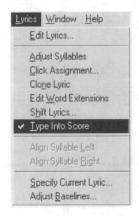

5. Click on the F♯ in measure 1 on the note head or stem.
6. A blinking cursor will appear. Type in the first word: Three.
7. Press the Space Bar or Tab key to move to the next note.
8. Enter the next word: blind.
9. When you come to the rest, press the Space Bar again to advance to the next measure.
10. Enter the lyrics for the first eight measures

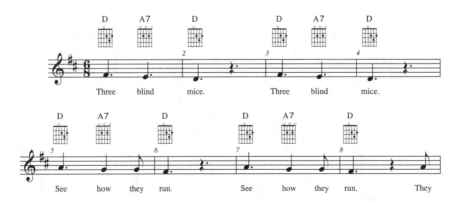

Entering a Syllable Break

When there is a syllable break, just type the first syllable, and enter a hyphen (-) after the syllable. Finale will automatically jump to the next note. Take your time, and be sure to enter the lyrics under the proper notes.

Enter the lyrics for measures 9 through the end of the piece.

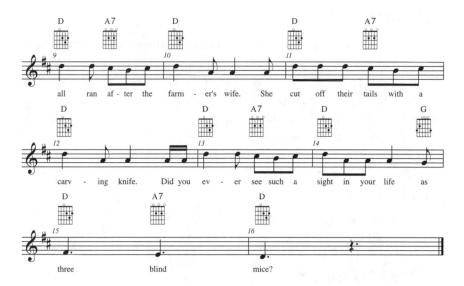

Fixing a Lyric

There will be times when you have to correct a lyric that was entered. Here are the steps:

1. Choose the Lyrics tool 🎵.
2. Select **Lyrics** > Type into Score.
3. Click on the notehead or note stem.
4. Press the Delete key to erase the lyric.
5. Re-enter the lyric.

Moving the Location of the Lyrics

When entering lyrics, a box with several arrows appears to the left of the staff. The arrow to the far left controls the position of the lyrics throughout the piece. To change the location of the lyrics for the entire piece:

- Click on the left arrow, and drag it up or down.

Click and drag the left arrow to change the position of the lyrics for the entire piece.

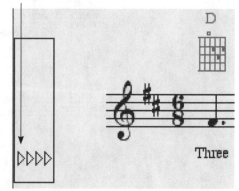

Lyric Baselines

Try to keep all of the arrows aligned (see page 56). Each one has a specific function:

- The leftmost triangle adjusts the baseline of the lyric for the entire piece.
- The second triangle controls the baseline for the selected staff only for the entire piece. Use this arrow if, for example, the tenor voice needs to be higher than the others.
- The third triangle controls the baseline for this staff, this system only.
- The rightmost triangle sets the baseline for the next syllable to be entered.

For most purposes, you will only need to adjust the leftmost triangle to control the position of the lyrics for the entire page. Try to keep these arrows aligned, unless you need to fine-tune your lyrics by adjusting the inner arrows as described above.

Changing the Size of the Lyrics

The size of the lyrics can be changed at any time. To change the size of the lyrics for the entire piece, use the Plug-ins menu.

1. From the Plug-ins menu, select Miscellaneous, and then Change Fonts.
2. Click on the Change Button next to Lyrics.
3. Choose the desired font and size, and click OK.

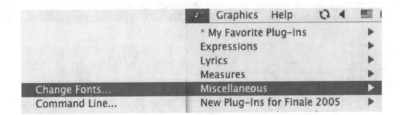

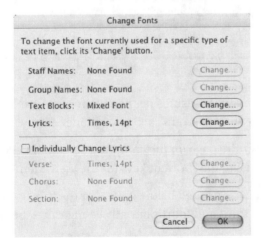

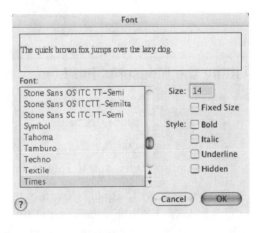

The normal size for most lyrics is 10 point. If there are a lot of lyrics in most measures, a smaller font size will permit more to be printed per line. For larger font size, use 12 or 14.

At point sizes of 10 or smaller, it is best to use a serif font, like Times, because they are easier to read than sans-serif fonts such as Helvetica. A serif is a small decorative line added as embellishment to the basic form of a letter. Typefaces are often described as being *serif* or *sans serif* (without serifs).

Entering and Adjusting the Titles

To enter the instrument name in the left-hand corner of the music:

1. Select **View** > Page View.
2. To enter the instrument name, select the Text tool .
3. Scroll to the top of the page, or use the Hand Grabber tool to move the music.
4. Double-click the mouse in the upper left-hand corner of the page.
5. Type in the instrument name: "Piano/Vocal."
6. Click the mouse outside of the text block.
7. Drag the handle of the instrument frame so that it aligns with the composer [your name] frame.
8. Left-justify the frame.

(See chapter 3 for detailed instructions on adding credits, changing the text size, and justifying left and right.)

😊 Have you saved lately?

 Use the shortcut commands to reduce or enlarge the display size of the piece so that it can be viewed on your monitor. This can be accessed from the View menu, but it is much faster to use the shortcuts (see page 10).

The View Percentage only controls the display on the monitor. Reducing the music for printout is done via the Resize tool and is described later in this chapter.

Fitting the Measures Per Line

So far, we have been grouping the measures per line to an even number of measures for the entire piece. It is also possible to group each line independently.

Make sure you can see the entire page on the computer screen. If necessary, reduce the view size to 75% or 50% by using the shortcut keys (or the View menu).

The goal is to group the piece as printed below. Note that the first two lines are grouped four measures per line, the third and fourth lines three measures per line, and the last line two measures per line.

Three Blind Mice

Piano/Vocal

entered by [your name]

To group the first eight measures to four on a line:

1. From the View menu, select Page View.
2. From the View menu, select the View Percentage so the entire piece is visible on the screen. View at 50% will work for most monitors.
3. Choose the Page Layout tool ⊙.
4. Select **Page Layout** > Fit Music.
5. Choose Lock Layout with "4" measures per system.
6. Click on the Measure button and enter measures 1 through 8.
7. Click OK to group the measures to four per line.

To group measures 9–14 to three measures per line:

Repeat the steps above. This time, enter "3 Measures per System," and change Measures to "9 through 14."

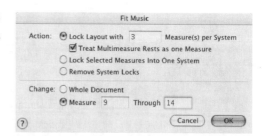

 There is a quick way to move a single measure to the line above or below.

1. Choose the Mass Edit tool.

2. Highlight the measure by clicking the mouse inside the staff.

3. Press the Up or Down Arrow key on the computer keyboard. This tells Finale to move the measure to the previous or next line. In this case, it will also move it to page 1. This method can be used from the beginning to the end of the piece, instead of using the Fit Music command.

When your example looks like the one below, you're done!

Are You Ready to Print?

- From the File menu, select Print.

Page Size

It is possible to change the page size of the document and to adjust the percentage size as well. For example, you could print this example the size of a choral octavo or the exact size of a choral hymnal.

To change the Page Size:

1. Choose the Page Layout tool 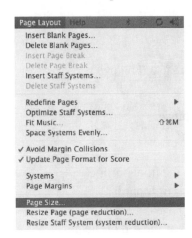.
2. From the Page Layout menu, select Page Size.
3. Click on the pull-down menu next to Page Size, and choose "Octavo."

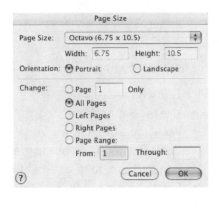

Be sure to check All Pages. The page will re-form to the selected size.

Changing the Size of the Printed Notation

The next step is to resize the music for the reduced page size. Typically, the percentage of the notation is also changed. For octavos, the percentage should be reduced from 100% to 85%.

1. Choose the Resize tool 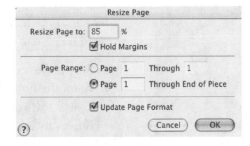.
2. From the View menu, select Page View.
3. Scroll to the top of the page so the Titles are visible.
4. Click the mouse at the top of the page. Be sure it reads "Resize Page." This tool can also resize staves and individual notes. For this purpose, we want Resize Page.
5. Change the percentage size to 85% or the desired percent. Then click OK.

The percentage can be changed from 0% to 1000%.

Do not use the Page Reduction Options in the Page Setup window for your printer. It is much more precise to control the print size in Finale.

Reviewing the Steps

Here are the basic steps to address when entering music in Finale

1. Set up the score.
2. Enter the notation, barlines, chords, lyrics, etc.
3. Reduce or enlarge the size of the music if needed.
4. Change the spacing between staves and address the number of measures per line.
5. Print the music.

Summary

The steps to enter "Three Blind Mice" are listed below.

- Launch Finale.
- Use the Setup Wizard to format the piece.
- Place measure numbers on every bar.
- Enter the notation for the piece.
- Delete the extra measures and insert the final barline.
- Enter the chords, then show the guitar fretboards.
- Enter the lyrics.
- Enter and adjust the titles and credits at the top of the page.
- In Page view, use Mass Edit to fit the music to specific measures per line.
- Save a copy to disk.
- Print the Score.

Review

1. Review the three ways to enter chords: type into score, manual input, and MIDI input. Each has its advantages.
2. We have now established the following general guidelines for creating notation in Finale. Try to reenter "Three Blind Mice" referring only to the general areas. If you need help, review the pages in this chapter or use Help.

   - Set up the score (key, time signature, measure numbers).
   - Enter the notation and chords. Use copy and paste to save time.
   - Delete the extra measures.
   - Enter any additional titles or credits.
   - Reduce the screen display so that the entire page can be seen.
   - Group the measures per line.
   - Print the music.

5

Articulations and Metatools ("Trumpet Voluntary")

Review the "Trumpet Voluntary" printout below. You will notice that the notation is more complex than the earlier examples. The chapter introduces a coda and the use of Metatools to speed the entry of articulations, dynamics, and other markings.

This arrangement copyright © 1997 by Tom Rudolph

The new areas in this example include:

- grace notes
- tuplets
- articulations entered with Metatools
- D.C. al Coda
- adjusting the positioning of staves (for the coda)

Preparing the Score

Open a new file in Finale. Use the Setup Wizard, and select Trumpet in C. Put in the title "Trumpet Voluntary" and "entered by [your name]." Select the time signature of 4/4, and enter the key of E (four sharps).

Enter the Copyright notice that will appear centered at the bottom of the page: This arrangement copyright 1977 by Tom Rudolph.

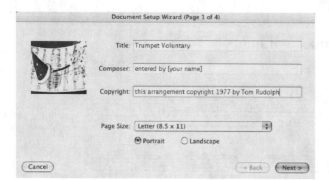

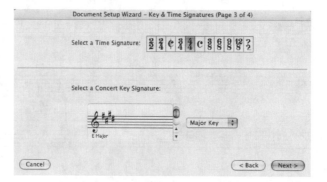

Use the Measure tool to display measure numbers below every measure. These steps should be almost second nature, if you've been entering each previous example. If you need assistance, review the previous chapters or consult Finale Help.

By now, you should be in the habit of saving frequently. I usually try to save after every step of entering the piece. Every time you begin a new section in this chapter, save the file.

Adding Measures to the Score

In this example, additional measures have to be added. When creating a file with the Setup Wizard, Finale creates one page of measures. "Trumpet Voluntary" has thirty-three measures. There are several ways to add measures. Finale will automatically create new measures as you are entering notation in Simple Entry. Just be sure that Create New Measures is checked in the Simple Entry Options dialog box.

1. Choose the Simple Entry tool ♪.
2. From the Simple Entry menu, select Simple Options, and be sure that the Create New Measures option is checked.

Now, when you enter notation at the end of the score, new measures will be automatically created.

Defining the Tuplet Positioning

Before entering complex tuplets (triplets, quintuplets, septuplets, and so forth), it is a good idea to check the Tuplet tool settings. In most cases, tuplets are positioned on the beam side of the group. To check the tuplet position setting:

Mac OS	Windows
Double-click on the Tuplet tool 🎵.	Control-click on the Tuplet tool 🎵.

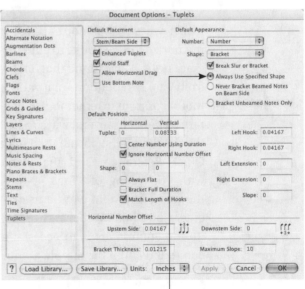

Various other options can also be controlled from this window. For example, if you want to display a bracket on every tuplet, check the box: Always Use Specified Shape. Publishers typically do not display tuplet brackets on beamed notes, but I find it is clearer to the performer when the brackets are displayed. I make this change every time I am using tuplets.

1. Select **Options** > Document Options, and then choose Tuplets.
2. Check the button next to the option "Always Use Specified Shape." Then click OK to close the window.

About Grace Notes

Finale does not automatically include the slash mark with the grace note. If you want to change it so every eighth note has a slash follow these steps:

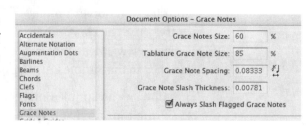

1. Select **Options** > Document Options.
2. Choose "Grace Notes."
3. Check the box: Always Slash Flagged Grace Notes.

Entering the Grace Notes

The easiest way to enter grace notes and tuplets is using Simple Entry. To enter the notation of the first measure:

1. Select the Simple Entry tool .
2. Enter the E half note.
3. To enter the G♯ grace note, first enter the note as an eighth note, by pressing the number 4 on the keypad for an eighth note and then playing the note G♯ on the MIDI keyboard.
4. To turn the G♯ eighth note to a grace note, press Option-G (Mac) or Alt-G (Windows).

Don't worry. You don't have to memorize the keystroke to enter the grace note. I have found that it takes from 7 to 21 repetitions of a various tool or shortcut to remember it long-term. There are several ways to find the shortcut. First, locate the Finale Quick Reference Card that came with your copy of Finale. Notice the many keys that can be used to enter notation. Another way to look up the commands is to access the commands from the Simple menu.

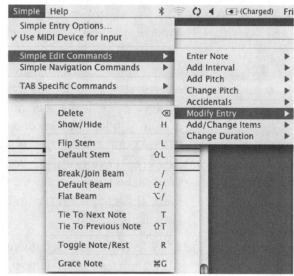

- Select **Simple** > Simple Edit Commands, and choose the Modify Entry option from the submenu.

Entering Tuplets

To enter the tuplet after you have entered the E half note and G♯ grace note:

1. Press 3 on the keypad to choose a sixteenth-note value.

2. Enter the first sixteenth note of the sextuplet, F♯.

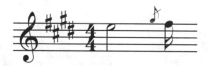

You will recall in chapter 3 that the number 9 was used to enter a triplet. To enter a custom tuplet of a value greater than 3, such as the sextuplet in this example:

3. Press Option-9 (Mac) or Alt-9 (Windows).
4. Enter "6" in the space of "4."
5. Finale will display rests. Ignore them, and enter the notes for the tuplet.

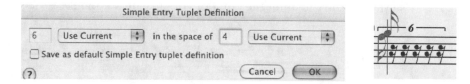

6. Enter the pitches for the sextuplet. Finale will group the six notes into a tuplet and place the bracket on the beam side of the group, as indicated previously.

7. Continue entering the first four measures of the piece.

Moving Tuplets

Sometimes, you will want to reposition a tuplet marking. To move the entire tuplet:

1. Press ESC (escape) to choose the Selection tool.
2. Double-click on the sextuplet.
3. Drag the tuplet handle (the clear box) to move it.
4. To edit the tuplet shape further, drag the small black handles.

Copy Measures 1 and 2 to Measures 5 and 6

Earlier, we copied measures by using the Mass Edit tool and dragging one measure onto another. Sometimes dragging is not possible—for example, when the target measures are on a different page than the source measures. In the *Finale User Manual,* this is called copying to off-screen locations. To facilitate this, select the desired measures, and then hold Option-Shift (Mac) or the Control-Shift (Windows) to copy and then paste.

1. Choose the Mass Edit tool .
2. Highlight measures 1 and 2 (source measures) by dragging a box around them.

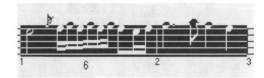

3. Advance to measure 5. (CAUTION: Do not click on the white portion of the screen or the selection will be cancelled).
4. Hold Option-Shift (Mac) or Control-Shift (Windows), and click the mouse in the staff of the target measure. Finale will copy the source measures to the new location.

Use Simple Entry to enter the notation for measures 7 and 8.

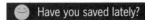

Have you saved lately?

Advancing to a Specific Measure

So far, we have advanced to measures using the scroll bars at the bottom of the screen. In Scroll View, Finale offers another way to jump from measure to measure. Measures can be selected using the Jump to Measure box at the bottom of the Finale Window.

To jump to a measure 11 in the score, in Scroll View:

1. At the bottom of the screen, double-click in the box next to the word "Measure."
2. Enter the number "11," and press Return/Enter. Finale will jump to that measure.

Going Home

Another helpful Finale option for immediately returning to the first measure of the piece is using the Home command. Go to the View menu, and select Home. (In Page View, this positions the top-left of your page in your monitor.)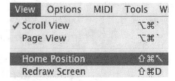

If there is a Home key on your computer keyboard, that will serve the same function. The End key will advance to the last measure of the piece (or the bottom-right of the page, in Page View).

Enter the notation for the measures 11 through 24:
- Use Copy and Paste for measures 17 and 18 and measures 21 and 22. *Do not enter the whole rests in measures 9, 10, 14, and 15*. Finale automatically places rests in measures without notation, which is a timesaving feature.

When you change from tool to tool, the Finale Simple Entry carat may not be in the correct measure. To move the Simple Entry caret, press the Right or Left Arrow key on the computer keyboard.

Entering Ties Across the Barline

Since Simple Entry is set to automatically move to the next measure, this can be used to save time entering ties across the barline.

1. Advance to measure 26.
2. Enter the rests. (Press 6 for half, 5 for quarter, and 4 for eighth.)

3. Instead of entering an eighth note at the end of measure 26, enter a B quarter note after the eighth rest on the and of beat 4.
4. Press Enter. Finale will automatically create a tie across the barline.

Enter the Remaining Notation

Remember, within a measure, enter ties by putting in the first note, pressing the letter T, and entering the second note of the tie.

Add the Double Barline in Measure 32

1. Choose the Measure tool 📖.
2. Double-click inside measure 32.
3. Select the double barline.

Adding Articulations

It is important to have a plan of attack when entering music in Finale. I have found that it saves time entering the notation and ties first, then going back to enter the articulations and other markings.

Articulations, such as accent and staccato markings, are usually entered using the Articulation tool. They also can be entered using the Simple Entry tool. I usually enter these in Scroll View.

1. Go to measure 1 using the Jump to Measure box, selecting **View** > Home Position, or by using the Home key.
2. Select the Articulation tool 🎵.
3. To enter the selected articulation, in this case an accent mark, click on the note-head or its stem.
4. Choose the accent marking, and click Select.

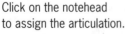
Click on the notehead
to assign the articulation.

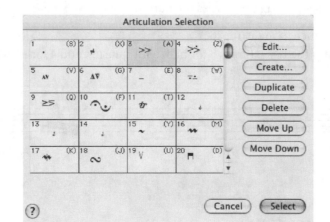

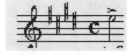

Notice that the Articulation Selection window, in some cases, displays two of each articulation. This indicates that the shape will automatically adjust to the note position according to the stem position. Finale can automatically position the marking above or below the note. In most cases, the articulation will be in the proper location. However, if it collides with another notation element in the score, it can be moved.

Moving or Deleting Articulation Markings

1. Press ESC (escape) to choose the Selection tool .
2. Click and drag the accent to a new location.
3. To delete or edit the accent marking, using the Selection tool, click on the accent. Press the Delete key on the keyboard.

Enter the rest of the articulations in the first sixteen measures of "Trumpet Voluntary."

> Articulations, like chord symbols, will copy when you copy and paste measures. With this in mind, it may be better to enter the notation and articulations before copying to other locations in the score.

Using Metatools to Enter Articulations

Entering articulations one at a time, as above, can be time consuming. Finale offers a quicker way to assign these common markings: Metatools. Metatools are pre-programmed keyboard shortcuts, built into Finale. These keyboard shortcuts reduce the time needed to enter articulations.

To view the Metatool assignments for articulations:

1. Choose the Articulation tool.
2. Click on a note head.

Notice that each articulation has a number or letter in parentheses in the upper right-hand corner of the Articulation Selection box. This number (or letter) is the Metatool assignment. These can be changed; however, I usually use the numbers that are built into Finale.

Metatool assignments

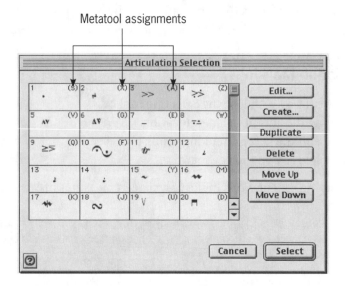

To assign accents by using Metatools, simply choose the Articulation tool, hold down the appropriate number or letter (S = staccato, A = accent, T = trill, P = pedal, etc.), and click on the note head to assign the articulation.

So, to enter the accent on the E half note in measure 1:

1. Choose the Articulation tool 🔈.
2. Hold down the letter A for an accent.
3. Click on the E half note. The accent marking should appear.

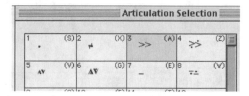

Assigning Multiple Articulations

It is also possible to drag-select a group of notes to apply an articulation. For example, in measure 3, there are three notes with accents in a row. To assign all three to the accent using Metatools:

1. Choose the Articulations tool 🔈.
2. Hold down the letter A for an accent.
3. Drag over the three notes (draw a box around the notes), and accents will be added to all three notes.

Entering Articulations using Simple Entry

Another articulation shortcut is to use Simple Entry's contextual menu. The advantage is the articulations can be entered when the notes are entered.

72

1. Choose the Simple Entry tool 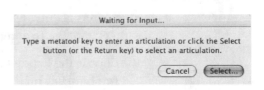.
2. Enter a note.
3. After the note is entered, press the asterisk (*) key on the numeric keypad.
4. Press the desired Metatool key (A = accent; S = staccato) to enter an articulation.

Enter the rest of the articulations in "Trumpet Voluntary." Try to use the Metatool assignments.

C Trumpet

Jeremiah Clarke

Trumpet Voluntary

entered by [your name]

This arrangement copyright © 1997 by Tom Rudolph

Adding Dynamic Markings (Expressions)

After entering notes and articulations, add the dynamic markings. These were entered in earlier chapters. To enter the dynamics:

1. Choose the Expression tool .
2. Double-click on the first note in the measure to enter the dynamic marking.
3. Drag the dynamic marking's handle to the desired location.

> Make sure you always leave the dynamic marking (or any other Expression) on the same notes to which you attached it. Avoid dragging a staff Expression to another note in the score. It will print fine, but when you go back to edit your document, it could take hours, weeks, or months to find the original note.

Adding Dynamics Using Simple Entry

Another option is to enter the dynamics using Simple Entry. As with articulations, the advantage is that the dynamics can be entered immediately after entering the notation in Simple Entry. Metatools are also available for Expressions, as we will soon discuss in greater detail.

1. Choose the Simple Entry tool 🎵 .
2. Enter a note.
3. After the note is entered, press X on the keyboard.
4. Press the Metatool key or click Select to choose an Expression.

> There are also Metatools for Expressions. Note the numbers and letters in parenthesis next to the selections. Memorize often-used Metatools to speed the notation entry process.

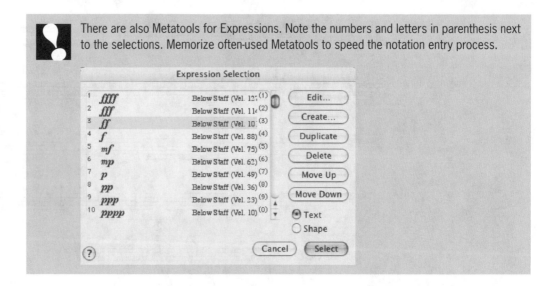

Creating a New Text Expression

The word "Stately" is printed at the beginning of the piece. Finale has several ways to enter text. We have already used the Text tool for entering titles. The best way to enter text within the score is to connect it to a specific measure. If the score's page layout changes, the Expression moves too. For this reason, I usually enter words such as Andante, Stately, Vivace, and the like, with the Expression tool.

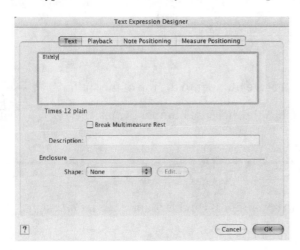

1. Choose the Expression tool 𝑚𝑓 .
2. Double-click on the notehead or stem of the first note in measure 1.
3. Click on the Note Expression button.
4. Click on the Create Button.
5. Type in the word "Stately" in the Text Expression Designer. Then click OK.

6. Click Select in the Staff Selection Expression box, then click OK in the Measure Expression Assignment box.
7. Drag the word "Stately" above the first measure.

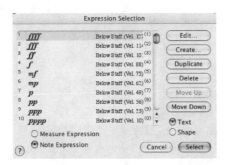

Boxing Measure Numbers

In the score, there are several locations where measure numbers are boxed. This occurs at measures 9, 17, and 25. To box a measure number:

1. Choose the Measure tool ▦.
2. Advance to measure 9.
3. Double-click on the handle of measure number 9.
4. Select the Rectangle Shape. Then click OK to close the window.

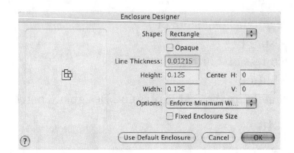

5. Drag the boxed measure number to the top of the staff.

Repeat these steps to box the measure number in measures 17 and 25.

Entering a D.C. al Coda

Use the Repeat tool to enter repeats and *D.S.* and *D.C. al Coda* signs.

1. Choose the Repeat tool ▤.
2. Advance to measure 32.
3. Click above the measure.
4. Choose "D.C. al Coda" from the Repeat Selection dialog box, and then click Select.

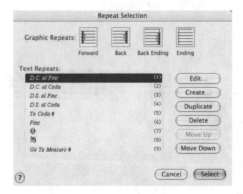

After closing the Repeat Selection window, the Repeat Assignment window appears. This window is used to input information to control the way the sign will repeat or jump to selected measures. Since D.C. means go back to the top (measure 1), the following change needs to be made in the Repeat Assignment window:

5. Enter 1 in the target measure box. Click OK.

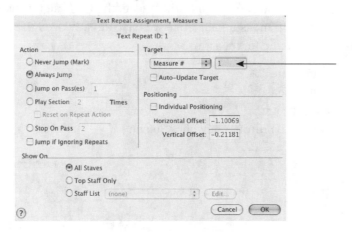

6. After entering the D.C. al Coda sign, drag it to the desired location in the measure.

😊 Have you saved lately?

Enter the Coda Signs

When entering the coda sign, it is very important to select the correct measure, especially if you want the sign to play back. The Repeat tool signs can be programmed for proper playback.

1. Advance to measure 7.
2. Click inside the staff in measure 7.
3. Choose the Coda sign, and click Select.

To enter the Repeat Assignment information so the piece will play pack properly:

1. Target measure = 33.
2. Jump on Total Passes = 2. Then click OK.
3. Drag the Coda sign to the desired location.

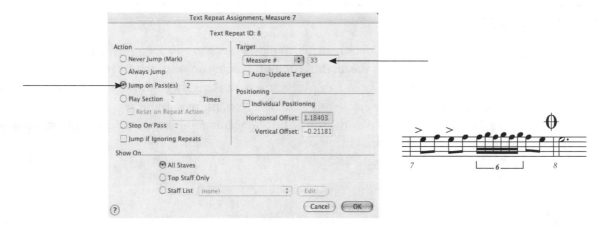

When entering multiple signs using the Repeat tool, it is important to create new copies of the signs each time they are used. In this piece, the Coda sign is used twice: once in measure 7 and again in measure 33. Since we have already used the sign in measure 7, we must create a new one for measure 33.

4.   Advance to measure 33.
5.   Click inside the measure.
6.   Choose the Coda Sign.
7.   Click the Duplicate button. Then click Select.

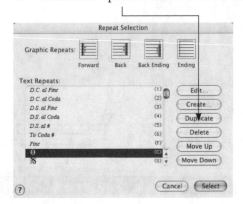
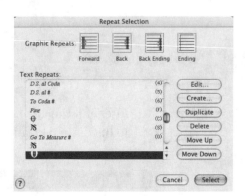

8.   Make no changes to the Repeat Assignment setting. Click OK.
9.   Drag the sign to the desired location in the measure.

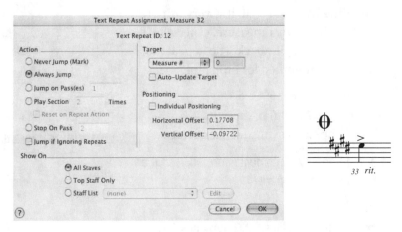

Sound the Trumpet

We have used the playback controls to play a piece to check for mistakes. Now, add the correct timbre for this piece: the trumpet. Finale can send the instrument number to your MIDI keyboard, or it can play various timbres through the computer's built-in speaker. If you are connected to a MIDI keyboard, read on. If you don't have a MIDI keyboard and want to play the sound through your computer's built-in synthesizer, skip to the following section.

MIDI Playback

To play back "Trumpet Voluntary" through your MIDI keyboard, you need to be familiar with how the keyboard sends and receives information. Most keyboards today are General MIDI compatible. If the keyboard is General MIDI compatible, refer to the keyboard's manual and set it up to send and receive General MIDI.

When a new file is opened in Finale, General MIDI is assumed. It is possible to play back and program specific sounds on non-General MIDI keyboards. The following example deals only with General MIDI. If you do not have a General MIDI compatible MIDI keyboard, consult the *Finale User Manual* from the Help menu, or read the *Installation & Tutorials* booklet: "Setting Up and Configuring MIDI."

To set a trumpet timbre:

If you selected a trumpet from the Setup Wizard, it automatically assigns a trumpet timbre. You can change the timbre if necessary.

1. Set your General MIDI instrument to multitimbral mode or to use the built-in sound of your computer. Consult your instrument's manual, if necessary.
2. Select **Windows** > Instrument List.
3. Display the Playback Controls, and click Play.

As you listen to the playback, you will notice that Finale also plays back the dynamics and the articulations.

To set a different instrument sound:

4. From the Instrument List, click on the word "Trumpet."
5. Choose New Instrument from this popup menu.
6. Type in a name for the new instrument, for example "Brass Section."
7. Choose the new instrument sound from the General MIDI popup menu. Then click OK to close the window.

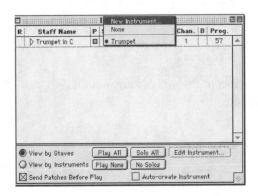
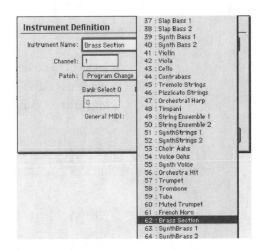

Computer Playback

Finale can also play back through the computer's built-in speaker. To play back through the computer's speaker:

Mac OS	Windows
1. Select **MIDI** > Internal Speaker Playback. 2. Choose "SmartMusic SoftSynth Playback."	1. Select **Options** > MIDI Setup. 2. Choose the SmartMusic SoftSynth for the MIDI Out device.

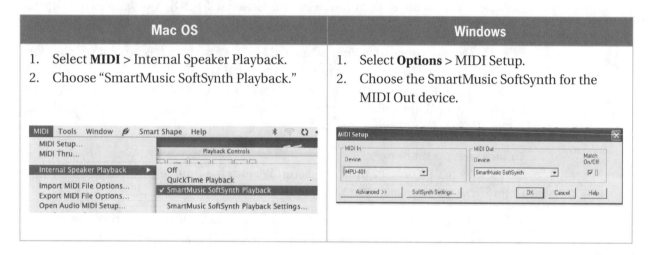

Page Layout

After the notation and entries are complete and the part has been checked for errors, the page layout can be addressed. The tuplets and other markings tend to look crowded on the screen. This can be adjusted using Music Spacing.

Adjusting the Music Spacing

As mentioned in chapter 1, Finale does automatically space notes and lyrics as they are entered, as long as this option is selected in the Edit menu. However, sometimes when entering complex notation, a manual application of note spacing is needed.

To manually apply note spacing:
1. Choose the Mass Edit tool 🔘.
2. Select **Edit** > Select All.
3. Select **Mass Edit** > Music Spacing > Apply Note Spacing.
4. Select **Edit** > Update Layout.

Gathered Rests

Finale can automatically create a gathered rest for a single part. Since there are two places in "Trumpet Voluntary" where there are more than one measure's rests, the following steps should be followed.

1. Choose the Measure tool .
2. Highlight measures 9 and 10.
3. Select **Measures** > Multimeasure Rests > Create.

If these steps do not create a gathered rest in your part, it is possible that you entered actual rests in these measures. When Finale sees any markings—notes or rests in a measure—it does not consider it a blank measure. Delete these entered rests, and the Gathered Rest function will work.

> It is not necessary to do this manually each time there are multiple measure rests. If you want to have Finale create them all for you, select the Measure tool and Select All, and then select **Measure** > Multimeasure Rests > Create. Finale will create all of the gathered rests in the entire piece.

Setting the Page Layout

The goal is to print the part on one page. The first step is to group the measures to four per line.

1. Choose the Page Layout tool .
2. Select **Page Layout** > Fit Music.
3. Group measures to "4" per line.

Next, the staff systems need to be adjusted so the entire piece fits on one page. (Of course, if time was of the essence, you could just print the part on two pages.) First view the pages:

4. Select **View** > Page View.
5. Scale the view to 50% to see the entire page on the monitor.

Indenting Individual Staff Systems

To make room for the Coda, the last staff system should be indented. This means moving the last staff system slightly to the right. To indent the last system to make room for the word Coda, use the Page Layout function in Finale. Page Layout allows you control over the margins and page size.

1. With the Page Layout tool selected, click the mouse inside the left box of system 9, and drag it to the right to the desired position.
2. Drag the right box of system 9 to the left.

Since the last system only has one measure, the right margin can be moved in slightly.

3. Drag the right handle of staff system 9 to the left.

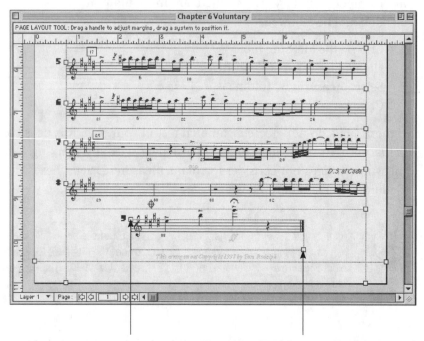

Click and drag the handle of system 9 and drag it to indent.

😊 Have you saved lately?

Moving a Staff System

There are times when you will want to change the space between one or more systems in the piece. For example, you might want to move the coda down slightly and give more space above the entire system. To do this:

1. Choose the Page Layout tool .
2. Scroll to the desired system.
3. Click anywhere *inside* the system, but not on the left or right handle, and drag the system up or down.

Adding Titles and Hiding the Staff Name

1. Choose the Text tool Ⓐ.
2. Select **View** > Page View.
3. Scroll to the top of the page.
4. Enter the text: "Jeremiah Clarke" and "C Trumpet."

C Trumpet   Jeremiah Clarke

Trumpet Voluntary

entered by (your name)

To hide the Staff Name (C Trumpet):

1. Press ESC to choose the Selection tool ⬉.
2. Double-click on the staff name: C Trumpet.
3. Open the contextual menu: Control-click (Mac) or Right-click (Windows) on the handle, and choose Edit Staff Attributes.
4. In the staff Attributes window, uncheck Staff Name.

Trumpet in C

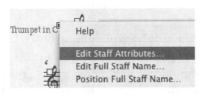

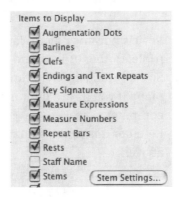

To enter the word "Coda":

1. In Page View, scroll to the bottom of the screen.
2. Double-click the mouse to make a text block.
3. Enter the word "Coda" before the last system.
4. Highlight or select the text: select **Edit** > Select All.
5. Select **Text** > Size, and change the font size to 18.

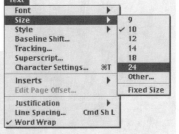

Printing

To print the piece, select **File** > Print.

Summary

This chapter added several new areas. The list of steps for entering music in Finale now includes:

- Set up the score, key, and meter.
- Display measure numbers in every bar, and box several at key places in the score.
- Enter the notation by using Simple Entry, and include tuplets and grace notes. Use the Mass Edit tool to copy and paste identical measures, to save time.
- Delete the extra measures, using Mass Edit.
- Enter the double barline, using the Measure tool.
- Enter the articulations, using the Articulation tool. Speed up the process by using Metatools.
- Enter the dynamic markings, using Staff Expressions. Enter a custom Expression at the beginning of the piece.
- Enter the D.C. and Coda signs, using the Repeat tool.
- Group the measures per systems, using the Page Layout tool.
- In Page Layout, drag the last staff to make room for the word Coda.
- Use the Text tool to enter the word Coda.
- Print the piece.

Review

1. Review how to enter tuplets and grace notes with Simple Entry. Practice entering triplets, other tuplets, and grace notes. Use Finale Help, if necessary.
2. Select several different timbres from Finale to play back through your MIDI instrument. If you have a multimedia computer, try sending the sound through the computer's speaker.
3. Re-enter this composition, or one like it, using the steps listed in the summary above.

6

HyperScribe: Real-Time Note Entry ("America")

All of the previous chapters dealt with some form of step entry of music notation. Select the value, and enter the pitch for each individual note. Simple Entry is my choice for entering the majority of notation in Finale. However, there are other helpful ways that Finale provides for the entry of notation. This chapter focuses Finale's HyperScribe tool, which lets you enter music by playing in a performance-like manner on your MIDI instrument.

HyperScribe Example 1: "America"

HyperScribe Example 2: "America" Counter-Melody

The new areas explored in this chapter include:

- creating a blank default document
- entering music in real-time using HyperScribe
- creating two sets of measure numbers in the same piece
- setting the Quantization level
- page formatting, forcing specific numbers of measures per system
- moving staves in Page Layout
- changing tempos for playback

Real-time Entry with HyperScribe

Imagine if Mozart had had a tool with which he could sit at the keyboard and play in all of the music already composed in his head, rather than drawing note heads on paper with ink and a quill pen. Using Finale's HyperScribe, it is possible to play music on the MIDI keyboard as Finale attempts to transcribe what is played. In some cases, Hyper-Scribe can be the fastest way to enter notation into your score. Entering music in this way is called "real-time entry." Simple Entry (see chapters 2 through 5) is a step-time tool. The HyperScribe tool is a real-time entry tool.

To demonstrate the use of HyperScribe, we are going to enter the melody, "America" and a counter-melody. These examples demonstrate the advantages and disadvantages of using HyperScribe.

In the computer world, the word "hyper" is used to indicate something with built-in intelligence. "Hypertext" is text that when you click on it with the mouse, provides additional information. "Hyperlinks" are used on the Internet to indicate text or pictures that link to other locations or sites. In Finale, HyperScribe is an intelligent tool for transcribing music.

Setting Up The Score

Prepare the score for the piece we are going to enter using the HyperScribe tool. The example on the previous page looks like two separate pieces, but they were created in one file in Finale and made to look like two separate pieces. Both examples have fourteen measures, for a total of twenty-eight measures in the piece.

Creating a Blank Document

There will be times when you will not want to use the Setup Wizard. For example, if you want a blank file with no title or instrument name. To select a blank default document:

1. Select **File** > Launch Window.
2. Click on Default Document.

Another option is to select **File** > New > Default Document.

Finale creates a piece with thirty-one measures. Since the example has twenty-eight measures, you will need to delete the extra measures. I usually enter all of the music and then delete the extra measures. These extra measures will be deleted later in this chapter.

Changing the Key Signature

With all our examples so far, the key signature was set by using the Setup Wizard. There are times when you will want to change the key, such as when using a default document or for entering a key change. There are two options. One is to use the Key Signature tool, by choosing the tool and then clicking inside a measure to enter the key signature. Another option is to use the contextual menus. To change the Key with Contextual Menus:

1. Press ESC (escape) to choose the Selection tool .
2. Go to the first measure and choose the contextual menu: Control-click (Mac) or Right-click (Windows).
3. Select Edit Key Signature from the contextual menu.
4. Change the key signature to G major from measure 1 to the end of the piece.

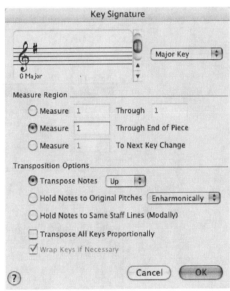

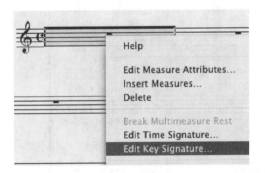

Changing the Meter with Contextual Menus

There will also be times when you will want to change the time signature for all or part of a piece. This can be done using the Time Signature tool. Click the tool and enter the change. The contextual menus can be an easier way to edit the meter.

1. Press ESC (escape) to choose the Selection tool .
2. Go to the first measure, and choose the contextual menu by clicking directly on the C common time marking. Control-click (Mac) or Right-click (Windows).
3. Select the "3/4" time signature.

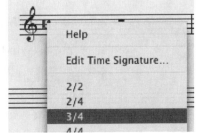

Creating Two Sets of Measure Numbers

Next, create the measure numbers by using the Measure tool. When you select **File** > New > Default Document, Finale automatically creates a piece with measure numbers displayed at the beginning of each staff system, numbered from 1 to the end of the piece. In this example, we need to create two sets, or "regions," of measure numbers to make the single page look like two separate pieces. The first region is measures 1 through 14.

Setting the First Measure-Number Region

First, create a region (Region 1) that includes measures 1 through 14. As usual, display the numbers beginning in measure 1 and positioned below the staff, just to the right of the left barline.

1. Choose the Measure tool 🔲.
2. Select **Measures** > Measure Numbers > Edit Regions.
3. Make the following changes in the dialog box that appears.

Enter 1 for first region.   Change to 14 for first section.

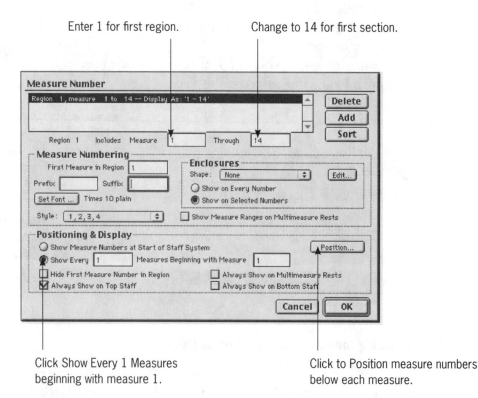

Click Show Every 1 Measures
beginning with measure 1.

Click to Position measure numbers
below each measure.

Adding Measure Numbers in the Second Region

To create a second region of numbers and display them on measures 15 through 28:

4. In the Measure Number dialog box, click the Add button, to create a new measure number region.
5. Enter the second region measure numbers: "15" through "28."
6. Select Show Every 1 Measures Beginning with Measure 1.
7. Uncheck Hide First Measure Number in Region.

Measure region 15–28

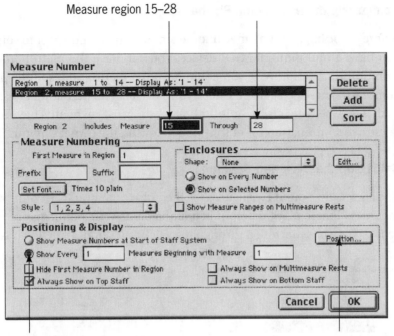

Click Show Every 1 Measures . . .　　　　　　　Click to adjust positioning

Finale looks at each region as a totally separate entity. Measure 1 in the second region is actually measure 15 in the piece. Before you exit this dialog window, click on the Position button and drag the measure numbers to the same location as measures 1 through 14.

In Scroll View, move around the score using the Jump to Measure box at the bottom of the screen. Notice that the box now displays two numbers. The number to the left of the colon is the region (1 or 2), while the right-hand number is the individual measure within that region. To go to measure 5 in Region 2, enter the numbers 2:5, and press Return/Enter.

left number = region

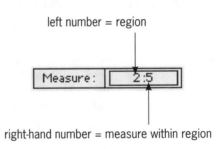

right-hand number = measure within region

Entering in Real-time with a Metronome

After the score is prepared, you can enter the notation for "America" using Hyper-Scribe. In order to use HyperScribe, a MIDI keyboard (or other MIDI controller) must be connected to your computer. See the MIDI chapter for more information on using MIDI controllers other than keyboards, as well as the information on MIDI in Help.

There are two ways to enter with HyperScribe: with the computer playing the pulse like a metronome, or you controlling the tempo with a note or foot pedal. Controlling the tempo is an option that is unique to Finale. First, let's use the traditional way to enter notation in real-time: with the computer supplying the pulse.

Configuring the Metronome Playback

Before recording, Finale's metronome sound source and specific sound must be set. If you have a multitimbral MIDI device, you can have the metronome sound a percussion timbre. Alternatively, you could have the metronome sounds played through the computer's internal speaker. Check your MIDI keyboard manual to see if it is multitimbral. If it is, be sure it is in Multitimbral mode. Most keyboards have a specific button or keystroke combination to set this mode. Consult the owner's manual if you are unsure.

Setting Up the Click and Countoff

The click is the sound Finale uses for the pulse or tempo. The countoff is the number of measures Finale plays before it actually records your performance or plays back your score. These are controlled through the Click and Countoff dialog box.

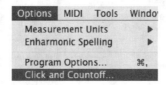

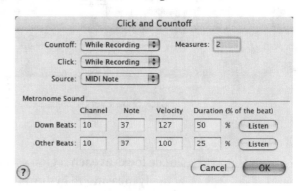

1. Select **Options** > Click and Countoff.
2. Set the values for playback in the Click and Countoff dialog window, as shown.

In the above settings, the metronome is set to MIDI channel 10—the channel reserved for percussion sounds. Note that number 37 is the General MIDI number for a rim-shot sound. These settings can be changed, if needed. I have also set the metronome to play only while recording.

In the Measures box, there is a 2. This means you will hear two countoff measures before the computer starts recording. This is extremely helpful, as it helps to set the tempo so that your note entry will be more accurate.

If your MIDI sound source is not multitimbral, then set the metronome to the tonic note of the key. In this example, choose the note G. Another option is to set the sound source to "internal speaker." The click will then come from the computer.

Setting the HyperScribe Options

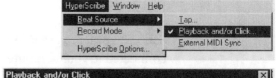

1. Choose the HyperScribe tool.
2. Select **HyperScribe** > Beat Source > Playback and/or Click.
3. Set the Starting Signal for Recording for the HyperScribe session.
4. Set the Tempo.

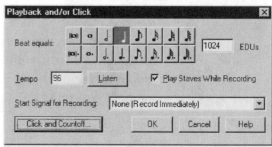

For the Start Signal for Recording, I usually choose None (Record Immediately), as a 2-measure lead-in was programmed in the Playback and/or Click dialog box. I recommend using a very slow tempo when using HyperScribe.

The next item to set in the HyperScribe menu is the Quantization level. Quantization refers to Finale's capability of rounding to the nearest note value. Perhaps you actually played a thirty-second note ahead of the beat. If you set the quantize to an eighth note, Finale will round your performance to the nearest eighth note.

To choose the best quantization level, let the music be your guide. In this case, examine the first fourteen measures of "America."

The smallest value in this piece is an eighth note (see the notation on page 92); therefore, set Finale to quantize, or round off, to the nearest eighth note. This will help forgive some of our timing problems when we enter in HyperScribe.

Setting the Quantization Level

1. Select **Options** > Quantization Settings. Since the smallest note value in the first fourteen measures is an eighth note, select that value from the quantization window.
2. Since there are no triplets in the "America" melody, click the No Tuplets button. Then click OK.

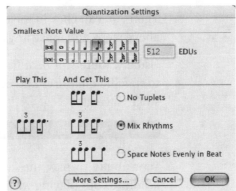

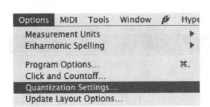

Setting the Record Mode and HyperScribe Options

1. Select **HyperScribe** > Record Mode > Record into One Staff.
2. Select **HyperScribe** > HyperScribe Options.

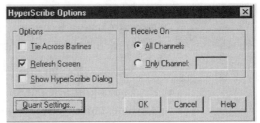

Usually, I activate Refresh Screen, which displays the music I'm playing on the screen. If you are using a slow computer, you may want to uncheck this option.

We are now ready to record. (Wouldn't you have had most, if not all, of the piece entered by now if you had just used Simple Entry? Possibly, but keep on reading because HyperScribe can be a time saver, in some cases.)

- Click the mouse inside the first measure of the piece. You should hear two measures of 3/4 as a countoff. Then start recording. Go ahead and give it a try.

If you don't like your first take, no problem! Just select **Edit** > Undo to erase your last recording.

Then you can click in the first measure and try it again, or you can go back through the above steps and make any necessary changes, such as slowing down the tempo.

Usually, there will be a few places where editing is necessary. Use Simple Entry to go to specific measures and edit the notation. And if you enter something that makes you smile, save it!

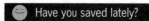 Have you saved lately?

Your ability to play the keyboard in tempo with the metronome will determine how accurate your playing will be. Don't give up after one or two tries. Usually, with practice, melodies such as "America" can be entered quite accurately in HyperScribe.

Erasing Music without Deleting Measures

To give this example another try, erase the notation in measures 1 to 14. We want the measure layout to remain, so **don't** use the Delete Measure command or the Delete key on your computer keyboard.

1. Choose the Mass Edit tool .
2. Select **Edit** > Select All.
3. Select **Mass Edit** > Clear Items.
4. In the Items to Erase window, choose "Everything." This will erase all of the notes and rests, but leave the blank measures.

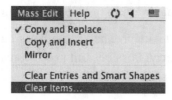

To Beat or Not To Beat

There is another option with HyperScribe that is worth considering: controlling the beat or tempo yourself, either with a key on the MIDI keyboard or with a foot pedal. When I use HyperScribe, I usually control the beat or tempo myself. This unique Finale feature can be the best way to enter music in real-time, since you control the metronome tempo.

Controlling the Beat/Tempo

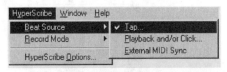

1. Choose the HyperScribe tool 🐟.
2. Select **HyperScribe** > Beat Source > Tap.
3. Choose the tap source you want to use from the Tap Source dialog box. This can be a pedal, any key on your MIDI keyboard, or other input device.

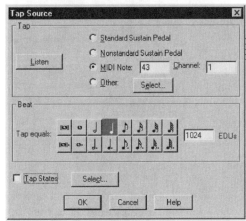

If you have a sustain pedal connected to your MIDI keyboard, this is the way I recommend that you enter notation. Simply tap your foot and play the melody. You can slow down or speed up the tempo as you are entering the notation. If you do not own a sustain pedal, use the tonic note of the piece, in this case G. Select the MIDI Note option, and then choose the Listen button and play the note G. The number 43 is the MIDI note number for G, two octaves below middle C.

- Click the mouse in the first measure of the piece.

Entering Example 2

Finale is waiting for you to supply the metronome with your hand or your foot. When you are ready, give it a try.

 I usually enter two or three measures of clicks just to help me establish the beat. After I record the melody, I delete these measures.

Now, we're ready to try part 2 of this example—the "America" counter-melody that follows. First, we need to examine the music to determine the quantization level.

HyperScribe Example 2: "America" Counter-Melody

After analyzing the above example, the quantization level must be reset because there are sixteenth notes and triplets.

To reset the Quantization Level:

1. Choose the HyperScribe tool 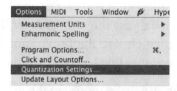.
2. Select **Options** > Quantization Settings.
3. Since there are sixteenth notes in the example, select the sixteenth note as the Smallest Note Value.
4. Since there are triplets, click the Mix Rhythms button.

The measure layout for the second example is complete. Finale records your last setting, so you are set up to enter the notation with you controlling the tempo without reentering the commands. If you want to switch back to Finale playing the metronome tempo, do so now.

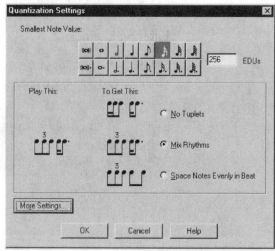

• Click on measure 1 of the second example, or use the Jump to Measure control by typing in 2:1. Play the "America" counter-melody.

HyperScribe Example 2: "America" Counter-Melody

Following is the printout of what I got after several tries (in other words, this is about as good as it gets....)

My HyperScribe attempt:

Minimizing Rests

Another useful HyperScribe option is that Finale can minimize the number of rests in its transcription. In the previous example, Finale eliminated some of the rests in an attempt to make the music look more readable. However, since this example has a great deal of rests, this feature can and should be turned off.

Let's retry the example, this time with the Minimize Rests feature turned off.

1. Select **Options** > Quantization Settings.
2. Click the More Settings button.
3. Match the settings in the graphic at right.
4. Select **Edit** > Undo HyperScribe Session to erase the last recording, or use the shortcut: ⌘-Z (Mac) or Control-Z (Windows).
5. Click in measure 15, and HyperScribe another attempt.

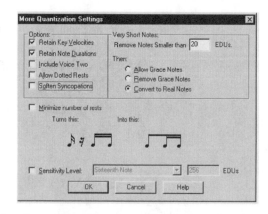

This time, some of the example transcribed more accurately. After several tries, the best I could do is printed below. Some parts are more accurate because we turned off the Minimize Rests feature.

Your own performance may print differently than mine, but you will likely find that, when there are many rests in the music, HyperScribe will do a fair-to-middlin' job of transcribing. Sure, we could go in and edit all of the errors, but my experience is that by the time I edit out all of the mistakes, I could have entered in more quickly if I just started in Simple Entry from the beginning.

This brings up a good point. You may use different entry tools for various parts of a piece. I would have chosen HyperScribe for the melody of "America" and used Simple Entry for the counter-melody.

 When you see triplets and lots of rests, it will most likely be faster to step-enter the notes using Simple Entry than to use HyperScribe. Another option is to make the Smallest Note Value in the Quantization dialog box a smaller value, such as an eighth note or sixteenth note. This could make the transcription more accurate.

Laying Out the Measures for Each Example

To make the examples line up properly on the page:
1. Choose the Page Layout tool.
2. Drag the upper-left handle of staff system 1 to the left, to align it with the other staves.
3. Select **Page Layout** > Fit Music.
4. Set Lock Layout to "4" measures per system.
5. Set Change to measures 1:1 through 1:14. Then click OK.

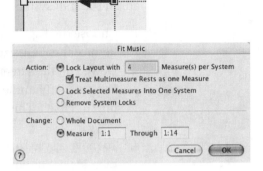

To move one measure from the line above:
1. Choose the Mass Edit tool.
2. Click in the white portion of the screen to deselect measures 1 through 14.
3. Click inside measure 12 to select just this measure.
4. Press the Down Arrow key on the computer keyboard to move the measure to the next line.

To group the measures for the counter-melody:
1. Choose the Page Layout tool.
2. Select **Page Layout** > Fit Music.
3. Set Lock Layout to "3" measures per system
4. Set Change to measures 2:1 through 2:14. Click OK.

Deleting the Extra Measures

Use the Measure tool to delete the extra measures. Select the measures from measure to the end, and then press the Delete key.

Page Layout: Fitting Both Examples on One Page

This example gives some good practice with creating two separate examples on the same page. First, let's get as many staves as possible on one page. This example requires nine staves to appear on one page. To change the space between **all** staves:

1. Select **View** > Page View.
2. Select **View** > Scale View To, and choose 50%, so that you can see ALL the staves on the screen.
3. Choose the Staff tool.
4. Scroll to the top of the screen, click on the top system handle, and drag it up until all nine systems appear on the first page.

Making Two Titles on the Same Page

To make room for the titles, two steps are needed: first, drag staff 1 up to the top of the page, and then drag staff 5 down, to make room for the title in the middle of the page. To adjust the staff systems:

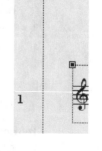

1. Choose the Page Layout tool .
2. Reduce the View size to 50% so the entire piece can be viewed on the screen.
3. Drag the left handle of staff system 1 down close to the staff itself. This will provide more room to drag the staves.
4. To move a system, drag it from anywhere inside its margins, up or down.
5. Go to system 5, which is the beginning of the second example. Drag it down, slightly, from inside the system's margins (not on the handles). Be sure that you don't force the last system to the next page.

To enter the titles:
1. Choose the Text tool .
2. Double-click the handle of the word "[Title]."
3. Select **Edit** > Select All, or use the shortcut ⌘-A (Mac) or Control-A (Windows).
4. Enter the title: HyperScribe Example 1: "America."
5. Drag the new title above the first staff.
5. Scroll to above system 5.
6. Double-click in the middle of the page, and enter the second title: HyperScribe Example 2: "America" Counter-Melody.
7. Adjust the font and size of the text as desired using the Text tool.

Changing Tempos for Playback

It is possible to change tempos in a piece for playback. For example, it is possible to set the first example (measures 1–14) to play at quarter note = 100, and the counter-melody to play at another tempo. In order to use tempo assignments, you will have to turn off Human Playback.

To turn off Human Playback:

Mac OS	Windows
Click on the arrow to the left of the Playback Controls. 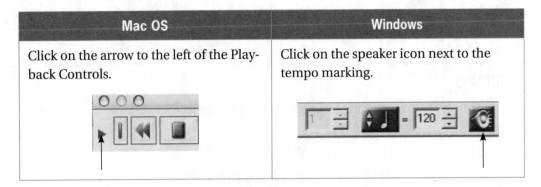	Click on the speaker icon next to the tempo marking.

- Click the pull-down menu next to Human Playback Style to make a selection.

To change the tempo:
1. Select the Tempo tool (Mac), or select **Tools** > Special > Tempo (Windows).
2. Click inside the first measure.
3. Set to "100" Beats Per Minute, Measure "1:1" Through "1:14."

To set a new tempo for the counter-melody:
4. With the Tempo tool selected, click in measure 15 (2:1).
5. Change the tempo to the desired speed (for example "120"), and enter Measure "2:1" Through End of Piece.

Select **Window** > Playback Controls, and click Play. The tempo should start at 100 and immediately change to 120 (or the tempo you entered) at the counter-melody.

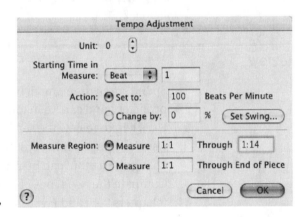

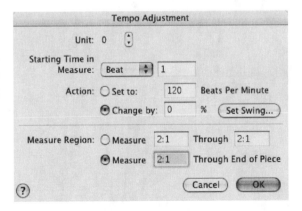

Printing

After the notation has been entered and edited, select **File** > Print to print out the two examples on one page.

Summary

This chapter focused on entering music in real-time using Finale's HyperScribe tool. The steps included:

- setting up the score
- entering two regions of measure numbers
- entering notation using HyperScribe, with the computer providing the click and by using a tap source to provide the tempo
- using Finale's Quantization feature to select the smallest note value in a particular passage or piece
- manually moving measures down to the next staff system in Page Layout
- dragging staff systems in Page Layout to make room for titles and text in the middle of the page
- using the Tempo tool to insert an initial tempo and to change the tempo during the playback

Review

1. Spend some time practicing with HyperScribe. This tool takes time to become proficient and can be helpful with some types of notation.
2. Use Help to review the setup and features of HyperScribe.
3. Use the Tempo tool to create a ritard at the end of the piece and other tempo changes. The tool can be programmed to change tempos by the beat, if needed.
4. Compare the two types of entry tools that have been covered so far: Simple Entry (chapters 2–5) and HyperScribe (chapter 6).

SECTION II
Grand-Staff and
Small-Ensemble Scores

7

Piano Piece Using HyperScribe ("Musette")

In this chapter, you'll notate a two-staff piano part. Begin by looking over the score to identify new areas to be addressed.

Musette in D
(from "Little Notebook for Anna Magdalena Bach")

Johann Sebastian Bach (1685-1750)

adapted by Tom Rudolph

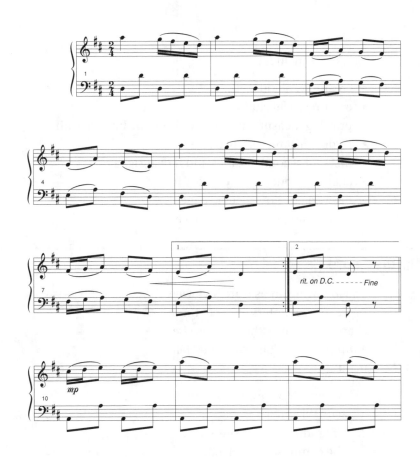

New areas include:

- creating a piano staff
- creating a clef change
- printing measure numbers only on the bottom staff
- HyperScribing with two hands
- first and second endings and repeat signs
- changing font size and style for text
- inserting text on specific pages
- transposing sections of a piece

Setting Up the Score

The following areas were reviewed in previous chapters. Refer to these chapters, or use the *Finale User Manual,* accessible from the Help menu.

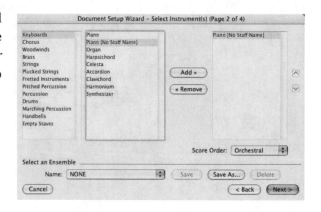

1. Select **File** > New > Document with Wizard Setup.
2. Enter the title "Musette" and the composer "J.S. Bach."
3. Select the instruments Keyboards, Piano [No Staff Name].
4. Change the key to D for the entire piece.
5. Change the time signature to 2/4.

Measure Numbers

Even though I plan to print measure numbers only at the start of each staff system, I display the numbers on every measure while I am entering the notation and markings. This helps me to see exactly where I am in the score.

- Use the Measure tool 🔘 to display measure numbers on every measure. For specific instructions, see chapter 3, page 33.

HyperScribing with Two Hands

If you are comfortable playing the piano and want to try enter two staves of notation at the same time, read on. If not, then you may want to try to HyperScribe one staff at a time. You could also skip playing anything in real-time, and use Simple Entry to enter the score. The latter would be my personal choice. However, my keyboard skills are limited so, that influences my preference. If you want to try HyperScribing with two hands:

1. Select **Options** > Quantization Settings.
2. Since there are sixteenth notes in the score, set the Smallest Note Value to a sixteenth note.

When using HyperScribe, it is important to go straight down the HyperScribe menu from the top and set each of the three areas: Beat Source, Record Mode, and HyperScribe Options.

3. Choose the HyperScribe tool 🐟.
4. Select **HyperScribe** > Beat Source, and choose "Tap" or "Playback and/or Click."

In other words, do you want Finale to play a click, or do you want to control the tempo or tap? See chapter 6 (HyperScribe) for a detailed description of this process. If you are going to supply the tap and play with two hands, you will need to have a sustain pedal connected to your keyboard. You will then tap the pedal with your foot to control the beat, while your two hands play the notes.

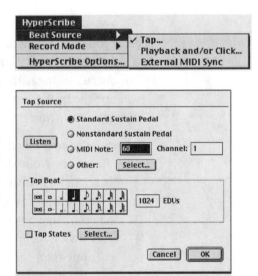

5. For two-hand keyboard input, select **HyperScribe** > Record Mode > Split into Two Staves.

You must choose the "split point" for the piece. Finale will set all notes from this note and above on the treble-clef staff, while those notes below the split point will go in the bass-clef staff. Since "Musette" has Ds in the bass clef, choose the note E♭ above middle C for the split point.

6. Click the Listen button, and play E♭ above middle C on the MIDI keyboard.

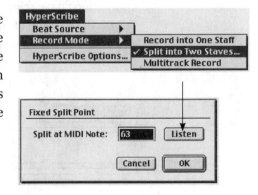

To enter the first four measures of the piece, HyperScribing with two hands:

1. Click inside the staff of the first measure.
2. Tap the Sustain pedal. Each tap represents one beat. Finale records your MIDI keyboard input as you tap.

After you enter the notation, you will notice that the split point works for most of the measures, but not all. In measure 4, the D below the staff will appear in the bass clef. This is easy to fix, using the Note Mover tool.

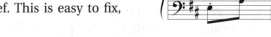

To move a note from one staff to another:

1. Choose the Note Mover tool . Windows only: Select **Tools** > Advanced Tools > Note Mover.
2. Select **Note Mover** > Delete After Merge.
3. In Scroll View, advance to measure 4.
4. Click inside the bass clef in measure 4. Handles will appear on each of the notes.
5. Drag the high D's handle to the treble-clef staff. You don't have to be precise. Just drag the note into the treble-clef staff's lines and spaces, and Finale will do the rest.

Drag this handle to the treble clef.

Use Simple Entry to make any necessary edits, then enter the rest of the piece. Remember, enter all notation and articulations before making any changes to barlines or repeats.

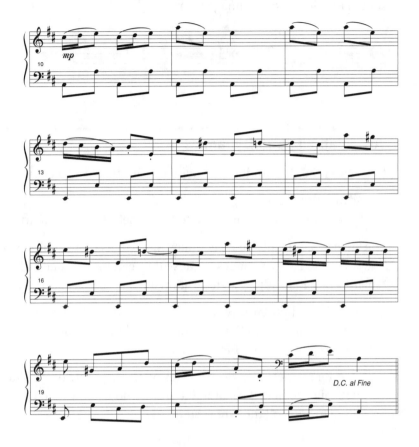

To begin HyperScribing in measure 10:

1.   Select the HyperScribe tool [icon].
2.   Click in measure 10. Tap the Sustain Pedal, and play in the rest of the notation.

After the notation is entered, use Simple Entry to edit any mistakes.

Entering a Clef Change

In this arrangement of Bach's "Musette," I included a clef change in the last measure (measure 21). To change clefs:

1.   Choose the Clef tool [icon].
2.   Click on the staff of measure 21.
3.   Choose the bass clef symbol, and set the range from measure 21 through 21.

Be careful when you select the clef. Finale offers many clef options, such as the baritone clef. Be sure to select the bass clef (see previous page) for this example. The last measure should now look like the image below.

Entering Slurs, Articulations, and Dynamics

Next, enter the slurs and phrase markings for the entire piece.

1. Advance to measure 3.
2. Choose the Smart Shape palette 🔘. Or select **Tools** > Smart Shapes.

The Smart Shape tool palette contains many tools that are used to enter graphic shapes. They are called Smart Shapes because they can be attached to individual notes and are "smart" enough to adjust their position if the notes are moved.

To enter slurs, choose the Slur tool 🔘. There are actually two tools that look like slurs. Choose the Slur tool, to the left. The Dashed Curve tool creates dashed slur markings, which is used in some choral music.

3. To enter a 2-note slur, double-click on the first note of the slur. Finale will automatically connect the slur to the second note of the slur. Use this double-click technique to enter all the 2-note slurs.

To enter a slur with three or more notes:

Go to measure 1 to enter the 4-note slur over the sixteenth notes. To assign a slur to groups of three notes or more, double-click the mouse, hold the second click, and drag through the note heads or stems to the last note of the group. The steps are as follows:

4. Double-click on the first note of the slur.
5. Hold down, or sustain, the second click.
6. Drag the mouse through the note stems.
7. Once the last note of the group is highlighted, release the button. Note how the slur snaps into position above the notes.

SmartFind and Paste

Finale has a handy feature to find and paste something in a score. In this case, there are several groups of four sixteenth notes with slurs. SmartFind and Paste can save time. After entering the first sextuplet slur in measure 1. Follow these steps to add a slur over all groups of four sixteenths:

1. Select **Edit** > Select Partial Measures. This will allow Finale to select just the part of measure 1 with the four sixteenths and the slur.
2. Choose the Mass Edit tool .
3. Drag-select beat 2 in measure 1.
4. Select **Mass Edit** > Set SmartFind Source Region.
5. Select **Mass Edit** > Apply SmartFind and Paste
6. Choose "Slurs" under Markings to Paint.
7. Click on the Paste All button.

Entering Crescendo Markings

The Smart Shape tool palette contains tools that are used to enter other markings, such as crescendo marks. Crescendo markings are sometimes called "hairpins" because they are shaped like hairpins, when set in a score.

The other Smart Shape tools work in a similar fashion to the Slur tool. The one difference is these markings are not attached to notes, but to measures. To enter crescendo markings:

1. Choose the Smart Shape tool palette .
2. Choose the Crescendo tool .
3. Advance to measure 7.
4. Double-click and drag to create the crescendo mark. The shape will become visible when you start dragging the mouse.

Finale's Smart Shapes expand and contract as the widths of their associated measures change. Measure widths change when adjusted manually (using the Measure tool) or when applying Note Spacing.

To edit a crescendo mark, choose the Selection tool (press ESC), and double-click on the marking. Select its handle, and a box

appears around the marking. Drag the diamond-shaped handles to adjust the size and position of the crescendo.

Deleting a Crescendo Marking

1. Press ESC (escape) to choose the Selection tool ⬉.
2. Click on the crescendo marking to select it.
3. Press Delete on the computer keyboard.

Enter the rest of the crescendo markings. To enter a decrescendo, first change to the Decrescendo tool ⊖.

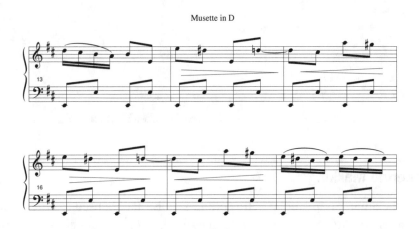

Musette in D

Dynamics

Use the Expression tool 𝑚𝑓 to enter the dynamic markings in measures 1 and 10. When working with a piano part, be sure to select This Staff Only in the Measure Assignment dialog. Here are the steps to enter a forte marking in measure 1:

1. Choose the Expression tool 𝑚𝑓.
2. Double-click in measure 1.
3. Choose the forte marking (*f*), and click Select.

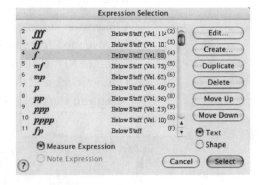

4. In the Measure Expression Assignment, choose This Staff Only.

5. Follow the steps mentioned previously and enter the *mp* marking in measure 10.

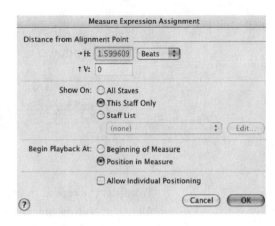

Entering Repeats

The repeat marks (first and second endings) and the D.C. al Fine markings all come from the same tool, the Repeat tool.

To enter the repeats and first and second endings:

1. Choose the Repeat tool 📧.

2. Highlight measures 1 through 8 by clicking in measure 1 and the Shift-clicking in measure 8.

3. Select **Repeat** > Create Simple Repeat. You can also Control-click (Mac) or Right-click (Windows) on a measure, and choose Create Simple Repeat.

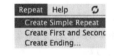

4. To add the first and second endings, select the first ending measure(s), in this case measure 8. Be sure to click on the white portion of the screen to deselect measures 1 to 8 and then click in measure 8 to select it.

5. Select **Repeat** > Create First and Second Ending, or Control-click (Mac) or Right-click (Windows) to access the contextual menu.

To adjust the repeat markings:

All of the ending markings can be moved. I usually move the ending number up and the back of the first ending forward a bit. All fine-tuning to the endings should be done in Page View.

1. Select **View** > Page View.
2. Choose the Repeat tool .
3. From the View menu, increase the view size to 200%. This makes it much easier to edit.
4. Click inside the measure where the repeat has been entered—in this example, measure 8.
5. Drag the handle next to the "1.," and pull it up slightly to keep it separate from the notation.
6. Drag the handle just above the repeat sign to the left, to separate the first and second repeats.

7. Click inside measure 9.
8. Drag up the "2." to match the position of the "1."

> ❗ Endings are another type of graphic that sometimes distort. As discussed earlier, the Redraw Screen command found in the View menu usually clears this up. Shortcut: ⌘-D (Mac) or Control-D (Windows)

Entering the *Fine* Mark

To enter the *Fine* marking in measure 9:

1. With the Repeat tool selected, double-click inside measure 9.
2. Select the *Fine* marking, and click Select.

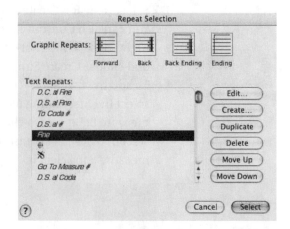

When you click the Select Button, you get the following dialog box.

3. Click Stop on Pass. In the box, the number 2 appears as the default.

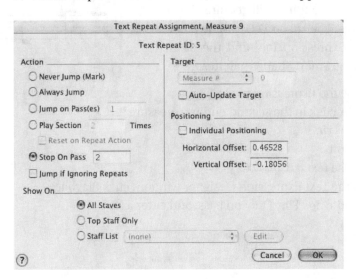

Entering the *D.C. al Fine* Marking

1. With the Repeat tool selected, advance to the last measure (21).
2. Double-click inside measure 21.
3. Select the *D.C. al Fine* marking, and click Select.
4. Enter the number 1 in the Target Measure box. This tells Finale to go back to the beginning of the piece (measure 1) when it sees the *D.C. al Fine* marking.

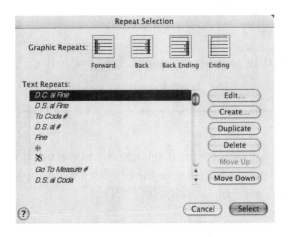

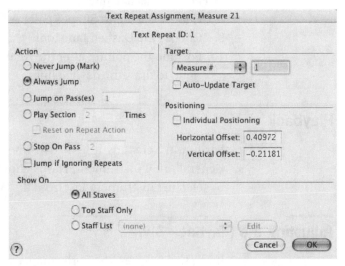

 It took me some practice to figure out how to make Finale play back the repeats and *D.C. al Fine* markings. If you don't care about the playback working exactly as it is printed, disregard the Repeat Assignment windows. However, if you do want the playback to be accurate, and you find it too mind-boggling to figure out how to program them properly, consider creating two versions of the files. One file looks correct but doesn't play back properly. The second file is designed to play back. Don't enter any repeats, but add measures and copy and paste the repeated sections so that it plays back properly.

The *Rit.* and Dashed Line

To enter the *rit. on D.C.* and the dashed line in the second ending will require the use of two tools. The *rit. on D.C.* will be created using the Expression tool and the dashed line from the Smart Shapes palette.

1. Choose the Expression tool .
2. Double-click in the second ending, measure 9.
3. Choose "*rit.*"
4. Click Edit.
5. Enter the text: *rit. on D.C.*
6. From the Text Expression Designer window, click Playback.
7. Check the box Play Only on Pass, and enter a "2."

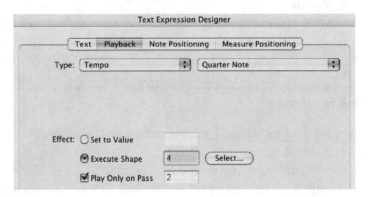

To enter the dashed line:

8. Choose the Smart Shapes palette .
9. Choose the Dashed Line tool .
10. Position the pointer after the *rit. on D.C.* in measure 9. Double-click-drag to the right, to draw the dashed line.

Playback

For fun, try creating a new instrument, Harpsichord, for playback. If you are using a General MIDI instrument, Harpsichord is number 7. Change the playback instrument by selecting Instrument List from the Window menu (see chapter 5).

Adjusting the Playback Style

If you want to hear the performance exactly as you played it, turn off Human Playback. If you want Finale to interpret the notation in one of its built-in Human Playback styles, and ignore what you played in, choose one of the options.

1. To access Human Playback (see chapter 6, page 99), click the arrow to the left of the Playback controls (Mac) or click on the speaker icon next to the tempo marking (Windows).
2. Click the pull-down menu next to Human Playback Style to make a selection.

The most appropriate Human Playback option for "Musette" would be Baroque. Human Playback will analyze the markings, including slurs, dynamics, crescendos, and so forth, and create a performance. When Human Playback is set, the performance information that you played is ignored. If you play piano like I do, this is a good thing!

Editing Performance Data with the MIDI Tool

There may be times when you want your exact performance to be preserved. In order to hear the exact performance you played, set Human Playback to "None" (see chapter 6, page 99).

Sometimes when recording using HyperScribe, an occasional note is played a little to loud or too soft. In my case, I played the first note in measure 1 too loud. To adjust this and any other aspect of the recorded performance, use the MIDI tool.

1. Choose the MIDI tool .
    Windows only: Select **Tools** > Advanced > MIDI Tool.
2. From the MIDI Tool menu, select the MIDI parameter you want adjust. In this case since the goal is to adjust the volume of the first note, select Key Velocities.

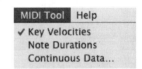

> If you are unfamiliar with MIDI and how it works, consult the *Finale User Guide* from the Help menu or read the *Finale Installation & Tutorial* guide.

3. Double-click the measures or measures that need to be adjusted. You can select the entire piece if necessary.
4. Select the note(s) that need to be adjusted.
5. Select **MIDI Tool** > Set To....
6. Type "75" for the value. (The value range is from 0–127). Then click OK.

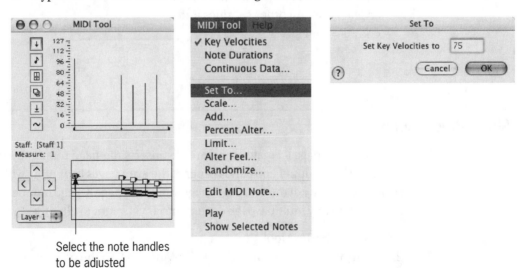

Select the note handles
to be adjusted

The graphic display will change and the recorded MIDI performance will be adjusted. The MIDI tool can be used to adjust note durations and any one of the MIDI controllers, such as sound (patch) changes and much more.

Remember, Finale is a notation program, and even though it has a lot of built-in MIDI control, it is not meant to be a MIDI Sequencer. If you want to have the best of both worlds, save the Finale file as a MIDI file, and open it in your MIDI sequencer software of choice.

Note Size Reduction, Page Layout, and Printing

After the notation is entered, address the final steps:

- Enter the titles, credits, and page number.
- Lay out the measures to three measures per line using Fit Music from the Page Layout or Mass Edit Menu.
- Print.

Entering the titles, credits, and page numbers:

1. Choose the Text tool Ⓐ.
2. Scroll to the top of the page to enter/edit the titles and credits. Enter each line as a separate text block.

Musette in D

(from "Little Notebook for Anna Magdalena Bach")   Johann Sebastian Bach (1685-1750)

adapted by Tom Rudolph

Use the Text menu to set the style and size of each title. To change the size and style:

3. After entering a title, select **Edit** > Select All.
4. From the Text menu, select the style and size: "Musette" = font size 24, style = Plain. All other subtitles and credits = font size 10.

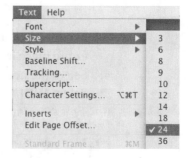

About Page Numbers

With multiple pages, Finale automatically inserts the page numbers for the score. This is displayed in the upper left-hand corner of the even pages beginning with page 2, and in the right-hand corner of the odd pages beginning with page 3. Page numbers will automatically be placed on any multiple page documents. If you want to alter these standard settings:

1. Choose the Text tool Ⓐ.
2. Control-click (Mac) or Right-click (Windows) on the page number's text-block handle to show the contextual menu.

3. Choose Edit Frame Attributes from the text block's contextual menu.

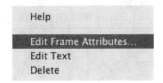

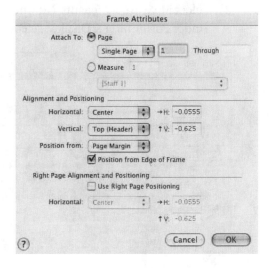

Text Inserts

Another way to insert text and other options is to use Finale inserts. It is sometimes helpful to use inserts to add the current time and date and other handy features, such as the copyright symbol © and performance time.

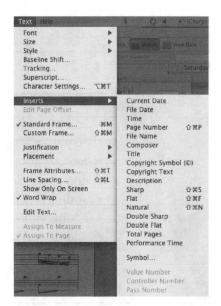

1. Choose the Text tool.
2. Select **Text** > Inserts and then any of the selections from the submenu.

Grouping Measures

To group the measures to three per line:
1. Choose the Page Layout tool 🔘.
2. Select **Page Layout** > Group Measures.
3. Group the measures to "3" per line.

Displaying Measure Numbers at the Start of Each System

Before printing, change the measure number display to the start of each staff system. Measure numbers could be displayed on every measure. However, they will frequently collide with notes and other score markings. For this reason, I recommend setting them to display at the start of each system.

1. Choose the Measure tool 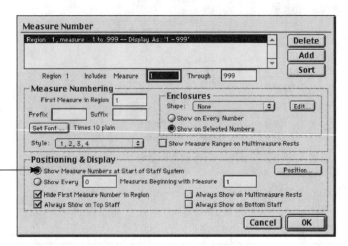.
2. Select **Measure** > Measure Numbers > Edit Regions.
3. Under Positioning & Display, select "Show Measure Numbers at Start of Staff System."

The file should be ready to print. Select **File** > Print.

Summary

This example included the following new Finale skills:

- creating a piano part using the Setup Wizard
- HyperScribing with two hands
- moving notes from one staff to another, using Note Mover
- entering a clef change
- adding repeat signs and a *D.C. al Fine*
- adding slurs and dynamic markings (hairpins)
- adding and modifying a *rit.* marking
- using the MIDI tool to adjust live performance mistakes
- adjusting the playback

Finale Advanced Input Steps

We have added several steps to creating a Finale document, which I like to refer to as the "Advanced Finale Procedures." The steps include:

1. Create the score (total number of measures, key, staves, etc.).
2. Enter the notation from beginning to end.
3. Enter the articulations, dynamic markings, endings, etc., one at a time, from beginning to end.
4. Enter the titles, credits, and page numbers.
5. Group the measures.
6. Adjust the staff systems if needed.
7. Make any adjustments to the score, such as printing measure numbers at the desired interval.
8. Print.

Review

1. Review the repeat, *D.C. al Fine,* and related markings that come from the Repeat tool. Read through the online help section on the Repeat tool now that you have had some experience using it.
2. Try HyperScribing other examples to see how accurately it prints. Change the quantization value to an eighth or sixteenth note to see if this improves the overall accuracy.
3. Experiment with the various options with Human Playback. Try various options such as Baroque, Jazz, Classical, and others.

8

Small Arrangements: Saxophone Quartet ("The Entertainer")

This is an arrangement of "The Entertainer" by Scott Joplin, scored for saxophone quartet. This chapter introduces some new situations presented by multi-stave scores, as well as entering music via scanning.

THE ENTERTAINER

for Saxophone Quartet

by SCOTT JOPLIN
arranged by *Vince Leonard*

What's New in This Chapter

- setting up a small-arrangement using the Setup Wizard
- scanning music
- importing TIFF files
- using Measure and Note Expressions
- enclosing text for rehearsal numbers
- combining fonts in a text expression
- setting up tempo marks that affect playback
- using the Cautionary Accidentals Plug-in
- using the Global Staff Attributes Plug-in
- using the Check Range Plug-in
- creating cue notes

- using EVPUs as a unit of measurement
- page formatting for multisystem score pages
- using Fixed-Size Text
- using Space Systems Evenly
- routing MIDI to software synthesizers
- determining the performance time
- extracting parts
- creating a piano reduction

 You will find Finale files for this chapter on our Web site at www.finalebook.com. These will allow you to work at any point in the chapter with all the steps up to that point completed.

123

Setting Up the Score File for "The Entertainer"

1. Select **File** > New > Document With Setup Wizard.
2. Enter the title, composer, and copyright (see right).

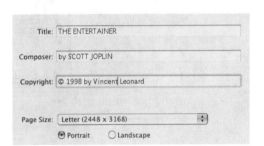

The page size and orientation are correct, so no changes are necessary.

3. Click Next.
4. Choose Woodwinds in the Instrument Family list.
5. Scroll down the Instrument list and select the Soprano Sax.
6. Click the Add button.
7. Choose Alto Sax.
8. Click the Add button.

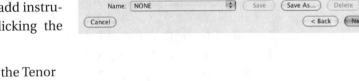

It is also possible to add instruments by double-clicking the name in the list.

9. Double-click on the Tenor and Baritone Saxophone to add them to the right-hand column.

 Finale allows you to save your instrumentations for repeated use. To do this, set up the desired instruments and score order in the right column of the dialog box, click Save As, name the ensemble, and click Save. The instrumentation will be added to the Name popup menu for one-click selection in the future.

10. Click Next, and advance to page 3 of the Wizard.
11. Click on 2/4 for the Time Signature.
12. The Concert key is C Major so no change is necessary for the key. Click Next, and advance to page 4 of the Wizard.

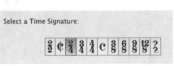
Select a Time Signature:

This example uses the default settings for page 4, for tempo, pickup measure, and font, so no changes are necessary.

13. Click Finish.

The Setup Wizard will set up a staff for each instrument with the proper transpositions, thus creating a transposed score.

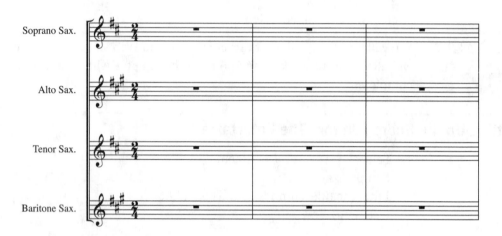

To save and organize your files:

1. Select **File** > Save As.
2. Name this document "Entertainer_Score."

> Proper organization of your files will help prevent files from getting lost or scattered all over your hard drive. This becomes more important when working with scores where parts will be extracted. Always check to see what folder you are in, when saving a document. In my Documents Folder, I have a specific folder for Finale projects. In that folder, I have separate folders for different pieces, projects, and clients. This way, they are easier to work with and to archive when the project is finished. This issue is magnified when working with scores and parts when many files belonging to the same project are created.

3. Locate to the Documents Folder.
4. Create a new folder. I suggest "Entertainer Folder" for the name. Move your file to that folder.

Make sure you have the correct number of measures for the score. The default score has thirty-one measures in it; you will need thirty-seven for "The Entertainer."

1. Choose the Measure tool .
2. Select **Measure** > Add.
3. Type "6" in the dialog box, and click OK. This adds six measures to the end of your score.

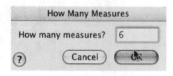

Measurement Units in Finale

Before I go on, a word about Measurement Units in Finale. I'll be using EVPUs, Enigma Value Percentage Units, as my unit of measurement. I learned them in Finale Version 1.0, and used them ever since. I find EVPUs easier to remember than fractions of inches. However, I will also include inches for all measurements. The scale is 288 EVPUs = 1 inch.

To choose a unit of measurement:

- Select **Options** > Measurement Units, then make a choice from the submenu. Choosing EVPUs or inches will make it easier to follow along with this chapter.

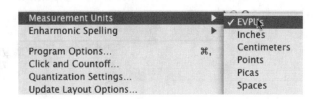

Changing The Distance Between Staves

The Document Setup Wizard places all staves it creates an equal distance apart. I don't always agree with this default spacing. I want to tighten things up a little, now, so the distance between the staves is finalized before I start adding and positioning Expressions. When creating scores, it is a good idea to try to tighten up the distance between the staves to help fit more on each page with less of a page reduction.

Respacing staves can be accomplished by using the Staff tool to drag the staves closer together, or by editing the numbers in the Respace Staves dialog box, found in the Staff menu. I want to add some space at the top of the score and tighten up the distance between the staves. Currently, there are 320 EVPUs (1.1111 inches) between the staves. I'm going to tighten that up to a distance of 256 EVPUs (0.8889 inches).

1. Choose the Staff tool ![staff tool icon].
2. Select **Staff** > Respace Staves.
3. Under the Top Staff Position, click the Set to button, and type "-140" EVPUs (0.2778 inches).
4. Under the Distance Between Settings heading, type -256 EVPUs (-0.8889 inches) for the Set to value. Then click OK.

This can be fine-tuned when performing the final page layout, but beginning the process now will keep Expression collisions to a minimum.

Boxed Rehearsal Numbers Using the Expression Tool

In chapter 5, boxed measure numbers were created using the Measure tool. This method is acceptable for single-stave projects, but when working with multi-staff scores, those changes would have to be made to every staff of the score. There is a more efficient way to handle the job in Finale: setting them up as Measure Expressions. This will place them on the desired staff or staves in the score, as well as all of the individual parts when they are extracted. If you are in a hurry, there are a few boxed rehearsal letters already in the Expressions library. Just duplicate them, and change the letter as needed.

To create a new rehearsal letter:

1. Choose the Expression tool .
2. Double-click on measure 5 of the score. This brings up the Expression Selection dialog box.
3. Note the radio buttons at the bottom of the selection window to choose between Measure or Note Expressions.
4. Click on the Create button.

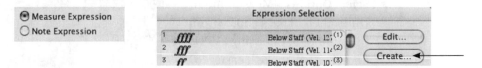

> Use a bold style for rehearsal numbers and make them a larger point size so that they stand out.

5. "Times" should already be selected as the font. To choose bold, select **Text** > Style > Bold, shortcut: ⌘ Shift-B (Mac) or Control-Shift-B (Windows).
6. To set the font size to 14 points, select **Text** > Size > 14, or increase the size using the shortcut ⌘ Shift-. [period] (Mac) or Control-Shift-. [period] (Windows).
7. Type the number 5.
8. Check the Break Multimeasure Rest checkbox.

> Checking the Break Multimeasure Rest box is essential for all performance related marks such as rehearsal numbers, tempo markings such as retards and accelerandos, and style or feel changes. This prevents them from being swallowed up in a gathered rest and being missed by the player.

9. Move down the dialog to the Enclosure heading.
10. From the Shape popup menu, select "Rectangle."

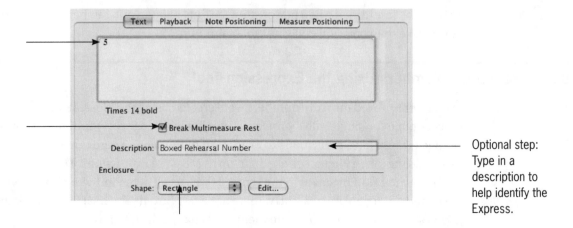

11. Click the Measure Positioning tab at the top of the dialog box.

It is possible to set a default automatic position—either horizontal, vertical, or both—that will be used every time this Expression is used as a Measure Expression. Note that all of the positioning choices will be represented, when selected, in the graphic display in the dialog box. Choose different options from these popup menus, and notice how the display changes.

12. Under the Horizontal heading, set the Expression Alignment Point popup to "Center."
13. From the Measure Alignment Point popup, select "Left Barline."
14. Under the Vertical heading, select "Above Staff Baseline."

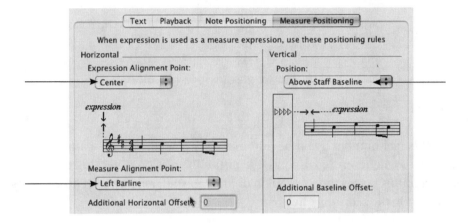

15. Click OK to leave the Text Expression Designer dialog box.
16. Click Select in the Expression Selection dialog box.

You will see the Measure Expression Assignment dialog box. At this point, decide if you want this Expression shown on all staves, just one staff, or only on selected staves. Since we want it to be displayed only on the top staff of the full score, but on all of the parts, it will require a Staff List—a chart that lets us choose exactly where our Expression will display.

17. Click the Staff List radio button.
18. Select New Staff List from the popup menu, to create a staff list.

First, name the Staff List, so that you will be able to recognize it and use it again later. I use the name Rehearsal for rehearsal numbers and anything else that appears above the top staff of the score, such as tempo or style indications. Again, I only want it to appear over the top staff now, but I'll need it on all the parts as well.

19. Click on Top Staff in the Staves column, to select both Score and Parts column.
20. Click OK to exit this window, and click OK again to return to the score.

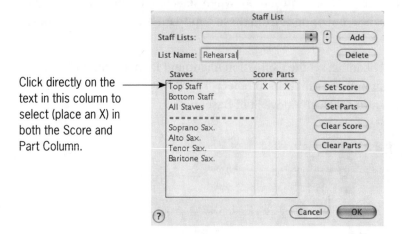

Click directly on the text in this column to select (place an X) in both the Score and Part Column.

The rehearsal number 5 will be automatically placed over the barline and retain that placement whenever it is used as a Measure Expression. Checking both the Score and Parts columns places the Expression on the top staff, regardless of how many staves are present, 4 in the score, or 1 in a part.

Duplicating an Expression

Duplicating Expressions allows you to skip a step or two in Expression creation. In this example, by duplicating the Expression we just created, you can skip the steps for setting the font, breaking a multimeasure rest, selecting the enclosure, and the horizontal and vertical positioning.

1. Advance to bar 17.
2. Double-click on bar 17 to open the Expressions dialog box.
3. Scroll down to the rehearsal number 5, at the bottom, and select it.
4. Click the Duplicate button.

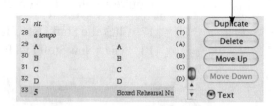

This creates a duplicate of the selected Expression and automatically selects the new Expression.

5. Click the Edit button.
6. Select all the existing text (the number "5"), using the shortcut ⌘-A (Mac) or Control-A (Windows).
7. Type 17 in the text field to replace the number 5.
8. Click OK, then Select.

In the Measure Expression Assignments dialog box, the Staff Sets button will be selected and the selection menu will show the last Staff Set selected.

9. Click OK. Then repeat the above procedure for measure 22.

I use Measure-Attached Expressions, rather than boxing measure numbers in Measure Tool (as shown in chapter 5), for several reasons. One is ease of editing. There are often several marks at a rehearsal number—dynamics, phrasing, or tempo indications—that are all entered as either Measure or Note Expressions. All can be edited easily without trips back and forth to the tool palette to switch from Expressions tool to Measure tool. Another reason is that with the Measure tool, boxed numbers must be copied down from staff to staff before extracting parts. This adds extra steps to the process. Also, if you are numbering every measure and the numbers are under the staff, all boxed numbers must be manually repositioned above the staff.

Barline Alterations

To insert a double barline at the end of measure 21:

1. Press ESC to choose the Selection tool.
2. Advance to measure 21.
3. Control-click or Right-click (Windows) inside the staff.
4. Select "Double Barline" from the contextual menu.

The final barline is automatically entered by Finale on the last measure of the file.

Setting Up the Repeat

To enter the repeat at measure 5:

1. Choose the Repeat tool.
2. Highlight measure 5.
3. Select **Repeat** > Create Forward Repeat Bar.
4. Advance to bar 20.
5. Highlight bar 20, the measure that will make up the first ending.
6. Select **Repeat** > Create First and Second Ending.

OOPS! The ending bracket is displayed on all four staves of the score, and we want it only on the top staff. We can control this by using the Repeat tool, but each ending would have to be handled separately. Displaying this only on the top staff is much easier to do using the Global Staff Attributes plug-in. Plug-ins are found in the Plug-ins menu and are grouped in folders by category. Plug-ins offer enhanced productivity—that is, speed—and additional features to Finale. Mac users, look for the plug icon in the tool bar . Window users will see the menu heading as text.

Setting the Global Staff Attributes Plug-in

1. Choose the Mass Edit tool .
2. Drag-select the Alto, Tenor, and Baritone Sax staves.
3. Select **Plug-ins** > Global Staff Attributes.
4. Under Items to Display, uncheck Endings and Text Repeats, and click OK. The ending brackets are now only visible on the top staff.

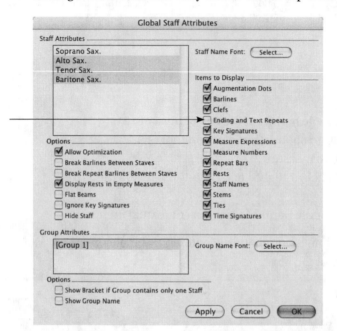

 In a score with a large number of staves, you may wish to display the ending brackets on several staves, for example at the top of each instrument family, for visual purposes. To do this, use the staff list under the Staff Attributes heading. Control-click (Mac) or Right-click (Windows) on a staff until only the staves to show repeats are highlighted. You can use this list to highlight groups of staves by Shift-clicking on the top and bottom staves of the group.

When you have multiple ending brackets in a measure of a score and need to position some differently to avoid collisions, check the Individual Positioning box in the Ending Repeat Bar Assignment dialog box. This will allow all brackets in the selected measure to have different heights and lengths.

To adjust the position of the repeat brackets or the number, with the Repeat tool selected, click on the desired measure. Positioning handles will appear. Drag the handles until the brackets are in the desired position. Be careful with the overlapping brackets in the first ending, making sure the brackets continue to overlap after you move them. You may need to view them at several different magnifications to make sure they are positioned properly.

For this example, the bracket collides with the measure number at bar 22. You need to drag the bracket clear of the number, using either of the handles on the end of the bracket. The left handle controls the

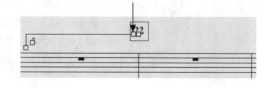

height of the horizontal line; the right handle can be used to create a vertical line to close the bracket.

To adjust the repeat bracket:
1. Select **View** > Scale View > 200% or press ⌘-2 (Mac) or Control-2 (Windows).
2. Choose the Repeat tool .
3. Click on measure 21.
4. Hold down the Shift key to constrain the drag to horizontal only.
5. Click on either the left or right handle of the Repeat shape.
6. Drag the bracket line to the left.
7. Release when there is a little white space visible between the bracket line and the box of the measure number.

131

8_Entertainer_1.mus

> Rehearsal numbers, key signatures, time signatures, double bars, and repeats all serve as guideposts when entering music. Once the guideposts are set, observe them. They can help you detect a skipped or repeated measure early in your piece, long before it becomes a major headache much later in the score.

🙂 Have you saved lately?

Scanning, Captain

Next, we will explore the scanning features that are included, free, with Finale. If you don't own a scanner, fear not; there are scanned files on the Web site for you to use, which are just like the files that you can create by scanning your own music. If you have no interest in scanning and would like to practice Simple Entry a little more, feel free to begin entering notes. Rejoin the tutorial at the "Accidentals Do Happen" heading, page 136.

Finale comes with a simplified version of SmartScore, a standalone music-scanning program. This "Lite" version will recognize clefs, key signatures, notes, accidentals, and ties. Additional elements of the score, such as lyrics, dynamics, and text, are only recognized by a full version of the software. An upgrade to the full version is available to registered Finale users for $199. A demo of the full version is available on the SmartScore Web site (www.smartscore.com), if you would like to load the included scans in for a comparison. Scanning technology is rapidly developing into a dependable tool for music entry of engraved music. Handwritten music is not supported

The scanner itself does not need to be top of the line, but do check the manufacturer's specifications to make sure that your computer meets the requirements of the scanner in both hardware and software before purchasing. Some older scanners may not work at all, so be aware of the return policy wherever you buy.

Entertainerpg1.tiff
Entertainerpg2.tiff

If you have a scanner and want to scan in the example for this chapter, print out the file 8_Entertainer_1.mus from the Web site and use that for the copy to be scanned. For those without a scanner, locate the "Chapter 8 Folder" on the Web site. In that folder, you will find the TIFF files (Entertainerpg1.tiff and Entertainerpg2.tiff) used in preparation of this chapter. Begin the tutorial at the point where the tiff files are imported into Finale.

Make sure your scanner is powered up and properly connected to the computer, and the scanner's software is installed. First, the sheet music of "The Entertainer" must be scanned into a specific graphic file format called TIFF, or TIF, short for Tagged Image File Format. Consult the manual for your scanner to find the location of the parameters we'll be checking or changing.

 ALWAYS make sure that the page to be scanned is straight. Pages scanned at too great an angle may not load successfully into Finale. If you are scanning from a book with a stiff binding, consider making a photocopy of the pages first so that positioning it is easier.

To scan "The Entertainer:"

1. Place page 1 of "The Entertainer" in the scanner.
2. Choose "Back and White" for the Color.
3. Choose 300 dpi (dots per inch) for the Resolution. (This is the dpi recommended by MakeMusic.)
4. Choose TIFF (or TIF) for the file type.
5. Scan the first page.
6. Scan the next page. (Before scanning, check the above settings in the scanner's software in case any have reverted to defaults.)

 Before scanning a large job, try importing the first page to see if the dpi setting is sufficient to produce a readable file for SmartScore Lite. Depending on the scanner, the dpi may need to be increased. The files on our Web site were scanned at 600 dpi after my first attempt at 300 failed to be recognized. Once the proper dpi is determined, use that value for all future scans.

To import your scanned notation into Finale:

1. Launch Finale.
2. In the Launch window, click the Scanning button.
3. Click the Add Files button.
4. Locate and select the TIFF file of page 1 (Entertainerpg1.tiff).

If there is a problem with the scan, an Error dialog box will appear at this point, and you will not be able to load the file. Try rescanning the example again at a higher resolution.

5. Click the Add Files button, and then locate and select the TIFF file of page 2. (Entertainerpg2.tiff)

Click on files in this column to display the contents in the Preview window.

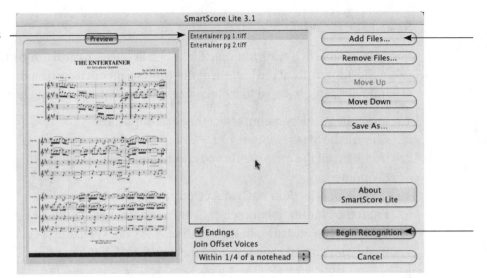

6. Click Begin Recognition.

If you get an error message saying that there is not enough memory, try importing one page at a time. This will result in each page being imported to a separate file in Finale.

A Finale file will be created with the staves, key, clefs, time signature, and notes from the scanned page. Click the About SmartScore button for more information about the full version. If you plan to do a lot of scanning, it may be worth $199 for the upgrade.

Note that multiple pages have been incorporated into a single file. The page breaks match the original but Finale still does not know what instruments are supposed to be in the score and, despite the appearance, what the correct transpositions are. Making this file useable as our version of "The Entertainer" will take more work and time than it is worth. A faster way is to create a new file in Finale, using the Setup Wizard. Then use Copy and Paste to copy the music from the scan import file to the new file.

Notation Station

It's time to enter the music, by Simple Entry, HyperScribe, or scanning. If you've closed the file created when the TIFF files were imported, then reopen it and skip to the next heading. If you are using Simple Entry, there are some new ways of entering articulations to come in this chapter, so hold off on entering them.

HyperScribers take note: when entering transposed notes onto transposed staves, Finale reads the pitches as concert and transposes them for display. The workaround for this is to transpose the MIDI keyboard the correct interval for the instrument: B-flat saxes up a whole tone, E-flat saxes up a major sixth. Then, play in the part. Enter the notes from start to finish, going staff by staff from the top of the score. Leave out the cue-size notes in the first three measures; they will be copied via Mass Edit later in this chapter. Refer back to the chapter on your selected method of input, if you have any difficulties. Do input the octave A notes in the bari sax. Also, leave the courtesy accidentals out until later. There is a plug-in that will take care of them.

Resume Scanning

Finale is capable of having multiple files open at once. To move from one file to another, select the desired file at the bottom of the Window menu. If you imported the scan in two separate files, adjust step 6 to include only the measures on the page being copied.

1. From the Window menu, select the scan import file.
2. Choose the Mass Edit tool .
3. Highlight all the measures in the original scan file: ⌘-A (Mac) or Control-A (Windows).
4. Copy your selection: ⌘-C (Mac) Control-C (Windows).
5. From the Window menu, select "The Entertainer Score" file.
6. Select All the measures in the new file: ⌘-A (Mac) or Control-A (Windows).
7. Paste your copied measures into the new file: ⌘-V (Mac) Control-V (Windows).

Proofreading is a necessary step for all scanned documents. This can be done with both the eye and the ear. First, compare your original notation with the screen display. You may notice that the tenor and baritone saxes are an octave too high. The scanning software was able to understand the staves being in different keys, but not the concept of transposing instruments.

To transpose selected measures:
1. Choose the Mass Edit tool .
2. Highlight the entire Tenor Sax staff by clicking in the left margin space between the words "Tenor Sax" and the system bracket.
3. Highlight the entire Baritone Sax staff by Shift-clicking in the space between the words "Baritone Sax" and the system bracket. Now, both the tenor and bari staves are highlighted.
4. Select **Mass Edit** > Transpose.
5. Click the Down button.
6. From the Interval popup menu, select Octave. Then click OK.

From here, I can only report on what the results are from my scan. If you have performed your own, there may be some differences in the results. For that reason, I won't go step by step through each correction, but I will discuss some common issues and fixes that you're likely to encounter in this process.

The first three measures contain the bulk of the problems. The half rests and the remnants of the cues need to be cleared using the Clear key (Mac) or Backspace key (Windows) in Mass Edit. The cues will be replaced later in this chapter.

Measure 4 in the tenor needs a quarter rest added on beat 1. Select the quarter rest from the Simple Entry Rest Palette and click on the eighth rest to change it to a quarter rest.

The most frequent problem is slurs being mistaken for ties in the soprano and alto parts. Select the Tie from the Simple Entry Palette, make sure no note value is selected, and click on the note where the tie originates, to delete it.

The last issue is the octave cue note in the baritone sax for all of the low A's. For this, I'll show you a little Mass Edit trick.

Creating Instant Octaves

Or, "how to create an eight-step interval in only six steps."

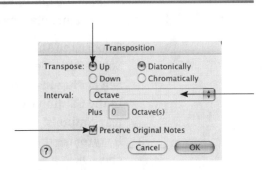

1. Choose the Mass Edit tool 🔲.
2. Highlight measure 8 in the Baritone Sax staff.
3. Select **Mass Edit** > Transpose.
4. Choose "Up."
5. From the Interval popup menu, select "Octave."
6. Check "Preserve Original Notes," and then click OK.

In the Mass Edit tool, the number keys 6, 7, 8, and 9 are user-programmable Metatools for transpositions. Here are the steps to program a Metatool key.

1. With the Mass Edit tool selected, press Shift-6 to bring up the Transposition dialog box.
2. Click the Transpose Up button.
3. From the Interval popup menu, select Octave, and then click OK.

To create a Metatool for transposing down an octave, repeat the steps, using the 7 key. Select Down for the Transpose direction and Octave for the interval. The 8 and 9 keys are available for other intervals

The Shift key is the key for programming Metatools in any tool that uses Metaltools. Hold down the Shift key and select the key you wish to program. Metatools are available in the Articulation, Expression, Tuplet, Time Signature, Clef, Chord, Mass Edit, Key Signature, Smart Shape, Staff, and Repeat Tools. All the letter and number keys are available for programming in all tools except Mass Edit. The Mass Edit tool has fixed Metatools for keys 1 through 5 and only allows user programmability for the transposition function, only using the 6 through 9 keys.

Repeat the steps for measure 16. In measures 20, 21, and to the end of the arrangement, begin with the following step.

- Select **Edit** > Select Partial Measures.

Drag-select only the low A's before transposing. This may take a little work to drag the correct area on the eighth note, but it is possible.

🙂 Have you saved lately?

Accidentals Do Happen

Cautionary accidentals are an important part of printed music. They help to clear up any ambiguity caused by chromatic alterations from one measure to the next. Even though the barline technically cancels out all accidentals from the previous measure, the player may still be thinking and playing C-natural instead of C-sharp. The problem has always been taking the time and trouble to decide where cautionary accidentals are needed and entering them. Finale has addressed this problem with a plug-in.

1. Choose the Mass Edit tool .
2. Select **Edit** > Select All.
3. Select **Plug-ins** > Note, Beam, and Rest Editing > Cautionary Accidentals.
4. In the Cautionary Accidental Options dialog box, uncheck everything except Courtesy Naturals.
5. If you'd like the accidentals to have parentheses, check the Parenthesize box. Then click OK.

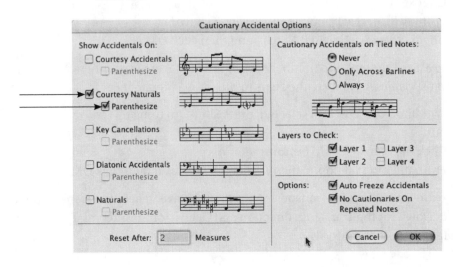

Music Spacing

The Auto Spacing feature does not automatically adjust to account for the accidentals added by the plug-in. A quick scan of the piece after adding the courtesy accidentals shows that the new additions are not properly spaced and are colliding with other entries. To remedy the situation, we'll use the Apply Note Spacing function of the Mass Edit tool.

Fix these collisions by applying Note Spacing.

1. Choose the Mass Edit tool .
2. Select all measures, either by selecting **Edit** > Select All, by using the keyboard shortcuts ⌘-A (Mac) or Control-A (Windows), or by using any other selection method.

8_Entertainer_2.mus

finalebook.com

3. Select **Mass Edit** > Music Spacing > Apply Note Spacing. All of the courtesy accidentals will now be spaced properly.

Entering Performance Information

Next, add the Articulations and dynamics to the score. I prefer to start with Articulations, since information such as Smart Shapes and Dynamics will have to be placed around them. The fastest method of Articulation entry is using Metatools.

To add articulations using Metatools:
1. Choose the Articulation tool.
2. Hold down the V key (Metatool for the marcato accent (**v**), and click on the B eighth note in bar 4 of the alto sax part.
3. Continue holding down the V key, and click on the C directly under in the tenor part and the E below, that in the bari sax.
4. Refer to chapter 5, page 71 for more about the Articulation Tool's Metatool assignments.

Make a key for yourself on a sheet of paper to track commonly used symbols until you memorize them.

137

Adjust your display so that measures 5 through 10 of the tenor sax are visible on the screen. Use the technique described in chapter 5, page 72 for selecting multiple notes to apply Articulations. You should have a highlighted region stretching from the first note, the A in measure 5, to the last note, the B in measure 10. Just remember, this technique can be used vertically as well as horizontally.

Every note in the highlighted region will now have a staccato dot assigned to it. This is a powerful extension of the Articulation Metatool. It can assign articulations to multiple staves and multiple measures at once, to a large region, from top to bottom of a score.

We need to add the front and back parentheses for the optional notes in the baritone saxophone. Enter them as Articulations. They are already in the library, but you need to use the scroll bar to view them in the Articulation Selection dialog box. Use the assigned Metatool keystrokes to enter them.

138

Entering and Positioning Dynamic Marks

Entering and positioning Expressions is one of the more time-consuming processes in music engraving. Fortunately, Finale has now combined these two tasks with smart Expressions containing their own positioning settings. You programmed these settings earlier in this chapter, when positioning the boxed measure numbers. All the Expressions in the Expression Selection Library have this kind of positioning data associated with them. For example, all the dynamics are set to position themselves on the Below Staff Baseline. These baselines are controllable using the same arrow system used in the Lyric and Chord tools.

Observe the cursor in the Expression tool as you move it around the music. The arrow will appear on the top or bottom, depending on the proximity to the staff, which indicates the staff to which the Expression will be defined. If the cursor also has a quarter note appearing under it, Finale detects an entry in the direction the arrow is pointing that you can attach an Expression to. This will make the Note Attached button active in the Expression Selection box. If no note is within the cursor's range, the Note-Attached option will not be available. Note-Attached Expressions are much easier to enter using a Metatool key. The default auto-positioning for dynamic marks will position the mark in proper relation to the note, below the staff, and adjust it down should the note be below the staff on ledger lines.

To define a *f* symbol as a note-attached Expression:
1. Choose the Expression tool 🔘 .
2. Select **Expression** > Adjust Below Staff Baseline.
3. Position the cursor under the first note in bar 1 of the Alto Sax, and look for the note symbol to appear on the cursor.
4. Press the 4 key (Metatool for the forte [*f*]), and click the mouse.

If the Expression requires further positioning, move one of its arrows to adjust the baseline, from left to right, global, staff, system (page view only) and next entry, or drag its handle to the desired position. Manually positioning an Expression does not affect its auto-position settings.

Measure Expressions, as described earlier, can appear on multiple staves of a score or only appear in one place on the score but on all the individual parts, as well. Another advantage of using Measure Expressions is that you can place many Expressions at once and have them line up vertically. They are assigned the same way Note Expressions are assigned, with one extra step:

1. With the Expression tool 🎵 selected, double-click on measure 4.
2. Choose the *sfz* Expression.

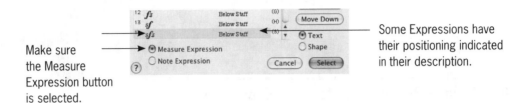

Make sure the Measure Expression button is selected.

Some Expressions have their positioning indicated in their description.

3. Click Select.
4. Under the Show On heading, click the Staff List radio button in the Score Expression Assignment dialog box (see page 127, step 18).
5. From the popup menu, select New Staff List to create a new staff list.
6. Give the staff list a name you can recognize, such as "All 4," so that you can use this list again.
7. Click on All Staves, and then click OK.

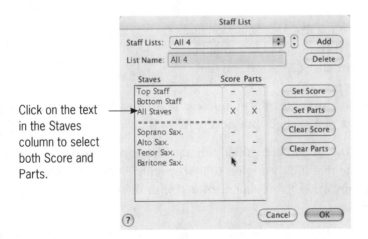

Click on the text in the Staves column to select both Score and Parts.

The staff list name will be displayed in the popup menu. To reuse a staff list, select any Expression, then select Measure-Attached at the bottom of the library window, and select the staff list from the Show On popup menu.

8. Align the Expression properly under the second beat. Use the vertical crosshair to position the mark. The line should be touching the front of the notehead on the upstemmed note and perfectly aligned with the stem of the downstemmed notes.

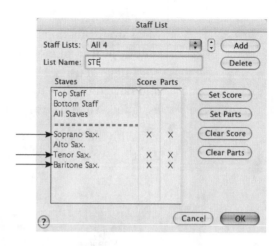

In measure 5, the piano mark is needed on three staves. Repeat the above steps (clicking in bar 5), and set up the Staff Set as follows.

1. Click the Soprano Sax text to select both Score and Parts.
2. Repeat for the Tenor and Bari Sax.
3. Name the set "STB." Click OK.

140

Individually Positioning Measure Expressions

In situations like measure 5, the Expressions don't align vertically, as in bar 4. The setting to fix this problem is called "Allow Individual Positioning," back in the Measure Expres-sion Assignment dialog box. I didn't do this before because I wanted to position the largest percentage of my Expressions while they still moved as one. This might seem trivial in a quartet score, but in a larger ensemble, it is a huge time savings.

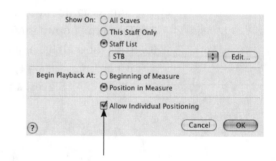

1. Press the ESC key (Selection tool), and then Control-click (Mac) or Right-click (Windows) on the Expression.
2. From the contextual menu, select Edit Measure Expression Assignment.
3. Click on the check box next to Allow Individual Positioning. Click OK.

This allows you to individually change the position of any single Expression in the staff list. Note that it only applies to that specific Expression in that specific bar. It does not effect any other Expressions entered with the same staff set, or any other uses of that Expression.

1. Move the Expression up by dragging it with the cursor or nudging it with the Up Arrow key.
2. Continue adding Expressions throughout the score, using the appropriate Expression.

Hold down the Shift key when dragging an Expression so it moves vertically but not hori-zontally. That will preserve a straight vertical line.

Expression Metatools

Now add dynamics to the score. Use Note-Assigned Expressions for single marks that do not occur in other staves or do not require vertical alignment. They can also be entered using Metatools.

1. Choose the Expression tool .
2. Double-click anywhere in the score to bring up the Expression Selection window.

As in the Articulation Selection window, the numbers in parentheses are the Metatool key assignments for the Expression. Anything without a number has not been assigned to a Metatool. The Measure Expression and Note Expression buttons at the bottom have no bearing on Metatool assignment.

Expression Metatool assignments are in the far right of the Selection window.

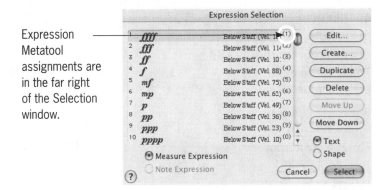

In the Expression menu, there are settings to default Metatool assignment to Attached To Measure, Attached To Note, or Context Sensitive. Expressions entered with the Attach To Measure option will be entered with Show On All Staves selected in Display Options. If you want the Expression to appear only on certain staves, you will need to use a Staff

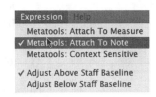

List. The Context Sensitive option will enter a Note-Attached Expression when you see the cursor display a note on the right side of the crosshair, and a Measure-Attached Expression when there is no note next to the crosshair.

> Once again, it may be helpful to create a key on a sheet of paper for frequently used Expressions. If you create or reprogram any Metatools, try to standardize the keys to which you assign specific marks or Expressions. This will help you to remember them.

Creating Tempo Marks with the Expression Tool

There is a Create Tempo Marking plug-ins (**Plug-ins** > Expressions > Create Tempo Markings) that will work with simple "quarter note equals number" markings, but the default font is not ideal. The Expressions tool allows for the mixing of fonts in a single Expression, so Expressions that call for text and a musical symbol are easy to create.

1. With the Expression tool 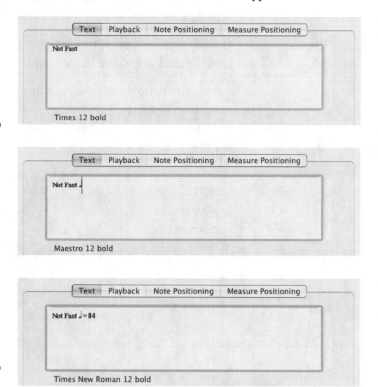 selected, double-click on measure 1.
2. Click the Create button.
3. Type ⌘-Shift-B (Mac) or Control-Shift-B (Windows) to bold the typeface.
4. Type "Not Fast," and press the Space Bar.
5. Select **Text** > Font > Maestro font.
6. Type ⌘-Shift-B (Mac) or Control-Shift-B (Windows) to unbold the typeface
7. Type a "Q" for the quarter note. (Refer to the Maestro Character Set in the Finale Help menu for a list of characters.)
8. Select **Text** > Font > Times New Roman.
9. Type ⌘-Shift-B (Mac) or Control-Shift-B (Windows) to bold the typeface.
10. Press the Space Bar, and type "=," add another space, and type "84."
11. Select the whole Expression, and increase the size to "14."

Now, set the Expression's playback value.

1. Choose the Playback tab at the top of the Expression dialog box.
2. From the Type popup menu, select Tempo.
3. In the Set to Value box, type "84."

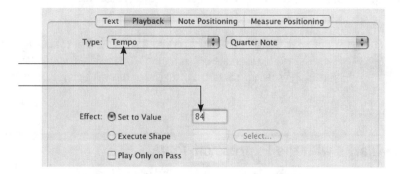

Next, set the auto-positioning for a Measure Expression.

1. Choose the Measure Positioning tab at the top of the Expression dialog box. The Expression Alignment point should be "left."
2. From the measure Alignment Point popup menu, select "Start Of Time Signature."

3. Under the Vertical Position heading, select Above Staff Baseline.

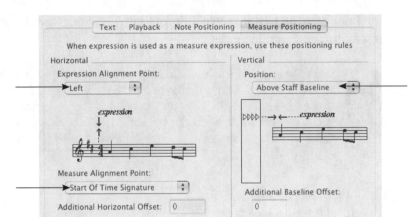

4. Click OK, then click Select.
5. Choose "Rehearsal" for the Staff List. Then click OK.

Determining the Performance Time

Once a tempo value is entered into a score, it is possible for Finale to determine the performance time of the piece or any selected part of it. Tempos that are entered as Expressions, and properly set up to play back, will override the tempo setting in the Playback Controls window.

Performance time is essential for timed presentations, from marching band shows, to concerts where overtime is an issue, to film scores where timing to the millisecond is critical.

To determine performance time:

1. Choose the Mass Edit tool .
2. Type ⌘-A (Mac) or Control-A (Windows) to select the whole score.
3. Select **Mass Edit** > Utilities > Check Elapsed Time.

Elapsed Time
Time at the Beginning of Measure 1
00:00:00:000
Time at the End of Measure 37
00:01:14:455
Elapsed Time of Section
00:01:14:455
(?) OK

Finale will give you the exact duration for the tempo entered. Finale can calculate the whole piece or a specific region selected in Mass Edit.

> This plug-in will help in any situation where time is a critical factor, such as concert length, competition show length, or film score.

Entering Slurs and Dynamics Shapes

Our final step of performance information is adding graphic elements: slurs and crescendo/decrescendo marks.

 Smart Shapes get their name because they recognize system and page breaks, and split themselves into two (or more) different and independently editable shapes. They will also reunite themselves if the layout changes. I prefer to input them in Scroll View. Smart Shape slurs are attached to notes just like Articulations or Note-Attached Expressions. All other Smart Shapes are attached to measures, in the same way that Measure-Attached Expressions are.

1. Choose the Slur tool 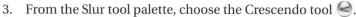.
2. Add all the slurs (see pages 121 and 122).
3. From the Slur tool palette, choose the Crescendo tool .
4. Add all the crescendo marks (see pages 121 and 122).

There are four handles that control the Crescendo shape. Zoom in, and drag the cursor over each handle. As you do this, the cursor will change into a graphic that indicates what function each handle controls. The square handle in the center will move the shape in any direction without changing its length or the size of the opening. The diamond to the left and right on the same horizontal plane will make the shape longer or shorter. Whichever diamond is on the closed end of the shape will also move it up or down. The diamond on the top of the shape's open end controls the width of its opening.

5. Continue to place the shapes as needed in the score.
6. Practice adjusting the size and width of the shapes to match the example.

When a hairpin crescendo leads to a dynamic mark, try to have both marks on the same horizontal plane. Also, try to avoid any collisions with other marks on the score. This should always be the first priority when positioning marks on a score.

Manually Adjusting Slurs

Occasionally, it is necessary to adjust the arc of a slur. In bars 5 and 6, the slur in the Alto Sax part collides with the staccato dot in the Soprano Sax part above.

Across the top of the slurs enclosure, there are three positioning diamonds.

1. Select the right diamond.
2. Drag the handle down until the shape clears the dot.

8_Entertainer_3.mus

Have you saved lately?

Playing the Score

When you use the Setup Wizard to create a score, each staff is assigned to a General MIDI sound based on the staff name. In the case of some of the more obscure instruments in the instrument library, it picks the closest sound. For example, the viola d'amore is assigned to String Ensemble 1, since there is no specific sound for the instrument in the General MIDI sound list. In the case of our sax quartet score, it is already set up for multitimbral playback with the appropriate General MIDI sounds assigned to each staff. If you are unfamiliar with MIDI, refer to your installation manual or the Help menu for Finale's MIDI setup and playback controls.

SoundFonts

When you installed Finale (version 2004 and higher), a custom group of sounds, called a "SoundFont," was installed on your computer. SoundFonts use the computer's engine for playback. These sounds are a better quality than the basic sound synthesizer of your computer. The technology is similar to that used in creating sounds for many synthesizers currently on the market. The SoundFont that ships with Finale is the same one used in the SmartMusic software system. In Finale 2005, the SoundFont has been expanded to include marching percussion sounds. Additional SoundFonts are available from music software vendors, and on the Web. Do a search for "SoundFonts" for a list of sites where you can purchase and download additional SoundFonts.

The controls for playback routing are located in the Instrument List window.

- Select **Window** > Instrument List.

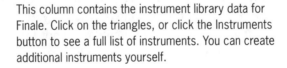

This column contains the instrument library data for Finale. Click on the triangles, or click the Instruments button to see a full list of instruments. You can create additional instruments yourself.

This column contains the staff controls for routing data out of Finale.

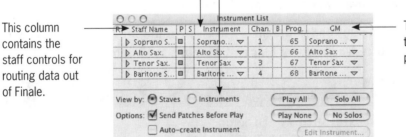

This column contains the full General MIDI patch list.

Libraries

Finale lets you create reusable libraries of information, which you can transfer between documents. If you want to create a library of instruments for your keyboard, set it up here, and use the Save Library command in the File menu to create a custom instrument library. Libraries are sets of data that can be saved and loaded into Finale documents to help customize documents or move data between documents. You can create libraries for Expressions, chord symbols, instrument assignments, and many other types of data.

To save a library of your instrument assignments:
*   Select **File** > Save Library.

The Save Library dialog box display buttons for all possible library groups.

To save a custom synthesizer library:
1.   Click the Instruments button, and click OK.
2.   Name the file, using the synth's name, and save it to a location you'll remember.

To import a library into a Finale document:
1.   Select **File** > Load Library.
2.   Choose the file, and click Open.

The Save Library dialog:

Save Library	
○ Articulations	○ Music Spacing
○ Chords & Fretboards	○ Page Format
○ Clefs	○ Percussion Maps
○ Default Fonts	○ Shapes
○ Document Options	○ Shape Expressions
○ Executable Shapes	○ Staff Styles
○ Fretboard Styles	○ Stem Connections
⦿ Instruments	○ Text Expressions
○ Key Signatures	○ Text Repeats

(?)   (Cancel)   (OK)

Using an External Device for Playback

If your playback device is a multitimbral General MIDI keyboard, Finale can communicate with it just as easily as the SoundFont. With the Send Patches Before Play setting checking the Instrument List window, Finale will load the appropriate sounds before playback begins.

To change a MIDI channel assignment:
1.   Double-click on the channel number in the Instrument List window.
2.   Type in the new channel number.

If your keyboard is not General MIDI, there are several other keyboard libraries in the Instrument Libraries folder that you can use. If your keyboard is not in the existing library, then there are two options. One is to set up your keyboard internally and uncheck Send Patches Before Play so that patch data is not transmitted. Otherwise, if you are adventurous, try setting up an instrument library for your keyboard.

Software Synthesizers and Samplers

Finale 2005 adds the ability to easily route MIDI data internally to a software sound source. The steps for Mac and Windows are different.

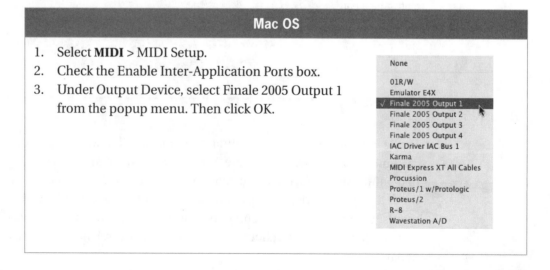

Mac OS

1.   Select **MIDI** > MIDI Setup.
2.   Check the Enable Inter-Application Ports box.
3.   Under Output Device, select Finale 2005 Output 1 from the popup menu. Then click OK.

None
01R/W
Emulator E4X
√ Finale 2005 Output 1
Finale 2005 Output 2
Finale 2005 Output 3
Finale 2005 Output 4
IAC Driver IAC Bus 1
Karma
MIDI Express XT All Cables
Procussion
Proteus/1 w/Protologic
Proteus/2
R-8
Wavestation A/D

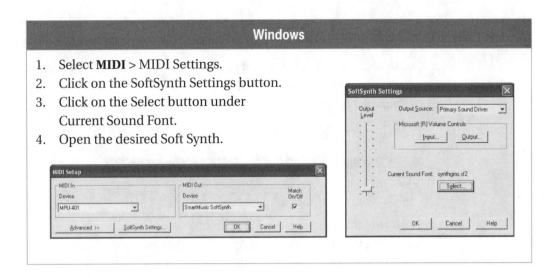

I'll now route this into Native Instruments Kontakt, a software sampler. A special version of Kontakt is used with both Garritan Personal Orchestra and EWQL Symphonic Orchestra Silver Edition. Garritan Personal orchestra can be purchased at www.garritan.com. The EWQL Symphonic Orchestra Silver Edition is available at www.soundsonline.com. The technique is the same for any software sound sources.

Routing into Kontakt (or other software sounds sources)

To play back using software sound sources:

1. Launch Kontakt.
2. From the Kontakt File menu, select Setup.
3. The Audio Setup window, click the MIDI tab.
4. In the Input Interface window, scroll down to Finale 2005 Finale 2005 Output 1.
5. Click the "off" indication in the right column, to change it to "on." Then click OK.

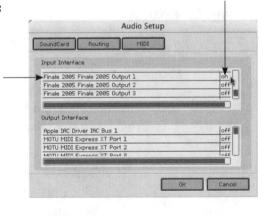

If you are using the Garritan Personal Orchestra, there is one additional setting, to deal with the unique performance controls available in

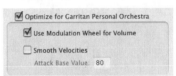

that collection. Expand the Playback Controls window, and click the HP Preferences button.

• Check the Optimize for Garritan Personal Orchestra box.

Check the documentation for both Finale and Garritan Personal Orchestra to determine the best settings for your work. There is a "Finale Users Resource Page" on the Garritan Web site (www.garritan.com). Consult this page for additional information and tips from other users.

Let's Really Burn! (an Audio CD)

Finale allows the direct export of playback to an audio file using a SoundFont. You can save your file as a WAV (Windows), AIFF (Mac), or MP3 (both) file that can be burned to a CD or uploaded to the Web.

1. Select **File** > Save Special > Save As Audio File.

2. Name the File.
3. Select the appropriate file type. The Standard Audio file format on the Mac is AIFF; on Windows, it is WAV. If you want to create an MP3, choose the MP3 button. Then click Save.

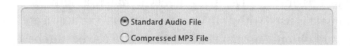

To create a CD, import the audio file into your CD burning software. On the Mac, there's iTunes or Toast. For Windows users, there's Easy CD Creator or the Windows version of iTunes.

Adding Cue Notes

Once you've proofed your work, go back and add the cue notes in the first three measures.

In this process, you'll be introduced to a feature called Layers. Each staff has four layers to it. Each layer can function as its own staff, independent of the other. To learn more about layers, see chapter 10.

1. Choose the Mass Edit tool ⬚ .
2. Highlight bar 1 of the alto sax part.
3. Select **Plug-ins** > Scoring and Arranging > Add Cue Notes.
4. Choose Soprano Sax in the Staff List window.
5. Enter "Alto Sax. Cue" in the "Name the cue:" box. Then click OK.

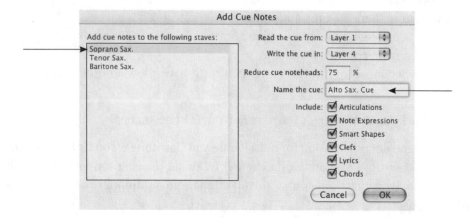

6. Repeat the process for the Tenor part.
7. For the Baritone Sax staff, first select **Edit** > Select Partial Measures.
8. Highlight all of measure 3 and the first eighth note of measure 4.
9. Create the cue using the above steps.

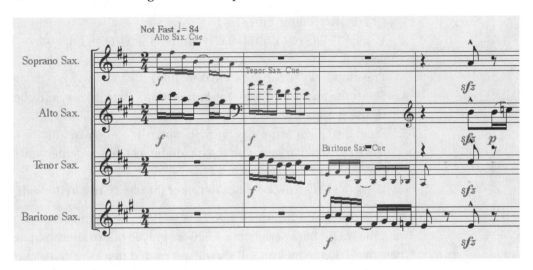

Through these steps, Finale has copied the music into the selected staves and added a Note Expression for the cue indication, which is red on the screen. The notes should be displayed in blue, since by default, cue notes are entered in Layer 4. A whole rest is placed in Layer 1. The dynamic mark has also been copied but must be repositioned, as does the text for the cue indications. Observe that, along with the notes, both the dynamic and the cue indications will be reduced to 75% of normal size. Any Articulation, chord symbol, or Note-Attached Expression will match the percentage of the entry to which it is attached.

> If you want more control over the size of the cue's text indication, it can be edited using the Expression tool.

The Alto Sax staff is wrongly displayed in bass clef. This needs to be corrected.

1. Choose the Clef tool .
2. Press the 1 key—the clef Metatool key for the treble clef.
3. Click on the first note of the Alto Sax in bar 2.

With the clef restored, the text can now be positioned for all staves.

1. Choose the Selection tool 🖈 (shortcut: ESC).
2. Click the alto cue, and drag it up.
3. Click on the dynamic mark for the alto cue, and drag it up.
4. Reposition the rest of the Expressions.

Measure 4 in the tenor sax contains a combination of cue- and normal-sized notes. The default Layer settings have kicked in and switched all of Layer 1 to Stems Up. However, I only want the cue to change the first beat of the measure. This will mean adjusting the stem direction of the eighth note on beat 2, and the staff position of the eighth rest it that follows it. In Layer 4, the stem direction of the eighth note on beat 1 must be changed and the eighth rest next to it switched from hidden to visible, and lowered a space in the staff.

1. Choose the Simple Entry tool 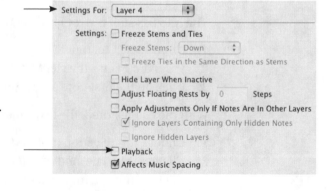.
2. ⌘-click (Mac) or Control-click (Windows) on the eighth note on beat 2 of bar 4 to select it.
3. Press the L key to flip the stem direction.
4. Select the eighth rest from the Simple Entry Rest Palette, and click on the eighth rest so it is highlighted.
5. Press the Down Arrow key once, to move the rest down into the staff. This step will leave it just a hair low, with the top of the rest on the center line rather than in the space above.
6. Press the Up Arrow key once to center the eighth rest in the staff.

The cue in Layer 4 has three eighth rests after the eighth note that display differently from the bright blue of the note. They are grayed out to show that even though they are there to fill up the measure. They will not print. I need the first eighth to become visible so that I have a complete beat in the cue. Complete the bar by flipping the stem direction of the eighth notes on beat 1.

1. In Simple Entry, select Layer 4 in the bottom-left corner of the Finale window.
2. With the Simple Entry eighth rest still selected, click on the first eighth rest, on beat 1 of Layer 4, so it is highlighted.
3. Press the H key to toggle the rest to show it, and print.
4. Press the Down Arrow key twice to position it a space lower in the staff.
5. From the Simple Entry Palette, select the eighth note.
6. ⌘-click (Mac) or Control-click (Windows) on the eighth note of Layer 4, beat 1.
7. Press the L key to flip the stem direction.
8. Tap the Space Bar to begin playback. The cue notes will now play. To eliminate the cue note's playback, disable the playback of Layer 4, since the cues are the only entries in that Layer.

To disable playback for Layer 4:
1. Select **Options** > Document Options.
2. Choose Layers in the left column.
3. Select the settings for Layer 4.
4. Uncheck the Playback box. Then click OK.

Checking Instrument Range

Whenever you copy and paste music from one instrument to another or transpose a score into a new key, it's a good idea to check your score for notes that are out of range or difficult to play for a particular instrument. If you're not that familiar with instrument ranges, it is a good idea to check your entire score. There is a plug-in to assist you. Let's check your cues.

1. Choose the Mass Edit tool ⊕.
2. Highlight the first four measures of the score.
3. Select **Plug-ins** > Scoring and Arranging > Check Range.

Finale selects the instrument based on the staff name entered in Staff Attributes.

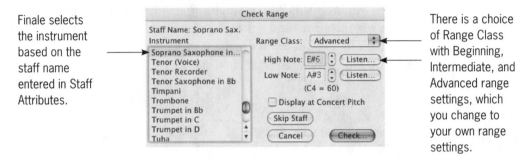

There is a choice of Range Class with Beginning, Intermediate, and Advanced range settings, which you change to your own range settings.

4. Click the Check button. Finale will check the region selected and report at the end of each staff if nothing is found.
5. Click OK, and continue checking.

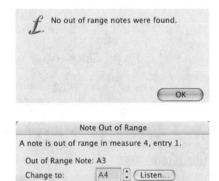

When you get to the Tenor Sax, you will find that the A in bar 4 is out of range. Note the choices you are given. Finale suggests raising the note up one octave.

6. If you agree with Finale's note change recommendation, click Change Note. If you don't agree with the recommendation, click Next and continue checking.

The offending note is transposed up an octave. The result is a leap on the end of the figure that will not sound right. The most musical solution is to transpose the entire cue up an octave.

1. Choose the Mass Edit tool ⊕.
2. Highlight bar 3 of the Tenor Sax part.
3. Select **Mass Edit** > Transpose, or press the 6 key, the Metatool for transposing one octave higher.
4. Choose "Up."
5. For Interval, choose "Octave." Then click OK.

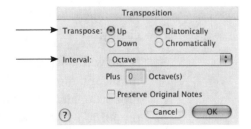

One final cosmetic adjustment needs to be made. The transposition process has moved the cue's text expression up too high. Select it, with the Expression tool, and move it down.

Cue-Sized Noteheads

Now, let's move on to measure 8 to resize the A cue notes in the Bari Sax part. The recommended size for cue notes is 75%.

1. Choose the Resize tool .
2. Click directly on the notehead of the A quarter note, in the second space. Be sure the window reads Resize Notehead; if not, click the notehead again. This tool can also resize staves and entire pages. It reacts to the location where you click, so be aware of this when you use the Resize tool.
3. Enter the percentage: 75. Then click OK.

ALWAYS check the dialog box heading in the Resize Tool to make sure you are changing the correct item. In this case, it should read "Resize Notehead."

4. Repeat the procedure in bars 16, 20, 21, 30, and 37.

Since you changed only an element of the entry, the parentheses will not change size.

If Finale crashed right now and you hadn't saved your work so far, would you:

1. Throw the computer out the window?
2. Make your downstairs neighbor think you joined the cast of Riverdance?
3. Blame me for not reminding you sooner?

8_Entertainer_4.mus

Have you saved lately?

Page Layout

It is time to turn your engraving masterpiece into a print suitable for framing. You need to be in Page View, so select it from the View menu.

There are two key factors involved in Finale page layout: margin settings and reduction percentages. First, look at the amount of space on the page to see if it is being used efficiently.

Begin with the page percentage. This changes the size of every element on the page, the music and the text, unless Fixed Size text is set. This allows all elements to be reduced proportionally, and at the same time. The idea is to have all elements readable and in proportion to one another. The default page percentage is 100%. Scores are usually anywhere from 75% down to 40%.

1. Choose the Resize tool .
2. Click in the upper-left corner of the page, away from any music. Be sure the Resize window says "Resize Page."

Position cursor above all music in this range

THE ENTERTAINER
for Saxophone Quartet

by SCOTT JOPLIN
arranged by *Vince Leonard*

3. Enter "75" for the percentage, then click OK.
4. Select **Edit** > Update Layout.

> After changing the page percentage, make it a habit to select **Edit** > Update Layout to re-layout the score with the new line spacing. When you change the percentage, there may be more, or less room on each staff depending on the size and direction of the change. This redistributes the music based on the new size and avoids problems of excess space or collisions.

Next, review how many systems and pages the piece is, now, and determine what the final goal for each will be. Right now, the piece is spread over four pages with a lot of blank space on each page. A publisher would consider this layout as unacceptable and want it on fewer pages. This piece will fit easily on two pages. Also, the music spacing can be loosened up a bit, since there is room for four systems on page 2.

1. Choose the Mass Edit tool 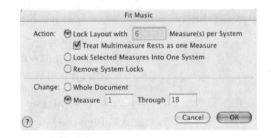.
2. Highlight measures 1 through 18.
3. Select **Mass Edit** > Fit Music: shortcut ⌘-Shift-M (Mac) or Control-Shift-M (Windows).
4. Enter "6" for Measure(s) per System, and click OK.

The music is now set at six measures to a line, and the lock icon is now visible at the end of each locked system. The remaining four systems should have five measures each, except for the last system, which contains four.

1. Highlight measures 19 through 37.
2. Use the shortcut for the Fit Music feature (see step 3 above).
3. Enter 5 for the number of measures, then click OK.

The music should now be properly set on seven systems. Now, it gets a bit subjective. This is the kind of layout a publisher would want—as few pages as possible with no blank or wasted space. If you were being paid to set four bars per line, you'd use the Fit Music command in Mass Edit to fit four bars to a system. If there are no other considerations, you could leave it the way it is, but what fun would that be? Besides, page layout skills are what separate great work from good work.

153

I'll take you through the changes I made, as we tackle the page and system margins to complete the layout.

Page Margins

In the previous chapters adjustments to the page layout were made by dragging the staff handle to alter the layout. For more precise positioning, I use the Page and System Margin Editing dialog boxes. Here I can edit a single system, a whole page or the entire document.

1.   Choose the Page Layout tool 🔘.
2.   Select **Page Layout** > Page Margins > Edit Page Margins.

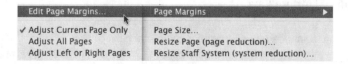

The Edit Page Margins dialog boxes for page margins and staff systems contain the margin settings and editing options. The Apply button allows changes to be applied and viewed without leaving the dialog box, in case additional changes are necessary. The OK button exits the dialog box and returns to Page View. All measurements in this book will be EVPUs/inches.

The page margins define the boundaries for the staff systems. The distance measured is the space between the edge of the paper and edge of the music. The page margin lines run horizontally on the top and bottom, vertically on the left and right side. All margin lines have handles along the edge of the page and can be manually dragged and positioned by editing the values in the dialog box. The dialog boxes below show the numbers for the default page margins. Edit the margin settings by entering new number in the boxes. Clicking Apply or OK will change the page margins to the new setting.

1.   Press the Tab key to advance the entry field to the Left page margin.
2.   Change the left page margin to 213 EVPUs (0.73985 inches).
3.   Click the All Pages button to apply the settings to both pages, and then click Apply. This will reduce the amount of empty space on the left side of the page.

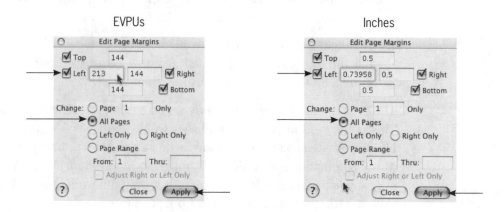

Page 1 Staff Systems

Even though the correct number of systems, three, are on page 1, the layout is far from correct. My first choice is to use the Space Systems Evenly feature in Page Layout tool.

1. With the Page Layout tool selected, select **Page Layout** > Space Systems Evenly.
2. Set Space Systems Evenly On: to "Page 1 Only."
3. Set Distribute Systems to "Do Not Change the Number of Systems on Each Page." Then click OK.

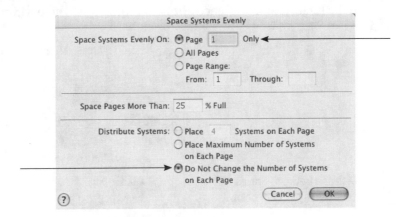

The results are close—too much space between the systems and not enough at the bottom of the page.

4. Select **Page Layout** > Systems > Edit Margins.

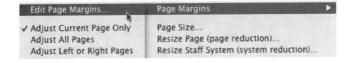

Staff System Margins control the size and position of each staff system on the page. Each system, in Page View, displays inside a box. Click the upper-left handle of box 2, the second system of the page. It is possible to go back and forth from the dialog box and the music without closing the dialog box. This is also true when the Page Margins dialog box is on the screen. Just remember to click on the System Margins dialog box to make it active again before entering any numbers.

 Use the numbers for uniform position of all margins and systems. Using the System Margins dialog box also allows for editing a single system, a group of systems (such as all those on a single page), or the entire document at once—all with precision that cannot be matched by manual positioning.

Referring to the graphic below, the Top field sets the distance between the top of the staff and the top of the system margin. Similarly, the Bottom field controls the distance between the bottom staff and the bottom dotted line of the system margin. Increase the numbers in either of these fields, and the system will occupy more vertical space on the page. The Left and Right fields control the distance of the box from the left and right page margins. Enter a number in either field, and the box will move away from the margin. The most common use will be using the left margin to create indents, as illustrated by the first system of the piece. Occasionally, the right-hand margin will need to be moved if the final system of a piece does not require the whole width of the page.

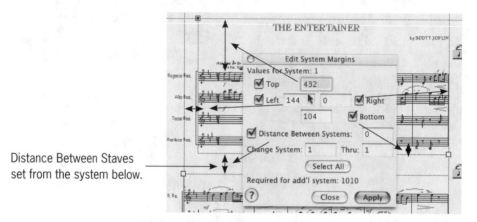

Distance Between Staves set from the system below.

The system boxes can be edited two ways: by dragging the handles or by entering numbers into the fields in this dialog box and clicking Apply. Entering the numbers will provide a more precise and even alignment of the systems, so mastering them will help you to give your work a much better look.

Underneath those four fields is another important field, Distance Between Staves. This number can be used to add space between a system box and the system or margin above it. In the above graphic, the arrows indicate the distance between the first and second systems. The dialog box is for system 1, where there is no space between it and the top page margin. That is why the value displayed is zero.

All these parameter fields have check boxes next to them. This allows for flexibility in editing. When you click the Apply button, only the values with check marks will be applied to the system or systems selected. This way, you can enter, say, a new Bottom value without changing the Top, Left, or Right.

The Change System fields allow editing from a single field to any number of contiguous systems. Clicking the Select All button allows editing of the entire piece at the same time.

To set the system margins for the first page:
1. Uncheck the boxes for Top, Left, and Bottom.
2. For Distance Between Systems, enter "150."
3. For Change System, enter "2" thru "3." Then click Apply.

There is no mystical wisdom hidden in what numbers you should use, as these parameters. My layouts use a little math, a little practiced eye, plus some trial and error. Finale provides the opportunity to tweak and tweak these numbers without doing any harm to to anything. The biggest mistake is usually just an Undo command away from never happening.

Page 2 Staff System Alterations

Page 2 requires more than just repositioning systems that are already on the page. Room needs to be created for systems on the continuing pages. Fortunately, Finale has a feature that will make this process a snap.

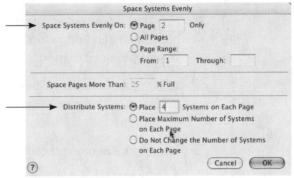

1. Select **Page Layout** > Space Systems Evenly.
2. Space Systems Evenly On: should be set to "Page 2 Only."
3. Distribute Systems should be set to "Place 4 Systems on Each Page." Then click OK.

At this point, check the graphic elements in the piece for proper positioning and alignment. Rehearsal numbers and tempo indications may need positioning. Smart Shapes and repeat brackets may need tweaking. On a score where several systems are on a page, make sure there are clean spaces between the systems.

Page Text

On publishing assignments, there are usually guidelines to be followed such that all of a particular company's music has the same look. For this example, I'll assume the publisher wants all text in the Times font.

According to the publisher's guidelines, the title should be in 24-point bold type and in all capital letters. The title text block's point size, 24, and style, bold, has already been preset correctly by the Setup Wizard. The problem is that by reducing the page, the printed size of the type is no longer 24 point; it is a 75% reduction of 24 point. To counteract this, Finale has added a setting called Fixed Size. This way, the text is no longer reduced with the page.

1. Choose the Text tool ⒶHandles will appear on all page text blocks.
2. Double-click the handle of the title.
3. Select **Edit** > Select All, or use ⌘-A (Mac) or Control-A (Windows).
4. Select **Text** > Size > Fixed Size. Click anywhere outside the text block when done.

To add the subtitle:
1. Double-click anywhere below the title, to create a new text block.
2. Select **Text** > Character Settings.

   a. Times should already be chosen as the font.
   b. Set Size to 14.
   c. Check Fixed Size.
   d. Check Italic, then click OK.

157

3. Type "For Saxophone Quartet" in the new text block, and then click anywhere outside the text block when done.

To center the text block on the page:

1. Select **Text** > Placement > Center Horizontally, or use the shortcut ⌘-Shift-' [apostrophe] (Mac) or Control-Shift-' [apostrophe] (Windows).
2. To adjust the distance between the title and subtitle, click the handle, and use the arrow keys to nudge the subtitle up or down until it looks good.

Now add the arranger's name to the writing credits. Rather than create a separate text block, you can add it to the composer credit. This makes one less block to position, should you need to move them later.

1. Double-click the "[Composer]" credit handle.
2. Position the cursor to the right of the composer's name, and press the Return/Enter key.

The arranger's name should be in italics, but the credit should be in plain text.

3. Type "Arranged by" and a space.
4. Select **Text** > Style > Italic.
5. Type the name, "Vince Leonard."

Now, set all the text in this frame for Fixed Size.

6. Use the Select All command.
7. Select **Text** > Size > Fixed Size, then click anywhere outside the text block when done.
8. Drag the text block handle down so the credit begins under the subtitle.

The "[Copyright]" frame requires a second line of text.

1. Double-click on the "[Copyright]" text block handle.
2. Press the Right Arrow key to move the cursor to the right of the existing text, and then press the Return/Enter key.
3. Type "All Rights Reserved."
4. Select **Edit** > Select All, or use the shortcut: ⌘-A (Mac) or Control-A (Windows).
5. Select **Text** > Size > 8.
6. Select **Text** > Size > Fixed Size. Then click anywhere on the page outside the text block when finished.

> Occasionally, text blocks need repositioning after the music is set. You can manually drag them with the mouse, but I would suggest using the arrow keys to nudge them, instead. This way, they retain their exact horizontal position. If there are several blocks that need to be positioned in relation to one another, it is possible to select and move them all as a unit.

Give the score one last visual inspection to make sure everything is where you want it to be.

 Have you saved lately?

Printing Your Score

Before printing, check the Page Setup settings.

1. Select **File** > Page Setup.
2. Confirm that "Letter" is selected for the Paper Size. If there is a Letter Small size, change it to Letter. The look of this window will depend on the computer's OS and the printer connected to it. This window is from a Macintosh running OS X connected to an HP LaserJet 5000.
3. Confirm that the proper printer is selected, after "Format for:".
4. Confirm that the proper page orientation is selected, and then click OK. Then, you're ready to print.

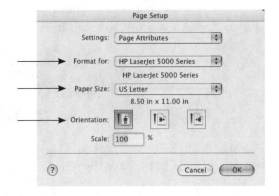

Extracting Parts

The next step in the evolution of a score is extracting parts. When I first started writing arrangements, this was the point where the fun ended and the work began. Since I was also a copyist, it also meant instead of working on a new and cool chart for a paying client, I was working for me for nothing. Thankfully, when working in Finale, parts are now an afterthought.

The Print Parts Option

There are three ways to create a printed part in Finale. The simplest is the Print Parts command in File menu. This is the Finale equivalent of taking the score and cutting it into strips, staff by staff, and pasting them on to a sheet of paper to create a part. It is strictly what you see is what you get—no editing of individual parts for spacing problems or layout. The good news is that this approach leaves the score file untouched, and it's fast. I use it for quick parts when there's no time to extract parts to separate files or when I'm still working on the arrangement.

Special Part Extraction

The second method is called Special Part Extraction. When using this process in a score, select the staff in Scroll View, and select **Edit** > Special Part Extraction. Go to Page View, and only the staff selected will be visible. Tweak the part as needed, and print it. This process is also relatively fast, but if the part needs to be reprinted later, the entire process must be repeated.

Extract Parts

The third way to create parts is to use the Extract Parts process, found in File menu. This separates each staff, or group of staves, into a separate and independent file. This file can be edited and printed and not affect the score or other part files. The resulting file is always there to be reprinted, as needed. This is my method of choice for 99% of my work, but some setup is recommended.

In my world, saving time is saving money, so I'm always interested in ways of doing things once instead of many times. Before I extract any parts, I do some things that need to be done for all parts. These changes affect the file in a way that will not be good for the score, so step 1 is to create a new file.

 Short file names allow for easier identification in the Open dialog box. I add "extr" to the file name to indicate that it is my master part extraction file. This becomes increasingly important when you create parts, as each file name will also need to include the name of the part, in addition to the name of the project.

160

1. Save the score as "Entertainer_extr.mus" (**File** > Save As).

Setting some formatting options for this new file will save us time later, as they will carry into the new part files we are about to create from this master score file.

2. Select **Options** > Page Format > Parts.

There are separate selections for Score and Part. The Part heading defines the size and scale of the page that File will automatically create when parts are extracted.

Here, I have a set page size and format that I use in most of my work. Try them in your own files.

EVPUs

Page Format for Parts

Page Size:	Letter (2448 x 3168)			System Margins		

Width: 2448
Height: 3168

Orientation: ● Portrait
○ Landscape

Scaling
Scale Page to: 88 %

System Scaling
Staff Height: 96
And Scale System: 100 %
Resulting System Scaling: 100 %

Units: EVPUs

System Margins
Top
0
Left 0   0   Right
134
Bottom

Distance
Between Systems: 0

☑ First Staff System Margins
Top
640
Left 0

Distance
from Top: 0

Page Margins
☐ Facing Pages

Left Page Margins
Top
300
Left 144   144   Right
72
Bottom

Right Page Margins
Top
180
Left 300   144   Right
72
Bottom

☐ First Page Top Margin: 180

Cancel   OK

Inches

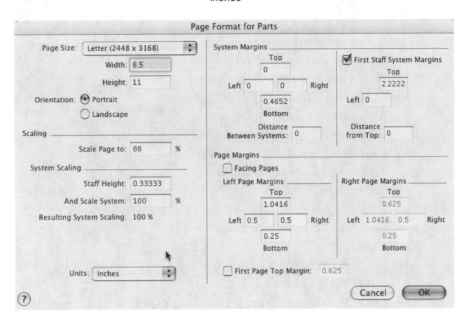

3. Transfer these setting to both the Page Format for Score and Page Format for Parts Dialogs.

4. Select **Page Layout** > Redefine Pages > All Pages.

The page has changed to the same size and percentage as what the extracted part page will require. Now, text can be positioned in the master score file exactly as it will be positioned in the extracted parts. The more text involved, the more time this step will save. Since this is a short arrangement, text on continuing pages is not a factor, in this case.

Now, it is time to extract parts. When Finale creates the new files for the extracted parts, it places them in the same folder as the master score file.

1. Select **File** > Extract Parts.

2. Uncheck Space Systems Evenly.

3. Under File Names, delete the "extr" extension and %n to shorten the file name.

4. Click the Options button, which opens the Page Options dialog box.

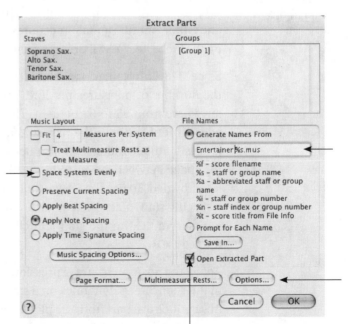

To have the extracted parts automatically open in Finale, check this box.

In Page Options, the staff name can be removed from the staff display and turned into a text block.

5. Under Items to Remove, uncheck "Single-Page Text Blocks and Graphics (Page 2+)."

6. Check "Staff or Group Names."

7. After Part Names, click the Set Font button, which opens the Font dialog box.

8. Set the font to 24 point Times, and then click OK.

9. Back in the Page Options dialog, set Resize Name to 100%.

10. Set the Vertical (V) position to 250 EVPUs (0.86806 inches).

Page Options

Staff Placement: ☑ New Staff Position
Top Staff: -80
Between Staves: -240

Items to Remove: ☐ Single-Page Text Blocks and Graphics (Page 1)
☐ Single-Page Text Blocks and Graphics (Page 2+)
☑ Staff or Group Names
☐ Multiple-Page Text Blocks and Graphics

Part Names: ☑ Create Staff or Group Name Header (Set Font...)
Resize Name to: 100 %
Page: 1   Through: 1
H: 0   V: 250

(Cancel) (OK)

11. Click OK to return to the Extract Parts dialog box, and then OK again to begin extracting.

Finale will create a separate file for each part and open those files automatically so you can inspect them, tweak them as desired, and then print them.

> For large-ensemble scores, extract one part first, just to make sure you've set up everything properly. If not, you can correct it before you've wasted the time extracting a large number of parts that need to be redone.

Part_Extraction.pdf

Space does not allow us to cover all the situations encountered when extracting parts or every technique I use in dealing with them. There will be an update of the "Part Extraction and Other Painful Dental Procedures" chapter, from the first edition of this book, posted on the Web site. We will present a few pointers here that you can explore on your own.

Since "The Entertainer" yields short, one-page parts, spread out the notation by reducing the number of measures per line. I usually employ the Resize tool to reduce the staff anywhere from 95 to 90 percent. This adds a bit of space to the part so that it feels a little less dense. It also helps the space between staves to be a little less crowded. To use the Resize tool on a specific staff, place the cursor in the left margin next to the staff and click the mouse.

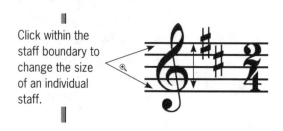

Click within the staff boundary to change the size of an individual staff.

Adjust the position of any Expressions that are tight to the staff, due to positioning issues in the score. Keep dynamics on a straight horizontal line so that they are easy to follow. Always look at a part from the player's perspective. Check the parts after printing to make sure you did not miss anything when viewing the part on the screen.

162

Creating a Piano Reduction

Creating a piano reduction of a score is just a plug-in away. The amount of work that it takes to produce a good reduction depends on the complexity of the score. "The Entertainer" provides an interesting example to work with, since it is an orchestration of a piano piece.

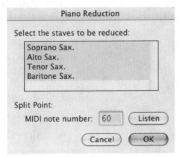

1. Choose the Mass Edit tool 🌐.
2. Select **Edit** > Select All, or use the shortcut command: ⌘-A (Mac) or Control-A (Windows).
3. Select **Plug-ins** > Scoring and Arranging > Piano Reduction.
4. Click "Soprano Sax" in the "Select the staves to be reduced" field, and then Shift-click "Baritone Sax" to select all four staves. Then click OK.

Finale will create a new grand staff with the reduced score. Make an inspection pass through it, to see how ready to print it is.

Ent_Piano_Red.mus

To view my results, download the file Ent_Piano_Red.mus from the Finale book Web site. I'll point out some issues encountered when creating a piano reduction.

1. Use Mass Edit to clear all cues before running the plug-in. In bars 1 through 4, the notes and the cues overlap, and since they are different sizes, it creates a confusing picture.
2. Measure Expressions set to appear on all staves appear on both treble and bass clef staves. Those set to appear only on specific staves do not appear on the reduction. In the rules of music notation, the brace of a grand staff carries the rule that any dynamic placed in between the staves applies to both. Only one mark, positioned between the staves, is necessary. In measure 4, the *sfz* expression appears on both treble and bass clef staves. In measure 5, the p is set to display on the Soprano, Tenor and Bari staves but does not appear on the piano reduction grand staff.
3. Smart Shape slurs are transferred, but they are multiplied by the number of occurrences in the score. In measure 7, select the slur's handle and drag it down, there will be a second slur underneath it, since there are two slurs on that figure in the original staves, the Soprano and Alto Sax.
4. There are some split-point issues where notes need to be placed in the other staff. In bars 5 and 6, middle C belongs in the bass clef staff.
5. Some figures have been combined, and need to edited into layers or voices to show different lines. In measure 24 the moving sixteenth-note line is split between two staves and the quarter note line is mixed with it in the treble clef staff, making it difficult to understand.

Expect these situations in every score reduction. It is part of the process, but at least it saves starting from scratch. For larger instrumentations, you might work in sections, creating several reductions, and then later, use Mass Edit tool to combine them to create a final composite reduced score. Further editing will depend on whether the reduction is to be used as a conductor's guide or piano part. As with any Finale tool, learning to use it most effectively, situation to situation, is key to good results.

Summary

This example included the following new Finale skills:

- setting up a score using the Setup Wizard
- scanning music
- importing TIFF files
- using Measure and Note Expressions
- enclosing text for rehearsal numbers
- combining fonts in a text expression
- setting up tempo marks that affect playback
- using the Cautionary Accidentals Plug-in
- using the Global Staff Attributes Plug-in
- using the Check Range Plug-in
- creating cue notes
- using EVPUs as a unit of measurement
- page formatting for multisystem score pages
- using Fixed-Size Text
- using Space Systems Evenly
- routing MIDI to software synthesizers
- determining the performance time
- extracting parts
- creating a piano reduction

Review

1. If you have access to a scanner, try scanning in another piece and recreate the layout of the original. Identify and correct any mistakes from the scanning process.
2. Review the Help sections for Metatools.
3. Change the instrumentation, using the Transposition settings to display in the proper key, and the Check Range plug-in to look for out-of-range notes for the new instrument. Alter the arrangement accordingly. Remember also to change the Staff names, because the Check Range plug-in uses that to determine what instrument to use.

   Go back to the Setup Wizard and create a new quartet score, this time using brass, strings, woodwinds, or mallet percussion. Copy and paste "The Entertainer" into the new score. Use the Check Range Plug-in to look for out-of-range notes for the new instruments. Look for problems caused by ranges or key. Explore changing the key or the orchestration to make it more playable.
4. Scan in another small ensemble piece. Identify and correct any mistakes from the scanning process.

9

Vocal Score with Percussion ("Simple Gifts")

This chapter discusses entering lyrics and polyphony. Begin by looking over the score to identify new areas that will be addressed.

Simple Gifts

SATB with Optional Percussion
Arranged by Tom Rudolph

New areas to be addressed include:

- customizing staves
- single-line percussion
- using and customizing percussion maps
- entering polyphonic parts on staves using layers
- multiple verses of lyrics
- entering percussion notation

Use the Setup Wizard to create the score.

1. Select **File** > New > Document from Setup Wizard, or use the shortcut command for a new document with the wizard: ⌘-N (Mac) or Control-N (Windows).

2. Using the Wizard, enter the following:

   Title: Simple Gifts
   Composer: Arranged by Tom Rudolph
   Copyright: Copyright 1997 by Tom Rudolph

3. Enter the following instruments:

   Chorus–Soprano
   Chorus–Tenor
   Percussion–Percussion
   Percussion–Cymbals

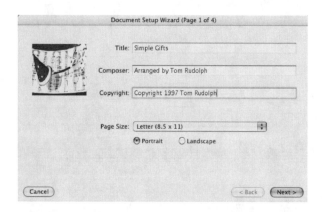
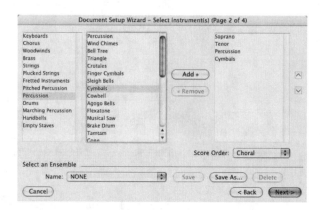

4. From the Score Order menu, select Choral. The standard instrument order for choral music order will be applied to your selected instruments. You can also control the instrument order manually by using the up and down arrows.

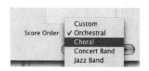

   Soprano
   Tenor
   Percussion
   Cymbals

5. Set the key signature to F major and the time signature to **C** (common time).

6. Since there is a pickup measure, be sure to check "Specify Pickup Measure," and choose the quarter note, as this pickup measure's duration is a total of one beat.

The score should look like the following:

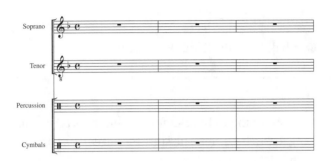

Simple Gifts

Arranged by Tom Rudolph

Customizing Staves using the Staff Tool

Use the Staff tool to customize the score setup, changing some of the elements set by the Setup Wizard. The Staff tool controls all of the aspects of each individual staff and can control just about every item that is displayed.

1. Choose the Staff tool .
2. Select **Staff** > Edit Staff Attributes. Or, use the contextual menus by Control-clicking (Mac) or Right-clicking (Windows) the staff and choosing Edit Staff Attributes.

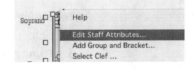

To put two instrument names on each staff:
3. Select the Staff Attributes for Soprano.
4. Click the Edit button next to Full name,
5. Press Enter or Return after Soprano, and type "Alto."

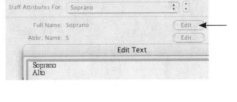

6. Click the Abbreviation button and enter:

   S
   A

7. Select "Tenor" from the Staff Attributes pulldown menu.
8. Click Edit, and after "Tenor," press Enter/Return and type "Bass."
9. Click the Abbreviation button and enter:

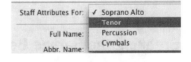

   T
   B

To set the names and abbreviations for the percussion staves:

10. Change the word "Percussion" to:

Snare Drum
Bass Drum

11. Set "Abbr. Name" to:

S.D.
B.D.

12. Change "Cymbals" to "Sus. Cym." Set its "Abbr. Name" to "Cym."

Changing The Starting Clef

The Setup Wizard chose the treble clef for the tenor part. For this arrangement, the clef needs to be changed to a bass clef. The starting clef can be changed using the Staff or Clef tool. To change the clef using the Staff tool:

1. Choose the Staff Tool, and select **Staff** > Edit Staff Attributes.
2. Select the Tenor Bass part from the pull-down menu.
3. Click Select next to First Clef.
4. Choose the Bass clef.

To change to a one-line staff:

5. Select the Staff Attributes for the Cymbals Staff from the pulldown menu.
6. Change the Staff popup menu from a 5-line to a 1-line staff.

The Staff names should now appear as:

Breaking the Barline Between Staves

The percussion parts pose another problem. They are part of the same group, but we want to break the barline between the two staves. This again requires using Staff Attributes.

1. Choose the Staff Tool 📧.
2. Select Edit Staff Attributes from the Staff menu or from the Staff Contextual menu.

3. Select Staff Attributes for Sus. Cym.
4. Check the "Break Barlines Between Staves" checkbox.

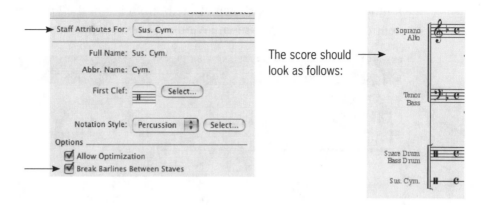

The score should look as follows:

Have you saved lately?

169

Polyphony = Layers

After the staves are formatted, it's time to enter the notation. In this "Simple Gifts" arrangement, there are two polyphonic parts in each of the top two staves and in the top percussion stave. You can identify polyphony when there are two independent parts on one staff: one with stems up and one with stems down.

Piano and vocal parts frequently have polyphony in one staff. Finale can handle four layers or polyphonic voices in each staff. With "Simple Gifts," only two layers are needed: Layer 1 for stems up and Layer 2 for stems down.

Before entering a piece with two or more layers, it is a good idea to check out the Layer Options that are set in Finale.

To access Layer Options:

1. Select **Options** > Document Settings > Layer Options.
2. Layer 1 is set to "Freeze Stems Up" and Layer 2 to "Freeze Stems Down." "Apply Settings Only if Notes are in Other Layers" should be checked.

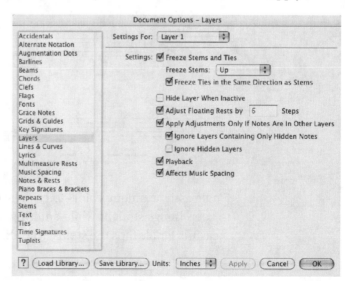

In Layer 1, enter the first eight measures plus the pickup measure in the Soprano part. Remember, Layer 1 will be all notes with stems up. Finale is in Layer 1 unless you tell it otherwise. The layer is shown at the bottom left of the Finale window. Mac lets you control layers via a popup menu; Windows uses four buttons.

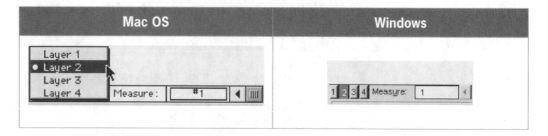

3. Confirm that Layer 1 is active, then enter the Soprano part for the first eight measures. Enter the notes any way you like: HyperScribe or Simple Entry.

Soprano Part: Layer 1.

To enter the Alto part, first switch to Layer 2.

4. Switch to Layer 2, and then enter the Alto part up through measure 8.

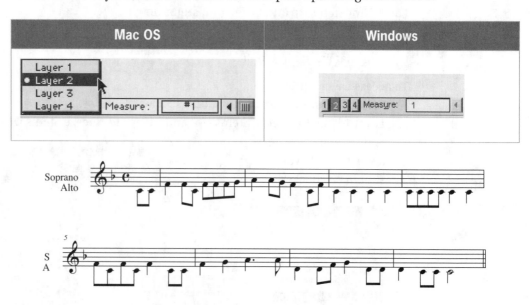

Finale assigns unique colors to each layer. Layer 1 is black, and layer 2 is red. This helps to keep things straight while entering and editing the notation. As you complete each measure, Finale flips the stems according to the settings in Layer Options.

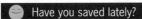 Have you saved lately?

To enter the Tenor and Bass parts:

One common misconception when using Layers is that it seems logical to enter the Soprano in Layer 1, Alto in Layer 2, Tenor in Layer 3, and the Bass in Layer 4. This is an option. However, I recommend viewing each staff as a separate entity, to keep things straight. For this reason, in the bass-clef staff, enter the Tenor in Layer 1 and the Bass in Layer 2.

6.   Switch back to Layer 1, and enter the Tenor part up through measure 8.

Tenor part—Layer 1.

7.   Switch to Layer 2, and enter the bass part.

Bass part—Layer 2.

To enter the Soprano and Alto parts for measures 9–17:

8.   Enter the continued Soprano part in layer 1.

9.   Enter the continued Alto part in Layer 2.

171

Copy, Paste, and Transpose

The Tenor and Bass parts are next. Looking at the arrangement, their parts in measures 10 and 11 are just like the Soprano/Alto parts in measures 9 and 10. It will save time to copy and paste these two measures, then transpose them down an octave.

1. Advance to measure 9.
2. Choose the Mass Edit tool , and highlight measures 9 and 10 in the Soprano/Alto part.
3. To copy the measures, hold Option-Shift (Mac) or Control-Shift (Windows), and click the mouse inside measure 10 in the Tenor/Bass part.

These two measures are copied an octave too high, because the staves are in different clefs. To transpose the copied measures down an octave:

4. With the Mass Edit tool, select the two copied measures. Then select **Mass Edit** > Transpose.
5. Set Transpose to "Down" and Interval to "Octave," and then click OK.

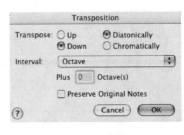

Transposing Metatools

As discussed in chapter 8, Mass Edit has four Metatools automatically assigned to transposition: the numbers 6, 7, 8, and 9—across the top of the computer keyboard and in the numeric keypad. The first time you use a particular number, Finale will ask you to set the transposition. After the interval is set, just highlight the desired measures and press the number.

To set 6 as the Metatool to transpose down an octave:

1. Choose the Mass Edit tool , and select the measures you wish to transpose.
2. Press the number 6 (a Mass Edit Metatool for Transposition).
3. Enter the direction and interval of transposition, for example, up an octave.

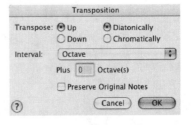

To access this Metatool, just highlight another measure and press the number 6. The notes will be transposed up an octave.

 Using the same Metatool assignments in all your files will help you keep track of them. For example, you could always use 6 for up an octave, 7 for down an octave, and 8 and 9 for other common transpositions.

- Enter the final measures of the Tenor and Bass parts: Tenor in Layer 1 and Bass in Layer 2.

Entering the Percussion Parts: Snare and Bass Drum

Before entering the notation in the percussion parts, review the following information on how percussion staves are formatted. It is helpful to have an understanding of how they function, especially if you are going to create your own custom percussion staves.

Finale uses "percussion maps" that assign sounds and percussion notation to specific lines and spaces. A percussion map also assigns playback information so that a snare sounds like a snare and a bass drum a bass drum.

The easiest way to enter percussion notation is to use the Setup Wizard and choose a percussion staff that most closely fits your needs. Since this step was taken at the beginning of this chapter, percussion map assignments have already been made.

 To add a staff after you have set up the score, choose the Staff tool and select **Staff** > New Staves with the Setup Wizard. To insert a staff in between existing staves, first highlight the staff handle beneath where you want to add the new staves.

Upon inspection of the Snare/Bass Drum part, since there is polyphony (stems up and stems down), layers must be used. Remember, Layer 1 is set to freeze stems up and Layer 2 stems down. So the best option is to use Layer 1 for the snare and layer 2 for the bass drum.

To enter the Snare part in Layer 1 using Simple Entry:
1. Switch to Layer 1.
2. Choose the Simple Entry tool 🎵, and choose the Quarter Rest in the Simple Entry Rest Palette. If the rest palette is not visible it can be turned on from the Simple Menu.
3. Enter a quarter rest in the pickup measure.
4. Enter a rest in measure 1, beat 1.
5. Enter the third-space C by clicking it in with the mouse or play MIDI note number 38. See chart below.

6. Press the Equal (=) key on the computer keyboard, as the snare is assigned to C#.
7. Enter a half rest on beat 3 and 4 of measure 1.

To enter the Bass Drum part in Layer 2:

8. Switch to Layer 2.
9. Enter the bass drum notation on the bottom space of the staff. See the notation above. Either click in the notes with the mouse or play the appropriate MIDI numbers, using the chart below.

You can also enter the drum parts from a MIDI keyboard. Play the note on the MIDI keyboard that corresponds to the proper percussion sound. This can be done in either Simple Entry or HyperScribe. Remember to play the proper note on the keyboard, so that it will be mapped to the proper line or space. A chart of the GM Percussion note assignments follows. The steps for entering percussion parts with a MIDI keyboard are covered in chapter 11, "Blues for a Hiccup"—see page 235.

General MIDI Percussion Note Assignments

GM Percussion Sounds: Assign to MIDI Channel 10

To copy measure 1 seven times:

10. Using the Mass Edit tool, select measure 1 of the Snare/Bass staff, and drag it to measure 2 to copy it. Specify "7" times, as there are a total of eight measures with the same pattern.

Entering the Suspended Cymbal and Editing the Percussion Map

The Suspended Cymbal (Sus. Cym.) part presents a bit of a challenge. This is a customized part, as there was no specific option for this instrument in the Setup Wizard. I chose Crash Cymbal, as this was the closest instrument in the Setup Wizard options. In order to get the third line to play a suspended cymbal, the percussion map must be edited.

1. Choose the Staff tool 🎚, and open the Staff Attributes dialog box for the Sus. Cym. part.
2. Next to Notation Style, click Select.
3. The Cymbals percussion map will be highlighted. This is the instrument originally selected using the Setup Wizard.
4. Click Edit.

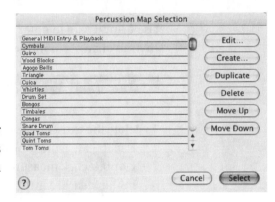

This reveals the Percussion Map Designer being used to assign percussion sounds and noteheads. Since this is a custom assignment, take the following steps:

5. Under Notes to use for "Sus. Cym.," click the None (Clear) button (see below).
6. In the Playback column, locate the Ride Cymbal, MIDI note 51. Click this to highlight it.
7. Make the changes to the map below.
8. Drag the notehead to the third line, as shown.
9. Be sure to activate the Highlighted Notes checkbox.

Drag the note to the third line of the staff.

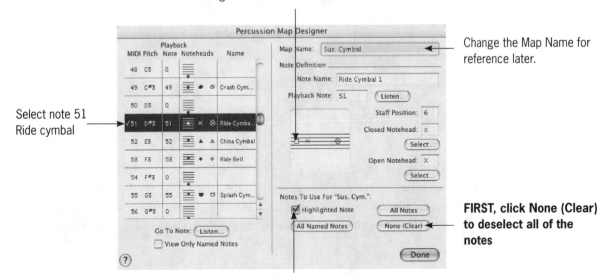

Select note 51 Ride cymbal

Change the Map Name for reference later.

FIRST, click None (Clear) to deselect all of the notes

Check Notes to Use checkbox.

Steps 1 through 9 remap the suspended cymbal sound to the third line. Now, the notation can be entered, beginning in measure 9. If you elect to enter it by using a MIDI keyboard, play MIDI note 51 or the D# below middle C. See the previously mentioned MIDI chart for reference.

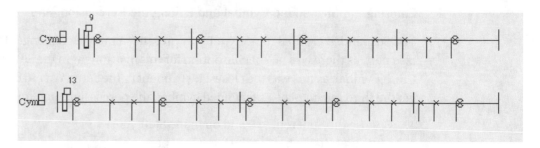

Use Copy/Paste to enter the part, rather than doing it one note at a time. Note that the rhythm changes in measures 12 and 17.

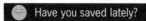

Have you saved lately?

To delete the extra measures and enter the double barline in measure 8:
1. Use the Measure tool ⬚ to delete any extra measures.
2. Double-click measure 8.
3. In the Measure Attributes window, choose the double barline, and then click OK.

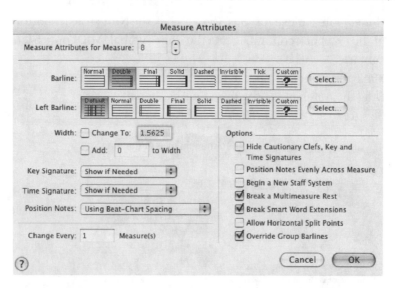

To enter the repeats and endings:
1. Choose the Repeat Tool ⬚, and highlight measure 1.
2. Select **Repeat** > Create Forward Repeat Bar, or use the contextual menu: Control-click (Mac) or Right-click (Windows) measure 1, and select Create Forward Repeat Bar.

Option 1:
Select from Menu

Option 2:
Control-click (Mac) or Right-click (Windows) the Measure

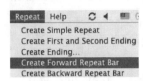

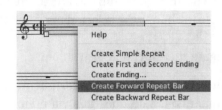

3. To enter the first ending, highlight measure 16. In other words, when you want a first and second ending, select just the first ending measure or measures.

4. Select **Repeat** > Create First and Second Ending, or choose it from the contextual menu.

5. Adjust the position of the numbers and brackets to avoid colliding with the top staff (see chapter 7, page 112).

To hide repeats in other staves:

The Repeat Tool displays repeats in every staff. Typically, in a choral score, the repeats would only be placed on the top staff. To hide the repeats in the lower staves:

1. Choose the Staff tool ![icon], and open a Staff Attributes dialog box for the Tenor/Bass part.

2. Under Items to Display, uncheck Endings and Text Repeats.

3. At the top of the Staff Attributes window, next to "Staff Attributes For," choose Snare/Bass from the pulldown menu. Now, this window is controlling the Snare/Bass staff.

4. Under Items to Display, uncheck Endings and Text Repeats.

5. Repeat this process for the Sus. Cymbal staff.

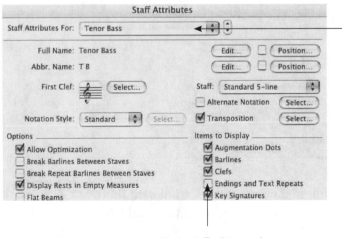

Select Staves from the pulldown menu

Uncheck Endings and Text Repeats

177

Playback

When you use the Setup Wizard to create a staff, the proper sound is selected. It is possible to change the selected instrument sound.

Changing the Playback Instruments

Templates.pdf
finalebook.com

If you want to change the instrument sounds for playback, you can preload a list of instruments. Finale does this via a Library. A library of General MIDI instruments is loaded when you install Finale. An advantage to using a GM library is it automatically loads sixteen of the most common GM sounds.

To load the General MIDI Instruments library:
1. Select **File** > Load Library. Finale will automatically go to the Libraries folder on your hard drive.
2. Choose General MIDI from the Instrument Libraries folder.

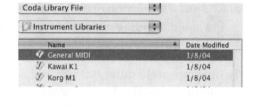

To change the playback sounds:
1. Select **Window** > Instruments.
2. Click an instrument in the Instrument column to change its playback sound.

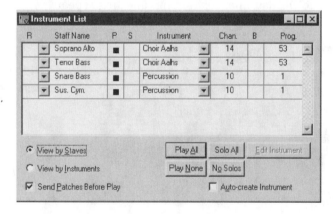

Another option in Finale is to send a different timbre to each layer. This way, different instrument sounds can be used for Layer 1 and Layer 2.

3. Click on the arrow next to Soprano Alto in the Staff Name column.
4. Enter different instruments for Layers 1 and 2.
5. Repeat this step for the Tenor Bass part.

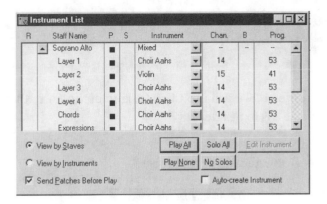

Entering Lyrics

After the notation is entered, enter the lyrics. In chapter 5, lyrics were entered one syllable, or word, at a time by typing them into the score. Now, we will use another way to enter lyrics: using Finale's built-in word processor. The first step is to enter the lyrics.

1. Choose the Lyric tool .
2. Select **Lyrics** > Edit Lyrics.
3. Type the song lyrics into the Edit Lyrics window. Start with verse 1. Be sure to enter the lyrics *exactly* as they are shown below. When Finale sees a hyphen (-) after a syllable, it knows to shift the next syllable to the next note.

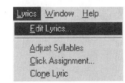

9_Gifts.mus
9_Gifts_No_Lyrics.mus

> The companion Web site contains two versions of "Simple Gifts." The file "Simple Gifts.mus" contains all of the music and lyrics. "Simple Notes.mus" contains the notation and the lyrics; however, the lyrics have not been inserted into the score.

'Tis the gift to be sim-ple, 'tis the gift to be free. 'Tis the gift to come down where we ought to be, and when we find our-selves in the place just right, 'twill be in the val-ley of love and de-light. When true sim-plic-i-ty is gained, to bow and to bend we shan't be a-shamed. To turn, turn will be our de-light 'til by turn-ing, turn-ing, we come 'round right.

> Take your time entering the lyrics, and check and double-check the syllable breaks. By confirming that they are correct, you will save much time when you flow these lyrics into the score.

After entering the first verse, type in the second verse.

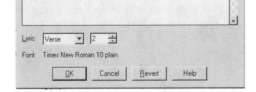

4. Next to Lyric, choose "Verse" and "2" at the bottom of the Edit Lyrics window.
5. Type in the lyrics for verse 2.

'Tis a gift to be gen-tle, 'tis the gift to be fair. 'Tis the gift to wake and breathe the morn-ing air. And eve-ry day to walk in the path we choose. A gift that we pray we may ne'er come to lose. When true sim-plic-i-ty is gained, to bow and to bend we shan't be a-shamed. To turn, turn will be our de-light 'til by turn-ing, turn-ing we come 'round right.

You can use your favorite word processor to enter your lyrics, and then Copy/Paste them into Finale's Edit Lyrics window.

After the lyrics are entered, we will use Click Assignment to enter them into the score. First, specify that verse 1 is to be added.

6. Select **Lyrics** > Specify Current Lyric.
7. Enter Number "1" to indicate the first verse.

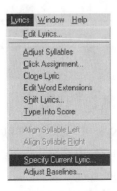
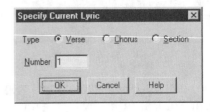

8. To enter the lyrics, select **Lyrics** > Click Assignment.

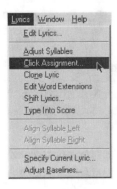
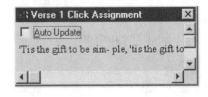

9. Scroll to the first note of "Simple Gifts."
10. Click the note head or stem to enter the lyrics. Be sure to click inside the lines and spaces. Click each word until the entire verse is entered.

Be careful in measure 11 because the first syllable of the word "a-shamed" has a syllable break over two notes.

Click here, then here:

11. Click the G eighth note.
12. Click the G dotted quarter note.

To enter the second verse:

13. Select **Lyrics** > Specify Current Lyric, and set it to Verse 2.

14. Select **Lyrics** > Click Assignment.

15. Advance to measure 17, and enter the first two words of verse 2 on the C eighth notes on beat 4. Note that verse 2 is printed below verse 1.

16. The lyrics "'Tis a" should be next to the word right. To move the lyrics, select **Lyrics** > Adjust Syllables.

17. Click on the note C. Drag the handle so that it aligns with the word Right in verse 1. Repeat the process for the word "a."

18. Now go to measure 1, and enter the rest of verse 2, clicking in the words, one at a time. The last three words of the verse must be entered in the last measure, 18.

 In order to flow in all of the lyrics at the speed of light, hold down Option (Mac) or Alt (Windows), and click on the first syllable. This can be a very fast way to enter lyrics. However, if you mistype one lyric or melisma, you may have to do a lot of editing. Review the Finale Help for more information.

181

Simple Gifts

SATB with Optional Percussion
Arranged by Tom Rudolph

Copyright 1977 Tom Rudolph

Cloning Lyrics

The lyrics are now entered in the Soprano and Alto parts. To enter the Tenor and Bass lyrics, Click Assignment can be used. Be careful, though, because the lyrics are slightly different in the second half of the piece.

Measures 1 through 8 have identical lyrics as the Soprano/Alto staff. Finale has a special way to handle copying lyrics from one staff to another by "cloning" the lyric.

To clone the lyrics from staff 1 to staff 2:

1. Choose the Lyric tool , and set **Specify Current Lyric** to Verse 1.
2. Select **Lyric** > Clone Lyric.
3. Highlight measures 1–8 in the Soprano/Alto staff.

4. Click inside the highlighted portion of the pickup measure, and drag to the second staff in the pickup measure.

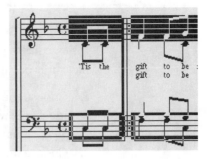

Verse 1 is copied to measures 1–8 in the Tenor/Bass. Then, copy the second verse.

5. Set Specify Current Lyric to be Verse 2.
6. Drag measure 1 in the Soprano/Alto to measure 1 in the Tenor/Bass, as before.

Cloning does not work for measures 9 through the end of the piece because the lyric assignments are not identical between the two staves, in that measure. Enter those lyrics using Click Assignment.

7. Advance to measure 9.
8. Set Specify Current Lyric to be Verse 1.
9. Select **Lyrics** > Click Assignment.
10. Manually advance the lyrics in the Click Assignment window so that the words "When true sim-plic-i-ty..." appear at the far left of the window (see below).

Remember, when using Click Assignment, the lyric that is located in the left-most position will be entered with the next mouse click.

SATB and optional percussion

Arranged by Tom Rudolph

Simple Gifts

Erasing Lyrics

Lyrics can be edited in the Edit Lyrics window. They also can be erased from entire measures or the entire piece, by using the Mass Edit tool. To erase just the lyrics:

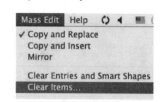

1. Choose the Mass Edit tool, and highlight the measures where lyrics are to be deleted.
2. Select **Mass Edit** > Clear Items.
3. Choose Entries.
4. From the Entry Items dialog box, check the Lyrics box, and then click OK.

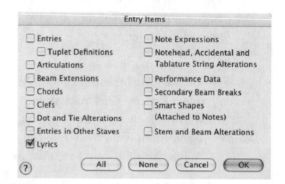

Finale will remove just the lyrics from the selected measures. This does not, however, delete them from file itself. They can still be re-inserted by using Click Assignment.

Changing the Score Size

In order to fit the systems of four staves on one page, we must reduce the overall size of the score, using the Resize tool. This tool was introduced in chapter 8. For this choral score, we'll reduce its size to 65%.

To reduce the score to 65%:

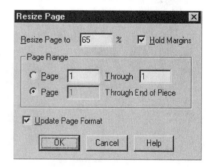

1. Select **View** > Page View and scroll to the top of the page so the Title is visible.
2. Choose the Resize tool, and click the mouse in the upper portion of the page.
3. Be sure the dialog box reads "Resize Page." This tool can also be used to resize staves and individual notes. Set a 65% reduction. This will affect the score when viewed in Page View and when it is printed.

Grouping Six Measures Per System

The next step, in making this piece fit on one page, is to group six measures per line. The 65% resize amount allows for more measures per line.

4. Choose the Page Layout tool, and select **Page Layout** > Fit Music.
5. Freeze the layout with "6" measures on a line.

Check to see if resizing the page to 65% and grouping six measures per line created enough room for the entire score to fit on one page. The number of staves per page depends on several factors. Earlier in this chapter, we used the Staff tool to drag staves to make room for the lyrics. The space created between staves will affect the layout.

If the score fits on one page, you are ready to enter the headers and footers, and then print the score. However, if the score is on two pages, the staff systems must be adjusted.

Adjusting the Location of the Lyrics

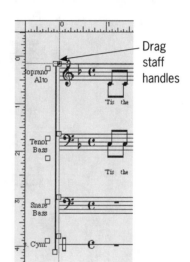

The distance between the staves can be adjusted to account for the lyrics. To adjust the staves:

1. Use the View menu to select Page View and show the rulers.
2. Choose the Staff tool 🎼.
3. Drag the staff handles to make room for the lyrics. The staff handles are the ones closest to the staff. Don't confuse them with the bracket handles.
4. Drag the staves as needed to make room for the lyrics. You can also move up the "Sus. Cym." staff to save space.

When you move the staves closer together, the lyrics may collide with note stems. To adjust the placement of the lyrics:

1. Choose the Lyrics tool 🎵, and select **Lyrics** > Click Assignment.
3. Use Specify Current Lyric to choose the lyric you wish to adjust, in this case, verse 2.
4. Drag the left-most arrow to position the lyrics. Be careful not to click anywhere on the score or you may enter a syllable without knowing it! The lyric positioning arrows are similar to the chord positioning arrows:

   - The left-most arrow controls the position of the verse throughout the entire song.
   - The second arrow from the left controls its position on the current page only.
   - The third arrow controls its position on just this current staff.
   - The arrow to the far right controls the position of the next syllable to be entered.

For most applications, the far left arrow is the only one that you'll need to use.

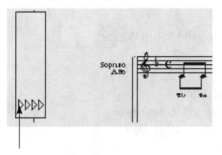

Drag the far left arrow to move the position of the lyrics for the entire piece.

Adjusting the Staff Systems (page formatting)

Making the final touches to the page layout can be done manually by dragging the systems as described in chapter 6, "HyperScribe." Another option is to use the automatic system spacing option.

1. Choose the Page Layout Tool .
2. Select **Page Layout** > Space Staves Evenly.
3. For this example, choose Place "3" Systems on Each page, and then click OK.

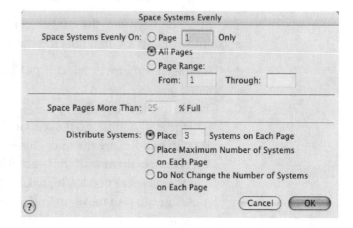

Entering a Custom Header

To enter the additional header at the top of the page:

1. Choose the Text tool 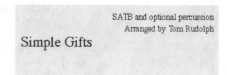.
2. Go to the top of the page and double-click above "Arranged by Tom Rudolph." Enter "SATB and Optional Percussion."

After entering the header, justify it to the right.

3. Control-click (Mac) or Right-click (Windows) on the new Text block's handle, choose Edit Frame Attributes. Under Alignment and Positioning, set Horizontal to "Right."

Save your file, and print out a copy. That was hard work! Congratulations.

Summary

This example included:

- custom score setup using the Setup Wizard
- customizing staves
- single-line percussion
- entering percussion notation
- using and customizing percussion maps
- entering polyphonic parts using layers
- multiple verses of lyrics

- playing back the score, including the percussion parts, and assigning different sounds for each voice on the staff
- resizing the score to 65%
- adjusting the staff systems to fit the score on one page

Review

1. Review the Lyric tool options in the *Finale User Manual*. Individual lyrics can be positioned, and the entire verse can be automatically assigned to the notes all at once. If you enter lyrics frequently, these additional functions can be helpful.

2. Practice setting up your own custom percussion map. Use this chapter and the *Finale User Manual* for reference. Remember, each staff should have its own percussion map.

3. View the QuickStart Videos for a review of lyrics and percussion maps.

10

The Art of the Piano Part
(Bach's "Fugue in G Minor")

Piano music can present some of the most complex challenges. For our journey into piano literature, we've selected J. S. Bach's "Fugue 16 in G Minor," mostly because he's not around to complain. Before starting this chapter, download and print the file Bach_Fugue.mus. Use this as a reference while working on the chapter.

Fugue 16 in G minor, BWV 861

J. S. Bach

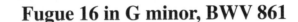

Edition (Your Name Here)

Edition (Your Name Here)

What's New in This Chapter

- creating a 34-measure double-stave part
- setting the key signature to G minor
- setting the Auto Save feature
- setting layer options
- Speedy Entry
- cross-staff notation
- manually positioning notes and rests
- manually altering stems and beams
- editing articulations
- entering fingerings

- creating S slurs
- preparing the page layout
- assigning playback of individual layers
- saving the moving van from the junkyard of forgotten Finale icons
- printing in color
- setting up a double-stave score

Get with the Program Options

Before getting started, with the Bach end of this project, I'd like to introduce some Program preferences that can be set in Finale to help with various tasks. The Program Options menu can be accessed either directly from the Launch Window, or once a file is open,

from the Options menu. I'm not going to go through all of the options available here, just a few I've found helpful. Refer to the Help menu if you want to learn about anything not covered.

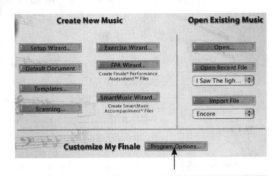

1. Launch Finale
2. From the Launch window, click the Program Options button.

New (Default File) Options

The New section controls startup and new documents. "Default Document" allows you to create a personalized Finale file to use every time Finale creates a new document. To use your own document as the "Default Document," set up a file with all your customized libraries and document settings, and then enter the file name in the space provided. Click the Default Document button to use your custom Finale document as the default file.

With the Startup Action menu, you can select which option Finale presents when launched. Choose between the Launch Window, Setup Wizard, or several other options. New Document Windows can be set to open in Scroll View or Page View, and in a set percentage. My personal preference is to do all of my note and expression entry in Scroll View, and then switch to Page View for page layout and printing; therefore, I set the initial layout to Scroll View. Rulers can be

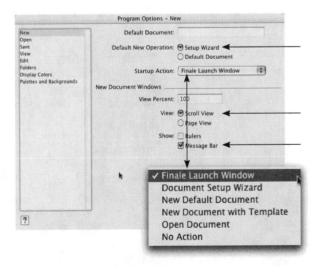

set to appear automatically, thought they are easy to toggle on and off. To buy a little more screen real estate for work, the Message Bar can also be turned off.

1. Click Apply when any changes are complete.
2. Click Save in the left column.

191

Save Options

Choose Save in the left column. Over the years, I've learned the hard way to save early and save often. Finale has a safety net, in case you have trouble thinking of it until it's too late, or if you have a shaky operating system that tends to crash a lot. Finale calls this special feature Auto Save. Checking the box for Auto Save tells Finale to automatically save your file, in the increments of time entered in the Minutes box. Just one word of caution: name your file immediately. If Auto Save attempts begin while you are in the process of saving and naming a document for the first time, the system may crash.

Auto Save is also a problem when using HyperScribe. It will interrupt your recording to save the file. If you are planning to use HyperScribe at all, disable Auto Save first.

We are about to do an exercise with a lot of positioning work. It would be a shame to lose hours of this kind of detailed work in a crash, so I recommend at least trying this feature out.

There is also a box that is checked for automatically creating backup files. This one has saved me a time or two when the main file has gotten corrupted. Keep the backups around while you are working on a project, then trash them when you've archived the finished project.

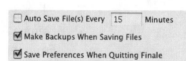

Folders Options

Templates.pdf

Select Folders in the left column. The Folders options allow you to select specific locations or folders for saving Finale files, backup files, and Auto Save files. You can also set specific folders where Finale will go to look for templates and libraries. To learn more about templates and libraries, download the PDF file Templates.pdf from the Finale Book Web site.

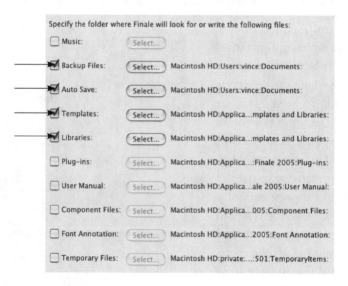

Palettes and Backgrounds Options

Select Palettes and Backgrounds in the left column. If you are bothered by some of the tool palettes cluttering up your workspace, the Action heading has a few settings you can check to keep your workspace clean and tidy. If you are tired of the plain gray background behind your work in Page View, you can select a graphic or solid color to display in the background under the Document Windows Background heading—change the background to match your mood, or the mood of the composition you are working on, but for us old-time Finale users, there is another reason to visit.

Old-Time Finale Users

Many of us lament the loss of the truck that, for so many years, was the symbol of the Mass Mover tool 🚚. Apparently, they thought that it just didn't seem fitting, when the tool's name was changed to Mass Edit. The symbol was changed from a Red Truck to a dotted rectangle (boring!). Whenever I'm feeling nostalgic for the ol' Moving Van (aka, "little truck"), I can come here and turn back the clock.

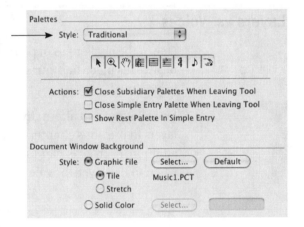

- Under Palettes, Select Traditional from the Style popup menu. Then click Apply, and then OK, to return to the Launch Window.

Feel free to check out the other tool palettes as well. A little change now and again can be refreshing.

Setting Up the Score

1. In the Launch window, select Setup Wizard, and set the following parameters:

   Title: Fugue 16 in G minor, BWV 861
   Composer: J. S. Bach
   Copyright: [leave this space empty]

2. The settings for page size and orientation are correct, so click Next to move on to the Choose Parts screen, and add Keyboards-Piano [No Staff Name]. Click Next.

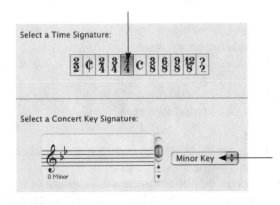

3. Select 4/4 for the time signature, not the C (common time) abbreviation.

4. Select Minor Key from the Key Signature popup menu, and set the key to G minor (two flats). Then click Next.

A comment about major and minor key signatures in Finale. For the most part, selecting a major or minor key will make no difference in the look or sound of the music entered or displayed. Functions where Finale does take the key into account are for changing key signatures, applying enharmonic spelling tables, and for chord symbols.

5.   Check Go to Document Options After Finish. Then click Finish.

Layers vs. Voices

One of the challenges of piano music is handling several independent voices simultaneously. This piece has four parts, with as many as three occurring on the same staff at the same time.

Finale offers two alternatives for handling polyphony: layers and voices. We have used layers in previous chapters. There are a maximum of four separate layers in each staff. In addition, each layer can support two voices. The result can be total confusion in deciding when to use layers or voices. Here is a table of features and drawbacks for each.

Layers	Voices
Pros • Independent of each other • Independent settings for stem direction • Independent settings for adjusting rest positions • Can assign separate MIDI channels for playback or mute playback • Displays in different colors • Can be displayed one layer at a time while hiding all other layers • Can edit one layer in Mass Edit without affecting others (including cut and paste) • Entries are not required in Layer 1 before you can use Layer 2, 3, or 4 • Can switch between layers in Speedy Entry or selected at the bottom of the screen	**Pros** • Can begin at any point in the measure where there is a voice 1 entry • Will explode and implode with entries on other staves **Cons** • Cannot have voice 2 without voice 1 • Stem flips only for first entry of voice 2, and cursor must be positioned under voice 1 to flip its stem up or over to flip it down. (You can change all stem directions manually in Speedy Entry or Special Tools.) • Voice 2 tie will not go beyond a voice 1 entry following it in a measure • Can't send to separate MIDI channels • Can't edit separately in Mass Edit • Can't display in different colors • Overlapping accidentals may require manual positioning
Cons • Easy to forget which layer you are in, especially if you jump around the score a lot • Will not explode or implode with voices in a different layer • Requires you to be in a specific layer to edit entries in that layer or to attach or edit expressions, articulations, or chord symbols, except for adding articulations via Mass Edit and drag-selecting with Metatools	

Use layers for anything that is a full measure or longer, and use voices only for divisi parts that are less than a measure long. When Finale was first released, the Layer feature was not a part of the program; voices were the only option for fitting two moving lines on the same staff. The Layer feature represents a dramatic improvement on the Voice feature, which is still a part of the program. Usually, you'll use Layers.

Setting Up Layers

Finale already has settings entered for Layers 1 and 2 that will control the direction of the stems and ties when there are two, or more, layers in the same measure. The position of the rests needs to be changed so that the default position better suits the demands of the music.

1. In the Document Options window (**Edit** > Document Options, if you're not already there), click on Layers in the left column.

Layer 1 settings are displayed in the dialog box. Layer 1 will function as follows: when there are entries in other layers (i.e., multiple voices on the staff), stems and ties will flip up, and rests will move up six steps. Otherwise, the music will be unaffected.

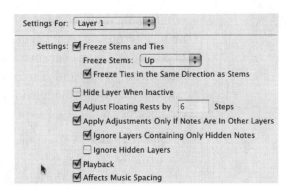

The Adjust Floating Rests setting controls the distance that rests are moved up (positive numbers) or down (negative numbers). A zero, or un-checking the box, will leave the rests unaffected. The purpose of floating the rests is to keep the rests more in line horizontally with the music and to avoid collisions. It's best to always use even numbers for the rest default, because odd numbers position the half and whole rests in the spaces instead of on the lines. Also, each layer can be set to a different number. The top layer may be okay with a float of 4, but the bottom layer may look best with –6 or –8. Remember, any rest can be manually repositioned in either Simple or Speedy Entry (discussed later in this chapter).

2. Change the Adjust Floating Rests number to 4.
3. Switch the Settings For popup menu to Layer 2.
4. Change the Adjust Floating Rests number to –4.

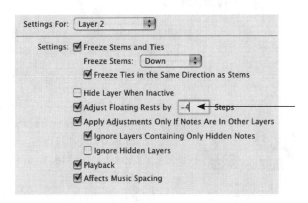

Note that the Layer 2 settings are the opposite of Layer 1. The negative number will move the rests down four steps. As with Layer 1, this will occur only if there are entries in another layer.

You will need Layer 3 for a few measures where there are three voices in the treble clef. Since the stem direction and rest offsets will be different for each case, we will position them manually, and not set anything up in Layer Options.

 It is possible to use layers even when you only need a second voice for part of a measure. Finale allows individual notes or rests to be hidden. These entries will appeared shadowed in the display but will not print. Enter all the notes and rests necessary for the second voice, then use the **H** key to hide any rests that are not needed. If you need to flip stems, press the **L** key. These keystrokes work in both Simple and Speedy Entry, which you will begin using for note entry later in this chapter.

Changing Stem Length

When using multiple layers, you must be aware of the default stem length. Finale is set up to shorten any stem when its direction is changed from the default direction. This is to reduce collisions between stems when there are up- and down-stemmed notes that are outside of the staff. The problem is that the change only effects half- and quarter-note stems, leaving them to look unnaturally short next to flagged to beamed groups, To change this and have all stems be full length:

1. Select **Options** > Document Options.
2. Choose Stems in the left column.
3. Change the value in the Short-ened Stem Length box to match the value in the Normal Stem Length box. I'm using EVPUs for measurement. If you're using anything else (such as inches), copy the appropriate number.

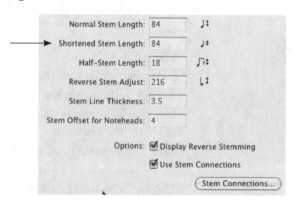

Measure Numbers

I recommend displaying the measure numbers on every measure. Review the steps in chapter 3, page 33, for using the Measure Tool to display them on every measure.

You should have a grand staff created and in the correct key. Let's prepare it to enter notes.

1. Save your file as "Bach_Fugue.mus."
2. Make sure you have 34 measures. Since the Setup Wizard creates 31 measures, you'll need to add three more.
   • Choose the Measure tool , select **Measure** > Add, and enter "3" measures. Then click OK.
3. Make sure that you are in Scroll View for note entry.

10_Bach_1.mus

Have you saved lately?

Speedy Entry

For those of us without killer keyboard chops but with a MIDI keyboard, it is my pleasure to introduce you to Speedy Entry. Speedy Entry dates back to the beginning of Finale, before Simple Entry could accept MIDI input. There are some differences between Simple and Speedy Entry to make it worth exploring, to see which method you prefer. Speedy Entry uses the same keys for rhythm as Simple Entry, but the pitch from the MIDI keyboard is played first. To enter rests, press the desired rhythmic value on the keypad without any key played on the MIDI keyboard.

So what makes Speedy Entry speedy? In music with notes and rests, it requires fewer keystrokes than Simple Entry. Those keystrokes can be a lot faster, since Finale buffers them. This allows you to continue entering notes while Finale is redrawing the screen and to quickly enter a passage consisting of different rhythmic values without having to wait before changing rhythms. You can enter notes as fast as you are able, and still get the correct notation.

1. Choose the Speedy Entry tool 🎵 .
2. The Speedy Entry window appears on the first visible measure.

Take a moment to review the Speedy Entry Keyboard Commands. This graphic is also available in Help under "Speedy Entry." Print it out, and keep it handy while learning the new keystrokes. This graphic is from the *Finale User Manual*. **Note:** Both the H and O keys work in Speedy Entry but the O does not work in Simple Entry, so my preference is to use the H key.

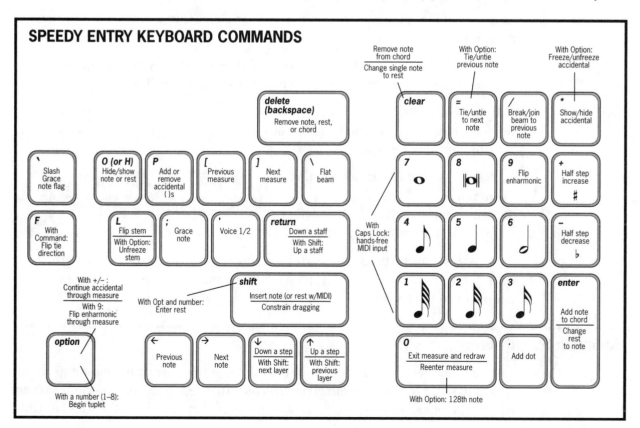

1. To enter the whole rest in measure 1, press the **7** key on the keypad, and then 4 for the eighth rest.
2. Hold down the G key on the MIDI keyboard.
3. Press the 4 key on the keypad for the G eighth rhythm.
4. Move up to the Bb on the MIDI keyboard and hold it.
5. Press 4 on the keypad for the Bb eighth rhythm.
6. Move down to the D on the MIDI keyboard and hold it.
7. Press 4 on the keypad.

The window auto-advances to the next measure. It may take a little while to get used to, since it is the opposite of Simple Entry, but the effort will be well rewarded.

Since the composition uses separate voices, I recommend entering it a layer at a time. For ease of reading, I separated the example into layers. Use the graphics on the following pages, and enter the piece layer by layer, for each staff. If you have any problems with Speedy Entry, consult the Help menu.

Treble Clef

Layer 1:

1. Continue note entry by playing the MIDI note, then pressing the key on the keypad the rhythm for notes. For rests, just press the key on the keypad.
2. Stop before entering the E eighth note at the end of bar 7.

Entering Ties Across The Barline in Speedy Entry

At the end of bar 7, the E ties over to the next bar. Here's a little trick to creating ties over the barline.

1. Press the E key on the MIDI keyboard, and type 5 on the keypad for a quarter note. (Any value greater than there is room for in the measure will do.)

This invokes a dialog box warning that we've been very naughty, and Finale will not continue until we behave.

2. Select "Move the extra notes to the next measure." Click OK.
3. Press 4 on the keypad for the rhythm of the E, and continue entering.

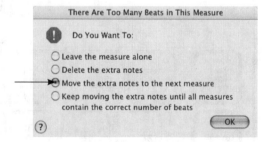

Try the steps again on the B at the end of measure 8. All you have to do is enter a rhythmic value greater than the amount of space left in the measure. This time, "Move the extra notes into the next measure" will remain selected, so all you need to do is click OK.

Editing in Speedy Entry

To fix an incorrect pitch in Speedy Entry, use the arrow keys or the mouse to set the cursor on the note, play the correct pitch on the MIDI keyboard, and press Enter. (Dragging the notehead with the mouse is also an option, but hold down the Shift key while dragging. This restricts the motion of the drag to vertical so that the note remains properly positioned, horizontally.)

To fix an incorrect rhythm, set the cursor on the note, and press the correct rhythm key on the keypad.

To fix an incorrect accidental, set the cursor on the note, and press the plus (+) key to go up in half steps, or the minus (–) key to go down in half steps.

To change an enharmonic spelling, set the cursor on the note, and press the 9 key to toggle the spelling.

 Sometimes, Finale will resist enharmonics such as F♭ or B♯, and other times, it seems to use them for no reason. If you encounter difficulty on a particular enharmonic, enter the natural note, and use the plus (+) or minus keys (–) to get the correct enharmonic.

Layer 2:

Let's enter Layer 2 of the treble-clef staff.

• Switch to Layer 2 in the bottom-left corner of the Finale window.

When entering multiple layers in Finale, each layer will be displayed in a different color, making them easier to distinguish for editing. This is for display only; they will not print in these colors.

When measures are blank, do not enter a whole rest. Just leave them blank, for now. To advance the Speedy Entry window to the next measure, use the Right Bracket (]) key, which is to the right of the P key on the computer keyboard.

The half rest in measure 7 must be hidden. Here are the steps for hiding an entry in Speedy Entry:

1. Choose the Speedy Entry tool .
2. Click on measure 7.
3. Position the cursor on the half rest.
4. Press the letter H key on your keyboard. This key is a toggle; to make the entry reappear, press the H key again.
5. Hide the half rest in measure 11.

A greyed image of the hidden rest can still be seen, but it will not print.

Layer 3:

Hide the half rests in the last two beats of measures 12, 30, and 34. By default, Finale automatically fills incomplete measures with rests.

Bass Clef

Layer 1:

No rest is necessary in measure 7. The half rest in measure 12 must be entered and hidden using the **H** key in Speedy Entry.

Layer 2:

Hopefully, you are getting some speed with Speedy Entry by now. For passages with a large number of rests, be careful, if using the right bracket key, that you have pressed the key the correct number of measures before continuing. Always check the bar numbers to keep your position.

10_Bach_2.mus

finalebook.com

☺ Have you saved lately?

Manual Positioning in Page View

Switch to Page View, and don't panic. Finale has taken care of a lot of the note spacing, but there are still quite a few things to be done manually.

> With any piece that requires a lot of special positioning of notes, it is best to do it in Page View, after Page Layout is complete. Nothing personal against Scroll View, but since Page View is ultimately what will be printed, it is important that it be the true representation of the final product.

- From the Edit menu, select Automatic Music Spacing, to turn it off. (Make sure it is unchecked.)

> Before you start any complex page editing, *always* turn off the Automatic Spacing Feature in the Edit menu so that any manual positioning is not accidentally undone.

The first issue is the overall size of the notation. Print out a page, and compare it to any piano books you may have. (No fair using big-note piano books!) Take into account any difference in overall page size if the printed piano music is larger than 8.5″ by 11″. It can be a lot smaller but still readable; larger does not always mean easier to read. Publishers often use reduced sizes, such as 80%, for their music.

To set the page percentage:

1. Choose the Resize tool %.
2. Click in the upper left-hand corner of the page, and select Resize Page from the contextual menu.
3. Enter 80 for the page percentage, and then click OK.

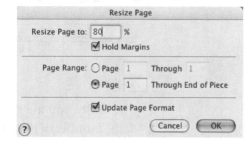

After formatting the music at the proper page percentage, see how many systems the music will need. The measure layout in the original calls for four measures in the first system of page 1, and three measures in all other systems, for a total of eleven systems. The easy way to group a large number of measures is with another Fit Music feature of Mass Edit.

1. Choose the Mass Edit tool ⊕.
2. Select **Mass Edit** > Fit Music, shortcut Shift-⌘-M (Mac) or Shift-Control-M (Windows).
3. For Action, choose Lock Layout with, and enter "3" Measure(s) per System.
4. For Change, choose "Measure" and enter "5" Through "34." Then click OK.

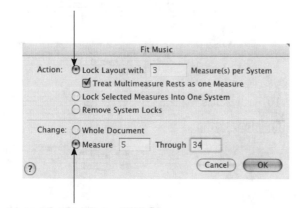

The Fit Music command is the same in the Mass Edit and in Page Layout tools, with the same dialog box and shortcut keystroke.

In addition to redistributing the measures, Mass Edit also locks the systems in place to assure that they won't move automatically with further changes. You can still unlock and move them, if you wish, by using the Unlock Systems command, which is right beneath the Lock Systems command in the Mass Edit menu.

Now that the staves are set, set their positioning on page 1.

1. Choose the Page Layout tool .
2. Select **Page Layout** > Space Systems Evenly.
3. Make sure "Page 1 Only" is selected.
4. Under the Distribute Systems heading, select "Do Not Change the Number of Systems on Each Page." Then click OK.

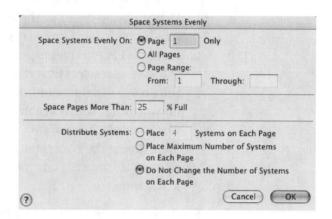

To add more space between systems:

Page 2 has some room at the bottom of the page. We can open up the distance between staves, to fill it in.

1. Select **Page Layout** > Systems > Edit System Margins.
2. Uncheck the Top, Left, Right, and Bottom boxes.
3. Enter "88" EVPUs (1.5 inches) for the Distance Between Staves.
4. For Change Staff System, enter "6" Thru "11." Click Apply, then Close.

Expand the distance here, for all staves to fill in the space at the bottom of the page.

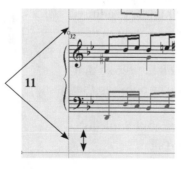

 You may occasionally find some music missing on the last page of a file. Music does not disappear from existence in Finale, but it may move off a page when systems are being edited. For the most part, Finale's Auto Update Layout feature will fix this, but once and a while I still encounter it. Just select **Edit** > Update Layout, and the music should reappear.

Cross-Staff Traffic

Once the system margins are set, go back through the piece and make all necessary positioning changes. This includes crossed voices, rests too close to notes, and something new: cross-staff notes. Cross-staff notes in Finale are notes that are entered on one staff but display on another. The first example of this is in bar 1. Remember that notes can display on other staves, though rests cannot. So, for measure 1 you need to have the notes entered in Layer 2 of the treble-clef staff.

1. Choose the Mass Edit tool.
2. Select **Edit** > Select Partial Measures, and highlight the last three notes in bar 1, treble clef.
3. From the Plug-ins menu, go to TG Tools, and select Cross Staff.
4. Uncheck "Fill empty destination measures with invisible whole rests." Click Go, and then Close. (The Cancel button changes to Close after the plug-in has run.)

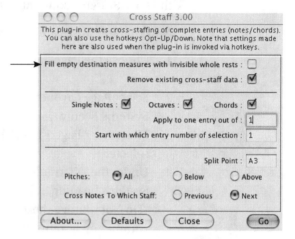

To adjust the angle of the eighth-note beam, use the Beam Angle tool. The Beam Angle tool is part of Special Tools, a group of tools for tweaking and editing notes and related items, such as ties, accidentals, stems, and beams. The Special Tools suite offers the ability to do the fine detailing often required by professional engravers.

1. Choose Special Tools, to show its palette. Windows users will find Special Tools under Advanced Tools: **Tools** > Advanced Tools > Special Tools > Beam Angle Tool. Mac users will find the Special Tools Pallet on the left side of the screen. Windows users will find it on the right side of the screen after it has been selected.
2. Choose the Beam Angle tool.
3. Click on the left handle to adjust the up and down position of the beam.
4. Drag down the left handle so that the beam is halfway between the two staves.
5. Drag the beam's right handle to give it an upward slant.

Now, flip the stems of the two quarter notes:

6. Choose the Stem Direction tool.
7. Click on the boxes above the treble staff to flip the stems up.

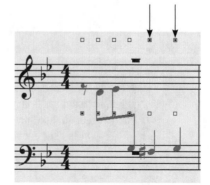

Remember, you are seeing the notes in the bass-clef staff. However, for any editing, Finale still considers them to be on the treble staff. To temporarily display cross-staffed notes in their staff of origin, in Document Options, check "Display Cross-Staffed Notes in Original Staff." Uncheck it when you are finished editing.

Next, there is the problem with the default whole rest in the bass-clef staff, despite the cross-staff notes displaying in those measures. There are several ways to fix this. Here's what I did:

1. Choose Speedy Entry .
2. Switch to Layer 1.
3. Press Return/Enter to move the Speedy Entry window to the bass clef.
4. Press 7 to enter a whole rest.
5. Press the Left Bracket key (or the Left Arrow key) to move the Speedy Entry window back to measure 1. Set the cursor on the whole rest.
6. Press the * (asterisk) key on the keypad (in Speedy Entry) to make the rest draggable.

The asterisk key is a toggle, so to undo the manual positioning, press the key again. The rest will return to its default positioning. Remember to hold down the Shift key to restrict the dragging to be vertical only.

7. Drag the rest to under the second line.

Bach_Fugue.mus

finalebook.com

Continue through the piece, adjusting the positions of notes and rests to match the example printed at the beginning of the chapter. I'll provide some specific steps for the more complex measures in the piece so follow along as we go from top to bottom. Refer to the finished example, if you are not sure of what I'm looking for when I give a direction to move something. Print the example from the Web site to save time flipping through the book.

Measure 7

In measure 7, lower the eighth rest on beat 1 of the treble and bass clef staves, and then the one on beat 3 of the treble clef.

1. Choose Speedy Entry .
2. Click on the treble-clef staff in bar 7.
3. Switch to Layer 2.
4. Place the cursor on the eighth rest, and press the * (asterisk) key.

This toggles the rest back to the normal mid-staff position.

5. Shift-drag the rest downward.
6. Go to Layer 2, and move the eighth rest in Layer 2 down slightly.

For the cross-staff notes in Layer 2 of the treble staff in bar 7, use the same steps as in bar 1. Select Show Active Layer Only first, so that the note in Layer 1 is not affected.

1. Select **Options** > Show Active Layer Only.
2. Switch to Layer 2 in the bottom left corner of the Finale window.
3. Choose Mass Edit tool ⬤.
4. Highlight the last two sixteenths in bar 7.
5. Select **Plug-ins** > TG Tools > Cross Staff. Click Go and then Close.
6. Choose the Beam Angle tool 🔧 from the Special Tools 🔲 palette.
7. Adjust the beam angle downward with the right handle.
8. Select **Options** > Show Active Layer Only, to toggle it off.

When adjusting the beam angle, remember that the beam is supposed to angle in the direction of the melodic line. If the line does not have a clear up or down direction, the beam should be closer to flat or horizontal. In all cases, avoid exaggerated angles on beamed groups. In Finale, the stem length of the two end notes usually determines the angle. This sometimes differs from what you will find in non-computer-generated scores. For example, in my original editions, the sixteenth notes on beat 1, Layer 2, measure 10 have a flat beam because the line is static. Finale uses the length of the stems as a guide, and since the B is higher than the A, the beam angles up.

Measure 7 also contains a bit of fake cross-staff displaying. The quarter notes C# and D in the bass clef are in Layer 1 of that staff, but the second half of that melodic line is entered in the treble staff, with a hidden half rest on the other two beats. The reason for doing this is that you cannot cross staff a rest.

Measure 12

Since the position of the notes in Layer 2 will dictate where elements in Layers 1 and 3 are repositioned, set Layer 2 first. I used more faux cross staffing between Layer 3 and Layer 1 of the bass-clef staff.

1. Choose Speedy Entry 🎵, and click the treble staff, measure 12.
2. In Layer 2:
   a. Drag the eighth rest in Layer 2 to the right of the quarter notes.
   b. Use the L key to flip up the stems of the eighth-note group and two quarter notes.
3. In Layer 3:
   a. Use the L key to flip the stem on the D quarter note.
   b. Reposition the quarter rest.
   c. Hide the half rest.
4. In Layer 1, drag the quarter and half rests above the staff.

Measure 13

1. Choose Speedy Entry , and click the treble staff, measure 13.
2. Reposition the eighth rest in Layer 1 of the treble staff by pressing the * (asterisk) key.
3. Hide the half rest in Layer 2 of the treble staff.
4. Hide the half rest in Layer 1 of the bass staff.

Measure 15

Where to start cleaning up this mess! Oh, I'm supposed to tell you? Okay, here we go.

> Before diving into deep waters, save your document. That way, between the Undo and Revert commands, you are never too far away from square one, if you need to start over.

1. Choose Speedy Entry , and click the treble-clef staff, measure 15.
2. Switch to Layer 2 by using the Speedy shortcut: Shift-Down Arrow.
3. Place the cursor on the E♭ sixteenth note in beat 1, and press the * (asterisk) key to display the accidental.

The big problem in this measure is horizontal space. We have to offset a lot of notes where voices cross, and Note Spacing did not allow enough room. We could use the Measure Tool to increase the size of the whole measure, but we need more space in specific areas of the measure—more than the measure as a whole.

1. Choose Speedy Entry , and click the treble-clef staff, measure 15.
2. Switch to Layer 2 using Shift-Down Arrow.
3. Place the cursor on the E♭ sixteenth note on beat 1, and press the * key to display the accidental.
4. Switch to Layer 4 using Shift-Down Arrow.

More room is required for beats 1, 2, and the first half of 3. A little extra space is needed on the second half of beat 1. To fool Mass Edit into allotting more space, temporarily add some smaller rhythms, then repeat the music spacing process.

5. Enter two 16th rests, four 32nd rests, two more 16th rests, four 32nd note rests, then eight 16th rests.

> Any time you need extra space in a specific place in a measure, just go to an empty layer or staff, and enter a group of invisible rests whose rhythmic value is less than the existing notes. Then use Beat or Entry Layout in Mass Edit to reposition the music, taking into account the new rests. The result will be more space exactly where you need it. If you don't have enough room yet, repeat with smaller value rests.

Just enter the rests you need where you need them. If you need space at the end of the measure, enter rhythms equal to the music already entered for the sections you don't want to change. That way, the spacing in those sections will remain the same.

1. Choose Mass Edit , and highlight both staves.
2. Select **Mass Edit** > Music Spacing > Apply Note Spacing.
3. Select **Edit** > Update Layout, or use the shortcut ⌘-/ (Mac) or Control-U (Windows).

To make these rests invisible, there are several options. You could return to Layer 4 and hide or delete the rests. Alternatively, you could use a Staff Style to make the rests in Layer 4 invisible. Staff Styles act like a mask, covering a layer—in this case, hiding the rests and displaying a blank, empty layer. Let's use the Staff Style; that way, the rests are still there, just in case. (See chapter 11 for more about Staff Styles.)

1. Choose the Staff tool, and highlight the treble staff, bar 15.
2. To open the contextual menu, Control-click (Mac) or Right-click (Windows) in the highlighted area in bar 15.
3. Select Blank Notation: Layer 4 from the popup menu.

It is possible to drag notes in Speedy Entry using the mouse. However, I recommend using the Note Position Tool, in Special Tools, for more precise control over placement. Check the numbers in the message bar as you drag, to see how far you are moving something. Press the Delete key to return to the default position to undo any positioning.

Now, there should be more space available to manually reposition notes.

1. Choose Speedy Entry, and move to Layer 3.
2. Drag the eighth rest in Layer 3 to above the staff.
3. Exit Speedy Entry by clicking away from the music or pressing the ESC key.
4. Choose the Special Tools icon. Then, choose the Note Position tool.

5. Use the Right Arrow key to nudge the A quarter note on the second half of beat 1, Layer 1, to the right. Place it in the space between the eighth note in Layer 3 and the E-flat's flat symbol in Layer 2.

The "Entry offset" display at the left side of the Message Bar will show the measurements, as you move items in Special Tools. The distance you move the note is displayed in the message bar in whatever unit of measurement you have selected. To reset the position of the note back to (0,0), select the handle, and press the Delete key.

In EVPUs

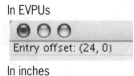

In inches

Entry offset: (0.08333, 0)

If the arrow key is nudging only in multiples of 2 or 4, use the Zoom Tool to enlarge the measure you are working on. This will get you down to single unit movements.

To set the stem directions:

We have already used the L key in Speedy Entry to change stem directions. Here is another way to do it.

1. Choose the Stem Direction tool.
2. Click the handles under the staff, to change the stem direction of the sixteenth notes on the second half of beat 2.

In most situations, Finale will adequately handle the rules and practices of music notation. In complex situations like measure 15, there are some problems that Finale has not solved properly. When two notes collide on any beat, only one note is moved, and it is moved to the right. Usually the down-stemmed note is moved to the right so that the stems are aligned. Following this practice will result in a change to the second half of beat 2.

1. Choose the Note Position tool.
2. Switch to Layer 3.
3. Highlight of the F eighth note's handle on the second half of beat 2.
4. Press the Delete key, and the note will return to the (0,0) position, overlapping the G sixteenth note.
5. Switch to Layer 1.
6. Highlight the G sixteenth note's handle, and use the right arrow key to nudge the note to right.

The stems should be close, without touching. My message bar indicates a displacement of 32 EVPUs (0.11111 inches).

On beat 3, the question is which to move: the B-flat eighth note or the quarter and dotted quarter note? The answer is, move the quarter and dotted quarter note, because it requires the smaller distance to offset. Moving the eighth note beyond the dot will give it the appearance of being on the second half of the beat. Move the C dotted quarter first, since it will require a larger distance because of the ledger line.

1. Switch to Layer 3.
2. Nudge the C dotted-quarter note to the right. Move it so that the ledger line is clear of the B-flat stem. Try 12 EVPUs or 0.04167 inches.
3. Switch to Layer 1.
4. Highlight the handle for the E quarter note, and nudge it the same distance to the right.

209

Now that the notes are positioned, we can fix the stem directions:

1. Switch to Layer 3.
2. Choose the Stem Direction tool ✳.
3. Click the handle under the C dotted-quarter note to flip the stem down.

The eighth-note beam is crowding the C, so it must be repositioned.

1. Choose the Beam Angle tool 🪁.
2. Switch to Layer 2.
3. Drag down the left handle of the eighth-note beam.

About (0, –32) EVPUs or (0, –0.1111) inches ought to do it. I have not forgotten about collisions being a big "no-no," but moving the eighth beam past the end of the C's stem makes it more difficult to read. Remember, rules must sometimes be broken.

On to the fourth beat, notes with opposing stem directions need to be offset.

1. Choose the Note Position tool ⬌.
2. Switch to Layer 2.
3. Use the Right arrow key to nudge the A quarter note to the right 32 EVPUs (0.11458 inches).
4. Choose the Tie tool 🎵.
5. Highlight the tie's handle, and then flip the tie using the keystroke command, ⌘-F (Mac) or Control-F (Windows).
6. Choose the Stem Direction tool ✳.
7. Switch to Layer 3.
8. Change the stem direction of the two sixteenths on the second half of beat 4. With beamed groups the entire group will flip when any one note in the group is flipped.

One last minor adjustment is to nudge the measure number away from the eighth rest.

9. Choose the Measure tool 🖼.
10. Click on the measure number's handle, and nudge it to the Left using the Left Arrow key.

There. All better.

Measure 17

There is one beaming change in Layer 1 of the bass clef in measure 17.

1. Choose Speedy Entry 🎵, and switch to Layer 1.
2. Press the Return/Enter key to move the Speedy Entry window to the bass-clef staff.
3. Use the Right Arrow key to position the cursor on the B-flat in beat 4.
4. Press the / (slash) key on the keypad to break the beam.

Measure 21

In this bar, there are some beaming alterations and one cross-voicing to attend to.

1. Choose Speedy Entry ![icon], and switch to Layer 1.
2. Use the / (slash) key to break the beam on the second half of beat 3.
3. Switch to Layer 2.
4. Break the beam between beats 1 and 2.
5. Switch to Layer 1.
6. Press Return/Enter to move to the bass-clef staff.
7. Break the beam between beats 3 and 4 in Layer 1.

On beat 3 in the treble clef, there is a cross-voicing problem. Normally the down-stemmed note would be moved, but in this case, that would place it almost under the eighth note on the second half of the beat. The solution is to nudge the eighth note to the right so the stems clearly do not touch the opposing voice's notehead.

1. Choose Note Position tool ![icon] from the Special Tools ![icon] palette.
2. Nudge the G eighth note to the right about 6 EVPUs (0.02083 inches).

Measure 24

There is another cross-voice problem in the treble staff to correct. Once again, it is a situation where moving the lower voice would create more of a problem, this time by colliding with the sharp. It is also much more readable if the A is just moved away from the opposing stem.

1. Choose the Note Position tool ![icon].
2. Nudge the A eighth note, Layer 1, beat 2, to the right about 6 EVPUs (0.021 inches).

There is also a beaming change in the bass-clef staff.

1. Choose Speedy Entry ![icon].
2. Click on the bass-clef staff.
3. Place the cursor on beat 2, and press the / key.

Measure 28

Here, there are more rests to move, as well as another cross-voice position problem.

1. Choose the Note Position tool.
2. Switch to Layer 1.
3. Nudge the quarter note G on beat 4 to the right, so that the noteheads do not touch the opposing stems. Nudge the same distance as in bar 24.
4. Choose Speedy Entry, and click the treble-clef staff.
5. Switch to Layer 2.
6. Drag the quarter and eighth rests below the staff.

Measure 29

To position the rests:

1. Choose Speedy Entry.
2. Switch to Layer 1.
3. Press the * (asterisk on the keypad) key, and then Shift-drag Layer 1's rests a little further above the staff.
4. Switch to Layer 2.
5. Press the * key to move the rests back to the center of the staff.
6. Switch to Layer 3.
7. Press the H key to hide the half rest.
8. Shift-drag the eighth rest beneath the down-stemmed eighth note.
9. Move the cursor to the sixteenth notes, and press the L key to change the stem direction.
10. Move to the group of notes on beat 4 and flip the stem direction.

To adjust the notes and beams:

1. Choose the Note Position tool.
2. Switch to Layer 1.
3. Nudge the sixteenth-note A on the second half of beat 1 to the right.
4. Nudge the sixteenth-note Bb on the second half of beat 2 to the right.
5. Choose the Beam Angle tool.
6. Highlight the right handle of the beam on beat 2, and raise it 6 EVPUs (0.021 inches) to give a little more space to the Eb in Layer 2.

Measure 30

1. Choose Speedy Entry.
2. Switch to Layer 2.
3. Drag the eighth rest on beat 1 up.

4. Move the cursor to the F♯ sixteenth, and press the L key to change the stem direction.
5. Switch to Layer 3.
6. Press the L key to change the stem direction of the B♭.
7. Press the H key to hide the half rest on beat 3.
8. Press the Return key to move to the bass-clef staff.
9. Switch to Layer 1.
10. Press the H key to hide the eighth rest.
11. Press ESC to leave the Speedy Entry window.

To reduce the size of the B♭:

1. Choose the Resize tool 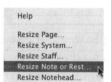.
2. Control-click (Mac) or Right-click (Windows) on the B♭ in Layer 1 of the bass staff, and Select Resize Note or Rest from the contextual menu.
3. Type "75" in the box, and then click OK.

Measure 31

1. Choose Speedy Entry .
2. Raise the eighth rest in Layer 1, beat 4 of the treble-clef staff.

Measure 33

1. Choose Speedy Entry .
2. Raise the eighth rest in Layer 1 of the bass-clef staff.

Measure 34

1. Choose Speedy Entry .
2. Switch to Layer 2.
3. Lower the eighth rest in Layer 2 of the treble staff.
4. Switch to Layer 3.
5. Hide the half rest in Layer 3.

On beat 2 of the treble staff, I want to offset the C eighth, not the quarter note.

1. Choose the Note Position tool .
2. Switch to Layer 3.
3. Select the handle for the D and F# quarter note on beat 2.

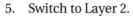

4. Press the Delete key to return it to the (0,0) position. It will now overlap the C in Layer 2.

5. Switch to Layer 2.

6. Highlight the handle for the C, and nudge it 27 EVPUs (0.094 inches) to the right.

🙂 Have you saved lately?

Adding Detail

For this exercise, I've added fingerings and a few other things for you to enter.

Articulations

To enter or edit articulations, you must be in the same layer as the entry you wish to attach an articulation to. Use the layers popup menu or keystroke commands to switch between layers.

In measure 1, the staccato dot should be on the stem side of the note. The default position for the dot is on the notehead side. The cross-staff positioning will confuse the auto placement function of the articulation, so we need to position the dot manually.

To create a manually positioned staccato dot:

1. Choose the Articulation tool 🎵.

2. Click the note position in the treble clef; look for the note on the cursor.

3. Choose the staccato dot, and click the Duplicate button.

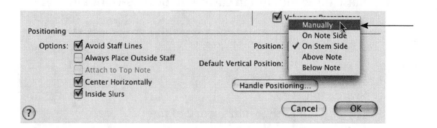

A new library entry will be created and automatically selected.

4. Click the Edit button.

5. Select "Manually" from the Position popup menu, and click OK.

6. Drag the dot to the correct position, above the beam.

Remember, Finale considers notes to be a part of the staff where they were entered. Therefore, you must click on the original staff to assign or edit a note or anything assigned to it. There are exceptions: any note, or notehead-attached shape entered with the Slur tool can be edited. Note-attached shapes are the Slur, Dashed Curve, and Bend Hat. Shapes that attach to a notehead are the Glissando, Guitar Bend, and TAB Slide shapes.

> Don't just think of Finale libraries (such as the Articulation and Expression libraries) as places to go to get something and go. Each library item also has customizable settings for positioning and MIDI playback options. You can change the size, the placement options, or create new items specially tailored for your work.

Phrase Markings

Slurs do not require you to be in a specific layer, or above or below the staff, to indicate direction. Finale calculates slur positions based on the stem direction of the notes in the phrase.

1. Choose the Slur tool ◯ from the Smart Shape ◯ palette.
2. Enter the phrase markings.

The crescendo in bar 10 is also entered with the Smart Shape tool. Other than slurs, most Smart Shapes are attached to the measure. When entering the crescendo, the cursor will behave exactly as it does in Expression Tool, with a little arrow that indicates the staff to which the mark will be applied. In the case of measure 10, there are down-stemmed notes, and the crescendo will have to be positioned under them. Position the cursor in the right spot, and the arrow points down, not up. In cases like these, the crescendo must be entered on top of the down-stemmed notes, then dragged down to the proper position, so that the mark is attached to the treble-clef staff.

1. Choose the Crescendo tool ◁.
2. Add the crescendo to the treble-clef staff of measure 10.
3. Drag down the mark to be underneath the down-stemmed notes.

215

Measure 30: S-Curves Using Slur Tool

1. Choose the Slur tool 🖱.
2. Double-click on the B♭ half note in Layer 3 of the treble staff.
3. Drag the slur down to the B♭ eighth note on beat 3 in the bass-clef staff.

A short Smart Slur anatomy lesson: Along the inside of the arc, or on top in this case, are three boxes. The left and right boxes control the end points of the shape, and the middle box controls the position of the entire shape. Consider these the positioning handles of a Smart Slur.

1. Drag the left positioning handle so that the left end of the slur is positioned to the right side of the B♭ half note.
2. Drag the right-end positioning handle down to right side of the B♭ on beat 3 on the bass-clef staff.

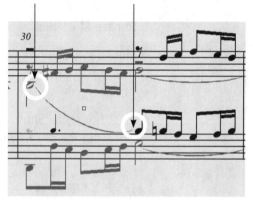

On the outside of the arc are three other boxes that control the contour of the arc itself. Each one can increase or decrease the height of the arc for fine-tuning of the shape.

3. Drag the right-contour handle up so that the curve is inverted from the original shape.
4. Drag the left-contour handle down a little to fine-tune the shape.

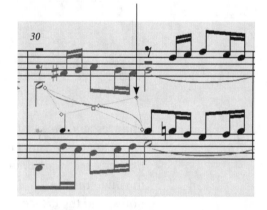

The right handle might need a little fine-tuning again after the left handle is moved. No numbers for this; just practice until you are satisfied with the curve.

Fingerings

Fingering numbers will be entered with the Articulation tool. The numbers, 1 through 5, are already in the Articulation library. The Metatools for entry are easy to remember, 1 is programmed to the 1 key, the 2 to 2 key, and so on, through 5. Articulations are programmed to auto-position above the note. Articulations can be dragged to another position after they are entered. This will be necessary in the cases where two fingering numbers are required, and also in cases where the fingerings go underneath the notes.

To enter fingering numbers:
1. Choose the Articulation tool 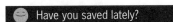.
2. Enter the numbers in the piece, as shown in the full score at the beginning of this chapter.

Dynamics

To enter dynamic markings, use the Expression tool with layers and voices. I attach all dynamics to the note they affect, even if the positioning places them under a rest that precedes the note. There are several reasons for this. First, there are MIDI velocity numbers assigned to the dynamics for playback, and I want them to take effect at the proper place. In the Expression selection window, along the right-hand column, there are velocity numbers for all the dynamics. These are the MIDI key velocity numbers, preset for each dynamic. They are user programmable. Look under the Playback tab in the Expression Designer to edit this number.

Remember the rules of placement! A brace implies that all dynamics between the staves apply for both staves, and all dynamics above the top staff or below the bottom staff apply only to that staff.

1. Choose the Expression tool 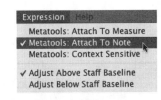.
2. Select **Expression** > Attach to Note, if you are using Metatools for Dynamics.
3. Enter the dynamics for the piece. Refer to the example at the beginning of the chapter.

10_Bach 4.mus

finalebook.com

😊 Have you saved lately?

Loading an Instrument Library

MIDI playback should be a familiar process by now. For this example, we will go a little deeper into this feature and use it to orchestrate the example you are working on.

To load the General MIDI library:
- Select **File** > Load Library > Instrument Libraries, and choose General MIDI.

Assigning Different Voices for Layers

The General MIDI library is a set of instrument names and patch numbers for General MIDI synths, such as the internal SoundFont. Now that you have loaded this library into your Finale file, these instruments can be assigned to the staff for playback. We will set several different instruments to play each staff.

1. Select **Window** > Instrument List.
2. Click on the triangle to the left of [Staff 1] to access the individual layer assignments.
3. To the right of Layer 1, click in the Instrument column.
4. Choose "Flute" from the popup menu.

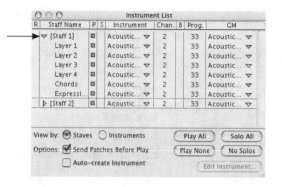

In the instrument column for Staff 1, the word Mixed now appears. That will remind you that the staff set is to more than one output routing when the list is minimized (using the triangle).

4. Set other instruments for the remaining layers:
   a. For the Layer 2 instrument, select Oboe.
   b. For the Layer 3 instrument, select Clarinet.
5. Click the triangle to the left of Staff 2 to expand the display for the bass-clef staff.
   a. For the Layer 1 instrument, select Clarinet.
   b. For the Layer 2 instrument, select Bassoon.

To close the Instrument List window, click the Close button in the window bar, or select Instrument List in the Window menu,

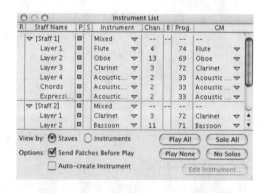

To play back the score:
1. Expand the Playback Controls window. On the Mac, click the expansion triangle to the left of the transport buttons. For Windows, click the Speaker icon.
2. From the Human Playback Style popup menu, select "Baroque."

The file is now ready to play back on a General MIDI synth or using the computer's internal synth. If your synth is not General MIDI, use your computer

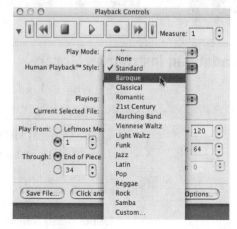

for this example. This will assure that the sounds we've selected will be the sounds used for playback. Finale has libraries for several different synths. If your brand is not in the Instrument libraries folder, you will have to create your own, or at least set up the synth manually.

Note the checkbox for Send Patches Before Play in the bottom section of the Instrument List dialog box. With this checked, Finale sends out patch data immediately before the MIDI data. If the library is not set for your synth, uncheck this before attempting a playback.

3. To begin playback, click the Play button, or press the Space Bar.

Changing the Tempo

Tempo can be controlled from two different places in a file: in the Tempo section of the Playback Controls, or in the Playback section of an expression. The Playback controls are more flexible, in terms of changing the tempo when you are still searching for the perfect setting.

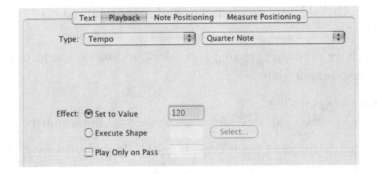

*   Use the Up or Down Arrow keys, or highlight the number and type in a new tempo value.

Tempo can also be a part of a text expression. Use this where there is more than one tempo in the piece. The text expression that indicates the change for the performer can also be set to change the tempo for MIDI playback.

To add tempo control to an expression:

1. Set up the expression, then click the Playback tab.
2. From the Type popup, select "Tempo."
3. Choose the beat value, in the menu to the right.
4. For Effect, click Set Value, and enter the tempo (beats per minute).

Tempos set by expressions will override the tempo set in the Playback Control window. Tempos set in the Setup Wizard are entered as expressions.

Creating and Editing Text Blocks

The text blocks for the title and composer of the piece are already entered, courtesy of the Setup Wizard. Use the Text Tool to edit the text, adjust text position, or create additional text blocks.

> When creating a text block, set the size and style of the font before typing, so that the text is entered in the desired form. Always check before typing.

To set the title to a custom font size:
1. Choose the Text tool .
2. Double-click on the title's handle, and select all the text in the frame.
3. Select **Text** > Size > Other.
4. Enter "32" for the point size of the type, and click OK. Then click anywhere away from the selected text block, to deselect it.

The composer credit needs to moved down and positioned approximately halfway between the title and the first system. This can be positioned visually. Use the positioning lines that appear when the handle is grabbed to maintain position on the right margin. The vertical line should always be flush with the right side barline. The text in this block needs to be a little larger.

To increase the size of the composer name:
1. Double-click the handle of the composer name, and select all the text using the shortcut ⌘-A (Mac) or Control-A (Windows).
2. Choose **Text** > Size > Other, and enter "16" for the point size of the type. Then click OK.
3. Drag the composer name down into position. Then click once anywhere away from the selected text block to deselect it.

We don't need the copyright text block, so select it and delete it. Use the Delete key, or Control-click (Mac) or Right-click (Window) the frame and choose "delete" from the popup menu.

Now, let's have a little fun creating a text block. Text blocks can be created anywhere on a page and positioned later.

To create a new text block:
1. Choose the Text tool, and double-click on the page, away from the existing text blocks.

The selected default of 12-point Times is fine for this block, so no change is required.

2. Type "Edition," followed by your name. Then click anywhere away from this text block to deselect it.

Now, position the text block in the bottom-outside corner, and set it to display on all pages. This text block will appear on the right side of the right-hand page and on the left side of the left-hand page.

1. Click on the "Edition" block's handle.
2. Select **Text** > Frame Attributes.
3. For Attach To Page, select "All Pages."

4. Under Alignment and Positioning, use the popup menu to set the horizontal position to "Left."
5. Set the vertical position to "Bottom (Footer)."
6. Set the H to "0" and V to "–84" EVPUs (–0.29167 inches).
7. Activate the Use Right Page Positioning box. This will allow the display to be different on the right and left pages of the book.
8. Set the H to "0" and V to "–84," and then click OK.

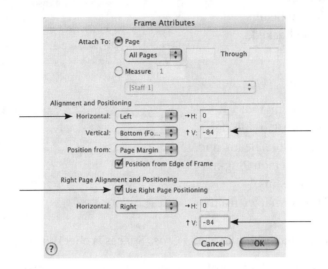

Check the second page to confirm that the text is positioned properly and not too close to the music.

Picking Nits: Plug-ins for Fine-Tuning

This chapter is an indication of the difference between churning out a quick piece and the art of engraving. There are plug-ins in Finale that help to reduce the time needed to individually adjust notation elements, when fine-tuning, as would be required by using the standard tools. The Cross Staff plug-in used in this chapter is one such time-saver. The introduction of this plug-in in version 2005 reduced the cross-staff process from three steps to one. It is a part of a larger group of plug-ins created by a third party, TGTools, for use with Finale. Open any of the Plug-ins in the TGTools folder, and click About to learn more about the full package. Use the Finale Help to learn more about the TGTools plug-ins included in Finale.

Another sample of plug-ins included with the Finale package is the Patterson Plug-ins Lite package, which is found in the Note, Rests and Beaming folder of the Plug-ins menu. One of the plug-ins, Patterson Beams, is designed to eliminate beam wedges. "Wedges" occur when the staff line passes through the gap between beams of a beamed group. There are many wedges in this chapter's example. The example at right is taken from measure 8. The wedge is located in the gap between the first and second stems. This can blur the distinction of the two beams—a small detail, but what is art without attention to every detail?

The Patterson Beams Plug-in will minutely adjust the beam angle and stem length to avoid the occurrence of wedges. In order for it to perform effectively, a few settings must be checked in the Beams dialog box in Document Options.

1. Select **Options** > Document Options.
2. Click Beams in the left column.
3. Check Allow Primary Beams Within a Space.
4. Make sure Extend Beams Over Rests is unchecked, and click OK.

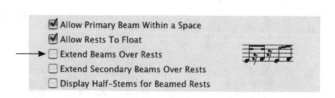

Now apply the plug-in.

1. Choose the Mass Edit tool 🌑.
2. Highlight measure 8, treble clef.
3. Select **Plug-ins** > Note, Beam, and Rest Editing > Patterson Plug-ins Lite > Patterson Beams.
4. Click OK. (This is what we fixed in advance.)

Patterson Beams is most effective with the following settings in your Finale Beaming Options:
Allow Primary Beam Within a Space CHECKED.
Extend Beams Over Edge Rests UNCHECKED.
Max Slope a multiple of 6 EVPU.

☐ Do not show again.   Cancel   OK

5. Make sure that Beams Should Never Cross Spaces is checked, and then click OK.

Go through the piece and look for other wedges, and use the Patterson Beams Plug-in to eliminate them.

Give it a final save, then send it to the printer.

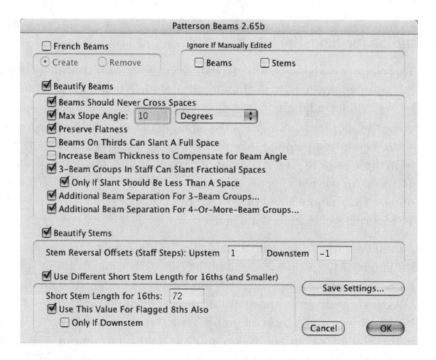

Printing in Color

We discussed that though Finale displays entries in different colors, those colors do not print. That is the default configuration for Finale, but if you have a color printer, and wish to print music in color, Finale makes this possible. The colors themselves can be turned on or off, or changed in Program Options in the display colors dialog box, or by selecting Select Display Colors from the View menu. With Use Score Colors activated, the final step is in the Print dialog box.

1. Select **File** > Print to open the Print dialog box.
2. Set it to print the colors.

Mac OS	Windows
a. From the Copies and Pages Menu, Select Finale 2005. b. Under the Print heading, select Display Colors.	a. Choose **File** > Print. b. In the Print dialog box, check the Print Display Colors option.

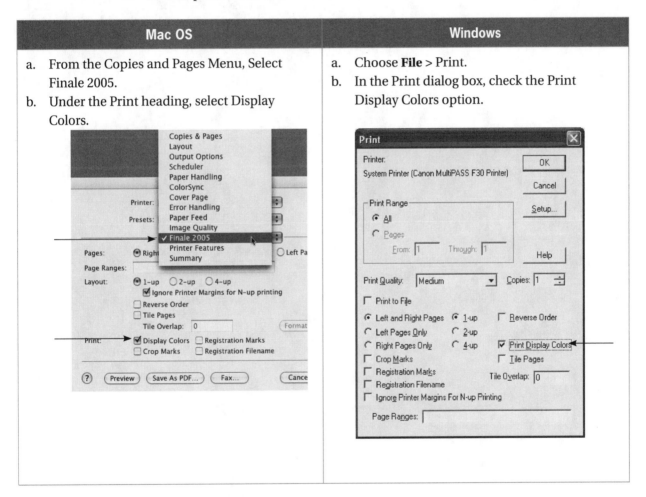

3. Click the Print button.

Summary

- creating a grand-staff file with the Setup Wizard
- set up layer attributes
- assign layers separate MIDI channels
- work with Special Tools, adjusting stem lengths and adjusting beam angles.
- cross-staff notation
- tips for creating additional space for offset notes

223

11

Jazz Notation: Leadsheets and Guitar Tab ("Blues for a Hiccup")

Hiccup_Sketch.mus

Before starting this chapter, download and print the file Hiccup_Sketch.mus. Use this as a reference while working on this chapter.

This chapter contains two parts. The first part focuses on constructing a rhythm-section sketch, just as a composer would do when writing. You will be creating an arrangement for a jazz composition that could be given to a rhythm section or small group for performance. In part 2, this sketch will be turned into a lead sheet, then into guitar tablature notation.

You will find Finale files for this chapter on the companion Web site. These will allow you to begin work at specific points in the chapter with all the steps up to that point completed.

In the previous chapters, we have been dealing with exact notation—every element clearly written out by the composer or arranger for all parts. However, for those who work with jazz and popular music, there are different problems to consider. Jazz is often expressed in a form of shorthand, which allows players to improvise their parts based on the guidelines set forth on the page. This includes elements such as chord symbols that define harmony, slashes that define rhythm, and improvised parts that are created by the performer. These symbols usually flow very fast from the pencil or pen, and speed encourages their use whenever possible. In Finale, these symbols sometimes require more effort to reproduce than parts that are exactly notated. For purposes of this exercise, I've incorporated as many examples of this shorthand as possible.

New in this chapter:

- creating a rhythm section score
- using the Jazz font
- using Staff Styles for slashes
- creating chord suffixes
- entering a drum set part
- opening a template file.
- using Jazz Human Playback
- guitar tab notation
- using FinaleScript
- creating a script

A Chart Is Born: Adding New Staves Manually

For this sketch, you'll need a grand staff for the guitar, piano, and bass, with a separate staff underneath for the drums. You'll also be using the Jazz font. This font is based on the look of *The Real Book*, the classic jazz fake book.

1. Launch Finale and click Setup Wizard in the Launch Window (or select **File** > New > Document With Setup Wizard).
2. In page 1:
   a. For the title, enter "Blues for a Hiccup."
   b. For the composer credit, enter "Vince Leonard."
   c. For the copyright, enter "© 2000 by Vince Leonard." Option-**G** is the Mac keystroke for the copyright symbol. In Windows, access this character using the Character Map utility. Then click the Next button.
3. In page 2:
   a. Add Keyboard-Piano, No Staff Name.
   b. Add Drums > Drum Set.
   c. For Score Order, select "Jazz Band." This will set the piano staff over the drums.
4. Click the Next button two times. No changes are necessary on the page 3 of the Setup Wizard.

5. In page 4:
   a. Activate "Specify Initial Tempo Marking," and enter "144" for the quarter-note value.
   b. For the Default Music Font, select Jazz. Then click Finish, and save the file as "Hiccup_Sketch.mus."

> Another way to create a document using the Jazz font is to open the Component Files folder in the Finale 2005 Folder, and select the Jazz Font Default file. This file has wider staff lines, stems, and ledger lines to accommodate the fatter noteheads, in addition to libraries and fonts using the JazzText and JazzChord fonts.

Hiding The Staff Name

To hide the staff name for the Drum Set staff:
1. Choose the Staff tool .
2. Highlight any measure of the Drum Set staff, and select **Staff** > Edit Staff Attributes, or just double-click the staff.
3. Under Items To Display, uncheck "Staff Name," and click OK.

Jazz Time-Signature Options

It is possible to remove the bracket following the time signature in Jazz font. There is an alternate C and a cut-time symbol in the Jazz font that does not have the bracket. Also, I prefer a different percussion clef that is also in the font. I've been asked to do both of these alterations in the past and will give you the steps for each.

1. Select **Options** > Document Options, and choose Time Signatures in the left column.
2. Click the Select button to the right of "Abbreviate Common Time to."
3. Scroll down to the next row of symbols, and double-click the C with no bracket (symbol 100), to select the shape and return to the Time Signature Options dialog box.

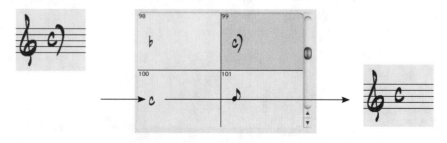

There should now be a lowercase "d" in the box for the common-time symbol; the cut-time symbol without the bracket is an uppercase D. Confirm this, and then click OK.

Setting the Measure Numbers

I recommend displaying measure numbers in every bar. There are benefits to doing this in both rehearsal and performance. Players will not need to count from main rehearsal markings to find a specific measure to ask a question or to pick a starting point. In a jazz setting, altering the arrangement during rehearsal or performance is a snap. This can be as simple as repeating sections for additional solos or for encores. In more extreme circumstances, it helps catch a soloist who just skipped ahead, or can help pull together an ensemble that has run amok.

To display numbers on every measure:
1. Choose the Measure tool 🔲.
2. Select **Measure** > Measure Numbers > Edit Regions.
3. Under Positioning & Display, set Display to Show Every "1" Measures Beginning with Measure "1."

Note that "Hide first measure in region" is activated, so the first measure number in the piece will not display. Hiding the first measure reduces clutter in a place where there are often many other notation symbols: time signature, tempo marking, and so on. Leave the measure number hidden here, unless either the measure is something other than the number 1, or if you are creating a full score.

4. For Always Show On, deactivate "Top Staff" and activate "Bottom Staff." Then click OK.

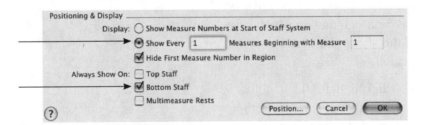

For Good Measure

Use the Measure tool to complete these measure layout tasks.

To set a double bar at the end of measure 12:
• Open the contextual menu in measure 12, using Control-click (Mac) or Right-click (Windows), and select "Double Barline."

To set measure 25 to begin a new staff system (for the coda):
1. Double-click inside measure 25.
2. In the Measure Attributes window, choose "Begin a New Staff System," for the start of the coda. Then click OK.

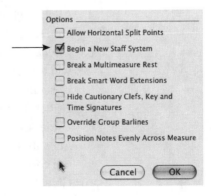

Setting the Repeat

1. Choose the Repeat tool 🔲.
2. Highlight measures 13 through 24.
3. Select **Repeat** > Create Simple Repeat. Alternatively, Control-click (Mac) or Right-click (Windows) the highlighted region, and select "Create Simple Repeat" from the contextual menu.

To set up the coda:

The repeat is entered and defined for playback. Next, the repeated section of music that precedes the coda must be indicated by symbols and text. In Finale these are referred to as Text Repeats. (If you are not interested in having the repeats affect music playback, it is possible to enter these as Measure Expressions.)

1. With the Repeat tool selected, double-click on measure 10. This brings up the Repeat Selection dialog box.
2. Scroll down, select the boxed coda sign, and then click Edit.

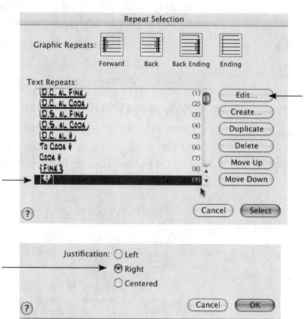

The coda sign should line up with the right-hand barline. By changing its Justification setting, you can select where Finale places the coda sign and on which side of the shape the handle will be located.

3. Click Right for the Justification setting. This places the handle to the right side of the coda sign. Click OK to return to the Repeat Selection window, and then click Select.

Now, let's set up the coda for playback. In the Text Repeat Assignment dialog, you'll input when to jump to the coda, and to what measure number.

4. Click the Jump on Passes button, and enter "2" in the box to the right.
5. Under the Target heading, enter "25" next to Measure #.
6. Check the Auto-Update Target box. When Auto-Update Target is activated, Finale will track the insertion or deletion of any measures in the file and adjust the target measure of the repeat accordingly.
7. Under the positioning Header, check Individual Positioning.
8. Under the Show On heading, choose Staff List, and then click Edit.
9. Activate Top Staff and Bottom Staff in both the Score and Parts columns, to make the coda display in those staves.
10. Give the list a name, such as "Piano & Drums," since they are the top and bottom staves of the score, respectively. Click OK twice to return to the score.

Click on the text in this column to select both
Score and Parts columns with a single click.

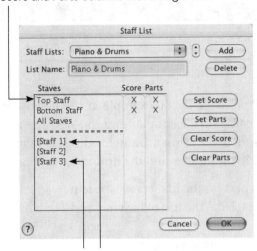

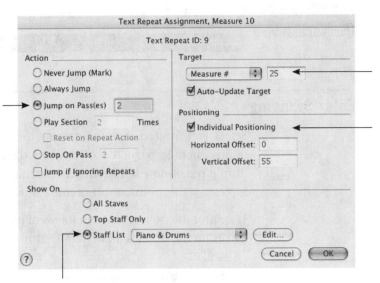

Another option is to check the Staff 1 and
Staff 3 display. Results with be the same.

This allows repeats to be placed on selected staves
and positioned similar to Measure Expressions.

11. Drag the coda sign so that the vertical
positioning crosshair aligns with the
right-hand barline of measure 10.

Setting Up the D.C. for Playback

Next, enter the D.C. al
Coda and configure it
to play back properly.

1. With the Repeat
Tool selected,
double-click on
measure 24.

2. In the Text
Repeats window,
double-click
"D.C. al Coda," to
choose it.

3. Under Action,
choose Jump on Passes, and enter "2" for the total.

4. Enter measure 1 as the target measure.

5. Activate Auto-Update Target. (You'll be glad you made this a habit, someday.)

6. Activate Individual Positioning.

7. Choose Staff List, and choose Piano & Drums, and then click OK to return to the score.

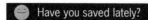
11_Hiccup_1.mus

8. Align the D.C al Coda mark with the right bar line, just like the coda sign.

😊 Have you saved lately?

Enter Swinging

Select your preferred note entry method. Refer back to the example at the beginning of this chapter, page 225, or download the completed example from the Web site and print it out. A note to HyperScribers: make sure that the quantization settings are for no tuplets. At this point, only enter the notes; skip the slashes and the drum part for now.

1. Enter the treble and bass staves of piano part for the first twelve measures.
2. Enter the treble staff of bars 13 through 24. Note the use of Layers 1 and 2 in bars 21 and 22.
3. Enter the treble and bass staves for the piano in the coda.

Swing Playback

So far, we've used Human Playback to add some phrasing and extra dynamic punch to Finale projects. Now, it's time to branch out and make it swing.

1. Expand the Playback Controls window. Mac users, click on the triangle to the left of the control buttons. Windows users, click on the Speaker button.
2. From the Human Playback Style menu, select Jazz.

None
✓ Standard
Baroque
Classical
Romantic
21st Century
Marching Band
Viennese Waltz
Light Waltz
Funk
Jazz
Latin
Pop
Reggae
Rock
Samba
Custom...

 For those of you who tried Human Playback out on tunes with multiple feels, such as "On Green Dolphin Street," take heart. Human Playback now comes in a handy-dandy plug-in version so it can be applied to a specific region allowing multiple feels in the same piece. This is done using Mass Edit tool to select the region and applying the Plug-in, located in the New Plug-Ins for 2005 submenu, to apply the selected style.

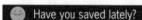
11_Hiccup_2.mus

😊 Have you saved lately?

Staff Styles—Just for Show

Staff Styles function as a mask for the staff or staves to which they are applied. You can hide notes completely, display them as rhythms with slashes, or transpose them to another key. In this chapter, we'll look at several different applications for Staff Styles, starting with one of the most common uses: slashes for rhythm-section parts.

In measure 4, the pianist is instructed to improvise a short phrase to fill in the space, since there is no written melody. This is indicated using chord slashes.

When preparing a part with chord slashes, I first enter rests in the measures, because chords and other markings will need to be attached to an entry. The rests will not affect playback and will help with proper spacing when applying allotments in Note or Beat Specific layouts.

To add the chord slashes:

1. Enter four quarter rests in measure 4.
2. Choose the Staff tool 📇.
3. Highlight only the treble staff of measure 4.
4. Select **Staff** > Apply Staff Styles.
5. Choose Slash Notation from the list, and then click OK.

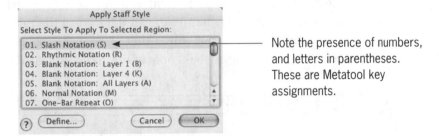

Note the presence of numbers, and letters in parentheses. These are Metatool key assignments.

Just like Expressions and Articulations, there are Metatools associated with Staff Styles. Try it using the Metatool for measures 8 and 12.

1. Using Simple Entry or Speedy Entry, enter four quarter rests in measures 8 and 12.
2. Choose the Staff tool.
3. Highlight only the treble-clef staff in measure 8.
4. Press the **S** key (the Metatool for Slash Notation).
5. Repeat for measure 12.

After a Staff Style has been applied, a blue bar will appear over the measure, when the Staff tool is active. This is so you can easily identify measures where Staff Styles have been used. This line is strictly for display purposes and will not print.

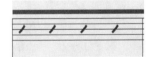

To keep track of the Staff Style used, the style's name can be added to the display.

• Select **Staff** > Show Staff Style Names.

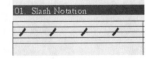

The blue Staff Style bars can be turned off.

• Select **Staff** > Show Staff Styles, to toggle it off.

When Show Staff Styles is unchecked, there are no lines over the measures, but the Staff Styles are all still active and displaying. Turning off Show Staff Styles does not turn off the styles themselves, just the blue lines.

233

In measure 11, there are slashes on beats 3 and 4. Staff Styles can be applied to a partial measure. First, the Select Partial Measure function has to be enabled.

1. Choose the Staff tool .
2. Select **Edit** > Select Partial Measures.
3. Drag-select to highlight only beats 3 and 4 of measure 11.
4. Select **Staff** > Apply Staff Styles and then choose "Slash Notation," or just use the Slash Notation Metatool (S). Then click OK.

Measures 13 through 24 contain a mix of alternate notation styles. The treble staff contains a background part that a horn section might play. The bass staff is for the rhythm section, and contains alternate notation that indicates what should be accented or played in a specific rhythm. The "Rhythmic Notation" Staff Style requires notes and rests to be entered. Pitch does not matter to the look of the final product, but for the purpose of playback, make it something that works harmonically with the rest of the composition. I suggest using the bass note of the chord indicated in the original.

Enter the notation in bars 13 through 24

Measures 13, 14, 16, 20, and 24 require Slash Notation.

*   Using the Staff tool, highlight each measure, and use the **S** key Metatool to quickly apply the Staff Style.

Measures 17, 18, 21, and 22 require Rhythmic Notation. Use the **R** key Metatool for applying Rhythmic Notation.

*   Using the Staff tool , highlight bars 17 and 18, and use the **R** key Metatool to apply the Rhythmic Notation style.

The other measures require a combination of slash and rhythmic notation. In measure 15, the first half of the measure requires Rhythmic Notation.

1. Confirm that **Edit** > Select Partial Measures is activated. This will enable you to select the specific beat or beats to be affected.
2. Drag-select to highlight the first two beats of measure 15.
3. Press the **R** key (Metatool for Rhythmic Notation).
4. Highlight beats 3 and 4 of measure 15.
5. Press the **S** key (Metatool for Slash Notation).
6. Enter the Staff Styles for measures 19, 21, 22, and 23.

Some Staff Styles can be copied with the Mass Edit tool. They are automatically included when Move Everything is selected in the Mass Edit menu.

Drummers Read?!?

Drummer jokes are many and widely told, but since they've gone through the trouble to set up all that equipment, you might as well give them something nice to look at.

 For notated drum parts, I use Layer 1 for all stems up notation, Layer 2 for the bass drum and any other stems down notation, and Layer 3 for any ensemble cues.

Remember, when entering with a MIDI keyboard, play the notes where the drums sound in the staff, not the pitches that appear on the staff. For a list of General MIDI percussion sounds and their respective MIDI note numbers, see chapter 9, page 174.

1. Enter the rhythm pattern in bar 1, layer 1, by either playing the following MIDI notes, or by entering the notes as they appear on the staff, if you are entering notes by using the mouse and Simple Entry's Note tools.

2. Go to Layer 2, and enter the bass drum part in measure 1 by playing the following notes.

The next nine measures are repeats of the above pattern. To enhance playback, copy the pattern, even though you'll eventually mask it with a Staff Style. Before reaching for the Mass Edit tool, there are a few details to consider. Selecting measure 1 of the drums and copying it 9 times will have the unintended effect of erasing the Coda sign from bar 10. This has to do with the default settings of the Copy/Paste function of the Mass Edit tool. Fortunately, this is a problem with a solution.

Selecting Specific Items to Copy in Mass Edit

1. Choose the Mass Edit tool 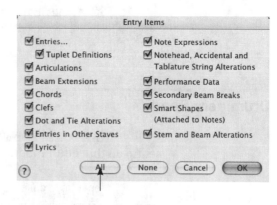.
2. Select **Mass Edit** > Copy Entry Items.
3. Click the All button, and then click OK.

Now, Mass Edit will only copy and paste these specific items, leaving other items uncopied and unchanged. A quick scan of the list confirms that Repeats are not on it. In case you are wondering, they can be found under **Mass Edit** > Copy Measure Items; more on that later.

4. Highlight measure 1 of the drum part, and drag it to measure 2.
5. Enter "9" for the number of times to copy, and click OK.

When reading a repetitive rhythmic pattern, it is easy to become lost. To combat this, most percussion parts contain single- or double-bar repeats. In many cases, these repeats are also numbered. Another advantage of repeat bars is that they take up less room, so the music fits on fewer pages. Measure-repeat symbols are staff styles.

1. Choose the Staff tool.
2. Highlight measures 2 through 10 of the drum part.
3. Press the letter O key (the Metatool for One-Bar Repeats).

A quick tap of the Space Bar for playback will show that our pattern is still there, playing back in every measure, but the performer will only need to read the pattern one time.

Numbering Repeated Measures

Next, add some numbers from the Number Repeated Measures Plug-in to help the performer count how many times to play it.

1. Choose the Mass Edit tool.
2. Highlight measures 1 through 10.
3. Select **Plug-ins** > Measures > Number Repeated Measures.

Each measure, 1 through 9, now has a number inserted as a Measure Expression. Note that the plug-in can only accommodate single digit numbers. There is an easy solution for measure 10. I don't think it is necessary to number bar 1. I'll delete that expression, edit it by adding a zero, and place it in measure 10.

1. Choose the Expression tool.
2. Click the handle for the "1" expression, and press Delete.

3. Double-click measure 10 on the drum staff.
4. Scroll down the Expression list and locate the number "1." You will see all nine numbers together.
5. Highlight the "1," and then click Edit.
6. Add the zero to make it a 10. Click OK, then Select.
7. Under the Show On heading, choose This Staff Only, and click OK.

Adjusting the Expression Baseline

One last cosmetic touch is to move the repeat numbers down closer to the staff.

1. With the Expression Tool activated, select **Expression** > Adjust Above Staff Baseline.
2. Click on the drum staff.
3. Drag the second baseline arrow (on the left) down towards the staff.

The baseline arrows function exactly as those in the Chord and Lyric tools. The second arrow lowers the baseline only for the drum staff.

Measure 11 has a different drumbeat, and therefore requires a little more note entry. Here's the pattern.

MIDI Entry   Mouse Entry

Using the Drum Groove Plug-In

The drum part for the solo section consists of slashes and cues for the background figures. I would still like to have something for playback, so I'm going to use the Drum Groove plug-in to add a little lift to this section of the piece.

Drum grooves are MIDI files that contain a specific drum pattern or groove that can be imported into an existing Finale file. The part can be added to an existing staff or the Plug-in can create a new one when the file is loaded.

1. Choose the Mass Edit tool ⊙.
2. Highlight measures 13 through 24.

3. Select **Plug-ins** > Scoring and Arranging > Drum Groove.
4. Scroll down, and choose "Straight Swing."
5. Click the Existing Staff button, and select "Drum Set" from the popup menu. Then click OK.

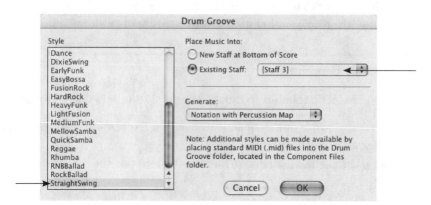

The notes are entered in the drum staff. Tap the Space Bar to audition the new part.

One last bit of notation to enter: ensemble cues, at the coda. Once again, I'll translate it into MIDI notes.

Ensemble Cues: The 75% Solution

Ensemble cues are a part of most drum set parts. My approach is to set aside a layer just for cues. That way, I can set up the layer for the stem direction, tie direction, and rest offsets that I need without affecting any other notation.

To set up a cue layer:
1. Select **Options** > Document Options, and then choose Layers from the list in the left column.
2. In the Settings For popup menu, choose "Layer 3."
3. Check Freeze Stems and Ties and choose "Up" from the popup menu.
4. Check Freeze Ties in the Same Direction as Stems.

5. Check Adjust Floating Rests by, and enter "8" for the number of Steps. Then click OK.

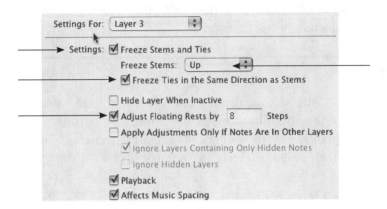

While you're in the Document Options neighborhood, there is one change required under the Beaming category. The current beam setting will interfere with placement of the rests. The will not move to the distances set in the Layers dialog box.

1. Choose "Beams" in the left column of the Document Options window.
2. Uncheck Include Rests When Beaming In Groups of Four.

One more thing: it's those pesky stems again. Just like in chapter 10, the quarter- and half-note stems are shorter than the eighth-note stems. Go to the Stems window, and make them all the same length (see chapter 10, page 196).

Disabling a Layer's Playback

The next setup issue is playback. I could have turned off playback for the entire layer in the Layers dialog box, but that might come back to haunt me later, if I want to add more parts to my sketch. I'd rather turn off the playback only for Layer 3 of the drum staff.

1. Select **Window** > Instrument List.
2. Click the triangle to the left of Staff 3 in the Staff Name column, to show playback information for its individual layers.
3. Click on the green square in the P column to the right of Layer 3, to deactivate it. This mutes playback only on Layer 3 of the selected staff.
4. Click the Close button in the window bar to close it.

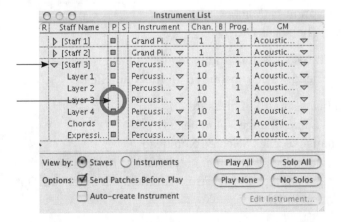

Enter the notes for the cues beginning in measure 15. If you are using MIDI for note entry, remember that you must play B♭ a ninth below middle C to place the note in the correct space. If you are entering notes with the mouse, click on top of the staff. Don't worry about the noteheads; that's next.

Changing Noteheads

One of the tradeoffs with the drum set parts is when solid noteheads and × noteheads need to occupy the same line or space. The choice is which one is formatted and which is altered later. In this case, the × noteheads are formatted to appear, and the cue notes will need to have their noteheads changed to the normal solid and open noteheads.

In the file you are working on, the × noteheads are programmed by the Setup Wizard when the staff is created.

The solid noteheads required for the cues will require changing the notehead symbol.

To change noteheads:
1. Switch to Layer 3, in the bottom-left corner of the document window.
2. Select **Options** > Show Active Layer Only.

Now only Layer 3 is displayed, and any changes we make using the Mass Edit tool will only affect the notes in Layer 3 of the region selected.

3. Choose the Mass Edit tool 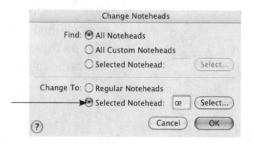.
4. Confirm that **Edit** > Select Partial Measures is activated.
5. Highlight measure 15 through the second beat of measure 21.
6. Select **Mass Edit** > Change > Noteheads.
7. Next to Change to, click Selected Notehead.
8. Click Select, and locate the Solid Notehead in the character list (character 207), or type the keystroke for the solid notehead: Option-Q (Mac) or Alt-Q (Windows). Then click OK.

The next note in bar 21 is a half note, so an open notehead needs to be substituted for the × notehead.

1. Highlight beats 3 and 4 of measure 21.
2. Select **Mass Edit** > Change > Noteheads.
3. Next to Change to, click Selected Notehead.
4. Click Select, and locate the open notehead (for half notes) in the character list (character 250), or type the keystroke for the open notehead, Option-H (Mac) or Alt-H (Windows). Then click OK.

5. Highlight beats 1 and 2 of bar 22, and repeat the steps for changing the noteheads to solid noteheads.
6. Highlight beats 3 and 4 of bar 22, and repeat the steps for changing the noteheads to open noteheads.
7. Highlight bar 23, and repeat the steps for changing the noteheads to solid noteheads.

Changing Note Size

Now that all the notes are entered, they must be reduced to cue-note size. I use 75% reduction for my cues. The fastest way to change the size of a full measure or more is to use Mass Edit.

1. Make sure Show Active Layer is still checked and that Layer 3 is the active layer.
2. Choose the Mass Edit tool 🔘.
3. Highlight measures 13 through measure 24.
4. Select **Mass Edit** > Change > Note Size.
5. Enter "75" for the percentage of reduction, and click OK.
6. Select **View** > Show Active Layer Only (so it is not checked in the menu). This will switch back to displaying all layers.

Staff Styles: Creating Your Own Style

One last detail is hiding the drum pattern imported by the Drum Groove Plug-in.

• In measure 13, select the Staff tool and use the **S** key for slashes,

Single-bar repeats present a new challenge. If we used the same single-bar repeat Staff Style from the first chorus of the piece, it would hide our cue notes, since it is set to mask entries in other layers. So for this application, a new Staff Style must be defined. I'll also let you in on another way of applying Staff Styles.

1. Choose the Staff tool 🔘.
2. Select **Staff** > Define Staff Styles.
3. Click the New button.
4. For Style name, enter "22. One Bar Repeat for Cues."
5. Check Copyable. (This allows coping of the style in Mass Edit.)
6. To the right of Alternate Notation, click Select.
7. Click the One-Bar Repeat(s) button.
8. Check Show Notes in Other Layers (the cues).
9. Check Show Items Attached To Notes In Other Layers. (Articulations will be added later.) Then click OK twice, to return to the score.

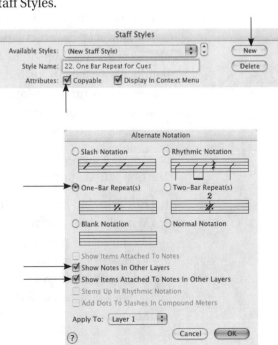

Staff Styles can also be applied by using the contextual menu.

1. Highlight measures 14 through 24.
2. To access the contextual menu, Control-click (Mac) or Right-click (Windows) inside the highlighted area.
3. Scroll down to the bottom of the popup menu, and choose "22. One-Bar Repeat for Cues."

16. Stemless Notes
17. Flute Transposition
18. Bb Clarinet Transposition
19. Eb Alto Saxophone Transposition
20. Bb Tenor Saxophone Transposition
21. Lyrics and Chords Only
22. One Bar Repeat for Cues

Next, enter the performance information. My preferred order of working is articulations first, followed by Smart Shapes for slurs and crescendos, all expressions, and then Chord Symbols. This order begins with the closest marks to each note, and works outward. The positioning of each subsequent item is based on the previous one so there are no collisions and minimal adjustments.

> Avoid going back and forth to the tool palette when working on a file. The larger the monitor, the longer those trips take. Do as much as you can with the tool selected before choosing the next tool you need to use.

Adding Expressions: Articulate Your Thoughts

The articulations available in the Jazz font set are a bit different from the more traditional Maestro font set, incorporating symbols predominantly found in the jazz idiom. I recommend clicking on an entry and scrolling down the library to become familiar with all the available shapes. The Metatools for commonly used articulations are the same in both the Jazz font and the Maestro font.

1. Choose the Articulation tool .
2. Enter the articulations for the piano part, except for the notes in measures 21 and 22 (see pg. 226).

The articulations in measures 21 and 22 need to be positioned on the stem side of the notes. However, the articulations in the library are set up to automatically position themselves on the note side of the entry. You could manually reposition them by dragging the handle above each note, but that is very time consuming and results in a non-uniform placement of the articulation. The solution is to duplicate the articulations required, change their automatic positioning defaults, and create new Metatools. Since the finger numbers are not used in this piece, I'll use the number 1 through 5 keys for the new Metatools.

The first articulation in bar 21 is the accent.

1. Confirm that Layer 1 is the active layer.
2. With the Articulation tool activated, hold down the Shift key and select the **1** key for assigning the new accent to Metatool 1.
3. Choose the accent (shape 2), and click the Duplicate button. This copies the selected shape, creating a new library item with its own number. Finale is not confused by two different accents; it's just a library number that gets displayed according to whatever display options you assign to it.

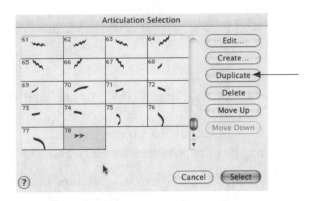

4. Click the Edit button.
5. Under the Positioning heading, choose "On Stem Side" from the Positioning popup menu.
6. Check Inside Slurs. Then click OK twice to return to the score.

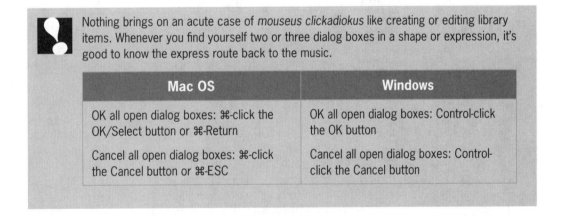

Nothing brings on an acute case of *mouseus clickadiokus* like creating or editing library items. Whenever you find yourself two or three dialog boxes in a shape or expression, it's good to know the express route back to the music.

Mac OS	Windows
OK all open dialog boxes: ⌘-click the OK/Select button or ⌘-Return	OK all open dialog boxes: Control-click the OK button
Cancel all open dialog boxes: ⌘-click the Cancel button or ⌘-ESC	Cancel all open dialog boxes: Control-click the Cancel button

Repeat these steps for the staccato dot and the tenuto mark. You will need this for the drum set cues in bar 17. Use the 2 and 3 keys for the stem-side shapes. Try the express route on step 6.

Slurs and Articulations

To enter the slurs:
1. Choose the Slur tool from the Smart Shape palette.
2. Enter the slurs in bars 2, 6, 10, 13, 21, 22, and 26.
3. Choose the Crescendo tool.
4. Enter the crescendo marks in bar 13 and 14.

If you see a collision between a slur and an articulation, check the articulation's designer dialog box. Chances are, an entire score's worth of collisions can be cleared up with a single click. The slurs on beat 4 of bars 2, 6, and 10 are colliding with the accents. Here's the solution.

1. Choose the Articulation tool .
2. To select the contextual menu, Control-click (Mac) or Right-click (windows) the accent's handle.
3. Select Edit Articulation Definition from the popup menu.
4. Under the Positioning heading, check Inside Slurs, and click OK.

The articulation now pushes the slur down, and all three marks are fixed at once. The upstemmed articulations already have this checked so they will not need to be edited.

Expressions in Jazz (Fonts)

1. Choose the Expression tool *mf*.
2. Add the dynamics in bar 1, 13, 15, 17, and 18, using Measure Expressions.

When using the JazzText font, it is possible to use the under and over brackets and boxes that a copyist would routinely make with a pen and ruler. Some samples already exist in the Expression Selection library.

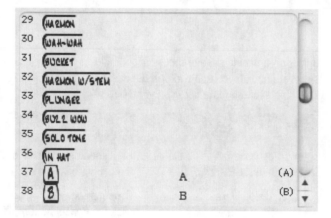

There are several components that make up these shapes. Brackets might include a left-side bracket that begins the over- or underline, characters that extend the over- or underline, and a right-side bracket, which also contains part of the over- or underline. For boxes, there are left and right sides as well as characters to extend the middle portion of the box, as necessary. The middle extenders for all shapes come in two varieties: those that add a space to the text and those that don't; more on this, in a bit. For rehearsal letters, there are characters that include both letter and box in the same character. To view the Jazz Text font's character set, select **Help** > Jazz Character Sets > JazzText Font Character Set (pages C61–C64).

OVER-TEXT BRACKETS

Left Brackets

Thin end, Short Line:	⌐	Option + Shift + O (Mac) Alt + 0175 (Win)
Thin end, Long Line:	⌐	Option + , (comma) (Mac) Alt + 0178 (Win)
Thick end, Short Line:	⌐	[(Mac and Win)
Thick end, Long Line:	⌐	Option + U, Shift + O (Mac) Alt + 0133 (Win)

Right Brackets

Thin end, Short Line:	⌐	Option + Shift + = (Mac) Alt + 0177 (Win)
Thin end, Long Line:	⌐	Option + Y (Mac) Alt + 0180 (Win)
Thick end, Short Line:	⌐	] (Mac and Win)
Thick end, Long Line:	⌐	Option + E, A (Mac) Alt + 0135 (Win)

Middle Extender Lines

Short Line (Single character):	–	\ or Option + 5 (Mac) \ (Win)
Medium Line (2 character):	–	Shift + 6 (Mac) Alt + 0176 (Win)
Long Line (5 characters):	—	Option + . (period) or Option + U, Shift + U (Mac) Alt + 0134 or Alt + 0179 (Win)

UNDER-TEXT BRACKETS

Left Brackets

Thin end, Short Line:	∟	Option + `, U (Mac) Alt + 0157 (Win)
Thin end, Long Line:	∟	Option + M or Option + T (Mac) Alt + 0160 or Alt + 0181 (Win)
Thick end, Short Line:	∟	Option + N, N (Mac) Alt + 0150 (Win)
Thick end, Long Line:	∟	Option + U, O (Mac) Alt + 0154 (Win)

Right Brackets

Thin end, Short Line:	⌐	Option + U, U (Mac) Alt + 0159 (Win)
Thin end, Long Line:	⌐	Option + 4 or Option + W (Mac) Alt + 0162 or Alt 0183 (Win)
Thick end, Short Line:	⌐	Option + `, O (Mac) Alt + 0152 (Win)
Thick end, Long Line:	⌐	Option + E, U (Mac) Alt + 0156 (Win)

Middle Extender Lines

Short Line (Single character):	–	Option +E, O (Mac) Alt + 0151 (Win)
Medium Line (2 character):	–	Option + I, U (Mac) Alt + 0158 (Win)
Long Line (5 characters):	—	Option + D or Shift + Option + 8 or Option + N, O (Mac) Alt + 0155 or Alt + 0161, or Alt + 0182 (Win)

JazzText Font Bracket Characters

TEXT BOXES

Complete Box

Single character size box:	◻	Shift + Option + ; (semicolon) (Mac) Alt + 242 (Win)

Left-Side Box

Single Character:	⊏	Shift + ' (apostrophe) (Mac and Win)
Two Character:	⊏	Shift + [(Mac and Win)
Four Character:	⊏	Option + U, Shift + A (Mac) Alt + 0128 (Win)
Single Character, Brace End:	⊱	Option + 3 (Mac) Alt + 0163 (Win)
Four Character, Brace End:	⊏	Option + 7 (Mac) Alt + 0166 (Win)

Right-Side Box

Single Character:	⊐	Shift +] (Mac and Win)
Three Character:	⊐	Option + Shift + C (Mac) Alt + 0130 (Win)
Single Character, Brace End:	⊐	Option + 8 (Mac) Alt + 0165 (Win)
Three Character, Brace End:	⊐	Option + R (Mac) Alt + 0168 (Win)

Middle Extender Lines

Single Character:	=	Shift + – (minus) or Option + 6 (Mac) Shift + – (minus) (Win)	Four Character:	=	Option + S or Option + Shift+ A (Mac) Alt + 0129 or Alt + 0167 (Win)
Two Character:	=	Shift + \ or Option +`, E (Mac) Shift + \ (Win)			

To create the "Fills" indication in bar 4, the \ (backslash) will be used to continue the over-text bracket from left to right. In the JazzText Font, the \ symbol will not add a space to the existing text—just the bracket line.

1. Choose the Expression tool .
2. Double-click on beat 1 of bar 4. Notice that with the Staff Style applied, the cursor does not display the note to indicate that a Note Expression is possible, but it will be available in the Expression Selection window.
3. Click the Create button, JazzText 12 (point) Plain should be automatically selected.
4. Type: **[Fl\l\l\s]**
5. Click the Note Positioning tab, and set both the Horizontal Alignments to "Left."
6. Set the Vertical Position to "Above Staff Baseline." Then close out of all the windows with one click: ⌘-click (Mac) or Control-click (Windows) the OK button.

(FILLS)

The trick is getting the bracket right, so that it does not extend past the right bracket and that there are no small gaps in the line extending over or under (or both) the text. Multiple word expressions present a challenge. The Ü character (Option-U then Shift-U, Mac, or Alt-U then Shift-U, Windows) is the longest version of the above text line; it's length is equal to five characters. The length of the expression requires the long line to be combined with one short-line character at the end, to meet the right bracket.

1. Double-click on beat 3 of bar 11.
2. Click the Create button
3. Type: [SÜolo [Space] ÜBre∞ak]
4. Click the Note Positioning tab and set the Horizontal Alignments, both of them, to Left.
5. Set the Vertical Position to "Above Staff Baseline." Then ⌘-click (Mac) or Control-click (Windows) OK.

(SOLO BREAK)

The DC al Coda signs are already entered with the correct under-bracket characters. For the Solos indication, use the box. Locate the characters in the Jazz Character Sets. These can be accessed in the Help menu.

> Anyone planning to make extensive use of bracketed expressions should spend some downtime building a library of commonly used expressions. These are keystroke intensive as well as mentally challenging. You'll thank yourself on the first all-nighter.

11_Hiccup_3.mus

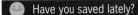

😊 Have you saved lately?

Untangling the Chords

In chapter 3, chords were entered using Type Into Score. In chapter 4, they were entered via MIDI. In this example, the chord symbols are a little bit more complex, and there are more chord entry options to help deal with them. We will also use Metatools to make the process of entering chord symbols more efficient.

 Before entering chord symbols, check to make sure the correct fonts and sizes are selected in the Document Options window (**Options** > Document Options, and then Fonts). For this example, the Symbol should be set to 18-point JazzCord Plain, the Suffix set to 12-point JazzText, and the Alteration set to 18-point Jazz.

Manual Input

Chords are entered into the score by clicking on an entry, and typing the letter and suffix into the Chord Definition dialog box. Suffixes can be typed in or selected from the library. The Select button is located in the Advanced settings area of the dialog box. If it it's not visible, click the Show Advanced button in the dialog box.

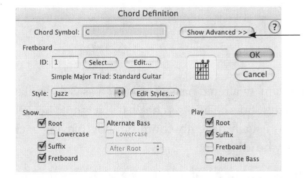

Click the Show Advanced button to access the chord definition controls.

 Program scale steps 1 through 7 as Metatools on the 1 through 7 number keys. I use the 8 for the minor 7, flat-5 suffix. The rest of the keyboard could be used to create Metatools with specific suffixes. This can be in a template, or set up piece by piece. Insert by clicking on an entry while holding down the appropriate key. To add or change a suffix, click on the handle and select the new suffix. (For more information about templates, please download the PDF from the Web site.)

In the Chord tool, Metatools can be used in Manual Input mode. By holding down the Metatool key and clicking a note or rest with a chord attached to it, this attached chord will instantly become the programmed chord for that Metatool key.

To program a chord Metatool:
1. Choose the Chord tool 🎵.
2. Select **Chord** > Manual Input.
3. Press Shift-1.

This brings up the Chord Definition dialog box. I want the 1 key to be the tonic of the key, so:

4. Next to Chord, enter "C" (the letter for the root of the key selected in the piece), or enter "1" in the box to the right of Root: Scale Tone.

Type the chord letter here, or the scale number here.

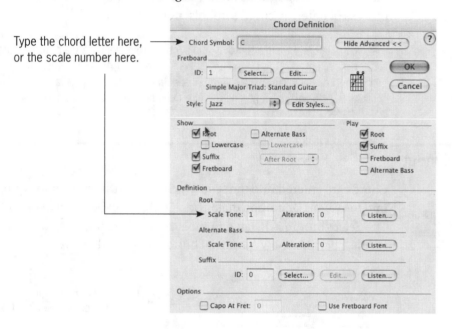

If you attempt to program an altered bass chord (such as **C/G**), make sure the checkbox for Altered Bass under the Show heading is checked; if it is not checked, the bass note will not be displayed. I don't usually have my chord symbols playing back, so I also uncheck all boxes under the Play heading.

5. Click OK, then repeat for the second scale step, assigning the Metatool to the 2 key, and typing the chord letter, or the number 2 in the Root Scale tone dialog box.
6. Continue for scale tones 3 through 7.

For the 8 key, I assign the minor 7, flat-5.

1. Enter the chord letter and a lowercase b for flat, or type **7** for the Root Scale Tone. (No alteration symbol is needed if a natural lowers the scale step.)
2. Unless you typed the letter, press the Tab key to advance to the Alteration box.
3. Enter "-1" in the Alteration box to lower the Root Scale Tone a half step. (Positive numbers raise the Root Scale Tone.) Then click OK.

Type Into Score

The Type Into Score method was presented in chapter 3, and will probably be the main method of entering chord symbols for most users. Here are a few things to remember when entering suffixes. For accidentals, use the lowercase b for a flat and the # (number sign, Shift-3) for the sharp, as necessary. Finale will automatically replace those symbols with the correct musical symbol from the selected music font.

For more complex suffixes it may be easier to select them from the library rather than type them. If you are not sure about a specific suffix and want to see what is in the library, follow these steps as well. I'll illustrate with the D♭9(♯11) chord in measure 2.

1. Choose the Chord tool .
2. Click on the E♭ in measure 2.
3. Type the D.
4. Type ":" (colon) then "0" (zero), and then press the Space Bar. This keystroke combination will bring up the Suffix Library window.
5. Choose the 9(♯11) suffix, library number 56, and click Select, or double-click the symbol.

In addition to the symbols already entered in the Jazz font's default suffix library, the JazzCord font contains suffixes that provide the entire suffix as one font character. Most of these are more complex chords, and using these characters will save a lot of manual positioning. Check the Jazz Character Sets in the documentation to see what suffixes are available before you begin constructing a custom suffix.

> Be aware of the letter case when typing suffixes. Finale will not recognize maj as Maj when it is typed into the score, and it will insist that a new suffix be created. If you are not sure, use the :-Return/Enter keystroke combination to select the suffix and remember it for next time, or learn the number. and use the colon-suffix number to save keystrokes on those long, complex chord suffixes.

MIDI Input, One- and Two-Staff Analysis

I've lumped MIDI Input, and One- and Two-Staff Analysis together because in all of them, Finale tries to interpret the information given to produce the chord symbol. Using Finale to analyze chords, played in via MIDI, works best with simple harmonic structures, since the program does not fill in missing chord tones or sort out inversions accurately. If Finale can't figure a chord out on its own, you will see the Unknown Chord Suffix dialog box.

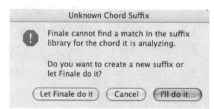

The choice becomes yours: to accept Finale's best guess or choose/define a symbol yourself. If you do it yourself, it will be the same process, and dialog box, as Manual Input.

To edit a chord symbol once it is entered, first press the ESC key to switch to the Selection tool. Edit a chord symbol by using Control-click (Mac) or Right-click (Windows), and from the contextual menu, choose Edit Chord Definition.

> For reasons of speed and accuracy, I recommend using either the Metatool option of Manual Input or Type into Score, instead of MIDI input.

Creating a Chord Suffix

Finale comes with a library of chord suffixes already installed. To view them:

1. With the Chord Tool selected, select **Chord** > Manual Input,
2. Click on any note.
3. When the Chord Definition Dialog box opens, check the button to the right of the Chord Symbol entry box, to show the advanced options. If the button reads Show Advanced, click it. If it reads Hide Advanced, proceed to the next step.

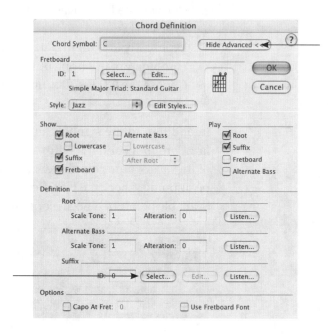

4. Under the Definition heading is the Suffix area. Click the Select button here, to view the Chord Suffix Selection window. Use the scroll bar to view the entire library.
5. Click Cancel twice to return to the music.

The Jazz font has its own chord symbol library and a separate chord symbol font. But even with all these choices, there are times when you must create a new suffix. In our example, we'll need to create two new suffixes. The first is in bar 3, the C7(13) chord.

For the first example, use Type Into Score as the entry method. Refer to the notation example at the beginning of this chapter (see page 225).

1. Enter the first three symbols, and position the cursor for the C7(13) chord.
2. Type "C7(13)," and press the Space Bar. The following dialog box appears whenever a suffix is entered that is not in Finale's library. Click Yes.

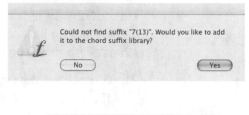

This brings up the Chord Suffix Editor dialog box. The suffix is already entered, but it is positioned on the baseline. In handwritten music, the numbers in the suffix are traditionally raised up off the baseline.

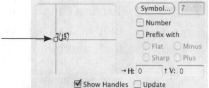

1. Press the Tab key twice to get to the V (Vertical) positioning box.
2. Enter 12 EVPUs (0.04167 inches) to raise the 7 a bit above the baseline.
3. Click the Next button, and similarly set the V value for the (character above the baseline.

4. Click Next again, and repeat this process until all the characters of the suffix are raised up off the baseline.

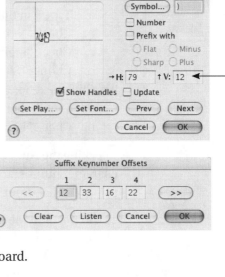

I'd Like to Teach the Chord to Sing

To make this chord symbol play back, and to help Finale correctly analyze it for the rest of the piece, follow these steps:

1. Click the Set Play button.
2. Click the Listen Button.
3. At the prompt, play the root on your MIDI keyboard.
4. At the prompt for the suffix, play the rest of the chord voicing on your MIDI keyboard.

Finale will display the distance from the root, in semitones away from the root, for each note of the chord you just played. If you made a mistake you can edit here or just press Listen and play the chord again.

5. Click OK when you are finished, or take the express route back to the music. Otherwise, four clicks await you, as you journey back.

Suffix with Two Chord Alterations

The next suffix you'll need to create is a bit more complex, since it contains two alterations to the basic chord structure. It's the C7(♯9,13) chord in bar 7. Create the symbol using Manual Input. The reason is the numbers of characters in the symbol. Everything except the 7 will be moved or altered in some way. Do not attempt to use spaces in a suffix for any reason. If there is a blank character in a suffix, Finale will not display anything entered after it. The space will be created by manual positioning.

1. With the Chord tool selected, select **Chord** > Manual Input.
2. Click on the note in bar 7, second half of beat 2
3. Under the Suffix heading, click the Select button.
4. Choose the 7 suffix.
5. Click the Duplicate button. The duplicate feature is a great way to build on basic suffixes in the Chord tool. This way part of the new suffix is already entered and positioned.
6. Click Edit. This opens the chord suffix editor.

I want to stack the alterations so the symbol takes up less room horizontally. This requires a larger set of parentheses.

7. Click Next, to advance beyond the 7 to where we'll create a ((open parenthesis) character.
   a. Click Set Font.
   b. Select JazzCord from the Font List.
   c. Enter 24 for the Font Size, and then click OK.
   d. Type < in the Symbol box for the large open parenthesis.

8. Click Next, to create the ♯9.
    a. Type 9 in the Symbol box.
    b. Check "Number."
    c. Check "Prefix with."
    d. Choose "Sharp."
9. Click Next, to create the "13."
    a. Type 13 in the Symbol box.
    b. Check Number.

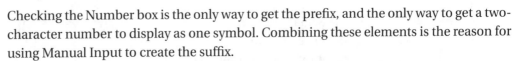

Checking the Number box is the only way to get the prefix, and the only way to get a two-character number to display as one symbol. Combining these elements is the reason for using Manual Input to create the suffix.

10. To position the alterations:
    a. Click the Prev button to return to the 9.
    b. Drag the 9 up to create room for the 13 to fit underneath it.
    c. Click Next, to advance to the 13.
    d. Drag the 13 underneath the 9.

No magic here, just going by eye. If it looks wrong in the score, return here to edit it further until it looks correct.

11. To add the close parenthesis:
    a. Click Next.
    b. Click the Set Font button.
    c. Choose JazzCord, set the size to 24 point, and click OK.
    d. Type > for the large close parenthesis.
    e. Make any positioning changes you feel necessary.
12. Take the express route back to the music and check the suffix.

Return to the Chord Suffix Editor to fix any spacing you don't like. For my taste, the open parenthesis is a little too close to the 7. Remember, this is trial and error time and you can always come back to it later.

If you want this symbol to play back, follow the steps from the previous chord symbol (see page 251).

There are many subtle variations on chord symbol nomenclature. For example, a major chord can be indicated with ma, Ma, maj, Maj, or a triangle. Music publishers each have their own preferences, and even they don't agree on one standard way of spelling chords. I've created several libraries of suffixes: one for my own work and a few others for different clients. Consider that option if the suffixes included with Finale do not suit your preferences.

Multiple Alterations with Fonts other than JazzCord

When using a font that does not have the larger parentheses, you have plenty of choices. Load a new document into Finale, and check the suffix library. You will see several options included in the library.

Option 1. Position the alterations horizontally. Note that in typing this suffix onto the score, Finale did not substitute the music font sharp for the number sign. This substitution only occurs when Finale can match a full suffix with something in the existing library.

$$C7(\#9,13)$$

Option 2. No parentheses. The next three examples were created manually, so the sharp is the music character.

$$C7\,\overset{\#9}{13}$$

Other possibilities include using a set of parentheses for each alteration or increasing the point size of a single set of parentheses, in this case 24 point, to cover both alterations.

$$C7\binom{(\#9)}{(13)} \qquad C7\begin{bmatrix}\#9\\13\end{bmatrix}$$

Chord with an Alternate Bass

In measure 9, there is a chord with an alternate bass note. If you are using Type Into Score or Manual Input:

- Type Dmi7/G.

The / mark indicates an alternate bass note. Finale automatically handles this in the Chord Definition dialog box.

For any other entry method, you will have to do this manually in the Chord Definition dialog box.

1. Enter the scale step number in the Alternate Bass box.
2. Check the Alternate Bass box or it will not display.
3. Select the Suffix. Then click OK, and return to the score.

Do not check Put Under Root! This checkbox is only used for polychords, where one symbol is above the other with a horizontal line between them.

Chord Alignment and Spacing

When chords are entered, they are centered over the entries to which they are attached. Most players I have encountered prefer the symbols to begin on the chord, or in Finale's terms, left aligned on the beat where they begin.

1. Choose the Chord tool [CM7].
2. Select **Chord** > Left Align chords.

The Automatic Spacing feature does not factor chord symbols into the equation for laying out music. This setting is a document option and can be enabled.

1. Select **Options** > Document Options.
2. Choose Music Spacing in the left column.
3. Under the Avoid Collision of heading, check Chords.

This does not automatically fix any spacing problems; the music must be re-spaced using the Music Spacing function of the Mass Edit tool, with the new parameter (chord symbols) added. There is one problem I have encountered with respacing and chord symbols, especially long chord symbols: The results can produce music that is awkwardly spaced due to the chord symbol (hence, the reason it is not active in the default settings). My advice is to only respace measures where there are chord symbol collisions, not the whole document. Sometimes, a little manual repositioning can do the trick, and these steps can be avoided.

1. Choose the Mass Edit tool .
2. Highlight the measure or measures where chord symbols are colliding.
3. Select **Mass Edit** > Music Spacing > Apply Note Spacing.

11_Hiccup_4.mus

For vertical space problems, the Chord tool uses the same baseline positioning as in Expression Tool and Lyric Tool. Use the baseline arrows to adjust the height of the symbols for the entire piece, or a specific system.

😊 Have you saved lately?

Layout—It No Longer Means Don't Play!

254

Time to get the score ready for printing. When entering the music, I recommend working from the inside out. When setting the page layout, I work from the outside in, beginning with the largest element: the page itself. Once the page size is set, then set the page margins, after that the staff systems, and then end with the measures and text. Begin by setting the overall percentage sizes.

1. Select **View** > Page View.
2. Choose the Resize tool %.
3. Click in the top-left corner of the page.
4. Change the Page Percentage to 88%, and click OK.

With the Update Page Format box checked, any changes made here will be amended to the defaults for the document. If any new pages are created, they will be created at 88%, not 100%.

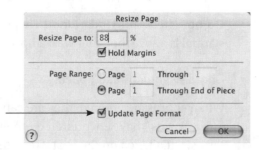

This choice of percentage (88%) is the amount a 9.5 by 12.5 inch of manuscript paper needs to be reduced to fit on a letter size (8.5 by 11) piece of paper. Next, eliminate the wide margin on the left of the page. Trim the margins to 144 EVPUs (0.5 inch) on all sides.

1. Choose the Page Layout tool .
2. Select **Page Layout** > Page Margins > Edit Page Margins.
3. Set the Left page margin to 144 EVPUs (0.5 inches).
4. Set Change to "All Pages," and then click Apply.

These settings will provide more horizontal room on both pages. This will allow more music to fit on each system.

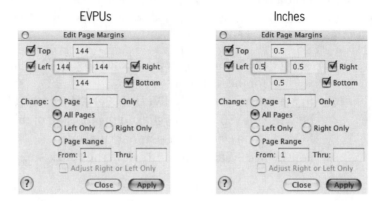

To update your document to use these new settings:

- Select **Edit** > Update Layout, or use the keystroke ⌘-\ (Mac) or Control-\ (Windows). The music will respace according to the new dimensions.

On "continuing pages" (pages after page 1), I like to have a little more room at the top of the page, or there could be a traffic jam with page numbers, titles, rehearsal numbers, and chords. In the example, this is only necessary for page 2.

1. Select **Page Layout** > Page Margins > Edit Page Margins.
2. Set the Top page margin 180 EVPUs (0.625 inches).
3. Set Change to Page 2 Only, and click Apply.

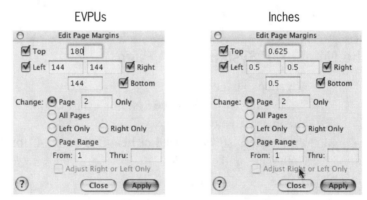

The next adjustment for page 1 is to distribute the systems more evenly on the page.

1. Select **Page Layout** > Space Systems Evenly.
2. Set Space Systems Evenly On to "Page 1 Only."
3. Set Distribute Systems to "Do Not Change the Number of Systems on Each Page." Then click OK.

Adding More Space for the Title

With extra room on a page, it looks best when that excess is spread around to all areas. Now focus on the staff systems. Some of the extra space can be transferred to the title area at the top of the page.

1. Select **Page Layout** > Systems > Edit Margins. The dialog box contains the margin settings for the first staff system.
2. In the Top box, enter 532 EVPUs (1.84722 inches). This number controls the space between the top Page margin and the top staff of the first system.
3. In the Left box, enter 0 to eliminate the indent.
4. For Change System, enter 1 Thru 1. Then click Apply.

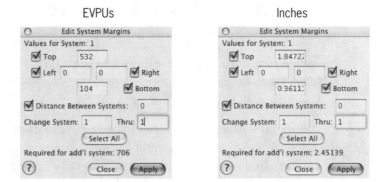

Leave the text alone, for now, and select page 2, to continue setting the page layout. This will help minimize going back and forth to the tool palette. Finish the page layout, before moving on to the text.

Changing the Number of Systems On A Page

1. Advance to page 2.
2. Select **Page Layout** > Space Systems Evenly. Note that Space Systems Evenly On is already set to page 2.
3. Under the Distribute Systems heading, enter "4" for the number of Systems on Each page, and click OK.

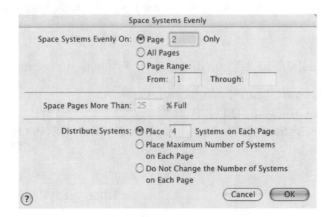

With a full page, Space Systems Evenly provides the perfect layout. The last system, which comprises the coda, will need to be indented on the left margin and shortened on the right margin.

Creating an Indented System for the Coda

Indenting a system can be accomplished by carefully dragging the system's handles, but I'll demonstrate using the Edit Margins dialog box, for greater precision.

1. Highlight the system handle for system 7, the coda.
2. Select **Page Layout** > Systems > Edit Margins. As you can see, when a system's (or set of systems') handle is highlighted, the Edit Margins dialog box appears with that system's number preset in the boxes, and with the Change System numbers set to your selection.
3. For the Left margin (indent), enter 244 EVPUs (0.84722 inches).
4. For the Right margin, enter 800 EVPUs (2.77778 inches). This is trial and error territory, so start with a round number and fine-tune to taste. Then click Apply.

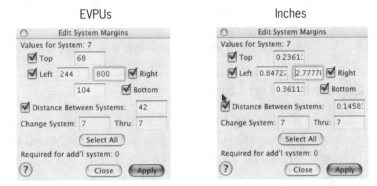

EVPUs   Inches

At this point, check the music on both pages of the example for any additional positioning changes that may be required. For example, you might need to move the chord symbols closer to the staff so that they do not collide with dynamics or measure numbers in the system above. Perhaps your dynamics should be moved up a little as well. Even when producing something informal, taking a few seconds to tweak the obvious positioning problems will help make rehearsals and performances easier.

Page Text and Coda Indications

The page size is set, the music has been entered, so it's now time to format the page text.

1. Go to page 1.
2. Choose the Text tool Ⓐ.
3. Double-click the handle of the title.
4. Select **Edit** > Select All the title text, or use the keystroke, ⌘-A (Mac) or Control-A (Windows).
5. Select **Text** > Size > 36.
6. Double-click the handle of the composer credit.

7. Select **Edit** > Select All the composer text, or use the keystroke, ⌘-A (Mac) or Control-A (Windows).
8. Select **Text** > Size > 18.

Create a text block for the instrumentation.

1. Double-click in the top-left corner of the page.
2. Select **Text** > Size > 24.
3. Type "Rhythm Section."
4. Click anywhere outside the text block to exit the block.
5. To position this new text element for positioning along the left margin, align the vertical crosshair line with the left barline of the music.
6. For the horizontal positioning, make sure it is above the title, but not closer than a quarter-inch to the top edge of the page.

The copyright needs a second line of text added to it.

1. Double-click the handle of the copyright.
2. Press the Option-Right Arrow key to move the cursor to the right side of the text.
3. Press Return/Enter.
4. Type "All Rights Reserved."
5. Click anywhere outside the text block to exit the block.

Positioning Elements in Tight Spaces

Go to page 2, and move to the top of the page. The top of the page is crowded, with chords, Expressions, and text blocks to be positioned around each other. In congested areas, use the Zoom tool to get a closer look.

1. Choose the Zoom tool ⊙.
2. Drag across the full top width of the page.
3. Select **View** > Show Rulers.

4. Choose the Expression tool 🔘.
5. Drag the "Solos" Expression closer to the staff.
6. Choose the Chord tool 🔘. If the baseline positioning arrows are not visible, click on the top staff.
7. Drag the third arrow from the left to lower the baseline closer to the staff.
8. Choose the Text tool 🅐.
9. Move up the page number and the continuing page title until they clear the Solos Expression, either by dragging their handles, or by using the Up Arrow key.

Adding the Coda to the Coda

The word "Coda" needs to be added in the space created by the indent. This could be added as a Text block, since there are no playback considerations for this text, but I recommend entering it as an Expression. Since I do a lot of score and parts work, I'd want this to be attached to each staff when I extract parts.

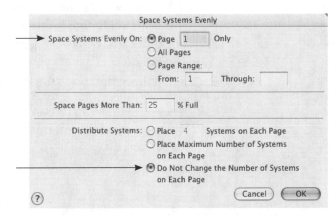

1. Choose the Expression tool .
2. Double-click on the top staff.
3. Create a new Measure Expression for the coda.
4. Set the font size to 36.
5. In the Measure Expression Assignment dialog box, set Show On to "Select This Staff Only."
6. Drag your new Coda Expression to the left of the staff, and use the horizontal crosshair to align it with the bottom line of the bass-clef staff.

> When using the Maestro font, I usually increase the point size of coda (and D.S.) signs. I've seen very good players read the most difficult pieces only to miss a coda indication. So, make them very visible. Note that there are alternate D.S. and coda signs without the boxes around them. Check the Repeat Selection window for the alternate symbols.

> 😊 Have you saved lately?

7. Select **File** > Print, and see if it's close enough for jazz.

Creating a Lead Sheet for "Blues for a Hiccup"

Creating a single-line lead-sheet version of this example is as simple as deleting the bottom two staves and adjusting the staff system size for the new layout.

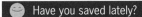

1. Select **File** > Save As.
2. Rename the file "Hiccup Lead Sheet.mus."
3. Choose the Staff tool 🗄.
4. Drag, to select the handles for the bass-clef and drumset staves.
5. Press the Delete key.
6. Choose the Page Layout tool ⬭.
7. Select **Page Layout** > Space Systems Evenly.
8. Set Space Systems Evenly to Page 1 Only.
9. Set Distribute Systems to "Do Not Change the Number of Systems on Each Page." Then click OK.
10. Drag the copyright down a little, and save the file. You now have a lead sheet.

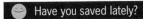 Have you saved lately?

FinaleScript

Finale has a programming language for creating scripts. A script can be a single function involving multiple steps, or multiple functions that can be triggered with a single command. Here are a couple of examples to help get your feet wet using it. Scripting will take some work on your part, in learning what it can do and how best to incorporate it into your work.

Search and Replace Script

We'll start with a simple Search/Replace command. The text block at the top left of the page needs to be changed from "Rhythm Section" to "Lead Sheet."

1. Select **Plug-ins** > Miscellaneous > FinaleScript Palette.
2. Click the New Script button. This brings up the FinaleScript Editor dialog box.

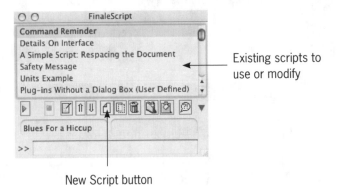

3. Name the script: "Replace Rhy Sec with Lead Sheet."
4. Click in the Editor window to begin creating the script.
5. Type: search "Rhythm Section" replace "Lead Sheet."
6. Click Close & Save. The script you just created appears, selected, in the Scripts window.
7. To Run the Script, press the Play Button.

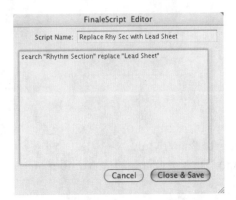

The text block now reads "Lead Sheet," and you have created your first FinaleScript. Scroll through the list, and see what existing scripts there are, and see if there are any for which you might have a need. As you are searching, begin to think about tasks for which you might want to attempt to create a script. Consult the Help menu for more information and ideas.

 Have you saved lately?

Batch Processing with FinaleScript

FinaleScript can work with open or closed files. It can also work with batches of files that all require the same modification. Let's use a FinaleScript to create a Bb Sax lead sheet, from our original. We will make some modifications to this script, to suit our current needs.

1. Select **File** > Save As.
2. Create a New Folder called "Lead Sheets to B-flat Folder."
3. Save the lead sheet file in this new folder, and then close the file.
4. Select **Plug-ins** > Miscellaneous > FinaleScript Palette.
5. Scroll down, and then highlight the "Voice to Sax Bb" script.
6. Click the View Current Script button. Scroll down and read all the text in the Editor window. Note the use of the two slashes (//) to disable a command line.
7. Delete the two slashes before "batch process folder."
8. Enter two slashes before "remove lyrics," since there are no lyrics.
9. Enter two slashes before "remove chord symbols." The player will need chord symbols for soloing.
10. Replace "voice" with "Lead Sheet" in the "search and replace" text command.
11. Delete the two slashes before "save."
12. Delete the two slashes before "close." Then click the Close & Save button.

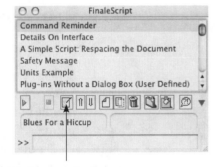

View Current Script button

To run the script:
1. Click the Choose Batch Folder button.
2. In the Choose a Folder window, highlight the "Lead Sheets to B-flat Folder."
3. Click the Choose button.
4. Click the Play button.
5. Open the file to see the results.

Had their been more than one file in this folder, all files would have been processed with the same changes.

 Have you saved lately?

261

Guitar Tab

While we are writing for rhythm section, there is a style of notation that is unique to the fretted-instrument family (guitar, bass, lute, and so on) called "tablature." The tablature staff is different in that the staff lines represent the strings of the instrument. Numbers take the place of notes on the tablature staff; they indicate the fret to finger for the note. Tablature notation strictly deals with the instrument. The key, rhythm, and other musical information still must be read from the music staff. (Finale does have a tablature staff that also includes stems for rhythms.)

To create a guitar tablature part for "Blues for a Hiccup:"
1. Open the original "Blues for a Hiccup" lead sheet file.
2. Select **File** > Save As, and rename the document "Hiccup Tablature.mus."
3. Select **Staff** > New Staves (with Setup Wizard).
4. Choose "Fretted Instruments-Guitar (TAB - No Staff Name)," and click Add. Then click Finish.

Some cosmetic adjustments need to be made; first, the measure numbers.

1. Choose the Measure tool 🖴.
2. Select **Measure** > Measure Numbers > Edit Regions.
3. Set Always Show On to "Top Staff" (not "Bottom Staff").

Next, the Score Expressions need to be hidden on the tablature staff.

1. Choose the Expression tool 𝑚𝑓.
2. To access the contextual menu, Control-click (Mac) or Right-click (Windows) the handle of the 𝑓 (forte) in measure 1, and choose Edit Measure Expression Assignment.
3. Under the Show On heading, click the Edit button next to Piano and Drums.
4. Click on the words Bottom Staff to remove the X's from both the score and parts columns.
5. Take the express route back to the music (see page 243).

Now, copy the music to the tablature staff.

1. Choose the Mass Edit tool 🖴.
2. Click to the left of the treble-clef staff to highlight the whole staff.
3. Drag the music down to the Tablature staff, and then release the mouse button.

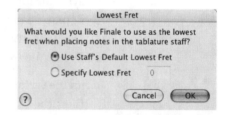

Here's where you need to know a little about the fretted instrument. Finale wants to know what fret to set as the lowest for the music being copied. A single note on guitar can be played a number of ways on a number of strings. A guitarist would make choices based on what lays best on the instrument, so if you are not sure, consult with a guitarist and get their opinion.

If I clicked Use Staff's Default Lowest Fret, the first phrase would look like this:

Clicking Specify Lowest Fret and entering "5" for the fret number yields the following results:

Note that Finale has grayed out the ties and rests. These elements are not represented in tablature notation. The chord voicing in the solo section would not be played in a closed position; they would be more open, as dictated by the strings and fret positions available.

 Have you saved lately?

Summary

This chapter included the following new Finale skills:

- creating a rhythm section score
- using the Jazz font
- using Staff Styles for slashes
- creating chord suffixes
- entering a drum-set part
- opening a template file
- using Jazz Human Playback
- guitar tab notation
- using FinaleScript
- creating a script

Review

1. Take a lead sheet of a song in a different style, and create a rhythm-section arrangement of it. See what challenges each style presents in terms of style, feel, drum patterns, and musical form.
2. Try a song with lyrics, and create a combo arrangement.
3. Transpose the vocal example into a new key, and adjust the position and arrangement as needed.

SECTION III
Large-Ensemble Scores

12

Big-Band Score ("Blues for a Hiccup")

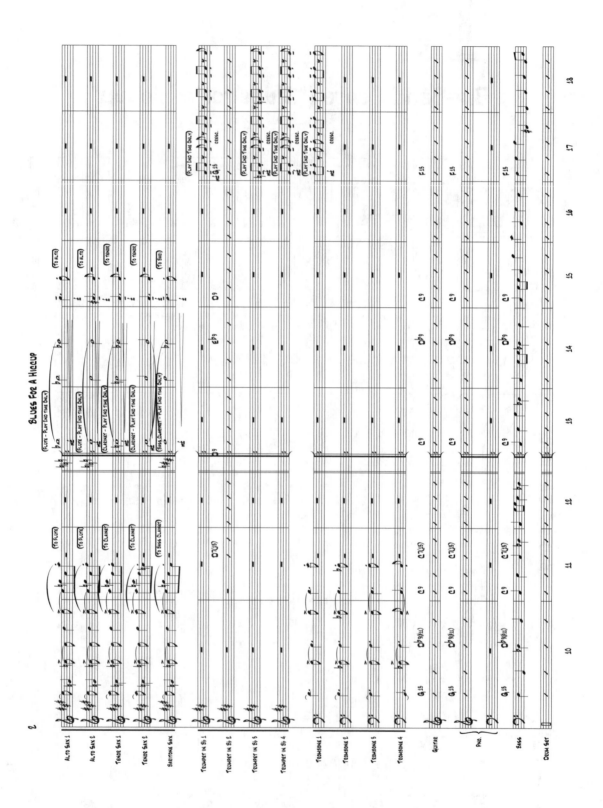

Blues For A Hiccup

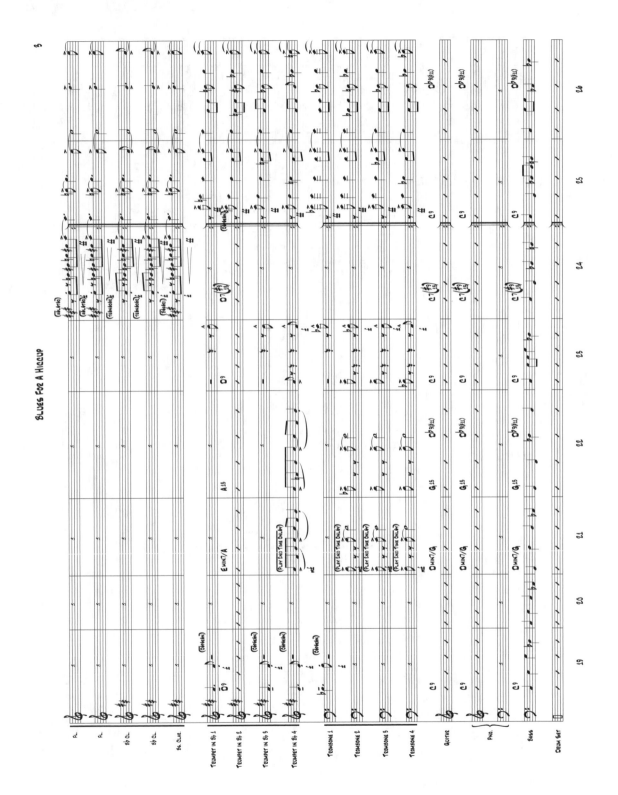

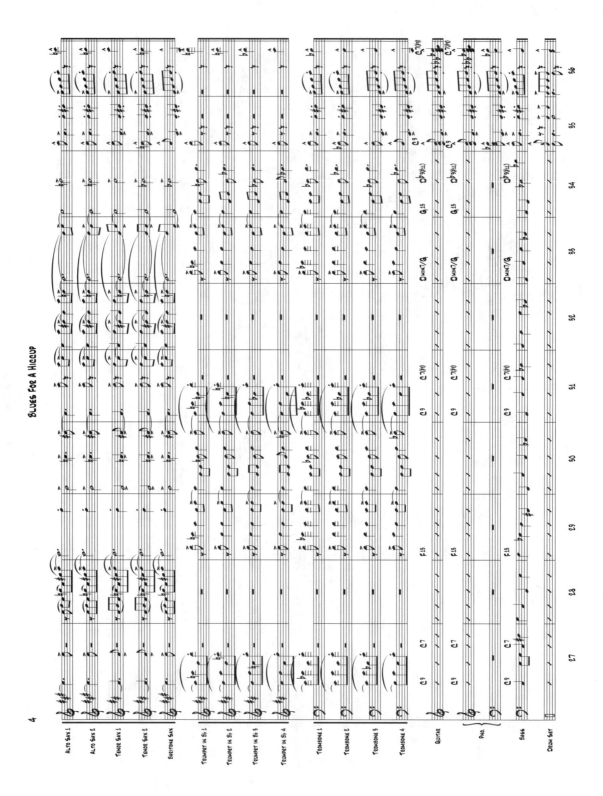

New in this chapter:

- creating a landscape-format score
- using the Band-in-a-Box Auto-Harmonization plug-in
- using the MiBAC Jazz Rhythm Section Generator plug-in
- using Staff Styles for transpositions
- creating expressions for MIDI Patch changes
- creating expressions for Play 2nd Time Only MIDI playback
- using Mass Edit to copy chord symbols
- printing a landscape-format score

Blues for Large Ensemble

In this chapter, you will create a big-band arrangement using the sketch of "Blues for a Hiccup," created in chapter 11. For this example, I'm not going to use the Setup Wizard. Instead, I've prepared a template for you to use. You can find it on our Web site at www.FinaleBook.com. Also on the Web site is a PDF that discusses the topic of templates.

BB_Score_temp.mus
Templates.pdf

In this chapter, you will learn some of Finale's powerful harmonization and orchestration tools. They provide a quick solution to creating a basic arrangement. In the course of creating arrangements in Finale, there are a few issues such as woodwind doubles, patch changes for accurate MIDI playback, and playing the second time only on repeats that will be addressed.

To copy your sketch from chapter 11 into the big-band score file:

1. Open both the "Blues for a Hiccup" file you just created and the "Blues Big Band Score Template" you downloaded from the Web site.
2. Select **View** > Scroll View for both files.

 Select **View** > Scale View To, and reduce the display size of both documents so more measures are visible on the screen. This makes drag-selecting large regions easier.

3. Choose the Mass Edit tool ⊕.
4. Select **Window** > Blues for a Hiccup (the rhythm section version).
5. Click to the left of the treble-clef staff to select the entire staff.
6. Shift-click to the left of the bass-clef staff so that it, too, is selected.
7. Select **Edit** > Copy, or use the keystroke, ⌘-C (Mac) or Control-C (Windows).
8. Select **Window** > Big Band Score Template.
9. Similarly, click to the left of the treble-clef staff and Shift-click to the left of the bass-clef staff.
10. Select **Edit** > Replace Entries, or use the keystroke, ⌘-V (Mac) or Control-V (Windows).
11. Select **File** > Save As, and name the score file "Blues_BB_Score."

With the sketch imported, set up the new file just as if it were a new example. The key of C is correct, but the double barlines and repeat need to be added.

1. Choose the Measure tool ⊜.
2. Advance to bar 12 if it is not visible on the screen.

3. Control-click (Mac) or Right-click (Windows) bar 12, and choose the Double Barline from the contextual menu.

Enter the Repeat for the Solo section, but not the DC al Coda. The Repeat Expressions did not transfer properly and will be deleted, since they are not necessary. The DC will be written out in this arrangement.

1. Choose the Repeat tool .
2. Delete the Fine in bar 10.
3. Highlight bars 13 through 24.
4. Select **Repeat** > Create Simple Repeat.
5. Delete the Fine in bar 25.

Before jumping into the orchestration process, a few things need to be cleaned up from the transfer. Long-time Finale users note: Measure Expressions copy from document to document now. The Staff Lists have copied as well, but the connection between the Expression and list has been lost. I'm going to delete them and re-enter what I need later.

1. Choose the Expression tool *mf*.
2. Delete the Tempo "quarter note = 120" Expression in bar 1.
3. Keep the "Bright Basic Swing" Expression.
4. Delete the repeated measure numbers from the Drum Set in bars 2 through 10.
5. Delete all dynamic Expressions from bar 1 to 19 in the wind staves.
6. Delete all Expressions from the piano staves.

Orchestrating Bars 1–12 with Mass Edit

With the score cleaned up, it is time to transform the sketch into a full arrangement. For the first twelve bars, the saxes will play the melody, unison, but breaking into harmony on the last note of each phrase.

> To view the score in concert pitch, select **Options** > Display In Concert Pitch. To return to the transposed view of the score, select this option again.

1. Choose the Mass Edit tool.
2. Select **Mass Edit** > Copy Entry Items. In this window:
    a. Click the All button.
    b. Uncheck Chords.
    c. Uncheck Clefs. Then click OK.
3. Highlight bars 1 through 11, treble clef, of the Piano.
4. Option-Shift-click (Mac) or Alt-Shift-click (Windows) on the first bar of the Alto Sax 1 staff, to copy the selected measures to this point.
5. Highlight bar 4, and press the Clear key to remove the quarter rests.
6. Highlight bar 8, and press the Clear key to remove the quarter rests.
7. Highlight bars 1 through 11 of the Alto Sax 1 staff, and copy it to the remaining four saxophone staves.
8. Highlight bars 1 through 11 of the Baritone Sax Staff.
9. Select **Mass Edit** > Transpose.
10. Transpose the part down one octave.

The harmony notes must be trimmed from the end of phrase notes. The top three sax parts contain the right note, along with two that must be deleted.

1. Highlight bars 1 through 11 of the Alto Sax 1 part.
2. Select **Plug-ins** > TG Tools > Process Extracted Parts.
3. With Extract voice line number "1" entered, click Go. Do not close the Plug-in window when the process finishes.
4. Click on the score, leaving the Plug-in window visible.
5. Highlight bars 1 through 11of the Alto Sax 2 part.
6. Click on the Plug-in window to make it active.

7. Enter "2" for the voice line number, and click Go.
8. Click on the score, leaving the Plug-in window visible.
9. Highlight bars 1 through 11 of the Tenor Sax 1 part.
10. Click on the Plug-in window to make it active.
11. Enter "3" for the voice line number, and click Go. Then click the Close button.

The bottom two saxes will need a note from the bass clef voicing in the piano. Enter the note by using Simple Entry's Repitch tool. The Tenor Sax 2 will play the B-flat (concert) on top of the bass-clef staff while the Bari plays the root, second-space C (concert).

1. Choose Simple Entry ♪.
2. Choose the Repitch ⬍ tool from the Simple Entry Palette.
3. Position the grey "Note" cursor in the correct position for the note to be entered. For the Tenor Sax 2 part, that note is the Bb below middle C concert (third-space C-natural, transposed).

4. Click to enter the note. The chord will be replaced by a single, purple-shaded, note.
5. Press the minus sign (–) on the keypad to lower it one half step.
6. Enter the same note for the Tenor Sax 2 in bars 7 and 11.

7. Scroll back to bar 3 of the Baritone Sax.
8. Position the grey "Note" cursor on the second-space C if the score is in concert, or A if it is transposed.
9. Click to enter the note.
10. Enter the same note for the Baritone Sax in bars 7 and 11.

The saxes are complete. The trombones will play the chord voicing in the bass-clef staff of the piano. While most of the part has four notes, the same end-of-phrase chord we just voiced for the saxes needs a fourth note to complete the voicing for the trombone section.

1. With Simple Entry selected, choose the eighth note from the Simple Entry palette.
2. Position the eighth-note cursor in the position to add the E above middle C to the bass-clef voicing.
3. Click to enter the note.
4. Scroll to bar 7.
5. In bar 7, position the eighth-note cursor in the position to add the E above middle C to the bass-clef voicing.
6. Press the minus key on the keypad to lower it to an E-flat.
7. At bar 11, position the eighth-note cursor in the position, and add the E above middle C to the bass-clef voicing.

Explode Music

The Explode feature allows a chord to be instantly voiced on any number of contiguous staves.

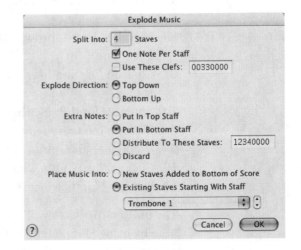

1. Choose the Mass Edit tool.
2. Highlight bars 1 through 11 of the bass clef Piano staff.
3. Press "2" on the keypad (the Metatool for Explode Music). In this window:
   a. Set Split Into to "4" Staves.
   b. Set Place Music Into to "Existing Staves Starting With Staff."
   c. Select Trombone 1 from the popup menu, and then click OK.
4. Select all four Trombone staves in bar 4, and press Clear.

The chord is now voiced on four separate staves and is still intact in the piano part. Any note-attached items such as articulations, note-attached Expressions, slurs, or chord symbols will be copied to each exploded staff along with the notes.

Explode Music has one disadvantage: it does not handle unisons. Therefore, it could not be used for the saxes. The Explode feature works best when the number of notes to be voiced is equal to, or greater than, the number of staves.

To complete the horn section for the first chorus, I want to have the Trumpet 2 play some jazz fills in the breaks between phrases.

1. Choose Speedy Entry .
2. Click on bar 3.
3. Press the 6 key on the keypad to enter a half rest.
4. Press the 5 key on the keypad six times to enter six quarter rests (the end of bar 3 and all of bar 4).
5. Choose the Staff tool .
6. Select **Edit** > Select Partial Measures.
7. Highlight the quarter rests in bars 3 and 4.
8. Press the **S** key (Metatool for Slash Notation).

These two bars can be copied to bars 7–8, and 11–12.

1. Choose the Mass Edit tool .
2. Select **Mass Edit** > Copy Measure Items.
3. Check the Staff Styles box, and click OK.
4. Highlight bars 3–4.
5. Copy them to 7–8 and 11–12.
6. Choose the Chord tool .
7. Enter C7(13) (concert) on the third beat of bars 3 and 11.
8. Enter a C7(#9, 13) (concert) on the third beat of bar 7.

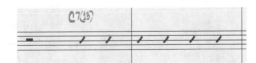

Select the Expression Tool to add the dynamics. A few slurs will need to be replaced in the saxes. Refer to the example at the beginning of the chapter on page 267.

The Solo Chorus: Bars 13–24

For the solo section, each of the backgrounds in the sketch will have a different orchestration. Woodwinds will play the first three bars. Three trumpets and one trombone will play the second phrase. One trumpet and three trombones will play the last phrase. The solo will be written in the Trumpet 2 part.

1. Choose the Mass Edit tool ⬤.
2. Select **Mass Edit** > Copy Entry Items.
3. In the Entry Items dialog box, check the Chords box.
4. Highlight bars 13 through 15 of the treble-clef Piano staff, and copy them to the Alto Sax 1 staff. The chords are necessary for the Plug-in that will be used shortly, but only for the saxes.
5. Select **Mass Edit** > Copy Entry Items.
6. In the Entry Items dialog box, uncheck the Chords box.
7. Highlight bars 21 through 23 of the treble-clef Piano staff, and copy them to the Trumpet 4 staff.
8. Highlight bars 21 through 22 of the treble clef Piano staff, and copy them to the Trombone 2 staff.

I want to have the saxes double on woodwinds and play the first three measures of the background figure with both altos on flute, both tenors on clarinet, and the bari on bass clarinet. With the change of instruments, I'll also change the voicing of the chord and the octave from the way is it voiced in the sketch file. I'll create the new voicing with a plug-in.

Band-in-a-Box Auto-Harmonizing: Five-Part Voicing

Finale contains some of the Auto-Harmonization features found in the Band-in-a-Box auto-accompaniment software package. Auto-Harmonization is applied from a plug-in. You don't need to own Band-in-a-Box.

1. With the Mass Edit tool still selected, highlight bars 13 through 15, and Transpose them up one octave.
2. With those measures still highlighted, select **Plug-ins** > Scoring and Arranging > Band-in-a-Box Auto-Harmonizing.
3. Set Number of Voices to "Five Part."
4. Choose "Swing Woodwinds" in the Style list.
5. Under Place New Voices Into, select "Four Existing Staves Starting with Staff," and from the popup menu, select "Alto Sax 1." Then click OK (ignoring the warning that the staff contains more than one melody note), and then click OK again.

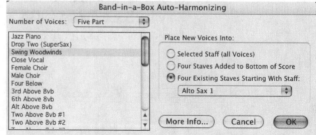

Saxophone Doubling using Staff Styles

Now that the notes are voiced on the staves, the proper transpositions must be applied to the staves. This is done using Staff Styles. The common practice is to have the new transposition, and the new key when necessary, begin on the first measure that the double plays, continuing until the first measure the sax plays. In this case, the Alto 1 begins playing flute in bar 13, and will switch back to alto for bar 24. So, that flute transposition will be in effect from bar 13 to bar 23, with the alto transposition being reintroduced at bar 24 for the alto's next entrance.

1. From the Options menu, uncheck Display In Concert Pitch, if it is selected.
2. Choose the Staff tool 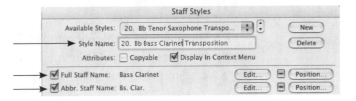.
3. Highlight bars 13 through 23 of the Alto Sax staves, since they both will double on flute.
4. Access the contextual menu by Control-clicking (Mac) or Right-clicking (Windows) the highlighted region.
5. Select "17. Flute Transposition" from the menu.

The tenor-to-clarinet double is not a change of key, but it is a change of transposition. There is also a little twist at the end to watch out for, but the process is the same as with the alto/flute Staff Style described above.

1. Highlight bars 13 through 23 of the two Tenor Sax staves, since they both will double on Clarinet.
2. Access the contextual menu by Control-clicking (Mac) or Right-clicking (Windows) the highlighted region.
3. Select "18. Bb Clarinet Transposition." The twist appears in the form of a bass clef in both staves. This is the result of the "First Clef" selected in Staff Attributes.
4. Double-click the Tenor Sax 1 staff.
5. Change the First Clef to Treble Clef.
6. Select Tenor Sax 2 from the popup menu.
7. Change the First Clef to Treble Clef, and then click OK.

There is no "Bass Clarinet Transposition" option, but the "Tenor Sax Transposition" is functionally similar, so use that for the Bari Sax. However, the Staff Style is set to change the Staff Name, so that must be changed.

1. Highlight bars 13 through 23 of the Bari Sax staff.
2. Access the contextual menu by Control-clicking (Mac) or Right-clicking (Windows) the highlighted region.
3. Select "20. Bb Tenor Saxophone Transposition."
4. Access the contextual menu again for this region, and select Define Staff Styles.
5. From the Available Styles menu, select "20. Bb Tenor Saxophone Transposition."
6. Change the Style Name of Tenor Saxophone to "Bass Clarinet."
7. Change the Full Staff Name to "Bass Clarinet."
8. Change the Abbr. Staff name to "Bs. Clar." and then click OK.

The woodwind voicing is complete but I have one small issue with the results. Finale has placed two B-sharps in the Tenor Sax 1 part. These notes, though correct in theory, will not make for a happy tenor player. Let's change notes such as B-sharps or F-flats to the more common enharmonic, to reduce player error.

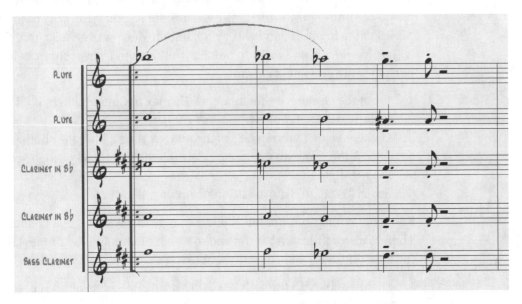

1. Choose Simple Entry ♪.
2. Use the Simple Entry Navigation keystrokes to move the cursor to the B-sharp whole note.
3. Press the \ (Backslash) key to toggle the enharmonic.
4. Press the Right Arrow key to advance to the half note.
5. Press the \ (Backslash) key to toggle the enharmonic.
6. Press the ESC key to exit Simple Entry.

Note that in bar 24, the E-flat saxes have key signatures for the sax transposition, so notes entered here will be in the correct key for the Altos and Bari. It is possible to do the whole part with Staff Styles alone, but I would only do this if there were a lot of changes. Use the transposition of the instrument that plays the most as the set transposition for the staff, as in the example, and then change for the instrument that plays the lesser amount of time.

 Have you saved lately?

Explosions for Brass

1. Choose the Mass Edit tool ⬚.
2. Highlight the treble-clef staff of the piano in bars 17 through 19.
3. Press the **2** key on the keypad (the Metatool for Explode Music). In this window:
   a. For Split Into, enter "4" Staves.

  b. For Place Music Into, select "Existing Staves Starting With," and select "Trumpet in Bb 2" from the popup menu. I know the Trumpet 2 will be soloing, not playing the background, but this will get the music to the proper staves with the least number of steps. Click OK.

4. Highlight the Trumpet 2 part in bars 17 through 19, and copy it up to the Trumpet 1 staff.
5. Select the part again in the Trumpet 2 staff, and press the Clear key.

The chord symbols did explode with the notes and must be deleted.

1. Choose the Chord tool .
2. Drag-select all chord handles in the Trumpets and Trombone 1.
3. Press the Delete key.

Copying Music Between Layers

The plan in bars 21 and 22 is to have the trumpet play the eighth-note line while Trombones 2, 3, and 4 play the accents. The Explode Music feature does not total up the number of parts in all voices before it distributes the music to the destination staves; it only views one layer at a time. Looking at the music, Layer 1 contains the Trumpet 4 part and Layer 2 contains the Trombone parts. In each staff, one layer needs to be cleared. The quick way to accomplish this is by copying the music between layers.

1. Choose the Mass Edit tool 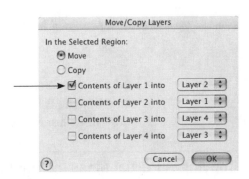.
2. Highlight bars 21 and 22 of the Trumpet 4 staff.
3. Select **Mass Edit** > Move/Copy Layers.
4. Check "Contents of Layer 1 into," and set the popup menu to "Layer 2." Then click OK (ignoring the warning about overwriting the music in Layer 2), and click OK again.
5. Highlight bars 21 and 22 of the Trumpet 4 down to the Trombone 2 staves.
6. Select **Mass Edit** > Move/Copy Layers.
7. Check "Contents of Layer 2 into" and set the popup menu to "Layer 1." Click OK.

Both parts need one additional tweak. The articulations are set to position on the stem side. Delete them, and replace them with note-side articulations. Then explode the Trombone parts.

1. Choose the Articulation tool.
2. Drag-select the articulation handles in the Trumpet 4 and Trombone staves.
3. Press the Delete key.
4. Reenter the articulations using the articulation Metatools.

5. Double-click on the first accent handle in the Trumpet 4 part.
6. In the Articulation Designer dialog box, under the Positioning heading, check the Inside Slurs box. Then click OK.
7. Choose the Mass Edit tool 🌑 .
8. Highlight bar 21 and 22 of the Trombone 2 staff.
9. Press the **2** key (the Metatool for Explode Music).
   a. Set Split Into to "3" Staves.
   b. Set Place Music Into to "Existing Staves Starting With Staff," and select "Trombone 2" from the popup menu. Then click OK.

Bar 23 presents a problem. I want the Trumpet 4 and Trombone 2, 3, and 4 to play the downbeat that concludes the background figure, and the whole brass section, except Trumpet 2, to play the note on beat 4. This cannot be accomplished with Explode Music. There is another tool that will work.

1. Choose the Note Mover tool 🌑 .
2. Select **Note Mover** > Delete After Merge. This will subtract each note moved from the chord, leaving a single note in the measure when done.
3. Click inside the staff of the Trumpet 4 part in bar 23. Handles will appear on all notes

Begin with the chord on the downbeat.

4. Select the bottom note of the chord, B-flat (concert).
5. Drag the handle down to the Trombone 4 staff. The note will appear, along with the articulation and appropriate rests, in the Trombone 4 part.
6. Drag the D in the Trumpet 4 staff down to the Trombone 3 staff.
7. Drag the E in the Trumpet 4 staff down to the Trombone 2 staff.

That completes the chord voicing on the downbeat. On to beat 4:

1. Select the top note of the chord, C (concert), and drag its handle up to the Trumpet 1 staff.
2. Drag the A (concert) up to the Trumpet 3 staff.
3. Drag the B-flat (concert) on the bottom of the chord down to the Trombone 1 staff. This will serve as a marker for copying a chord voicing for the trombones.

Copying A Partial Measure from an Off-Screen Location

For the trombones, a little surgical copy/paste is in order.

1. Choose the Mass Edit tool 🌑 .
2. Select **Edit** > Select Partial Measures.
3. Scroll to bar 7.
4. Select the eighth note in beat 2, for all four staves.
5. Scroll to bar 23, and Shift-Option-click (Mac) or Shift-Control-click (Windows) on the B-flat in the Trombone 1 staff, on the second half of the fourth beat.

Copying Staff Styles

To finish off this section in the wind section, the Trumpet 2 part needs twelve bars of slashes.

1. Choose the Mass Edit tool .
2. Select **Mass Edit** > Copy Measure Items.
3. Check only the Staff Styles box, and click OK.
4. Highlight bar 12 of the Trumpet 2 part.
5. Copy it into bar 13.
6. Enter "12" for the number of times, and click OK.

Copying Chord Symbols

1. Select **Mass Edit** > Select Copy Measure Items.
2. Click the None button.
3. Check the Chords box, and click OK.
4. Highlight bars 13 through 24 of the treble clef of the Piano staff.
5. Copy this region to the Trumpet 2 staff beginning in bar 13.
6. Choose the Chord tool.
7. Enter the C7(#9, 13) (concert) in bar 24.

> When using Mass Edit to copy individual items such as chord symbols, make sure that Select Partial Measures is turned off, in the Edit menu. Finale will not copy items attached to entries without the entries themselves, when a partial measure is selected.

Expressions for Patch Changes

There are a lot of ways Expressions can be used to effect MIDI playback. In the example, the saxes change instruments. An Expression alerts the player to the change. That Expression can also tell the MIDI playback device to change sounds. The Expression indicating the instrument change should occur as soon as the passage before the change is finished.

1. Choose the Expression tool.
2. Scroll to bar 11, and double-click on the Alto Sax 1 staff.
3. In the Text window, enter "To Flute" (Jazz font brackets optional).
4. Click the Playback Tab.
   a. From the Type menu, select Patch.
   b. From the GM menu, select 74 Flute.

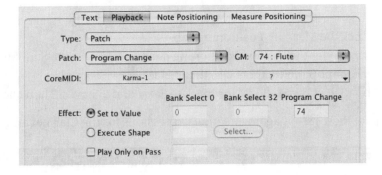

5. Click the Measure Positioning Tab.
6. Under the Vertical Positioning header, select Above Staff baseline from the popup menu. Then, click OK, and then Select.
7. Create a new Staff List for the Alto Sax 1 and 2 Staves. Click OK.

Repeat the same steps to create an Expression for the Tenor Sax 1 and 2 staves, indicating "To Clarinet" and changing the patch to the Clarinet.

Repeat the steps again for the Bass Clarinet Expression. There is no General MIDI patch for Bass Clarinet, so use the Clarinet patch.

Expressions for "Play 2nd Time Only"

When the new instrument begins playing, it is indicated by another Expression. In this example, the woodwinds begin playing at the beginning of a repeated section. The part is only played the second time through, so an Expression should also be entered to indicate that direction. Finale is capable of executing a "Play 2nd Time Only" command, but it does it backwards, sorta kinda. Finale cannot ignore the notes for playback on a repeat, but you can change the key velocity of those notes to zero, rendering them inaudible. The first expression you will create sets them to zero. This will apply to all staves where the expression is entered, including the MIDI channels to which those staves are assigned.

1. With the Expression tool active, double-click on the Alto Sax 1 staff in bar 13.
2. Click Create.
3. For Text, enter "Flute – Play 2nd Time Only."
4. Click the Playback Tab.
    a. Set Type to "Key Velocity."
    b. Set Effect to Set To Value "0." This turns the key velocity of the staff to zero.
    c. Check "Play Only On Pass 1." The means the velocity will be zero only on the first pass (time) through the repeat.

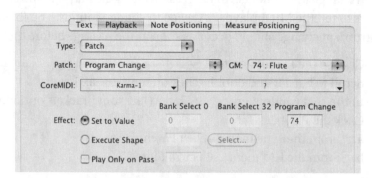

5. Click the Measure Positioning Tab.
    a. Under the Vertical Positioning header, select Above Staff baseline from the popup menu. Click OK, then Select.
    b. Select the Staff List for the Alto Sax 1 and 2 Staves. Then click OK.

Repeat theses steps again, creating Expressions for the Clarinet and Bass Clarinet staves.

 Have you saved lately?

Dynamic Dynamics

The velocity is now set to zero for all MIDI channels assigned to the staves where the expression has been applied. The velocities will remain at that level until they are reset by another expression, such as a dynamic mark.

This is a problem, since the next dynamic mark encountered is not set to recognize the repeat, and will reset the key velocity to the proper amount for the dynamic. This will immediately undo all the work done to create the "2nd Time Only" effect. The answer is to duplicate the dynamic marks required in the repeated section and amend their playback settings to only take effect on the second pass. In the graphic above, the change to the f (forte) Expression is shown.

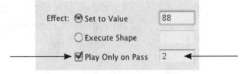

Check the Play Only on Pass box, and enter "2." This Expression resets the key velocity to the proper level. I recommend placing one at the beginning of the phrase, even if it is redundant.

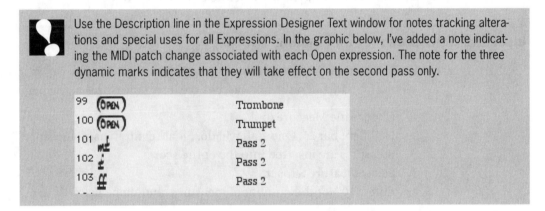

In measure 15, the woodwinds change back to saxes. Go back to the Expressions for the Patch Changes section. Use the steps to create Expressions indicating a change to saxophone, and also change the MIDI patch to the proper saxophone sound. Check Play on Pass and enter "2," since the change needs to be made on the repeat only.

In measure 24 each sax needs an Expression indicating the sax now being played.

The trumpets need an Expression indicating Harmon Mute. This needs to be in bar 1 of the piece, and there is an Expression already in the library. It does need to be edited for playback, so it sends Muted Trumpet patch in the GM menu.

In bar 17, the trumpets and trombone playing the background figure need a "2nd Time Only" Expression. This should also be programmed to set the key velocity to zero for the first pass. If needed, review the steps in the "Play 2nd Time Only" section. The Trombone needs an Expression for "Straight Mute." Since there is no General MIDI sound for a muted trombone, use the Muted Trumpet patch.

In bar 19, the trumpets need an Expression to remove the Harmon mute—just use the word "Open." The Expression should also switch the MIDI patch to the unmated Trumpet sound. The Trombone 1 will need an "Open" Expression, but the same one cannot be used; a separate Expression with the Trombone General MIDI patch must be entered.

283

In bar 21, the Trombone 2, 3, and 4 staves need the same "2nd Time Only" Expression entered in the bar 17. If needed, review the steps in the "Play 2nd Time Only" section.

Using the power contained in Expressions will make MIDI playback of Finale files much more interesting. Just remember that each separate patch requires its own MIDI channel. For example, if I had the Alto Sax 1 double on flute, and the Alto Sax 2 double on clarinet, then they would need to be on separate MIDI channels instead of sharing the same one.

The Shout Chorus

Since this is a different musical setting from the Rhythm Section arrangement, I've decided that a shout chorus is a more appropriate way of bringing the arrangement to a conclusion. I have constructed a small variation on the original melody to be played by the brass, while the saxes will play a unison countermelody with fills in the phrase breaks. This eliminates the DC al Coda repeat. However, room must be made for the new section by inserting measure before the final two bars.

Inserting Measures into an Existing Score

When inserting measures into a score, select the bar after the insert point. This may seem a bit odd, but only this way, can we insert measures at the beginning of a piece.

1. Choose the Measure tool 🖦.
2. Highlight bar 25. One staff will do. Finale cannot insert measures into just one staff; measures are inserted into the entire score.
3. Select **Measure** > Insert.
4. Enter "10" for the number of measures, and then click OK.

Entering the New Melody and Counter-Melody

Enter the notation below on the treble-clef staff of the piano. It is a subtle variation on the original melody. The change on beats 1 and 2 of the beginning of each phrase, and beats 2 and 3 of the second bar of each phrase, make copying from the original tedious since the chord symbols will have to be reentered. It's just as easy to enter it from scratch. Choose whichever note entry method you prefer.

Enter the notation below on the Alto Sax 1 staff, beginning in bar 23. Check in the Options menu, to make sure Display In Concert Pitch is activated before beginning.

Band-in-a-Box Auto-Harmonization: Four Voice

The first order of business will be the brass. I want the new melody harmonized with a tight four-part voicing. The trumpets will play it up an octave; the trombones will double the voicing as written.

1. Choose the Mass Edit tool.
2. Select **Mass Edit** > Copy Entry Items.
3. In the Entry Items dialog box, check the Chords box, and then click OK.
4. Highlight bars 25 through 36 of the treble-clef staff of the piano.
5. Copy the highlighted measures to the Trumpet 1 staff, measures 25 to 34.
6. Highlight bars 25 through 34 of the Trumpet 1 staff.
7. Select **Plug-ins** > Scoring and Arranging > Band-in-a-Box Auto-Harmonization. In its dialog box:
   a. Set Number of Voices to "Four Part."
   b. Choose "3 Below #1" in the Style list.
   c. Set Place New Voices Into heading to "Selected Staff (all Voices)." Then click OK.

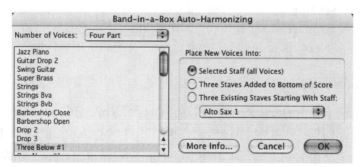

The chord symbols are no longer needed in the trumpet part, so remove them now, before exploding.

1. Choose the Chord tool.
2. Highlight the handles of all the chord symbols in the Trumpet 1 staff from bar 25 to the end of the piece.
3. Press the Delete key.

Exploding the Trumpets

1. Choose the Mass Edit tool 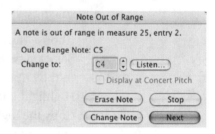.
2. Highlight bars 25 through 34 of the Trumpet 1 staff.
3. Copy the highlighted measures to the Trombone 1 staff, using Option-Shift-click (Mac) or Control-Shift-click (Windows).
4. With the Trumpet 1 measures still selected, transpose them up one octave.
5. With the Trumpet 1 Staff still selected, press the **2** key (Metatool for Explode Music). In this dialog window:
   a. Set Split Into to "4" Staves.
   b. Set Place Music Into to "Existing Staves Starting With Staff."
   c. Select Trumpet 1 from the popup menu. Then click OK.

Dem Bones

The trombone register seems a little high in places. To be on the safe side, use the check Range Plug-in, to fix anything that is out of range.

1. With Mass Edit still active, highlight bars 25 through 34 of the Trombone 1 staff.
2. Select **Plug-ins** > Scoring and Arranging > Check Range.
3. With Trombone selected in the Instrument List, click Check. Finale flags the high Cs.
4. Click Change Note. Finale will lower the note one octave, and leave the rest of the voicing untouched.
5. Change all the C5s to C4s. Then click OK when the plug-in is finished.

With the range issues cleared up, explode the staff.

6. With 25 through 34 of the Trombone 1 staff still selected, press the 2 key. In the dialog window:
   a. Set Split Into to "4" Staves.
   b. Set Place Music Into to "Existing Staves Starting With Staff."
   c. Select "Trombone 1" from the popup menu, then click OK.

Explode the Saxes

The saxophones have a counter line that is unison, with two voiced chords at the end as a build to the coda. Begin by exploding the chords in the last two measures.

1. With Mass Edit still selected, highlight measures 33 and 34 of the Alto Sax 1 part, and press the **2** key. In this dialog window:
   a. Set Split Into to "4" Staves.
   b. Set Place Music Into to "Existing Staves Starting With Staff."
   c. Select Alto Sax 1 from the popup menu. Then click OK.

Next, copy the unison line from measure 24 to the downbeat of beat 4 in bar 33 to all sax parts. Use care when Select Partial Measures is active; the position of the mouse is critical for proper placement of the music in the destination staff.

2. Select **Edit** > Select Partial Measures.
3. With Mass Edit active, highlight measure 24 to the downbeat of 4 in bar 33 in the Alto Sax 1 part.
    a. Copy it to the Alto Sax 2 staff.
    b. Copy it to the Tenor Sax 1 staff
    c. Copy it to the Tenor Sax 2 staff.
4. Highlight measures 24 to the downbeat of 4 in bar 33 in both Tenor Sax staves.
    • Transpose this selection down one octave.
5. Highlight measures 24 through 34 in the Tenor Sax 2 staff.
    • Copy this selection to the Bari Sax staff.

The Bari needs to have some repitching done for the two voiced chords in bars 33 and 34. Both notes will be changed to the root of the chord.

1. Choose the Repitch ⬍ tool from the Simple Entry Palette.
2. Click on the last eighth note in bar 33, to highlight it.
3. Play, or click in a first-line G concert (first-line E, transposed).
4. Change the first half note in bar 34 to the same pitch.
5. Change the second half note to a third-line Db concert (third-line Bb, transposed).
6. Select the tie, and retie the eighth in 33 to the half in 34. Then press the ESC key to deselect it.

Have you saved lately?

The Coda

The last two measures of the piece need to be treated differently because of the unison figure. The trumpets will be wailing away up high and will not play the unison line at all. Enter the following in the Trumpet 1 staff, and use Explode Music to distribute the voicing to all four trumpet staves. The notes in the example are in concert pitch.

The saxes will play chords and the unison line. Use Explode Music to distribute the chords, then use Mass Edit (with Select Partial Measures active) to copy the unison line down. Transpose both Tenor Sax unisons down one octave. There are only four parts here: the Bari will double the Trombone 4 part.

The Trombones can be handled in the same way as the saxes. Use Explode Music to distribute the chords onto four staves, then copy the unison line down to all four parts. Transpose the unison down one octave for the Trombone 3 and 4 parts. When finished, copy the Trombone 4 part for the coda to the Bari Sax staff, and to the rhythm-section bass staff as well.

Deleting Extra Measures

Here is a tip for deleting a large number of measures at the end of a score.

1. Choose the Mass Edit tool ⬭.
2. Click on measure 37, to highlight it.
3. Press Shift-Right Arrow.
4. Press the Delete key.

The Rhythm Section Generator Plug-in

The MiBAC Jazz Rhythm Section Generator plug-in uses chord symbols to generate a MIDI accompaniment and enters it into the selected staves in the document. These staves can be the actual staves used to generate parts, or staves used only for playback and not printed or extracted. There are currently four styles available: ballad, swing, bebop, and bossa nova. The generated part can be displayed as notation or slashes, with or without chord symbols, or hidden from view completely. To create the piano, bass, and drum parts for playback, I'm going to use a plug-in. I will need the chord symbols, but they must be out of the Piano staff.

1. Choose the Mass Edit tool ⬭.
2. Select **Mass Edit** > Copy Everything.
3. Select **Edit** > Select Region. In this window:
   a. Under From, set the Staff to "Piano TC" and Measure to "1."
   b. Under Through, set Staff to "Piano TC" and Measure to "34" (I want to leave the coda untouched.) Then click OK.
4. Copy the highlighted region to the Guitar staff.
5. Highlight both piano staves from bar 1 through 34.
6. Press the Clear key.
7. Choose the Staff tool ⬚.
8. With the region still highlighted, select **Staff** > Clear Staff Styles.

The Plug-in would still work for creating the notation using the information if it were in the Piano staff, but the chord symbols would be lost.

One limitation of the plug-in is that it does not recognize user-created chord symbols. Before this plug-in is applied, the C7(13) and the C7(♯9,13) chords must be deleted and replaced with the closest suffix to the intended harmony.

- Choose the Chord tool 🄲, and replace the C7(13) with a C7 in bars 3 and 11. Replace the C7(♯9,13) with a C7(♯9) in bars 7 and 23.

To generate rhythm-section parts for playback:
1. Choose the Mass Edit tool 🄴.
2. Highlight bars 1 through 34 of the Guitar staff.
3. Select **Plug-ins** > Scoring and Arranging > Rhythm Section Generator.
   a. Set Style to "Swing."
   b. For Generate:
      - Set Piano to "Slashes w/Chord Symbols."
      - Set Bass to "Notation w/Chord Symbols."
      - Set Drum Set to "Slashes."
   c. Set Place Music Into to "Existing Staves as Specified."
      - For the Piano, select The Piano TC. The part is generated on a single line.
      - Set Bass and Drum Set respectively to "Bass" and "Drum Set." Then click OK.
4. Copy the drum part for the coda from the Rhythm Section.
5. Play back the file.

The rhythm section is now a little closer to the sound of a live band. There are some issues with the visual aspect of the parts generated by this plug-in. The chord symbols attached to the anticipations, for the most part, did not copy. This is due to entries not existing on those parts of the beat. There are two choices, and I've seen both of them in practice: to place the chords on the next downbeat and leave the interpretation up to the player, or to rework the part.

The style interpretation that the MiBAC plug-in leans towards is the former, and jazz is supposed to be about player interpretation. The horns are playing the anticipations, so in that way, the composition is still true to the original. Use the Chord tool to enter the displaced chords on the next downbeat. At this point, the two suffixes that were deleted

289

can be entered in their proper place. Refer to the example at the beginning of the chapter, if you have any placement questions.

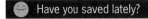 Have you saved lately?

Printing Landscape Scores

This piece requires a landscape-formatted page (8.5" by 11" wide). This is set in the Page Setup dialog box, located in the File menu. Here, Finale communicates information about the orientation, portrait or landscape, and size of the page to be printed. Unless the size and orientation are set here, the document will not print properly. The exact look and available settings in the dialog box will vary depending on your computer's OS and your printer's specific make and model.

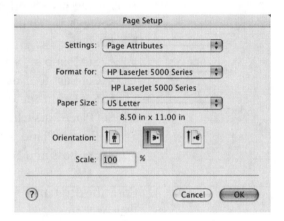

1. Select **File** > Page Setup.
2. Confirm that your printer is indicated and that Page Size is set to "US Letter."
3. Set the proper orientation (landscape). Then click OK.
4. Select **File** > Print, then click OK.

Summary

- creating a landscape-format score
- using the Band-in-a-Box Auto-Harmonization plug-in
- using the MiBAC Jazz Rhythm Section Generator plug-in
- using Staff Styles for transpositions
- creating expressions for MIDI Patch changes
- creating expressions for Play 2nd Time Only MIDI playback
- using Mass Edit to copy chord symbols
- printing a landscape-format score

Review

1. Enter a melody and chords and explore the Band-in-a-Box Auto harmonization plug-in. Experiment with different numbers of voices, and note the stylistic compatibility of the results.
2. Take the previous step a little further by taking those harmonizations and orchestrating them for different combinations of instruments. Note the qualities of each variation.
3. Try creating some jazz solo-practice recordings using the Rhythm Section Generator Plug-in.
4. Create a rhythm section from a tune, then delete the melody. Compose a new one based on the changes.

13

Orchestral Excerpt (*Petrushka*)

13_Petrushka_Score.mus

Before starting this chapter, download and print the file 13_Petrushka_Score.mus. Use this as a reference while working on the chapter.

An Organ-Grinder Appears in the Crowd with a [Woman] Dancer.

For this chapter, we'll pretend we've been "hired" to create a score for Igor Stravinsky's ballet, *Petrushka*. Okay, we're just going to do a small excerpt from the score, but just to illustrate certain problems and their possible solutions, we'll set up the score as if we're doing the entire piece.

What's New in This Chapter

- creating a custom ensemble in the Setup Wizard
- breaking barlines between staves
- formatting staves for stems up display
- adding staves to an existing score
- setting up staff groups and brackets
- setting up staff sets
- using the Time Signature tool
- using the Shape Designer
- entering tremolos
- rebeaming measures according to the time signature
- entering complex tuplets
- optimizing a score
- creating beams across the barline
- positioning staves in Page View

The Score: Igor, 47—You, 1

The first thing to do, besides taking some Russian language lessons, is to look at the instrumentation required for the score template.

2 Piccolos (on one staff)	Tamtam
2 Flutes (on one staff)	Triangle
4 Oboes (on two staves): Oboe 4 doubles on English Horn	Tambourine
	Side Drum (offstage)
3 Clarinets (B♭, A, on two staves)	Long Drum (offstage; grouped with
Bass Clarinet (B♭)	the Side Drum)
3 Bassoons (on two staves)	Glockenspiel
Contrabassoon	Celeste
4 Horns in F (on two staves)	Piano
2 Cornets (B♭, A) (on one staff)	2 Harps (on one grand staff)
2 Trumpets (B♭, A) (on one staff)	Xylophone
3 Trombones (on two staves)	Violin 1
Tuba (grouped with the Trombones)	Violin 2
Timpani	Viola
Bass Drum	Cello
Cymbals	Bass

This score is based on several published study scores, in which the instrumentation changes frequently, system to system, depending on who is playing. Setting this up requires a little time and effort. If this were for a commercial situation, speed most likely would dictate displaying all staves on all score pages. However, the size of the score may make this impractical, unless you can print at sizes larger than 8.5 x 11. The compromise will be to choose one basic staff layout that you will configure as a study score for printing.

Setting Up a Score Template

Setting up a score of this size and complexity takes a lot of work, though Finale makes it much easier than would be the same process in pen and ink. To set it up precisely is beyond even the Setup Wizard's power, but we can use the Wizard to get us started.

 For large-scale works, especially multi-movement works, it is advisable to break the piece up over several files—say, one for each movement. The larger the file, the more RAM and processor power required by your computer.

1   From the Launch Window, click Setup Wizard, or if Finale is already open, select **File** > New > Document With Setup Wizard.

2.   Click Next in page 1, since we don't need the title and credits for this example.

3.   Under the Select an Ensemble heading, select "Orchestra (Full)" from the popup menu.

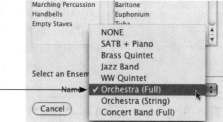

This provides a basic ensemble that will be edited to meet the needs of the project. Now go up to the instrument list and see what needs to be added or removed.

4.   To remove an instrument from this list, highlight it and click the Remove button. Remove the following:
   •   one Flute staff
   •   E♭ Clarinet
   •   one Trumpet staff
   •   Tuba (it will be combined with the Trombones)
   •   Percussion

5.   To add a cornet, choose the Brass family in the left column, and add one cornet staff to the score: Brass > Cornet.
   •   Use the Up Arrow (on the right) to move it up, over the trumpet, in the list of current instruments.

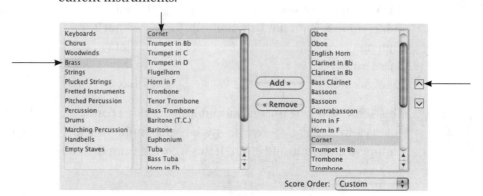

Note that the Score Order popup menu has switched from Orchestra to Custom.

6. Add a Bass Drum staff: Drums > Bass Drum (Single Line)
   - Use the Up Arrow key to place it under the Timpani.
7. Add the following instruments from the Percussion family:
   - Cymbals: Use the Up Arrow key to place it under the Bass Drum.
   - Tamtam: Use the Up Arrow key to place it under the Cymbals.
   - Triangle: Use the Up Arrow key to place it under the Tamtam.
   - Tambourine: Use the Up Arrow key to place it under the Triangle.
   - Log Drum: Use the Up Arrow key to place it under the Percussion.
8. Add the following instruments from the Pitched Percussion family:
   - Glockenspiel: Use the Up Arrow key to place it under the Log Drum.
   - Xylophone: Last is fine.
9. Add a celesta: Keyboard > Celesta.
   - Use the Up Arrow key to place it under the Xylophone.
10. Add a Harp: Plucked String > Harp.
    - Use the Up Arrow key to place it under the Piano.

The instrumentation is complete. Save this instrumentation list so you can select it here should you need it again.

1. Under the Select An Ensemble heading, click the Save As button.
2. Enter "Petrushka Orchestra" for the name. Then click OK. The "Petrushka Orchestra" instrument list has been added to the Name popup menu, and can be accessed at any time in the future. Continue on with the Setup Wizard.
3. Click Next and set the Time and Key Signatures.
4. Click Next and Finish to complete the Wizard.
5. Select Save As and name the file "Petrushka_Score.mus."
6. Go to Scroll View. We'll do the rest of the formatting and entry work there.

Staff Attributes

Now that we have our basic template, we can put the final touches on it. We'll begin in the Staff tool.

1. Choose the Staff tool ⬚.
2. Select **Staff** > Edit Staff Attributes, or Control-click (Mac) or Right-click (Windows) on the staff to access the contextual menu.

The top staff is selected. We need to add "1 & 2" to the piccolo for both the Full Name and the Abbr. Name.

3. Click the Full Name's Edit button.
4. Click to the right side of "Piccolo," and type "[space] 1&2" in this field.

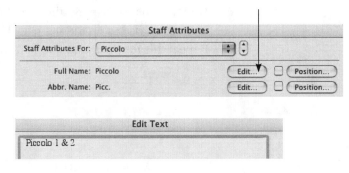

Since we need to do a lot of this, let's just copy and paste this text to all the other lines that need a "[space] 1 & 2."

5. Highlight the "[Space] 1&2" and use the Copy keystroke: ⌘-C (Mac) or Control-C (Windows). Click OK to exit the Full Name dialog box.

6. Click the Abbr. Name Edit button.

7. Position the cursor to the right of the "Picc." and use the Paste keystroke, ⌘-V (Mac) or Control-V (Windows).

8. Set the Staff Attributes For popup menu to "Flute," to display the staff attributes for the Flute staff. Add the 1 & 2 to both names.

9. The Oboe has a 1 but for the sake of expedience, just select the space and the number and paste the 1 & 2 over it.

10. Continue through the score, adding the "[Space] 1&2" to the Full and Abbr. names for the Oboe (top), Clarinet, Bassoon, Horn in F (top), Cornet, Trumpet, and Trombone (top) staves.

11. Repeat the process adding "[Space] 3 & 4" to the Oboe (bottom) and Horn in F (bottom) staff.

12. Change the "2" to "3" in the bottom Clarinet and Bassoon staves.

13. Change the bottom Trombone from "2" to "3," then press Return/Enter and add "Tuba."

14. Select the Log Drum Staff, and change the Full Name to "Side Drum," press Return/Enter, and type "Long Drum" on the line underneath.

15. For the Abbr. Name use "S. Dr." and "L. Dr.," also on two lines.

Hidden Staff Names

Perhaps you've noticed in the popup menu that the grand staff names are not listed in Staff Attributes. Their names are controlled by the Group Attributes dialog box; don't worry, we'll get there shortly. The reason I'm bringing this up while we are in Staff Attributes is to name the staves here, manually, as well. In doing so, the staves will have a name in staff lists for Measure Expressions and for part extraction. There is no need to enter an Abbr. Name.

Though we are naming these staves, we don't want them to display. Therefore, we'll hide these names, after we name them.

1. In the Staff Attributes window, choose "Staff 28."

2. Click the Edit button for the Full Name, and type "Celeste."

3. Under Items To Display, uncheck "Staff Name," so it will not be visible on the score itself.

4. Repeat this for the Piano (Staff 30) and Harp (Staff 32).

Breaking Barlines Between Staves

The next task is breaking the barlines between instrument types within an instrument group, in order to see more separation in the score. It's a subtle, visual nuance that helps distinguish between instruments more easily.

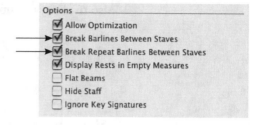

1. In the Staff Attributes window, select the Oboe 1 & 2 staff.
2. Under the Options heading, check Break Barlines Between Staves.
3. Also check Break Repeat Barlines Between Staves, even though there are no repeats in this example. These two go hand-in-hand, so it's just a good habit to do both automatically.

These two parameters affect the barlines to the staff above the current staff. So to continue down the score, go to the top staff of each instrument group.

4. Select the "Clarinet 1 & 2" Staff from the popup menu.
5. Break the barlines between the clarinets and oboes.
6. Move down to the Bass Clarinet and Bassoons, and repeat step 5.

The brass begins a new group, so there is no need to break barlines between the horns and bassoons or between anywhere else the barlines are already broken. In the *Petrushka* score, the Setup Wizard created the groups you are working with. Groups can also be created and edited using the Staff tool. The group settings determine the number of staves included in the group, which bracket or brace is displayed on the left side of the score, and if the group has a name, that name is displayed. In the *Petrushka* score, the "Harp" is a group name, not a staff name. Groups are also important when extracting parts using the Extract Parts command in the File menu.

7. Continue down to the cornet and trombone staves, adding the breaks. Don't click OK yet; there's still a little more to do in Staff Attributes.

Setting Up Non-Pitched Percussion Staves

Each of the non-pitched percussion requires a single-line staff. Therefore, we will have to change the Cymbals and Side Drum staves.

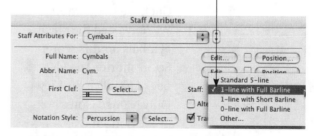

1. View the Staff Attributes window for the Cymbals staff.
2. Set the Staff popup menu to "1-Line with Full Barline."
3. Choose the Side Drum Staff, and repeat step (2) above.

Next is the staff itself. The Wizard has given us a single-line staff for the bass drum, but Finale is capable of so much more, in creating and formatting a staff. What I'd like to have is a single-line staff that automatically flips the note stems up. For the metallic percussion, I'd like to use ×-noteheads that appear on the staff line.

1. View the Staff Attributes for the Bass Drum staff.
2. Under Items to Display, click the Stem Settings button. This brings up the Staff Stem Settings dialog box.
3. Set Stem Direction to "Always Up." Then click OK.
4. View the Staff Attributes for the Cymbals staff, and set the Stem Settings for this also to always go up.

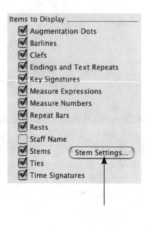 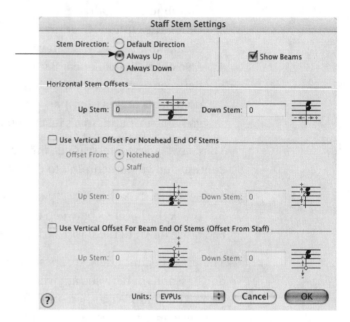

Continue down the non-pitched percussion family setting the stem direction. Then return to the Cymbals staff for our next task.

X-Noteheads and Percussion Maps

The final phase of our odyssey through Staff Attributes is to set the playback, note positioning, and noteheads for the non-pitched percussion parts.

1. In the Staff Attributes for the Cymbals staff, click the Select button to the right of the Notation Style popup menu. This opens the Percussion Map Selection dialog box, where Cymbals will be selected.
2. Click the Edit button.
3. We only need the crash cymbals for this score. So, to shorten the Playback List, click the View Only Named Notes box at the bottom.

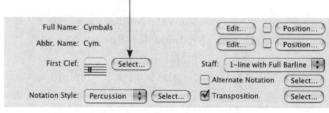

4. Select MIDI pitch 49/C♯3/Crash Cymbals. (As a reference, middle C is MIDI note 60.)
5. Click the Select button beneath Closed Notehead.
6. Locate the × notehead in the font library (symbol 121), and click Select.

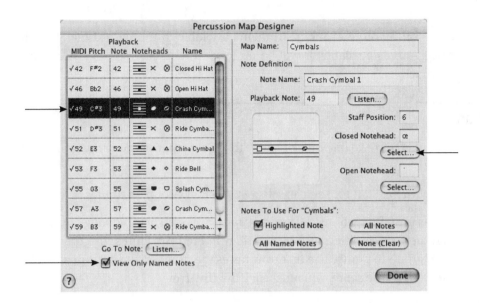

The closed note in the example will change to reflect the symbol you have selected.

7. Click the Select button for the Open Notehead, and select the ⊗ in a circle notehead (symbol 89). Click Done, and then Select.

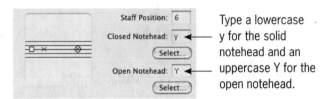

Type a lowercase y for the solid notehead and an uppercase Y for the open notehead.

There are a few details worth taking note of here. First, the note for the Crash Cymbals is C♯, MIDI note 49. When entering the part by using a MIDI keyboard, the Cymbals part must be played in on the C♯ one octave below middle C. All of the metallic percussion parts will be set to the same noteheads for solid and open notes. To save time scrolling through the character lists, learn the characters for each notehead, and type them in the Closed Notehead and Open Notehead boxes. For example, the character for a "Closed Notehead" is a lowercase "y," and for an Open Notead, uppercase "Y."

8. Set the percussion map for the Tamtam by displaying its Staff Attributes. Then:
    a. Click the Notation Style Select button.
    b. Click Edit.
    c. Click the View Only Named Notes box.
    d. Select "Tamtam."
    e. Enter a lowercase y in the Solid Notehead box.
    f. Enter an uppercase Y in the Open Notehead box. Click Done and then Select.

Remember, the Tamtam is on E3, MIDI note 52. Play this note to enter the Tamtam part.

9. Repeat the selection process for the Triangle. For the triangle, there are two pitches in the Percussion map: one for the open sound, one for the muted sound. They are a half step apart, so they will display on the same line with the accidental hidden. Change the noteheads for both pitches. Remember the MIDI notes for entry, later.
10. Select Tambourine and go through the steps one last time. Then click OK to exit Staff Attributes, and save your document.

Some of the more exotic instruments available in the Wizard many not have General MIDI sounds available. It will be up for you to decide on a substitution or to disable playback.

Group Attributes

You need to make one quick change to the harp part, adding the designation for Harp 1 & 2.

1. With the Staff tool active, select **Staff** > Edit Group Attributes.

Just as in Staff Attributes, all groups can be accessed in this dialog box. The popup menus here perform a different function than in Staff Attributes, use the arrows to navigate from group to group. The up arrow raises the number, the bottom arrow lowers it, so to move down the score, you must click the Up Arrow.

2. Click the Up Arrow until you reach the Harp group, ID 12.
3. Click the Edit button for the Full Name.
4. Type 1 for Harp 1, press Return/Enter, and type Harp 2 on the line under it. Then click OK.
5. Add the Abbr. Name info. Then click OK twice to return to the score.

Adding Staves to an Existing Score

After looking further at the printed editions, I've made an editorial decision to split the Violin I, II, and Viola staves each onto two staves for the last two pages of the example. This will require adding and grouping new staves to the score. Later in this chapter, you will learn how to hide the unwanted or unused staves from individual pages. Each staff will actually exist for the entire score and be visible in Scroll View, but in Page View, it is possible to hide staves selectively. I want those staves in a specific place, with the existing string staves.

1. Choose the Staff tool.
2. Highlight the staff handle of the Violin II staff by clicking once anywhere on the staff. The new staves will be inserted above the selected staff.

3. Select **Staff** > New Staves, or Control-click (Mac) or Right-click (Windows) to access the contextual menu. The Wizard won't be much help in this situation.
4. Enter "2" for the Number of Staves, and click OK.

Creating a Group and Adding the Bracket

1. Click anywhere on the two new staves.
2. Select **Staff** > Add Group and Bracket. In this dialog box:
   a. Click the Edit button for the Full Group Name, and enter "Violin I."

b. Click the button for the Abbr. Group Name, and enter "Vln. I."
c. Under the Bracket heading, select the rightmost bracket.
d. Enter "–24" for the Distance from Left Edge of Staff. This positions it to the left of the existing bracket. Then click OK.

3. Select the handle of the Viola staff, and repeat the steps to add the Violin II staves, name them, and add the group and bracket information.
4. Select the handle of the Cello staff, and repeat the steps to add the Viola staves, name them, and add the group and bracket information.

The new staves have not been assigned for MIDI playback; only the Wizard can do that when creating staves. When you create new staves using the Staff menu, you must manually assign the playback timbre.

1. Select **Window** > Instrument List.
2. Scroll down, locate the new staves, and assign to them the proper Instrument for playback.
3. Choose "String Ensemble" from the Instrument popup menu. The channel and patch number will change automatically.
4. Repeat this for all of the staves you just added.

Anyone Make an IMAX Monitor?

I use a 20-inch monitor, and I can only see down to the Bass Clarinet staff at 100% viewing size. Even at 50%, I only make it to the Trombone 3/Tuba staff. It is difficult to manage large-size scores on a computer screen, but it was also difficult to manage large-size scores using manuscript paper. The advantage in Finale is that you can view the score up as smaller sets of staves called Staff Sets. Finale gives you the option of setting up eight different staff sets in a document, and they can contain any number or combination of staves in the score.

The first thing I do with a new score layout is set up Staff Sets for each section of the orchestra: woodwinds, brass, percussion, and strings. Depending on the piece, I may also set up additional sets of instruments that combine specific parts such as the woodwinds and strings. Other combinations possible are all the low instruments such as the bassoons, tuba, timpani, cello, and bass, or the high instruments: flutes, oboes, clarinets, trumpets, bells, and violins. Wherever I see an advantage to having a particular group of staves right next to one another on the screen, I'll create a specific Staff Set.

Creating Staff Sets

1. Select **View** > Scroll View. You can only define Staff Sets in Scroll View.
2. Choose the Staff tool .
3. Select **View** > Scale View to, and then adjust the view percentage so all the woodwind staves are visible on the screen.
4. Drag-select all the woodwind staves.
5. Hold Option (Mac) or Control (Windows), and select **View** > Program Staff Sets > Staff Set 1. Then release the Option or Control key.

Now, you will see only the woodwind staves of the score on the screen. To return to the full score, select **View** > Select Staff Sets > All Staves. Note the keystroke options displayed in the submenu for each Staff Set. They can be used in creating Staff Sets, on the Mac side; Windows users will need program using Control key and selecting via the menu.

1. Drag-select over all the brass instrument staves, Horns through Tuba.
2. Press Option-Control-2 (Mac) or Control-select **View** > Program Staff Sets > Staff Set 2 (Windows).
3. Repeat the above steps, and create a Staff Set for Percussion for Staff Set 3.
4. Assign Staff Set 4 to the Keyboard instruments.

For Staff Sets consisting of non-adjacent staves, use Shift-click to select the staff handles. For non-contiguous staves you must specifically select the handles, not click on the staves themselves.

1. Drag-select the handles for the Woodwinds again.
2. Scroll down the score to Strings.
3. Shift-drag to select the String staves.
4. Press Option-Control-5 (Mac) or Control-select **View** > Program Staff Sets > Staff Set 5 (Windows) to assign the woodwinds and strings to Staff Set 5.
5. Select the single-staff Violins and Viola, with the Cello and Bass.
   - Press Option-Control-6 (Mac) or Control-select **View** > Program Staff Sets > Staff Set 6 (Windows) to assign these to Staff Set 6.
6. Select the double-staff Violins and Viola, with the Cello and Bass.
   - Press Option-Control-7 (Mac) or Control-select **View** > Program Staff Sets > Staff Set 7 (Windows) to assign these to Staff Set 7.

Any combination is possible. Sets can be selected from **View** > Staff Sets or by using the keystroke equivalents assigned to the Staff Sets. This enables you to move quickly from one to another, or back to the full score. You can even move directly from a Staff Set to Page View, where all the staves will be visible.

Here's the complete list of Staff Sets I created for *Petrushka* and the keyboard shortcuts for accessing them:

Staff Set	Mac	Windows
Staff Set 1: Woodwinds	Control-1	Alt-V, F, 1
Staff Set 2: Brass	Control-2	Alt-V, F, 2
Staff Set 3: Percussion	Control-3	Alt-V, F, 3
Staff Set 4: Piano, Harp, and Celeste	Control-4	Alt-V, F, 4
Staff Set 5: Woodwinds and Strings	Control-5	Alt-V, F, 5
Staff Set 6: Single-Staff Strings	Control-6	Alt-V, F, 6
Staff Set 7: Double-Staff Strings	Control-7	Alt-V, F, 7

Run The Checklist

Here is a list of other things to set up in this (or any) template. Keep in mind, you can edit your templates, so if later there are any additions, changes, or omissions, it is generally easy to update them.

1. Edit any settings in the Options menu, and the Document Settings dialog window.
2. Set up or create Metatools, Expressions, Articulations, Chord Symbols, Shapes, or other library items.
3. Load or edit any libraries.

Normally, I would also go through a Page Layout phase in setting up a template, since it is important that it prints properly. For this assignment, the score pages will be optimized, so the staves on each page will have to be positioned manually after the music is entered.

You have just completed setting up a score template.

> 😊 Have you saved lately?

Given all the work that goes into setting up a score template, I always keep a clean copy as backup, for several reasons. One reason is to create a backup, just in case it is needed due to a disk error or crash. Also, if I am working on the entire *Petrushka* score, I'll break the complete work into four separate pieces, by "Tableau" (the label Stravinsky gives to each section of *Petrushka*). With a master template specific to *Petrushka*, I don't have to repeat setting up the template for each section, based on a more generic orchestral template. Templates can also serve as starting points for creating other templates that require slightly different variations in instrumentation.

To safeguard your templates, you can lock them so that you don't accidentally overwrite them. This is done in your computer's OS; open the contextual menu by Control-clicking (Mac) or Right-clicking (Windows) on the file icon.

Preparing the Score for Note Entry

Before entering notes, set the correct number of measures, barlines, meters, key changes, if any, and rehearsal and tempo marks. These will become the landmarks that keep you from getting lost in a sea of measures and staves.

To set the measures and double-barlines:

1. Choose the Measure tool .
2. Select **Measure** > Add, and enter "24" for the number of measures to add.
3. Control-click (Mac) or Right-click (Windows) measure 17, and select "Double Barline" from the contextual menu.
4. Continue through the score entering the double barlines, including the one at the last measure.

Time Signature Tool

The Time Signature tool hasn't seen much action in this book so far, since time signatures can be entered in the Setup Wizard, but there is a lot to learn about time signatures in Finale.

To change time signatures:

1. Choose the Time Signature tool .

2. Set measure 18 to 3/4 time by selecting 3/4 from the contextual menu, using Control-click (Mac) or Right-click (Windows).
3. Set the other time signatures, using the contextual menus:
   - Set measure 19 to 2/4.
   - Set measure 28 to 3/4.
   - Set measure 29 to 2/4.
   - Set measure 33 to 3/8.

Better Beaming through Time Signatures

Time signatures control beaming. This is a common issue for time signatures where the eighth note gets the beat. Having to manually beam notes (using / in Simple Entry to connect flags) can be a major time drain, especially for something that occurs automatically in other time signatures. A time signature of 4/8 is easy enough to create in the Time Signature tool, but, as illustrated in the graphic below, it will not automatically beam them together, without our setting some parameters. Time to dig deeper into the Time Signature tool.

To open the Time Signature dialog box, choose the Time Signature tool, and double-click the measure you wish to edit. Click the More Choices button.

In the expanded Time Signatures window, you can set the numeric time signature independently of how Finale will beam the notes together. This is done via two windows. The top section sets the measure size and beaming, and the bottom section sets the time signature symbol that will display.

In this case, we need four eighth notes beamed together, with a time signature symbol displayed as 4/8. The best time signature for beaming that also has the same number of beats as 4/8 is 1/2. In other words, all notes within a half-note duration will get beamed together.

1. Double-click measure 34, or select Edit Time Signature from its contextual menu via Control-click (Mac) or Right-click (Windows).

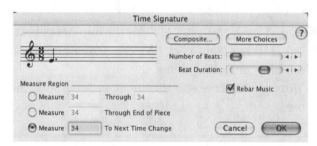

2. Set the Beat Duration, which will control the beaming behavior. Click the scroll bar's right arrow one time to create a 1/2 time signature.
3. Set Measure Region to "Measure 34 Through 34."
4. Click the More Choices button, to expand the Time Signatures dialog box.

5. Check "Use A Different Time Signature for Display." Now set the lower time signature for 4/8.

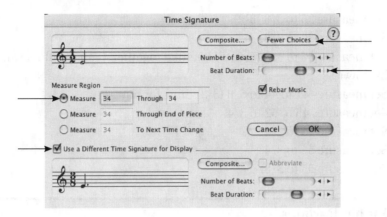

6. Click the left Beat Duration arrow three times, to display "1/8."
7. Click the right Number of Beats arrow three times, to display "4/8," and click OK.

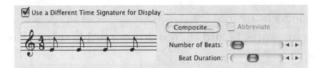

Now, all of the beamed notes in the bar will automatically beam in 1/2 time, but the time signature symbol displayed in the score will be 4/8. Measure 35 has half the problem, a 2/8 time signature, so you can solve it with half the time: 1/4.

8. Follow the setup procedures discussed previously to set the time signature to 1/4, while displaying 2/8 in the score.

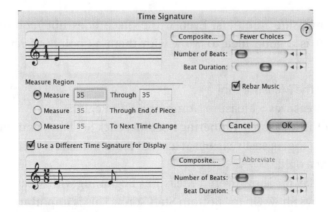

Measures 36 through 38 are in 5/8 time with all five eighths beamed together. For now, we'll set this as 3+2, as grouping all five beats requires some special techniques that we'll discuss later in the chapter.

To set the remaining time signatures for this example, use the contextual menu, via Control-click (Mac) or Right-click (Windows):

9. Set measure 35 to 5/8 (3-2).
10. Set measure 39 to 3/8.
11. Set measure 40 to 4/8 time, all beamed together. (You should be an old pro at this, by now.)
12. Set measures 41 to 44 to 5/8 (3-2) time, for now.
13. Set measures 45 to 52 to 3/4.
14. Set measure 53 to 2/4.
15. Set measure 54 to 3/4.
16. Set measure 55 to 3/8.

Entering Multiple Double Barlines

Our example contains quite a few double bars, all of them occurring in groups of two or more. It is possible to select and change more than one barline at a time, using the Measure tool.

1. Choose the Measure tool .
2. Highlight measures 17 and 18. You do not need to select all of the staves, in this instance.
3. Double-click the highlighted measures to bring up the Measure Attributes dialog box, or access the contextual menu via Control-click (Mac) or Right-click (Windows).
4. Choose "Double Barline," and click OK, if you're using the dialog box.
5. Repeat the steps for the rest of the double barline combinations. Remember that the right-hand barline is the one that changes.

Measure Numbers

Next add measure numbers. Even if the piece does not require individual measure numbers, it is a good idea to work with them as points of reference when entering music.

1. Choose the Measure tool .
2. Select **Measures** > Measure Numbers > Edit Regions.
3. Under the Measure Numbering heading, click Set Font, and select something big and bold that is easily visible at a small reduction size. I recommend 18-point Helvetica bold.
4. Set Display to "Show Every 1 Measures Beginning with Measure 1."
5. Set Always Show On to "Bottom Staff" only. This is important for staff sets where the bottom staff—the bass part, in this case—is not included.

When setting up the measure numbers, select Always Show on Bottom Staff so they will be visible in all Staff Sets.

6. Click the Position button, and position the number in the center of the measure, far enough below the music so it does not collide with the music on the bottom staff. In most cases, –275 to –300 EVPUs (–0.95486 to –1.04167 inches) will provide enough room under the bottom staff for dynamics, unless it's the tuba. Then click OK twice.

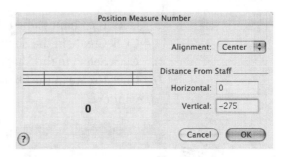

Expressions: the Shape of Things to Come

Creating boxed rehearsal numbers should be old hat by now (see chapter 8). In a score that will require a large percentage of reduction to fit on letter-sized paper, the point size needs to be increased significantly.

1. Choose the Expression tool 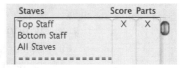.
2. Double-click on measure 1.
3. Click the Create button.
4. In the Text pane:
    a. Select **Text** > Size > 24.
    b. Select **Text** > Style > Bold.
    c. Enter a "5" for the rehearsal number.
    d. Check "Break A Multimeasure Rest."
    e. Set Enclosure Shape to "Rectangle."
5. In the Measure Positioning pane:
    a. Set Horizontal: Expression Alignment Point to "Left."
    b. Set Measure Alignment Point to "Left Barline."
    c. Set Vertical: Position to "Above Staff Baseline." Then click OK and Select.
6. Create a new Staff Set called "Rehearsal."
7. For the Top Staff, click to indicate both "Score" and "Parts." Then click OK.

Staves	Score	Parts	
Top Staff	X	X	
Bottom Staff			
All Staves			
===============			

Continue though the score, adding the rehearsal numbers and text. Leave out the tempo indications, for now.

Shape Designer: Mixed-Font Tempo Indications

The "Stringendo ♩. ♩ = 144" tempo indication in measure 33 presents a unique challenge. Normally, the mixed font would not be a problem in a Text Expression, but there is one character here that rules out our using Text Expression for this object: the tie between the two notes. There is no text character for this in the Maestro font. However, the Shape side of the Expression tool will allow the mix of text and graphics.

First, enter the text of this composite shape:

1. Choose the Expression tool .
2. Double-click in measure 33.

3. Click the Shape radio button at the bottom of the Expression Selection window.
4. Click Create in the Shape Expression window.
5. Click Select in the Shape Expression Designer window.
6. Click Create in the Shape Selection window. You are now in the Shape Designer window.

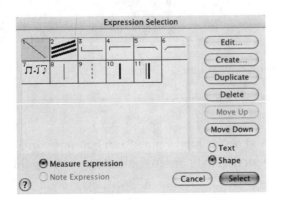

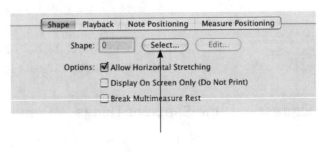

The Shape Designer window is like a drawing program inside Finale. Graphic symbols can be custom created or combined with text, as you are about to do.

7. Select **Shape Designer** > Show > Grid. Rows of dots will appear in the window. These are for spacing purposes only and will not become a part of the shape or print.
8. Click the Text tool icon in the Shape Designer window.
9. Select **Shape Designer** > Select Font.
    a. Set the font to "Times."
    b. Set the point size to "18."
    c. Set Style to Bold, and then click OK to return to the Shape Designer window.
10. Move the cursor to the circle in the center of the window. This will become the handle for the shape.
11. Click once, so the blinking line appears on the screen.
12. Type "Stringendo," followed by a space.

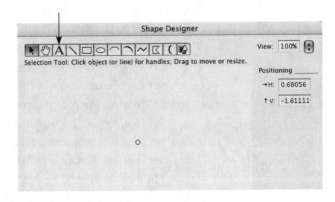

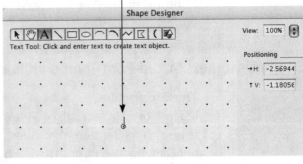

13. Select **Shape Designer** > Select Font.
    a. Set the font to "Maestro."
    b. Set the point size to "18."
    c. Uncheck Bold under Style, so the characters are plain. Then click OK.
14. Next, enter the Maestro characters for the notes. Type:
    a. Lowercase Q for the quarter note.
    b. Period (.) for the dot.
    c. Four spaces (space for the tie), then lowercase H for the half note.
    d. Two more spaces.
15. Select **Shape Designer** > Select Font.
    a. Set the font to "Times."
    b. Set Size to 18 point.
    c. Set Style to "Bold," and then click OK.
16. Type the equals sign (=), a space, and the number 46.

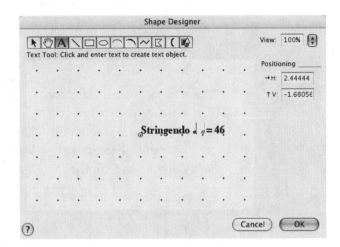

Now, add the graphic element (tie) to the Expression, and ultimately, make the text and the graphics a single shape.

1. To aid in positioning, set the View popup menu (in the top-right corner) to "800%."
2. Choose the Shape Designer's Hand Grabber tool 🖐, and move the shape so that the notes are visible.
3. Choose the Shape Designer's Slur tool ⌐.
4. Position the cursor by the half note, at the right end of the slur. The slur will draw from right to left.
5. Drag to the left, and release the button when you reach the quarter note.
6. Choose the Shape Designer's Selection tool 🔺, and click on the tie.
7. Drag the tie's center handle downward, to give the tie a bit more arc.

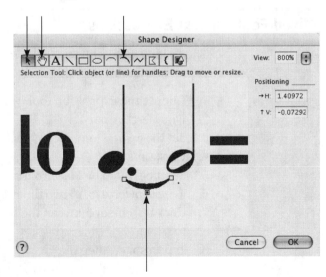

Once all the elements are entered, they must be grouped so that Finale will treat them as one shape.

1. Select **Edit** > Select All.

2. Select **Shape Designer** > Group, and then click OK to exit the Shape Designer's editing window.

In the Shape Expression Designer window, there are two tasks to accomplish. First, prevent horizontal stretching of this shape (which would distort it).

3. Uncheck the Allow Horizontal Stretching box.

Finally, set the shape to cause the piece to play back at the correct tempo, and then select it for our score.

4. In the Playback pane:
    a. Set Type to "Tempo."

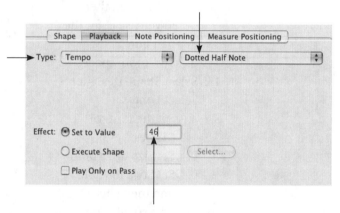

There is no menu item for this note value, so select a dotted half, or a whole note for the value. I choose the faster of the two tempos.

    b. Enter "46" for Effect: Set to Value, and click OK.

5. Click Select in the Shape Expression window.
6. Choose the "Rehearsal" Staff List for this Measure Expression, and click OK.

The Shape Designer seems a bit mysterious, but once you get the hang of it, the roughest part is getting there and back.

Have you saved lately?

Mixed Fonts in Text Expressions

The "eighth note equals eighth note" expression in measure 41 is easy work for the Expression Tool.

1. Choose the Expression tool 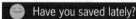.
2. Double-click bar 41.
3. Set the expression type to "Text."
4. Click Create.
5. Set the Font to be Maestro, 18 point.
6. Type a lowercase "e" two times, for the two eighth notes.
7. Click the cursor between the two eighth notes. Set the Font to "Times" and the Style to "Bold."
8. Type a space, then the = (equals sign), then another space. Spaces in Maestro are very small, so be sure that you are adding them while you're in Times.

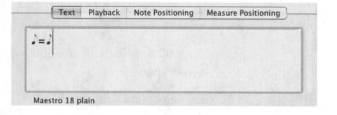

9. Click Select.

10. Choose "Rehearsal" for the Staff List, and click OK.

Try creating the tempo indications in measures 45 and 50 using the Expression tool and the same fonts: 18 point Times bold for the text, and 18 point Maestro plain for the music notes.

The first tempo mark we created comes back in measure 55 with a slight twist. Due to the amount of available space, it has been split onto two lines. We'll need to copy the original shape and do a little shape-shifting in the Shape Designer.

1. Choose the Expression tool 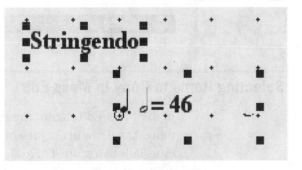.
2. Double-click measure 55.
3. Choose Shape in the Expression Selection window.
4. Highlight the Stringendo shape you created earlier, and click Duplicate.
5. Highlight the duplicated shape, and click Edit.
6. Click Select in the Shape Expression Designer.
7. Click Edit in the Shape Selection window.

This will place us back in the Shape Designer's editing window. The goal is to change this single-line Expression into a two-line Expression. Unfortunately, making a two-line Expression out of the current one by placing a line break after "Stringendo" will not work. There would be too much space between the top and bottom line. We need to create two separate elements, in order to control the positioning.

1. Choose the Text tool A from the Shape Designer palette.
2. Select **Shape Designer** > Ungroup.
3. Turn the Grid display on.
4. Place the cursor to the right of "Stringendo," and use Delete/Backspace to delete the word "Stringendo." This word is the easiest thing to re-enter. The metronome marking notes and value remain. Note that the slur did not move. It will be repositioned later.
5. Position the cursor above and to the left of the remaining original text.
6. Set the font to 18-point Times bold.
7. Re-enter "Stringendo."

I've selected both elements with the Shape Designer's Selection tool (not to be confused with the Finale Selection tool). Each element is in its own box and can be moved separately. The grid dot by the dotted quarter note is where the handle of the shape will be in the score. Make that dot the left margin for the shape.

Now there are two separate elements in the window, or three if you count the slur, which has retained its original position. To help with repositioning the elements, turn on the grid display in the Shape Designer window.

8. Choose the Selection tool from the Shape Designer palette.
9. Click on the word "Stringendo."
10. Drag it over the bottom line, using the grid dots to left align the two elements. Increase the view percentage as the elements get closer together.
11. Drag the slur to the correct position between the notes. You will have to drag both end handles to their new position, as the shape cannot be moved whole.
12. Once all of the elements are in place, the shape needs to be rejoined as a whole.
13. Select **Edit** > Select All.
14. Select **Shape Designer** > Group.
15. Click OK, and follow the trail back to insert the shape into the score, using the "Rehearsal" Staff Set.

> For difficult alignments, use the Line Tool in Shape Designer to create a guideline to position the text or graphics. Delete the line once the positioning is set.

13_Petrushka_1.mus

> 😊 Have you saved lately?

Enter the Notes

As you enter the music (I recommend using Speedy Entry for this example), scan the original for any unisons, octave doubling, or repeated sections. These only need to be entered once, then copied via the Mass Edit tool. This can save you a lot of time, but a word of caution. Make sure you've got it right the first time, or you may multiply mistakes. (Been there, done that, hid under the t-shirt.)

If you are interested in arranging and orchestration, copying can be an excellent analysis tool. Identifying doubled or repeated sections can speed along note entry, and help with learning some useful techniques for your own work. Continue reading ahead for tutorials on copying repeated or doubled sections in Mass Edit, and entering grace notes (bar 32 for example), tremolos, tuplets, and beaming across the barline.

13_Petrushka_2.mus

> 😊 Have you saved lately?

Selecting Items to Copy in Mass Edit

In the Mass Edit menu, the default setting for copying and pasting is to Move Everything. As we saw in the previous chapter, "everything" isn't always what we want to move, especially in a score. For example, if you copy notes from bar 1 of Petrushka to bar 2, the rehearsal number and text entered in Expressions would be copied as well. But fear not: Mass Edit is not only powerful; it can be taught.

To set which Entry Items will be copied:

1. Choose the Mass Edit tool 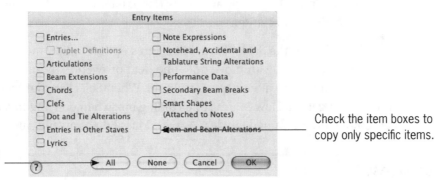.
2. Select **Mass Edit** > Copy Entry Items.

Click the All button to select everything.

Check the item boxes to copy only specific items.

3. Click the Entries checkbox. The Entry Modifications dialog box allows you to make additional modifications to the entries that you are moving. This is the only category that allows additional modifications to be made while copying, though we will go with the default settings. Click OK to return to the Entry items dialog box.

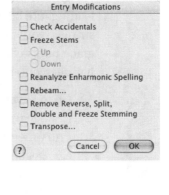

4. In the entry Items dialog box, click the All button.
5. Uncheck the Clefs box, and then click OK.

This is my standard setting for Mass Edit copying. The Clefs box is important because I do a lot of copying across treble, bass, and alto clefs. Failing to check this would result in time spent with the clef tool repairing the unintended clef changes. Measure items can be copied along with Entry items or on their own.

To set which Measure Items will be copied:

1. Select **Edit** > Copy Measure Items.

This dialog box controls what measure items Mass Edit will copy. It works the same way as the Entries dialog box: Check only what you want to copy. This is most useful in formatting or copying out large sections of formatted music. I usually enable Smart Shapes (Assigned to Measures) for copying crescendos so that they line up vertically in a score.

2. Click Smart Shapes (Assigned to Measures), and click OK.
3. Let's find some things to copy. First, enter the Piccolo and Flute notes in bars 6, 7, and 8. Then copy them into bars 10, 11, and 12.
   a. Enter "2" Times in the dialog, and then also copy it to bars 13, 14, and 15.
   b. Copy the same measures in the Clarinet staves.

317

4. Select **View** > Staff Sets > Staff Set 6.
5. Copy the Piccolo in bars 1 through 15 to the Violin 1.
6. Enter the first two measures of the Cymbals.
   - Use Mass Edit to copy and paste it into bars 1 through 17 and 19 of both the Cymbals and Tamtam part.

Don't forget about the Select Partial Measures option in Edit menu. By checking Select Partial Measures, you can move only one beat or twenty-and-a-half measures, adding more flexibility to an already powerful tool. When Select Partial Measures is activated, you will not get the How Many Times dialog box when copying to a different measure. Remember, only a trained Finale user with Mass Edit as an ally can defeat Stravinsky.

Grace Notes across the Barline

For grace notes like those in measure 32 leading into 33 in the low woodwinds and strings, you must first understand that grace notes can be entered after the note has been entered.

1. Go to Layer 2 in Speedy Entry.
2. Change two behaviors in the Speedy Entry menu:
   a. Deactivate **Speedy Entry** > Jump To Next Measure.
   b. Deactivate **Speedy Entry** > Check For Extra Notes.

This will allow you to place note values greater than those in the time signature without getting the "Too Many Notes" dialog box or having the Speedy Entry window advance to the next measure when the measure is full.

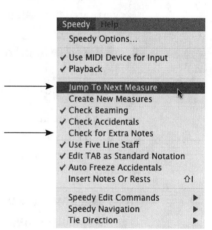

3. Enter a half rest in measure 32. This half rest is there strictly for positioning the notes and must be hidden.
4. Enter three sixteenth notes in bar 32.
   a. Use the ; (semicolon) key to convert them to grace notes.
   b. Place the cursor on the second and third sixteenth notes, and use the / (slash) key on the keypad to beam them together.
5. Place the cursor on the half rest.
   a. Press the H key to hide the half rest.
   b. Switch to Layer 1.
   c. Enter a whole rest. The Layer Options settings will kick in and place the rest above the staff because of the entries in Layer 2.
   d. Position the cursor on the whole rest and press the * (asterisk) key on the keypad to place it in the default position.

6. Reset the Speedy Entry menu settings of step (2), after all of the grace notes have been entered.

Use the same technique for the cross-barline grace notes in the rest of the score. Make adjustments in the number of rests entered based on the time signature.

The Whole Rest and Nothing But The Rest

Whenever two instruments share a staff, there is the possibility of one playing while the other is resting. There are two ways of handling this situation. Both are illustrated in the Oboe parts at bar 34. For the Oboe 1 and 2 staff, the Roman numeral "I" indicates that only Oboe 1 is playing. This continues until the "a2" indication at bar 45. The Oboe 3 and 4 staff uses whole rests, stem directions, and a Roman numeral to indicate which part is the Oboe 3 and which is Oboe 4.

Entering a whole rest is simple in 4/4 or 2/2 time, but for any other time signature, entering a whole rest means four beats of rest. That brings you face to face with our old nemesis, the "There are too many beats in this measure" dialog box. Simply click the "Leave the measure alone" button, and everything will be fine. Your music will space properly when laying out entries in Mass Edit.

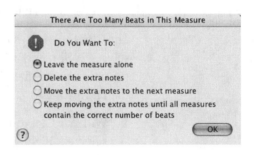

> Add the rests when you are finished entering the music, and deactivate the Check for Extra Notes setting in the Speedy Entry menu, so that you don't end up having to face "the box" again.

Clef Changes

There are two ways of setting a clef at the start of a piece. The first is in the Staff Attributes dialog box; the second is with the Clef tool. Keep an eye out for the clef changes in this piece. In fact, you may want to do this when you are setting up your key signatures and measure attributes. The Trombone 1 & 2 staff begins with tenor clef, and it stays in that clef for the length of the example. That is a situation where Staff Attributes would be the best solution.

1. Choose the Staff tool .
2. Double-click the Trombone 1 & 2 staff.
3. Next to First Clef, click the Select button.
4. Choose the Tenor clef. Then click OK twice to return to the music.

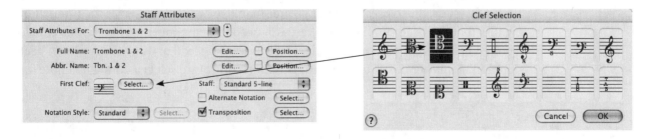

The next clef change is in the bass-clef staff of the harp in bar 20. This change continues to the end of the example.

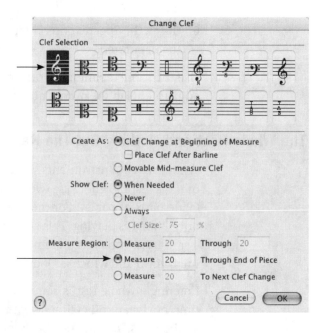

1. Choose the Clef tool 𝄢.
2. Option-double-click (Mac) or Alt-double-click (Windows) in bar 20.
3. Under the Clef Selection heading, choose the Treble clef.
4. Set Measure Region to "Measure 20 Through End of Piece." Then click OK.

The Clef Tool makes it possible to select a region and use a Metatool to apply a particular clef. The Viola part changes to Treble clef beginning in measure 22, then returning to Alto clef at bar 33.

1. With the Clef tool still selected, highlight measure 22 of the Viola staff, and Shift-click on measure 32 to select the region.
2. Double-click on the high-lighted section to choose the clef from the Clef Selection window, or press "1," the Clef Metatool key for the Treble clef.

The Cello staff also changes clef in measure 22, but ends a bar earlier in 32 because of the grace notes. If you don't know the Metatool key for the Tenor clef, follow these steps.

1. With the Clef tool still selected, highlight measures 22 to 31 of the Cello staff.
2. Double-click on the highlighted region.
3. Select the Tenor clef from the Clef Selection dialog box. Then click OK.

Polka Dots and 5/8 Beams

Remember those 5/8 measures back in the Time Signature tool? Well, time to face the music and dance, er, beam them together. First, enter all the eighth notes with the default beaming. Now the fun begins. How can we get all five notes in the 5/8 bars to beam together? Finale beams in multiples of two or three. Since five is not a multiple of two or three, use the closest number greater than five, which is six. Six is the number of eighth's that the beaming time signature will need to beam together. Six eighths equals a dotted half note so a 3/4 meter is the place to start. Instead of using the common beat duration of quarter notes, use the Beat Duration controls to select a dotted half note for the value.

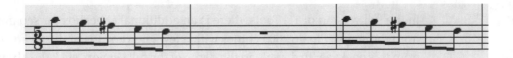

1. Choose the Mass Edit tool.
2. Highlight bars 36 through 38.
3. Select **Mass Edit** > Rebeam > Rebeam to Time Signature.

4. Choose 3/4 time with a dotted half as the indicated rhythm (top arrow 3 clicks to the left, bottom arrow 3 clicks to the right).
5. Repeat for bars 41 through 44.

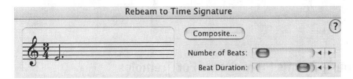

Entering the Tremolos in Bars 45–48

The secret to tremolos is to enter them as half the displayed value. Enter a whole note tremolo as two half notes, or in this example, enter a dotted-half-note tremolo as two dotted-quarter notes.

1. Enter two dotted-quarter notes for all tremolos.
2. Choose the Mass Edit tool.
3. Select **Plug-ins** > TG Tools > Easy Tremolos.
   a. For Total number of beams, enter "2."
   b. Check "Create playback notes," if you want the tremolo to play back. Then click OK.

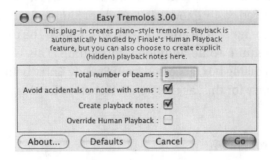

For Tremolos on divisi staves, select **Options** > Show Active Layer Only before applying the plug-in.

321

In the full version of TG Tools, there is an additional checkbox for separating the beams from the stems. Finale 2005 comes with a few Lite versions of the more popular plug-ins from this package. To download the demo of the full version, click the About button in any of the TG plug-ins, in the **Plug-ins** > TG Tools submenu. The full package currently sells for $99.95 for professionals, $69.95 for home use, and $49.95 for students. The price includes full documentation, and you will receive e-mails when fixes or upgrades are available.

Using the full version, you would be done with tremolos and ready to move on. Using the Easy version, you've skipped some complex and tedious steps at a great time savings, but there's one more task left: separating the beams from the stems. We'll do this using another technique.

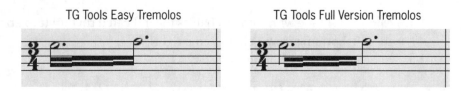

TG Tools Easy Tremolos · · · TG Tools Full Version Tremolos

Separating Beams From Stems For Tremolos

1. Choose the Beam Extension tool 🎵 from the Special Tools 🔻 palette.
2. Double-click on the beam handle in measure 45.
3. Check both the 8th and 16th box, and click OK.
4. Drag the beam's left handle to the right, just beyond the dot.
5. Drag its right handle to the left the same distance as the left handle.
6. Repeat the steps for all the woodwind tremolos.

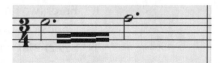

Tuplets

There are three variations of tuplets in the score. The triplets in bars 40 through 46 in the woodwinds are produced easily enough in Speedy or Simple Entry with some extra positioning required using Tuplet Tool after they are all entered. The tuplets in section 9, bars 49 through 54, will require some additional formatting. This will be accomplished in the Tuplet Definition dialog box, accessed from Speedy Entry before you begin entering notes. Use Speedy Entry for this, as there are fewer steps for this process than in Simple Entry.

Lucky 7s: Bar 49 through 54

1. Choose the Speedy Entry tool 🎵.
2. Click in bar 49 of the Oboe 1 & 2 staff.
3. Type Option-1 (Mac) or Control-1 (Windows) to set the tuplet parameters:
   a. Set the Tuplet Definitions for "7 Eighths in the space of 6 Eighths."

b. Under the Placement heading, select "Note Side" or "Beam Side" from the popup menu, as indicated.
   - Check the Enhanced Tuplets box.
   - Uncheck the Allow Horizontal Drag box.
   - Check the Use Bottom Note box, if there is more than one note in the first voicing.

c. Uncheck the Break Bracket or Slur box.

d. Click Always Use Specified Shape.

e. Under the Position heading, enter "25" for the Shape: Vertical. This will raise it up over, or down under, the number. Click OK.

4. Enter the notes in bars 49 through 54.

Make sure the number is under the bracket and not touching it. Use the Tuplet tool to adjust the positioning. Use these steps for entering the rest of the quintuplets and septuplets.

The Same Thing Only Different

In measures 50 through 54, the flutes have a sextuplet pattern. There is a slur instead of a bracket, and there is also a beam break. First things first: enter the notation.

1. Choose the Speedy Entry tool.
2. Click in bar 50 of the Piccolo staff, and enter the two quarter rests.
3. Type Option-1 (Mac) or Control-1 (Windows) to set the tuplet parameters:

   a. Under the Placement heading, select "Note Side" or "Beam Side" from the popup menu, as indicated.
      - Check the Enhanced Tuplets box.
      - Uncheck the Allow Horizontal Drag box.
      - Check the Use Bottom Note box, if there is more than one note in the first voicing.

   b. Uncheck the Break Bracket or Slur box.

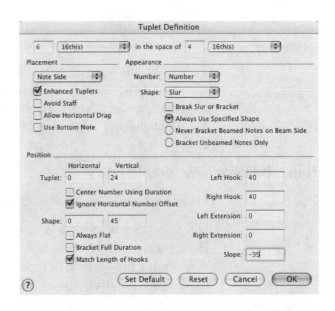

   c.   Click Always Use Specified Shape.

   d.   Under the Position heading, enter "45" for the Shape: Vertical, to get the slur over the number.

   e.   Press the Tab key, and enter "40" for the Left Hook and "40" for the Right Hook.

   f.   Enter "–35" for the Slope. The Hook and Slope number will give the slur a good arc. Then click OK.

4.   Enter the sextuplet in bars 50 and 51, then exit the Speedy Entry window.

Make sure the tuplet number is underneath the slur and not touching it.

As you see, complex tuplets are very time intensive. If you didn't tweak the numbers in the dialog boxes, you'd be dragging shapes on the screen. Since I am all about the time saving, the rest of the sextuplets will spring from these three.

1.   Choose the Mass Edit tool .
2.   Select **Edit** > Select Partial Measures.
3.   Highlight the sextuplet on beat 3 of bar 50.
4.   Copy/Paste the selected sextuplet into beat 1 of bar 53.

Next, tackle the beam break. The reason I'm not able to copy and paste one sextuplet for the whole passage is that the beam break will not copy to a partial measure. (It will copy when Select Partial measures is not checked.)

1.   Choose the Secondary Beam Break tool 🎵 from the Special Tools 🌳 palette.
2.   Click the fourth handle from the left.

   a.   Click the Break Only button.

   b.   Check 16th, then click OK.

3.   Repeat the steps on the other three sextuplets.

Now the sextuplets are ready for mass production.

1.   Choose the Mass Edit tool .
2.   Select **Edit** > Select Partial Measures, to toggle it off.
3.   Highlight bar 51 of the Piccolo part, and copy it to bars 52 and 54.
4.   Highlight bars 50 through 54 of the Piccolo, and copy them to the Flute.

Repitch Notes with Simple Entry

Time to apply a little digital pitch-correction, Finale style.

For passages where there is a lot of detailed work involved, copying the passage and changing the pitches of the notes may be easier than entering the whole phrase. In this case, setting the position of tuplet brackets and entering beam breaks can be done four times instead of twelve times, so it's a good shortcut.

1. Choose the Repitch tool from the Simple Entry 🎵 Palette.
2. Click to highlight the first note on beat 3 of bar 52.
3. Play E-flat on the MIDI keyboard, or press the Up Arrow key and the minus sign.
4. Press the Right arrow key twice advance to the next incorrect note, and repeat the E-flat.
5. Fix the E-flats in bar 53.
6. Click on the first note of the Flute in bar 50, and correct the pitches through bar 54.

> ❗ Whenever you have a complex passage for reasons of Expressions, Articulation, or Tuplets, the Repitch tool can save you a lot of work.

Copying Articulations with Mass Edit

For *Petrushka*, you will need string bowings and "soft accent" ◦ markings, in addition to the usual accents. You can use Mass Edit to move only the articulations. This technique is useful when there is an extended passage of mixed articulations.

1. Choose the Mass Edit tool ⬤.
2. Select **Mass Edit** > Copy Entry Items.
3. Check Articulations, and click OK.
4. Enter the bowing for the Violin I (only) in bars 1 through 20.
5. Highlight bars 1 through 20 in Mass Edit. Then drag the highlighted region down to measure 1 of the Violin II part. When a black box appears around the measures of the Violin II part, release the mouse button.
6. Highlight both the Violin I and II staves, and copy them to the Viola and Cello.
7. Enter additional bowings in bars 2, 8, 12, 13, and 15.
8. Highlight the Cello, and copy it to the Bass.

Entry Items

☐ Entries...	☐ Note Expressions
☐ Tuplet Definitions	☐ Notehead, Accidental and
☑ Articulations	Tablature String Alterations
☐ Beam Extensions	☐ Performance Data
☐ Chords	☐ Secondary Beam Breaks
☐ Clefs	☐ Smart Shapes
☐ Dot and Tie Alterations	(Attached to Notes)
☐ Entries in Other Staves	☐ Stem and Beam Alterations
☐ Lyrics	

(?)   (All)   (None)   (Cancel)   (OK)

325

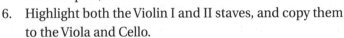

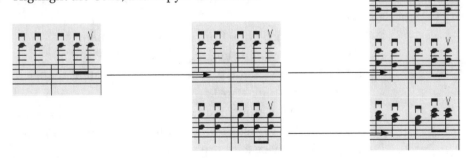

Articulations—Not a Real Drag

By now, you've used Articulation Metatools enough that you probably have the basic set memorized. There are quite a few that are used less frequently, depending on the kind of work you do. When you come to a situation where an unfamiliar articulation is used, drag-select the region and select the articulation from the Apply Articulation dialog

CHAPTER 13 | Orchestral Excerpt

box. Measures 34 through 40 of the top three string parts require a soft accent symbol ›. Unless you do a lot of string writing, this is probably one articulation Metatool that you can't just pull out of the hat.

1. Choose the Articulation tool .
2. Drag over measures 34 through 40 of the Violin I, Violin II, and Viola staves, and then release the mouse button. This brings up the Apply Articulation dialog box.
3. Click the Select button. This brings up the Selection window.
4. Select the soft accent, shape 2. Then click Select and OK.

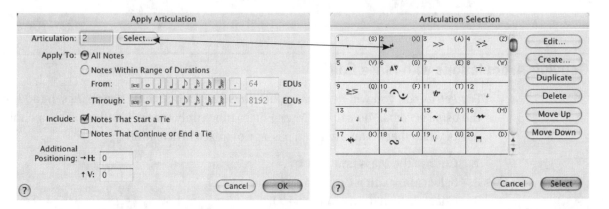

> The Apply Articulation dialog also contains other placement options, such as the ability to select a specific rhythm or group of rhythms to receive the articulation, placing articulations on tied notes, and adding extra distance to the automatic positioning values already assigned to the selected mark.

Adjusting the Handle Position of Articulations

Occasionally, for my taste, the position of an articulation is a little close to the note or staff, or a little distant. Here, I think the soft accent could use a little fine-tuning.

To edit an articulation's distance from the note or staff:

1. Control-click (Mac) or Right-click (Windows) the handle of any soft accent articulation.
2. Select Edit Articulation from the contextual menu.
3. Under the Positioning heading, click Handle Positioning.
   a. To raise the articulation higher above the staff, change the Main Symbol V (Vertical) from –8 to 0.
   b. To move the articulation closer when it's below the staff, change the Flipped Symbol V (Vertical) number from –32 to –24.
   c. Click OK twice to return to the score.

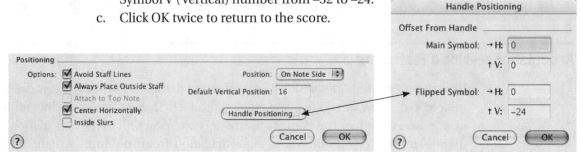

Stem-Side Articulations

For the drum set part in chapter 11, you created stem-side positioning articulations. In this score, there are staccato dots and accents that require special positioning for divisi parts, such as the oboes and clarinets in bars 34 through 38. See, this isn't algebra; you do actually use this stuff again! Duplicate the articulations and change the auto-positioning before entering.

Expressions

Positioning Expressions in this score will take some work. The distance between staves will not be finalized until after the page layout process is complete. Enter the Expressions and dynamics now, since their presence will help determine how much room a particular staff requires, but be prepared for a longer than normal adjustment process. I suggest adjusting the below-staff baseline as close to the staff as possible.

Moving and Positioning Notes

Whenever two independent parts share the same staff, some repositioning of notes or accidentals may be necessary. This is best done with the Note Position tool, in the Special Tools palette, but it can also be handled in the Speedy Entry window. Rests also may need to be moved vertically, which can be done only in Speedy Entry.

The dotted quarter note in the F Horn 3 part in bar 37 must be moved off of the eighth note in the F Horn 4 part. Even though the noteheads are of the same type, dotted notes must always be offset, to clearly show which rhythm and voice has the dot.

In bar 43 of the Trumpet, there are two C-sharps. Only one is necessary.

In bar 48 of the Clarinet 1 & 2 and Bassoon 1 & 2 staves, the dotted half note in the first part must be separated from the eighth note in the second part. It is easiest to move the dotted half, for a variety of reasons. In these situations, use your best judgment to make the music easy to follow.

13_Petrushka_3.mus

😊 Have you saved lately?

Page Layout and the Big O: Optimization

As you've no doubt noticed, there are more staff lines in our score template than are used in the example. Why include them at all if they are not used? Answer: to illustrate the awesome power of Optimization. You are probably familiar with study scores of classical symphonic literature. This format reduces a score to only the instruments playing for however many measures there are on a specific system. Finale allows you to do exactly the same thing in Page View, with a process called "Optimization." Finale scans each staff in a system and looks for entries. Remember, Finale considers rests entries as well as notes. If Finale does not detect an entry, it assumes that the staff can be removed from that system. The advantages are many: you can fit multiple systems on a page in sparsely orchestrated sections, you can use lesser percentages of reduction on pages with fewer staves on them, and you can adjust stave distances to allow for more information such as dynamics, ledger lines, or text.

Optimizing staff systems takes a little time, since each page must be tweaked manually. If time is a factor, you may want to consider other options, such as reducing the score until all staves fit on the page, or pairing up as many instruments as possible to reduce the number of staves.

Set the number of measures per staff system first. Optimization does not automatically readjust when measures are moved. If you decide to move measures after you have optimized your score, you must remove the optimization and reapply to update the layout. If systems are locked and only two pages are altered, then remove and reapply optimization for those two pages, if systems are not locked, then re-optimize from the change to the end of the document.

Since this is not the beginning of the piece, select the Text tool and delete the title, credit and copyright text blocks on the first page. Also delete the continuing page title on page 2, but leave the page numbers.

Begin with Resizing the Score Overall

Finale has attempted to place the entire score onto one letter-size page, with a large margin on the top and the left side of the page. In addition to optimizing out the unused staves, the staff size, page percentage, and page margins will also be adjusted. The Setup Wizard uses the size of the staff as a way of fitting staves on a page. This preserves the page size so that the text is not reduced as well, but the staff reduction is a harder element to work with during the trial-and-error phase. I'll be going through that process and giving you the resulting steps here, but sooner or later you may be doing this on your own.

1. Select **Options** > Page Format > Score.
   a. Set the System Scaling to "96" EVPUs (0.33333 inches) for the Staff Height.
   b. Press the Tab key, and enter "100" for And Scale System. You will see no change until you redefine the score. Click OK.
2. Choose the Page Layout tool.
3. Select **Page Layout** > Redefine Pages > All Pages. Click OK.

EVPUs

Inches

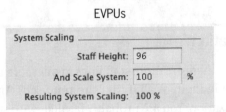

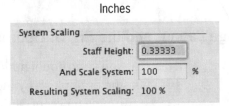

4. Choose the Resize tool 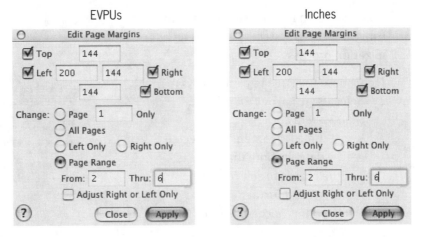 .
   a. Click in the upper-left corner of the first score page. Be sure the window reads "Resize Page." This tool can also resize staves and notes.
   b. Resize the page to "50%," a good place to start on a large score.
   c. Choose "Page 1 Through End of Piece." Click OK.
5. Select **Edit** > Update Layout. Since the scale of the music has changed dramatically, updating the layout is a must.

Next the margins need some tweaking. There is a lot of music to get onto each page and every last EVPU and inch needs to be used efficiently.

1. Choose the Page Layout tool .

The first page requires a larger margin to give ample room to the full staff names. On pages 2 through 6, the left margin can be trimmed.

2. Select **Page Layout** > Page Margins > Edit Page Margins.
   a. For the Left margin, enter 200 EVPUs (1 nch).
   b. Set Change to "Page Range."
   c. Enter "2 Thru: 6."
   d. Click Apply.

3. Select **Page Layout** > Systems > Edit Margins.
   a. Click the Select All button to select all the staff systems.
   b. For the Top, enter "80" EVPUs (0.27778 inches). Then click Apply.

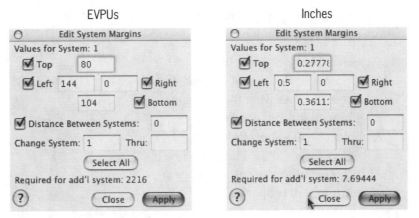

The score is down to six pages, but there is room to loosen up the layout a little since there is room on the last page. Use the Mass Edit tool to set the number of measures for each system, and lock them.

> When preparing a score for optimizing, try to look for changes in the orchestration to set the system breaks.

1. Choose the Mass Edit tool .
2. Highlight measures 1 through 11. Use **Edit** > Select Region, if it is hard to judge in the score.
3. Select **Mass Edit** > Fit Music.
    -   Under the Action heading, choose "Lock Selected Measures Into One System."
4. Highlight measures 12 through 22, and repeat the steps for locking them onto one system.
5. Continue locking the required number of measures for each remaining page of the example.

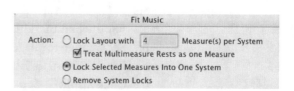

Now that the pages are set, it's time to trim the unused systems with the Optimization process.

1. Choose the Page Layout tool 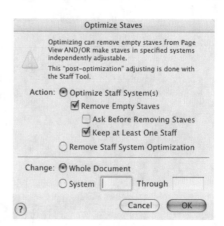.
2. Select **Page Layout** > Optimize Staff Systems.
    -   "Whole Document" is selected by default. Note that there is the option to select specific systems if further editing becomes necessary. Click OK.

Page through the score, and you'll notice that only page 4 actually fits. All staves will need to be positioned manually.

Page Positioning Aides

Guides will help you position elements on a page. They do not print.

1. Select **View** > Show Grid.
2. Choose the Zoom tool 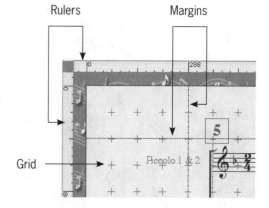, and zoom in to see what the page looks like with the grid displaying.
3. Select **View** > Show Rulers.
4. Select **View** > Show Margins. This will help most with positioning the bottom staff properly.

Use one or all of these aids in positioning the staves and other page elements. To turn any of them off, select them again in the View menu.

Positioning Individual Staves

- Choose the Staff tool . Every staff now has two handles to the left of the clef. These allow you to drag the staff in an optimized score to a new vertical position.

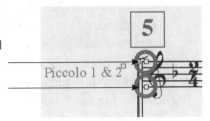

The top handle controls that staff for all optimized systems for the entire score.

The bottom handle controls that staff for the current system only.

In the example, pages 1, 2, 3, 5, and 6 each have a few staves hanging off the bottom of the page. Use the bottom handle to begin closing up the space between the staves on the page until they all fit within the page margin. Move down the score until the Bass staff fits with room to spare for the measure numbers. Once the Bass is in an acceptable position, work back up through the score repositioning anything that looks too close together.

Pages 4 actually has room to spare, but not enough to fit an additional system—so drag the bottom handle of the Bass staff down to the bottom of the page, and spread everything else out in between. On pages 4 and 6, drag the Piccolo handle down to allow more room for the tempo, rehearsal, and Text Expressions at the top.

Trial and error is the way to go here. Once again, go with whatever looks clearest to your eye. Try to avoid collisions and crowding dynamics or text, as best as you can. Use the Show Rulers and/or Show Margins display options in the View menu to help you position things as close to the margins as possible without going over. Print a test page if you are still not sure.

> Close the distance between a group of staves with the same instrument (oboes, clarinets, horns, etc.), and leave a little larger space between those groups—oboes and clarinets, horns and cornets, and so on. That will help the eye group instruments together and to follow a score that changes from page to page more easily.

Beaming Across the Barline

Finale does not directly support beaming over barlines, so over the years, some workarounds were developed to fake it. The Beam Over Barlines plug-in takes the best of them and saves several steps in applying them. Just as with the Cross-Staff plug-in, this is a lite version of a more powerful product that is available separately from Patterson (http://RobertGPatterson.com) for $59. To learn more about Robert Patterson's plug-ins, select **Plug-ins** > Note, Beam, and Rest Editing > Patterson Beams Lite > Options and Info. It will take you to directly to the Web site.

To beam across a barline:

1. Make sure you are in Page View.
2. Choose the Mass Edit tool .
3. Select **Options** > Show Active Layer Only.
4. Select Layer 2.
5. Highlight bars 34 to 36 of the Oboe 3 & 4 staff.
6. Select **Plug-ins** > Note, Beam, and Rest Editing > Patterson Beams Lite > Beam Over Barlines.
7. Highlight bars 34 to 36 of the Clarinet 1 & 2 staff.
8. Select **Plug-ins** > Note, Beam, and Rest Editing > Patterson Beams Lite > Beam Over Barlines.
9. Switch to Layer 1 and repeat the steps for the Bassoon 1 & 2.
10. Advance to page 5, and apply the plug-in to the bottom staff of Violin I and the top staff of Violin II.

In the same collection, there is also a Beam Over Barlines/ Remove plug-in as well. I recommend that you remove the cross-barline beaming if you have to edit the note in any way. That includes changing the pitch or adding Expressions, Articulations, or Note-Attached Slurs. Beams Over Barlines may also adversely effect playback, especially Human Playback.

Page Numbers

There are currently numbers on page 2 through 6, but no number on page 1. Usually, the title page of a score does not have a page number, but in this case, page 1 of our document is not page 1 of the score.

1. Choose the Text tool Ⓐ.
2. Go to page 2.
3. Control-click (Mac) or Right-click (Windows) the page number's handle.

   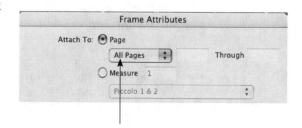

   • From the contextual menu, select Edit Frame Attributes.
   • Under the Attach To heading, choose "All Pages." Click OK.

The numbers are set up for book-style display, with the numbers always on the outside corner of the page. They should be moved up and out of the way of the music.

4. Select **View** > Show Rulers.
5. With page 2 still displaying, drag the page number handle up and to the left. Position it a quarter-inch in from the left side and a quarter-inch down from the top of the page.
6. Go to page 1.
7. Drag the page number's handle up and to the right, and position it a quarter-inch in from the right side and a quarter-inch down from the top of the page.

332

Expression and Articulation Playback

Dynamics play back, and their key velocity is programmable. For our purposes, key velocity = relative volume. If you played the passage in, it would come from your performance, but if you entered the notation in Simple or Speedy Entry, those notes are all at the same key velocity. The dynamic Expressions have key velocity data programmed.

The first measure of the example is marked triple forte (*fff*). To make this as loud as possible in the MIDI world, change the value to the highest velocity possible.

To reprogram the key velocity of a dynamic mark:
1. Choose the Expression tool.
2. Control-click (Mac) or Right-click (Windows) the handle, and select Edit Measure/Note Text Definition from the contextual menu.
3. Click the Playback Tab.
4. Set the number in the Set To Value box to "127," and then click OK. Note: MIDI velocity numbers are 0 to 127, where 0 is the lowest (silence) and 127 is the highest (loud).

Articulations also have playback settings. Not all articulations in the default library are configured to play back. The staccato dot is one articulation that does have a playback setting. The effect is to shorten the duration of the note to 40 percent of its length. Depending on the sound or sample used for playback and the tempo involved, this could cause the notes to sound clipped or hardly sound at all. To allow the note to sound longer, increase the percentage.

To set the playback effect of a staccato articulation:
1. Choose the Articulation tool.
2. Advance to measure 34 and the staccato dot in the Oboe 1 & 2 staff.
3. Double-click the staccato's handle to access the Articulation Designer dialog box.
4. Under the Playback Effect heading, increase the value to "60" in both Top and Bottom Note boxes. Trial and error rules apply, depending upon the sound and the tempo.

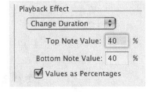

Reverb? Reverb!

Yes, Finale can simulate reverb in Human Playback.

1. Expand the Playback Controls Window, via the triangle in the playback controls (Mac) or the speaker icon (Windows).
2. Click the HP Preferences.
3. Under the Reverb Room Type heading, use the popup menu to change the room size to Taj Mahal. Click Save when you are done, and play back the file to hear the difference.

Chances are that the example will sound best in a smaller space setting. Repeat the procedure and try the large and small halls in the menu. The best room size will depend on the style of the composition, combined with what your ears tell you is right.

333

Check out the HP Preferences dialog when you have a minute. There are plenty of settings there that might enhance playback a little more with some tweaking. This is a personal taste situation, so no steps or numbers. Just look through the Help menu and experiment.

Instruments

If your synthesizer is not multitimbral, it might be helpful for you to listen to the piece in sections first, so you can focus separately on the woodwinds, strings, brass, and percussion. Be prepared for unisons to sound strange. Notes being struck more than once result in a phasing of the sound.

In the Instrument List (**Window** > Instrument List), click the square in the P (Play) column to toggle the staff off (no square) or on (square).

If you have one multitimbral keyboard, you have sixteen channels at your disposal to play back an orchestration. However, you're still limited by your instrument's polyphony. It may be a good idea to check section by section, to make sure no mistake gets by, due to a polyphony limitation. You will experience some phasing on any unisons assigned to the same sound.

If you have more than one MIDI keyboard or tone module, how come you have money left over to buy Finale and this book? The good news is you should be able to avoid the polyphony problem.

Just remember, when Finale transmits a patch change through MIDI, it uses the numbers 1 through 128. If your synthesizer's patch bank begins with zero, the numbers will have to be adjusted by one, so patch 1 in Finale will be patch 0 (or 00, or 000) on your synth.

Saving a Playback File

With a large file, it is better to save it as a Playback File than play it from the score. This places less demand on the computer because it is just playing a MIDI file, as opposed to creating and playing one at the same time. If you make changes to the score, you must create a new playback file. Finale does not update the file automatically.

1. Open the Playback window, and expand it to see all the parameters.
2. Click the Save File button in the lower left corner.
3. Name the file, and click OK.
4. Choose "Select Playback File" in the Playing popup menu.
5. Open the file you just created.
6, Choose "Playback File" from the Playing menu.
7. Click the Play button on the transport controls.

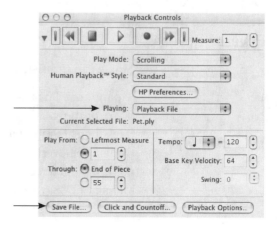

If you make any updates to the score, you'll need to resave the playback file.

If You Want to Know the Score. . .

To view the score in concert pitch:

1. Select **Options** > Display in Concert Pitch.
2. Select it again to return to transposed view.

Leave this on, if you prefer to have the score printed in concert. As long as the transpositions are set up on the individual staves, Finale will turn off the concert pitch display for the part files when they are extracted.

Cut, Print It!

Time to print, so make sure your printer is on and loaded with paper. If you print a lot of scores, consider a printer with a duplex feature. Duplexing involves some additional hardware that will enable the printer to print on both sides of the paper. It hits the output tray ready to be bound.

Creating Parts for Large (Long) Works

The examples in this book are not long enough to get into every copying situation, but in any work longer than two pages, you must be aware of page turns. Use the Smart Page Turns Plug-in on a newly extracted file of two pages or longer, to look for the best location to turn the page. Be sure to check the results, and avoid situations where a page turn appears in the middle of a prominent feature passage or during a difficult instrument change.

In orchestral literature, it is not uncommon for string parts not to have page turns. In these cases, the inside player will stop playing to turn the page while the outside player continues playing. In situations where no page turn is possible, care must be taken to avoid page turns during loud passages where the sound of half the section dropping out will be noticeable. Also be aware of the size of the section. Many recording-size orchestras cannot afford to lose half the players and need turns on rests, no matter how short, or how much paper is left blank.

The Smart Page Turns plug-in has plenty of user-definable controls to set allowable times for turns, as well as warning text to be inserted into the part. Consult the Help menu for more information to using this plug-in.

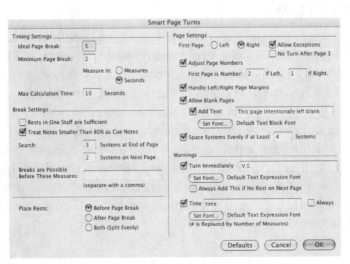

Cue Notes

The next situation is cue notes—
not the "doubling another part"
kind of cue but the "put the cards
down and get ready to play"
cue. The Smart Cue Note plug-
in scans the score and locates
long rests where cues might be
recommended and even looks
for a passage to cue. Consult the
Help menu for more information
to using this plug-in.

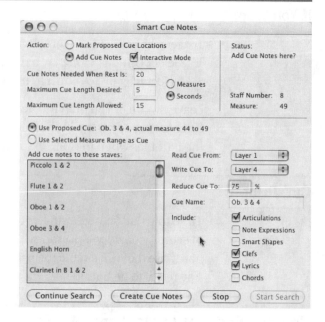

Extracting Two Parts from the Same Staff

In extracting the parts for *Petrushka*, there is the issue of multiple parts on a staff. Split-
ting the 1st and 2nd Flutes or 1st and 2nd Clarinets onto separate staves to create separate parts was enough work to make me avoid the situation altogether, until I discovered
TG Tools. The Process Extracted Part plug-in is another Lite version of a plug-in from the
full TG Tools package.

After you extract the combined-part staff into
a separate file, save the file with the first part
name, then the second part name. Run the plug-
in on the first part with 1 entered in the "Extract
voice line number" box. Load the second part,
and run the plug-in again, entering "2" for the
voice line number.

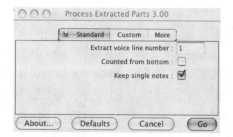

Archiving Your Work on CD or DVD

If you are backing up projects regularly, or even if you back up irregularly, to CD or DVD,
here is some food for thought. I recommend keeping a copy of Finale NotePad (see
chapter 14) around and adding the current version to every disc you burn. Every now
and then, there have been versions of Finale that do strange things to files created in
previous versions. Having a version of NotePad on the disc will give you a limited version
of Finale that will handle the file more closely than the newer version. Also, if the music
is going on the road and a part gets lost, someone can take the disc to a Kinko's and
access the part through NotePad to print a replacement. This also helps with giving discs
to clients, allowing them to reprint parts as needed without tying up your time to reload
and print the files. NotePad can also come to the rescue if you are working with someone
who has a different version of Finale.

Summary

This example included the following new Finale skills:

- creating a custom ensemble in the Setup Wizard
- breaking barlines between staves
- formatting staves for stems up display
- adding staves to an existing score
- setting up staff groups and brackets
- setting up staff sets
- using the Time Signature tool
- using the Shape Designer
- entering tremolos
- rebeaming measures according to the time signature
- entering complex tuplets
- optimizing a score
- creating beams across the barline
- positioning staves in Page View

Review

1. Notate an excerpt from a study score of a modern orchestral piece and see what graphic challenges you can overcome by using Special Tools and Custom Shape Creation.
2. Practice using Staff Optimization with an excerpt from any classical study score. Enter music from a printed score or import a MIDI file. MIDI files can be downloaded form the Classical MIDI Archives (www.classicalarchives.com) or the Choral Public Domain Library (www.cpdl.org).
3. Find an excerpt you'd like to analyze harmonically, and enter it, format it, and print it while you're analyzing it.
4. Many vocal scores use optimization for staves assigned to specific characters' vocal parts during a piece. Search your collection for a large ensemble number with a lot of parts that weave in and out.

337

SECTION IV
Getting the Most out of Finale

14

Importing and Exporting

This chapter deals with exporting or sending files to other programs and importing MIDI files and graphics into your Finale scores. It is possible to exchange Finale files, send Finale files to other programs, and import MIDI files into Finale. It is also possible to purchase MIDI files or download them from the Internet and read them into Finale. All of these options can be an enhancement to Finale users.

The areas to be addressed in this chapter include:

- sharing files between Mac and Windows
- exporting Finale files in Standard MIDI File (SMF) format
- importing a Finale MIDI file to a MIDI sequencer
- downloading MIDI files from the Internet
- translating and quantizing MIDI files
- scanning music
- importing graphics files into a Finale document
- exporting Finale files as TIFF, PICT, or EPS files to be read by other programs

Sharing Files Between Mac and Windows

Since Finale version 97, Macintosh and Windows files are totally compatible. It is as simple as saving a file on one computer and moving to the other and opening it. It is helpful to include the Finale file suffix ".mus" at the end of the file name.

Sometimes, it is helpful to open the file specifying that you want Finale to open it. To do this in Windows and Mac, use the contextual menus:

1. Open the folder that contains the Finale file to be opened.
2. To open the contextual menu, Control-click (Mac) or Right-click (Windows) on the file icon, and then select "Open With" and then choose "Finale 2005" (or the most recent version of Finale you own).

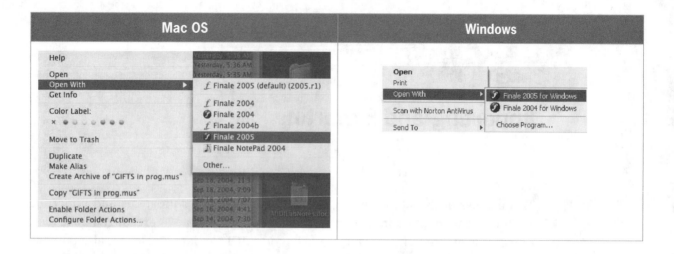

Exporting Finale Files as MIDI Files

Chapter 1 mentioned that Finale has one major purpose: creating printed notation. There are times when it is helpful to send a Finale file to another program, such as a MIDI Sequencer, when a Finale file is needed for background tracks or for making an expressive sound recording. For example, some users export a Finale file to a MIDI sequencer and then enter ritards, crescendos, and other data that is easier to manipulate in a sequencer or add digital audio tracks.

All MIDI sequencers can read MIDI files in Standard MIDI File format. If the file to be transported is a multiple-stave score, it can be sent as a multiple track file, or all staves can be combined to one track. In most instances, it is better to have each Finale staff transfer to a separate track in the sequencer. If this is the desired output, be sure to assign a different instrument to each staff.

To save staves as separate tracks in MIDI file format:

1. Select **Windows** > Instrument List.
2. Assign each staff to a different instrument.
3. Select **File** > Save As.
   - In the Save As dialog box, choose "Standard MIDI File" (Mac OS) or "MIDI File" (Windows). Then click Save.

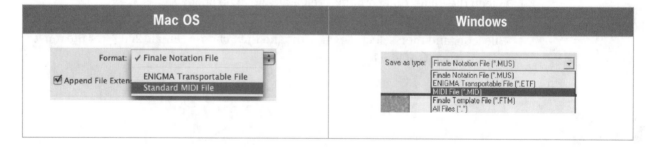

4. Finale then asks what type of MIDI file. For files where all of the staves are saved to separate tracks, choose "Format 1—All Instruments Saved to Separate Tracks." This will place every instrument that you have identified on a separate track. "Format 0,

All Instruments Saved into a Single Track," would be used if you were transferring a Finale file to play on a Web page or in a multimedia presentation. I use Format 0 only on rare occasions.

- Select a format, and then click OK.

Importing a Finale MIDI File to a MIDI Sequencer

It is possible to translate MIDI files into Finale. The main reason to transfer in a MIDI file is to save time entering the notation manually using Speedy Entry, Simple Entry, or HyperScribe. Depending on how the file was created, this can be time-saving. Also, some composers/arrangers prefer to work in a MIDI sequencer and then go to Finale for the printout.

Be sure to follow the following steps when opening a MIDI file into Finale:

1. In Finale, select **File** > Open.
2. Choose the MIDI file to be opened. If the MIDI file does not appear, try selecting "All Files."
3. Make any necessary changes to the Import MIDI File Options window. I sometimes change the Quantization settings to reflect the smallest note value in the piece being imported. Click OK.

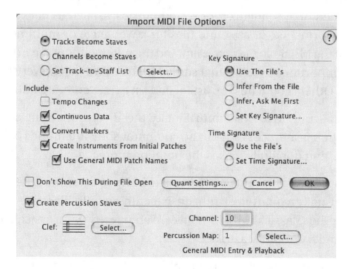

Sources of MIDI Files to Import into Finale

There are various ways to locate and create MIDI files that can be read into Finale. MIDI files can be purchased from music publishers such as Hal Leonard, Warner Brothers, Silver Burdette, and others. MIDI files can be downloaded from the Internet and scanned using MIDI scanning software

Downloading MIDI Files from the Internet

MIDI files can be downloaded from Web pages on the Internet. There are thousands of MIDI files available via the Internet. To locate sources of MIDI files, use an Internet search engine such as www.google.com or www.yahoo.com and search for pages with

MIDI files. An excellent source of MIDI files is the Classical MIDI Archives (www.classicalarchives.com). There are many other pages that offer MIDI files; use a Web search tool (such as Google or Yahoo) to locate additional pages.

The first step is to find a MIDI file that you want to download. This may take some time, browsing and listening to files. When you find a file on a Web page, listen to it by clicking on the name of the file. After you listen to the file and you decide you want to copy it or download it to your hard drive:

1. Control-click (Mac) or Right-click (Windows) "Save Link as" or "Download Link."
2. Rename the file if necessary and save it to your hard drive. Rename the file to something that you will remember. Be sure, however, to leave the suffix ".mid" at the end of the file.
3. To open a MIDI file in Finale, use the Open With options described above.

After the file opens, save it as a Finale file. In this way, you can download countless MIDI files from the Internet. Be sure to review the copyright restrictions of the MIDI files. Check with the site to be sure you have permission to copy and use the file.

Translating and Quantizing MIDI Files

Some MIDI files that are translated into Finale may not be very readable. Most MIDI files were created on a sequencer for sound purposes, such as background tracks for practice or performance, or as sound files for a Web page or multimedia presentation. The creator of the MIDI file may have entered the notes without regard for how they will print out. It is important to realize that some MIDI files will not be very useful, once imported in Finale. Others could be very useful and save time entering notation by hand.

When importing MIDI files into Finale, the most important aspect is quantization. Quantization is a process where the computer software rounds off the notes to a specified value, and hopefully makes the notation more readable.

Before importing a file into Finale, listen to it. Try to determine the lowest rhythmic value, which is usually a quarter, eighth, or sixteenth note. To illustrate this, I downloaded two files from the Classical MIDI Archives Web page (www.classicalarchives.com): a Bach Chorale and a Chopin Mazurka.

First, I listened to the file using my Web browser, by clicking on the name of the piece. After listening to the piece, I downloaded it using the techniques mentioned previously. After the file was copied to my hard drive, I imported it into Finale.

1. In Finale, select **File** > Open. Sometimes when downloading files from the Internet or opening commercial MIDI files, they will not appear when you select MIDI or MIDI Sequencer Format. Try the selection "All Files."

   Finale Notation File
   ENIGMA Transportable File
   Standard MIDI File
   Lesson File
   Finale Performance Assessment

   All Readable Files
   ✓ All Files

2. Select the MIDI file name that you saved on the hard drive. Finale presents the transcribe window.
3. Set the Quant Settings (Quantization settings) to the lowest note value in the piece. Then click OK. Finale will transcribe the MIDI file into notation.

The Bach chorale translated into Finale with most of the notation correctly transcribed. The staff names and titles need to be edited, but other than that, the piece is ready to print. This is an example of a MIDI file that requires minimal editing, and therefore will reduce the amount of time needed to input the notation by hand. However, this is not always the case.

Next, I downloaded a Chopin mazurka, "Op. 6, no. 1." This example does not work as well. There will be significant editing required. In this case, I would not use the MIDI file at all, but simply enter the notation from scratch.

 If you open a MIDI file that requires significant editing, it is often faster to enter the piece by hand.

Transcribing Tips and Techniques

There are some techniques that can be used in Finale once a MIDI file is imported. To illustrate these techniques, there is a MIDI file that I downloaded from Classical MIDI Archives of "Canzona No. 7" by Gabrielli. First, I listened to the MIDI file, and determined that most of the file contained eighth notes. Then, to open the file in Finale:

1. Select **File** > Open, and choose MIDI file that has been downloaded ("Canzona No. 7" from www.classicalarchives.com).
2. Select "eighth note" as the quantization level.

This file translates into Finale in nearly perfect notation. There are only a few measures that need to be edited.

One option is to use Simple or Speedy Entry to edit the notation. However, Finale offers one additional option to retranscribe selected portions of the piece. In this example, measures 46 and 53 contain notation values that were not read well with the chosen settings. Since most of the notation is accurate, use the Retranscribe function for these measures.

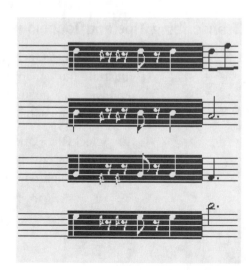

3. Advance to measure 46.
4. Choose the Mass Edit tool ⊕.
5. Highlight the imported notation in measure 46. Click on the top staff in measure 46 and Shift-click on the fourth staff down. This highlights the block of music that printed with grace notes (and is unreadable).

6. Select **Options** > Quantization Settings. and choose the eighth note as the smallest value.
7. Select **Mass Edit** > Retranscribe, and Finale will retranscribe the highlighted measures using the new Quantization Settings.

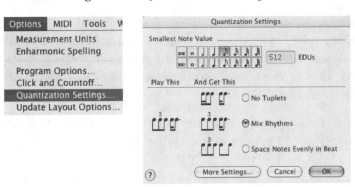 

The new, retranscribed notation in measure 46 looks much better.

The retranscribing process can be continued as needed throughout the piece. Another option is to delete the notes in the specific measures and reenter them using Speedy or Simple Entry.

Scanning Notation

With the proper software and hardware, it is also possible to scan printed music into Finale. See chapter 8, for a detailed overview of this option.

Importing Graphic Files into Finale

Graphic files can be imported into Finale documents. Perhaps you want to import a graphic logo into a Finale file, or maybe you just want to spice up your Finale printouts with some added graphics such as pictures of instruments or fingering charts.

Finale notation can also go the other direction. Pages or portion of pages in Finale documents can be exported to other programs, including word processing applications (such as Microsoft Word or Word Perfect) and page layout software, such as InDesign, Page-Maker, or QuarkXpress.

Types of Graphic Files

There are several types of common graphic files that can be imported into Finale. On the Mac side, Finale can send (export) and read (import) three types of graphic files: EPS (Encapsulated Postscript), PICT (picture files), and TIFF (tagged image file format). Windows users can send (export) and read (import) TIFF, Windows Metafile, and Encapsulated Postscript (EPS).

The most common graphic file formats are TIFF or PICT format. The EPS format is primarily used for print output. When importing graphics files into Finale, I recommend using either TIFF or PICT formats. Graphic files can be purchased, created using drawing programs, photographed, scanned, and downloaded from the Internet. Most word processors include some graphics or clip art.

Incorporating Graphics

Perhaps you would like to include graphics such as a timpani icon or graphics of fingerings in Finale. For example, a friend of mine was working on a percussion method book using Finale and wanted to include icons. He created the icon in a graphics program (or you could search for graphics on the Web), and then imported that graphic in Finale.

Once you have the graphic in one of the above-mentioned file formats, it can be imported into a Finale document.

1. Select **View** > Page View.
2. Choose the Graphics tool (⬤). In Windows, select **Tools** > Advanced Tools > Graphics Tool.
3. Select **Graphics** > Place Graphic, or double-click where you want the graphic.
   • Select the graphic file you wish to import.
4. Click the mouse to place the graphic.

Exporting Graphics from Finale to Other Programs

The Finale Graphics tool can also be used to create graphics to send to other programs. Perhaps you would like to include a high quality graphic of music notation in a word processing document, page layout file, or other applications. Using the Graphics tool, it is possible to export entire pages and portions of pages. As a matter of fact, all of the high quality graphics in this book were exported from Finale using the Graphics tool.

To export an entire page:
1. Choose the Graphics tool (⬤). In Windows, select **Tools** > Advanced Tools > Graphics Tool.
2. Select **Graphics** > Export Pages.
3. Choose the desired file format, and click OK.

When you click OK you will be prompted for what to name the file and where to save it. Be sure to leave the suffix after the file name (.tif, .eps; Mac OS can also save as .pct). This is important for the files to be properly read.

Exporting Portions of a Page

More often than not, you will want just a portion of a page. To select a portion of a page in Finale:

1. Select **View** > Page View. Selecting portions of a page cannot be done in Scroll View.
2. Center the music on the screen. You must be able to see the portion of the page you wish to export.
3. Choose the Graphics tool 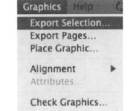. In Windows, select **Tools** > Advanced Tools > Graphics Tool.
4. To select the portion of the page, move the mouse to the desired location, double-click-the mouse, and sustain or hold down the mouse button on the second click. While holding the button, drag the mouse to outline the example you wish to export.
5. Select **Graphics** > Export Selection.
6. Choose the type of file format, and save it to the desired location.

To use this file, open your word processor or page layout program. Choose Insert Picture, or consult the manual for the program you are using. Be sure that it is capable of reading the type of file format you exported from Finale.

Summary

This chapter included the following areas:

- sharing files between Mac and Windows
- exporting Finale files in Standard MIDI File format
- importing a Finale MIDI File for use in a MIDI sequencer
- downloading MIDI files from the Internet
- translating and quantizing MIDI files
- scanning music
- importing graphics files into a Finale document
- exporting Finale files as TIFF, PICT, or EPS files to be read by other programs

Review

1. In Finale, retrieve the "Canzona" piece, but use a variety of settings. Experiment with different transcription settings to see their effects. It is important to realize that you can retranscribe a piece as many times as you like, to try to get the closest notation realization.
2. Search for MIDI files on the Internet. When you find some, download them, and read them into Finale. Try several different quantization levels to see their effect on the piece.
3. Save a Finale file as a MIDI file and open it in another music program, such as a sequencer.
4. Try exporting Finale graphics output to other programs, such as a word processor or page layout program.

15

Music Education Applications

Notation software in general, and Finale in particular, can be applied in music education in many diverse ways. Finale can be used by both teachers and by students. There are many applications that can be grouped into teacher and student tasks:

Teacher use:

- To print out scores and parts
- To prepare practice and assessment exercises
- To post files on educational Web sites

Student use:

- To compose and print original music
- To use for practice, accompaniment, and assessment

Finale for Teachers

Creating Custom Exercises for Students

Finale can be an invaluable tool for a wide variety of education applications. The most obvious reasons for using a notation program are to save time and to produce more readable pieces of music. I am a middle school band director. No matter which arrangement I purchase, minor revisions are needed to suit the abilities of my students, so I often rewrite some of the parts. With the help of Finale, I hand out music that looks professionally typeset. Students are able to read my revisions as easily as they read published music. Another advantage of using Finale is the way it helps find mistakes. Simply play back the composition, and "proof listen" to the piece. It is often easier to find mistakes by listening than by solely inspecting the printed score. There are many ways to use Finale in music education. Some applications include:

Simplify parts for students

For example, you might need a custom clarinet part for students not yet over the break; or perhaps the range of a particular piece goes above that which is comfortable for your soprano section. Finale can be used to reduce the difficulty level of the part.

Re-orchestrate an existing arrangement

In my middle school band, I currently have eighteen alto saxes and two trombones. Yet, the arrangements I purchase are usually written for three trombones and two alto saxes.

I enter or scan the second and third trombone parts, and print them out for alto sax. Parts for all ensembles can be re-orchestrated in this manner.

Creating warm-up and practice exercises

Finale can help you to print out your custom-designed exercises. A scale study is easy to create, and then copied into an entire score. Use the Extract parts command to print individual parts.

C Instrument Scales

Create readiness exercises for performing groups

Before I pass out a new arrangement to one of my performing groups, I sit down and create a page or two of exercises that will help the students prepare for playing the piece. I include scales, rhythm patterns, and important melodies. Once the C part is completed, I simply copy and paste the music to create the other parts. I often use the Score template that is installed with Finale. I also use the Extract Parts techniques described in earlier chapters to save time printing the individual parts.

Create rhythm parts and exercises

It is very easy to create rhythm parts using Finale's Staff Styles (see chapter 11). Staff Styles convert standard notation to a variety of options, including rhythmic and slash notation. For example, I often create a set of rhythm patterns for students when we are learning a piece. Alternate notation can also be used to create rhythm parts for the jazz ensemble.

Kodaly/Stick Notation

Finale comes with templates that are automatically loaded when you install the program. One of these templates facilitates the creation of solfeggio and stick notation. To access this template:

1. Select **File** > New > Document From Template. (You can also open the Launch Window and select Template)
   a. From the Templates Folder, open Education Templates.
   b. Open the file "Kodaly 2" if you want to create solfeggio, or "Kodaly 1" if you want to create stick notation.

2. Select the clef, and enter the notation in the bottom clef.
3. Using Mass Edit, copy the notation from the bottom to the top staff.

Consult the QuickStart Videos for a detailed demo of this template.

The Exercise Wizard

Finale includes a built-in exercise generator that can be used to create thousands of exercises for complete ensembles. The Exercise Wizard will create parts based upon the exercises you select and will print out copies of parts transposed and ready to play.

1. Select **File** > Launch Window.
   a. Click on the Exercise Wizard button.
   b. Create a new title for your exercises, such as "Scales and Intervals," and click Next.

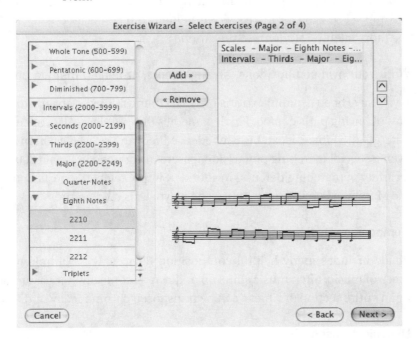

2. Choose the type of exercise you want.
3. Set the key and articulation of each exercise
4. Define the type of ensemble and parts that you want Finale to print. You can create a customized ensemble that you can use and reuse to save time.
5. Print the parts.

My only criticism of the Exercise Wizard is it does not currently create a score in Finale. It creates separate parts. However, teachers will find the Exercise Wizard to be a fast way to create printouts of exercises for students. For more detailed instruction on the Exercise Wizard, watch the QuickStart Video and consult the *Finale User Manual*.

Create ensemble music such as duets, trios, and quartets

As long as the music is your original composition or is in the public domain, you can create your own chamber music for any instrument combination. Imagine having duets that any instrument combination can play. I use Finale to create 2-, 3-, and 4-part pieces for my students to perform in chamber groups. As described above, once you have created a version of the duet or trio in concert pitch, you can transpose and shift the music for any combination of instruments.

Reduce a piano part, so students can accompany a chorus or other ensemble

Many times with published arrangements, the piano accompaniment part is too difficult for student accompanists. Finale can help the teacher simplify the part so it can be played by students.

Compose difficult parts, such as descants, to challenge the more advanced students in the ensemble.

How many times have you heard the better students in your ensembles complain that the music is boring, or too easy? With Finale, directors can create challenging parts for the more talented students in the group.

Write your own compositions, arrangements, or even a method book

If you have been avoiding writing original compositions or arrangements because of the cost of having parts copied, Finale remedies this problem. Also, once the composition is entered into Finale, it can be listened to, edited, and revised as often as you like. There is even a special marching percussion feature introduced in Finale 2005. This can include a variety of marching percussion sounds. Simply select the parts in the Setup Wizard in the Marching Percussion column. The playback is most impressive.

Composition Devices

Finale includes many helpful composition devices. For example, when composing a piece of music, often music shifts up or down diatonically. A measure, several measures, or an entire section of a piece can be transposed chromatically or diatonically.

Diatonic Transposition

To transpose a passage diatonically:

1. Enter the notation. In this example, the notation shifts up a second in the next measure.
2. Copy the measure from measure 1 to measure 2. Using the Mass Edit tool, highlight measure 1, and drag it to measure 2.

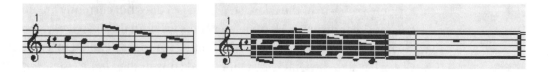

3. To transpose the second measure diatonically up a second, highlight the measure (still in Mass Edit).
4. Select **Mass Edit** > Transpose.

5. Choose Transpose "Up," "Diatonically," and set Interval to "Second."

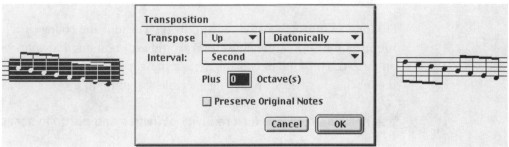

Finale in the Hands of Students

Finale is a fascinating tool in the hands of students. Finale will not teach students how to compose any more than a word processor will teach them how to write. However, just as a word processor can assist a student with editing, cutting, copying/pasting, spell-checking, and so forth, Finale can assist in the music composition process. Finale gives students a fast and legible way to enter and print music, and then hear what they have written.

Teach student librarians to use Finale

Many of the applications mentioned in this chapter, such as re-orchestrating parts from an arrangement, could be delegated to students.

Allow students to use Finale to create original music

Students can learn to use Finale and begin to print out their own compositions. Every year, I ask my middle school band members to compose a duet. I provide them with a melody and they write the harmony part. Notation software gives them the opportunity to hear their composition as it is being composed. Also, they can produce a professional-looking printout.

Teach students to transcribe melodies—perhaps, the parts they are playing in the ensemble

Through the process of entering the notation, they will "discover" many aspects of music, such as note values, number of beats per measure, direction of stems, etc.

Use notation software as a tool for students to apply concepts as they are learned

For example, if students are learning about theme and variations, ask them to compose their own variations using Finale. This can be applied to any musical concept.

Take classes to the school computer lab and use Finale to compose and arrange music

Since notes can be entered with the mouse or typewriter keyboard using Simple or Speedy Entry, students can compose using the computers in the computer lab. A site license or lab pack must be purchased in order to legally make multiple copies of software.

Provide notation software for students to use to create legible theory class assignments

Students in music theory classes at the high school and college level should have access to computers to create legible exercises and assignments. Four-part writing can be greatly enhanced. The student gets the benefit of hearing the exercise as it is being entered and the teacher benefits by receiving a legible assignment.

Use notation software for creativity activities and portfolio assessment

Finale provides a tool for students to create and print out music. A printed piece of music is a tangible outcome that can be used for assessment.

Finale NotePad

MakeMusic, the company who publishes Finale, also offers a free notation program to Mac and Windows users. The program can be downloaded and used for from www.finalenotepad.com. NotePad is a "lite" version of Finale. It can be used by students to compose and print Finale files.

MakeMusic offers a complete family of Finale products that are designed for a variety of users and applications. Finale is the high-end offering. Another product is PrintMusic, a "lite" version of Finale that costs under $100 and is an excellent option for students and especially in music technology labs where cost is a factor. Consult the www.makemusic.com Web site for information on the other offerings. Also, be sure to take advantage of the education discounts offered by MakeMusic and their education dealers. There are significant discounts offered to teachers and church musicians.

Finale Performance Assessment

A totally cool feature has been added in Finale 2005: Finale Performance Assessment. A teacher can create an exercise in Finale and save it as a Performance Assessment file. Students can open the file, attach a microphone to their computer, and play their instrument or MIDI keyboard. The program will assess the pitch and rhythm accuracy. On the student's end, all they need to do is download the free Performance Assessment software from the www.makemusic.com Web site.

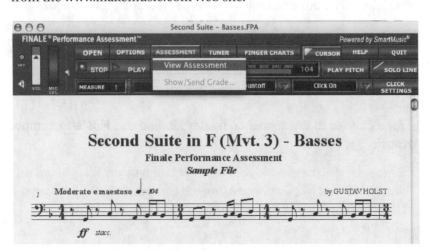

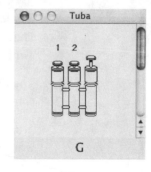

In addition to the assessment options, woodwind and brass players have access to complete fingering charts. Simply select an instrument, click on a note, and the fingering for that note appears.

Finale Performance Assessment is a separate application that is included on the install disc with Finale version 2005 (and presumably, later versions). Consult the Finale Help menu for the steps on how to create assessment materials.

SmartMusic Accompaniments

MakeMusic also produces a very popular practice and accompaniment application called SmartMusic. Many schools and students are using this application. Teachers who have Finale can create their own practice accompaniments to be used in SmartMusic. For example, as a band director, I converted my Finale practice materials so they could be opened by students using SmartMusic. This option makes it possible to create virtually any accompaniment.

To create SmartMusic accompaniments:
1. Select **File** > Launch Window.
2. Click on the SmartMusic Wizard button.
3. After going through the SmartMusic Accompaniment Wizard, save the application in a folder that can easily be accessed by SmartMusic. I usually put these files in the computer's SmartMusic folder.

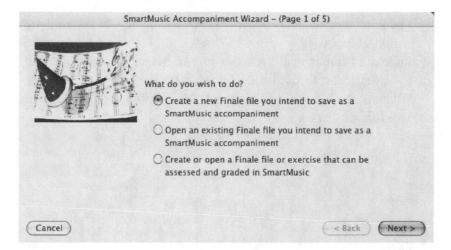

Students can open teacher-created SmartMusic exercises for practice and performance. If you are unfamiliar with the options SmartMusic offers, check out www.smartmusic.com.

Administrative Applications

Finale can also help instructors to create worksheets, handouts, tests, and the like. Questions can be typed directly into the score. With the skills presented in the chapters in this book, you will have the capability to layout out the page any way you like.

Finale includes several templates that can help teachers create tests and worksheets. These are in the Templates folder in the Education subfolder. There are 2-measure- and 4-measure-per-line files that can be opened and changed as needed.

The Education Templates folder also contains a file for printing blank manuscript. This can save time and money when printing music paper for students.

Another option is to capture notation in Finale and export it to other programs, such as word processors and page layout software. See chapter 13 for information, or consult the Finale Help menu.

Summary

There are many ways to use Finale to enhance teaching and learning. This chapter explored a variety of ways both teachers and students can use Finale to make a positive impact on education.

Review

1. List all the ways you can use Finale to improve your teaching.
2. List the ways students can use Finale as a composition tool.
3. Select one piece you intend to teach this year. Make a list of the Finale techniques you can employ to create readiness exercises for the students.

Reference Books

Rudolph, Thomas. *Teaching Music with Technology*. 2nd edition. Chicago: GIA publications, Inc., 2004.

Rudolph, Thomas, et al. *Technology Strategies for Music Education*. Wyncote, PA: Technology Institute for Music Educators, 1997.

Williams, D.; Webster, P. *Experiencing Music Technology*. 3rd edition. New York: Schirmer, 2004.

16

Finale Support

Finale is a complex program. There will still be times when you have questions about some aspect of Finale and need assistance. This chapter will highlight how you can get connected to help find the answers to your questions about Finale.

- using the most up-to-date version of Finale
- maintenance upgrades
- documentation from the Finale Help menu
- Finale Web site
- tech support via e-mail
- tech support via voice
- vendor support
- joining a Finale mailing list
- Finale courses
- third party Finale products

Use The Latest Version

The best way to eliminate unnecessary problems is to upgrade to the latest version of Finale. When Finale is upgraded, many times, it corrects problems or bugs in the program. I once met a Finale user who complained about many problems and, after asking a few questions, I found out he was running Finale 97. After upgrading, most of his problems were solved.

To upgrade, contact MakeMusic either by telephone 800-843-2066 (M–F, 8:30–5:00 CST), via e-mail finalesales@makemusic.com, or visit the Finale Web site (www.finalemusic.com). The cost of the upgrade is usually in the $99 range, depending upon which version you are using.

Maintenance Upgrades

It is also important to use the latest maintenance upgrade of Finale. Typically, MakeMusic issues one or more maintenance upgrades during the year. These maintenance upgrades have versions such as Finale 2005a, 2005b, and so forth. Maintenance upgrades are free and can be downloaded from the www.makemusic.com Web site. The only requirement is to register on the site, so have your serial number handy.

Documentation from the Finale Help Menu

Finale 97 and later versions include a complete manual that is included with the program and accessed via the Help menu (see chapter 1). Be sure to try to find the answer to your questions using this valuable tool before calling MakeMusic tech support or looking for other ways to get answers. Becoming familiar with the Help documentation will save you a lot of time.

Finale Web Site

MakeMusic maintains an extremely helpful Web site with extensive information and resources for Finale users. The address is www.finalemusic.com. Go to the site, and check out the Support options. The Knowledge Database can be an excellent place to ask questions when you don't find the answer in this book or the Help documentation. Most every answer is in the documentation, but sometimes you won't know the proper Finale term to look for. When this happens, try the Knowledge Database.

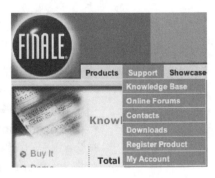

There are also several online forums where you can connect with other Finale users around the world.

Finale QuickStart Videos

Finale contains a host of videos that can be most helpful with all aspects of the program. Simply select QuickStart Videos from the Finale Help menu. I find myself using these videos when I purchase the latest Finale upgrade to see what is new or has changed.

Tech Support via E-Mail

When I have a problem I can't solve myself after consulting the Help documentation, I usually send an e-mail to MakeMusic. I have been extremely impressed with the quick responses I have received, and it's free! Simply send an e-mail address to one of the addresses below. Be sure to include your Finale serial number.

Macintosh: macsupport@makemusic.com

Windows: winsupport@makeemusic.com

Tech Support: Voice

If you have a question that has you stumped and you can't find the answer from the Help documentation or via e-mail, then the next step is to call tech support. Be sure to register your software after purchasing it, and write down your serial number and key number. This is important information you will need when calling the Finale Tech Support line.

With your key number in hand, call the Finale tech support number: 952-937-9703 (M–F, 8:30–5:00 CST). For best results, have your computer up and running, with Finale, and the problem you are experiencing on the screen. When you do speak with a tech support person, explain the problem succinctly. You will be asked to provide your key number and serial number. The call is not toll free, so use the voice tech support only if other options have been explored or if you have a lot of free minutes left on your cell phone.

Vendor Support

Another way to get help is to call the company or vendor who sold you Finale, if you purchased it through a software company and not directly from MakeMusic. I recommend buying Finale, and all of your music software, from a reputable music dealer. The advantage to purchasing in this manner is that you have another person to call if you have questions. Many music companies have people on staff who are familiar with Finale and can offer support.

Finale Mailing Lists

Another popular way to stay connected with other users is to join a Finale mailing list. To do so, you must have your own Internet e-mail address. There is an excellent mailing list designed for Finale users. Once you subscribe, you will receive e-mail messages from the mailing list and you can post your own questions and messages. To subscribe to the Finale list offered by Sam Houston University, send an e-mail message to listserv@shsu.edu, consisting of "subscribe Finale." If you want to stop receiving messages from the list, send a message to listserv@shsu.edu, with the message "signoff Finale."

It is also possible to subscribe to the list and receive a digest version. The digest contains one complete day's worth of messages. You don't want to be on both lists, so pick either the Finale list or the digest. To subscribe to just the digest, write "Subscribe Finale-Digest ["Your Real Name in Quotes"]" in the body of a mail message to listserv@shsu.edu.

Finale Courses

Finale can also be learned by enrolling in traditional or online courses. Some institutions offer Finale courses. Check with a school's Web site to see if they offer one. An excellent source for education course listings is on the Teachnology Institute for Music Educators (TI:ME) Web site www.ti-me.org. Check in the Summer Study section for courses dealing specifically with Finale.

Online Finale courses are also available from Berkleemusic.com (www.berkleemusic.com).

Third Party Products

There is an amazing amount of third party products available for Finale. This includes a host of things such as fonts and specialty items, such as education fonts and even Medieval music notation. One of the best places to find the current list of Finale support sites is: http://www.musicprep.com/coda/.

This Web page lists a wide variety of third party products for Finale on the site. The site is updated regularly and is an excellent resource. Another popular independent site is The Finale Forum, www.finaleforum.com.

Summary

This chapter included the following information on how to get support for Finale from various resources:

- using the most up-to-date version of Finale
- maintenance upgrades
- documentation from the Finale Help menu
- Finale Web site
- tech support via e-mail
- tech support via voice
- vendor support
- joining a Finale mailing list
- Finale courses
- third party Finale products

Review

1. Make a list of the ways to solve problems using Finale including using the Help menu, calling MakeMusic tech support, e-mailing Finale support, reading the FAQs on the FinaleMusic Web site, and joining a Finale mailing list.
2. Visit the FinaleMusic.com Web site, and review the various support areas listed for Finale.
3. Join a Finale mailing list. Read the messages and contribute to the list when possible.

Appendix
The Finale Book Web Site: File Index

On the Finale Book Web site, you will find the Finale files referenced in this book, along with other supplemental material. The URL is: www.finalebook.com. The Finale files are available for Macintosh and Windows. Text information is provided in Adobe PDF format—the same format used by Help.

The files posted fall into three categories. The first category contains Finale files related to the examples in the book. For chapters 2 through 12, there are completed Finale files of each example. These files were used to generate the graphics in the book. These files can be downloaded, printed, and used for referral while you create your own version. In section II of the book, there are partially completed files that allow you to begin work at specified points in the chapter.

The second category is "Templates and Libraries." These Finale files have been specially prepared by Vince Leonard for this book and contain many of the templates and libraries he uses in his work.

The third category contains supplemental text in Adobe PDF format. For those readers familiar with the first edition of the book, the "Templates" and "Part Extraction" chapters have been updated and posted here. The Templates PDF also contains a listing of all of the templates available in section II.

Finale Book Chapter Files

Chapters 1 through 7

2_Aura Lee.mus

3_Amazing.mus

4_Mice.mus

5_Voluntary.mus

6_HyperScribe.mus

7_Musette.mus

Chapter 8. Small Arrangement: Saxophone Quartet ("The Entertainer")

Entertainer_Score.mus

8_Entertainer_1.mus

8_Entertainer_2.mus

8_Entertainer_3.mus

8_Entertainer_4.mus

Entertainerpg1.tiff

Entertainerpg2.tiff

Ent_Piano_Red.mus

Chapter 9. Vocal Score with Percussion ("Simple Gifts")

9_Gifts.mus

9_Gifts_No_Lyrics.mus

Chapter 10. The Art of the Piano Part ("Bach Fugue in G minor")

Bach_L1_TC.mus

Bach_L2_TC.mus

Bach_L3_TC.mus

Bach_L1_BC.mus

Bach_L2_BC.mus

Bach_Fugue.mus

10_Bach_1.mus

10_Bach_2.mus

10_Bach_3.mus

10_Bach_4.mus

Chapter 11. Jazz Notation: Leadsheets and Guitar Tab ("Blues for a Hiccup")

Hiccup_Sketch.mus

11_Hiccup_1.mus

11_Hiccup_2.mus

11_Hiccup_3.mus

11_Hiccup_4.mus

11_Hiccup_LS.mus

11_Hiccup_TAB.mus

Chapter 12: Big-Band Scores ("Blues for a Hiccup")

BB_Score_Temp.mus

Blues_BB_Score.mus

Chapter 13. Orchestral Excerpt (Petrushka)

13_Petrushka_Score.mus

13_Petrushka_1.mus

13_Petrushka_2.mus

13_Petrushka_3.mus

Templates and Libraries

Choral Templates

Choral_1.mus

Choral_1Oct.mus

Choral_2.mus

Choral_2Oct.mus

Choral_3.mus

Choral_3Oct.mus

Choral_4.mus

Choral_4Oct.mus

Concert Band Templates

Small_1.mus

Small_2.mus

Concert_1.mus

Concert_1_leg.mus

Concert_1_tab.mus

Concert_2_leg.mus

Concert_2_tab.mus

Jazz Ensembles Templates

Jazz_Combo.mus

Jazz_1.mus

Jazz_1_leg.mus

Jazz_1_tab.mus

Jazz_2.mus

Jazz_3.mus

Jazz_4.mus

Jazz_5.mus

Jazz_6.mus

Jazz_7.mus

Jazz_8.mus

Marching Band Templates

Marching_1.mus

Marching_2.mus

Marching_3.mus

Marching_4.mus

Orchestra Templates

Sym_1_leg.mus

Sym_1_tab.mus

Sym_2.mus

Sym_2_leg.mus

Sym_2_tab.mus

Sym_3_leg.mus

Sym_3_tab.mus

Sym_4_leg.mus

Sym_4_tab.mus

Sym_5.mus

Pops_1_leg.mus

Pops_1_tab.mus

Pops_2_leg.mus

Pops_2_tab.mus

Opera_leg.mus

Opera_tab.mus

Parts Templates

8_10_Stave.mus

8_10_Piano.mus

10_12_Stave.mus

10_12_Piano.mus

Marching_Parts.mus

Concert_Parts.mus

Sym_Parts.mus

365

Pit/Show Templates

PV_1.mus

Pit_Show_2.mus

Pit_Show_3.mus

Pit_Show_4.mus

Pit_Show_5.mus

Pit_Show_5_leg.mus

Pit_Show_5_tab.mus

Sketch_Utilities Templates

4_Line.mus

5_Line.mus

5_Line_Film.mus

6_Line_Film.mus

Cue_Sheet.mus

Cue_Sheet_tab.mus

PDF Files

Part_Extraction.pdf
A deeper look into the processes of part extraction and formatting. Learn pre-extraction tips and post-extraction tricks for creating better-looking parts faster than ever.

Templates.pdf
The second edition of the Templates chapter PDF includes tips for customizing your Finale environment, from tweaking default settings to creating custom libraries to developing personalized scores.

About the Authors

© 2001 joel perlish photography

Thomas E. Rudolph, Ed. D. is the Director of Music and middle school music instructor for Haverford Township School District, in Havertown, Pennsylvania. He is an adjunct Assistant Professor at The University of the Arts. Dr. Rudolph has authored seven books on music technology including *Teaching Music with Technology 2nd edition*, *Finding Funds for Music Technology*, and *The SoundTree General Music Curriculum*. He is the co-author of *Finale: An Easy Guide to Music Notation, 1st edition*, and *Recording in the Digital World*. Rudolph's articles have appeared in the *Music Educators Journal*, *The Instrumentalist*, *Down Beat* magazinge, and *Jazz Educator Journal*. In addition, he is a regular contributor to *Music Education Technology* magazine.

Dr. Rudolph was one of the founders of the Technology Institute for Music Educators (TI:ME at www.TI-ME.org) and currently serves as President of the organization. He has taught workshops in music technology at 17 institutions of higher learning and has trained over 4,000 music educators in his acclaimed workshops. Dr. Rudolph presented the keynote address for the Massachusetts State Conference in 1999, the MENC/TI:ME National Conference in 2002, the Missouri State Conference in 2003, and the Alabama State Conference in 2005.

Producer and composer **Vincent A. Leonard, Jr.** has had works premiered nationally and internationally. He is published by Arrangers, Publishing Company and Educational Programs Publications. He is co-author of *Recording in the Digital World* and *Finale: An Easy Guide to Music Notation, 1st edition*, both published by Berklee Press. In 1996, he and fellow producer and engineer Jack Klotz, Jr. formed Invinceable Entertainment, 3 IPS Studio and have released two CDs, *Magic Up Our Sleeve* and *On The Brink of Tomorrow*. Compositional credits include theme and episode music for the *Captain Courteous* radio series, the musical *Mainstreamed*, numerous theater pieces, and industrials. Leonard has provided orchestrations for world premier productions of *Redwall* for Opera Delaware, *Elliot and the Magic Bed*, *Isabell and the Pretty Ugly Spell*, and *The Little Princess* for Upper Darby Summer Stage. Also widely known as a copyist and arranger, he has worked on projects with Peter Nero, the Philly Pops Orchestra, Doc Severinsen, the London Symphony Orchestra, Chuck Mangione, Leslie Burrs, and in musicals by Duke Ellington, Alan Mencken, Kurt Weil, and Mitch Leigh. Leonard is a member of NARAS and ASCAP, a TI:ME instructor, and is active as a clinician and beta tester for music software for Macintosh computers.

Index

A

accent marks, entering, 70, 137, 242–43,
    325–26
accidentals
    cautionary, 136
    chord symbol suffixes and, 248–49
    enharmonics and, 199
    entering, 21, 37
Acrobat Reader, 14
Add Cue Notes plug-in, 148
administrative applications, 357–58
AIFF file format, 148
alternate bass notes, 253
Alternate Notation dialog box, 241
"Amazing Grace," 31–46
"America," 85–100
Apply Articulation dialog box, 325–26
Apply Staff Style dialog box, 233–34
archiving on CD or DVD, 336
arrangements, small, 121–64
arranger's name, entering, 158
Articulation Designer dialog box, 243–44,
    280, 333
Articulation Selection dialog box, 38,
    70–71, 72, 138, 214, 243, 326
Articulation tool, 38, 70, 71–72, 137, 214,
    217, 279–80, 333
    contextual menu, 244, 326
articulations. *See also* slurs
    adding, 70–71
    assigning multiple, 72
    automatic positioning of, 71
    copying with Mass Edit, 325
    entering with Metatools, 71–73, 137–
        38, 217, 242–43, 325–26
    entering with Simple Entry, 72–73
    Jazz font, 242–43
    layers and, 214–15
    moving or deleting, 71
    playback settings, 333
    stem-side positioning, 242–43, 327
asterisk key toggle, 205
audio file formats, 148
Audio Setup window, 147
"Aura Lee," 17–29
Auto-Harmonization, 276, 285–87
Auto Save Files, 28, 192
Automatic Music Spacing, 12, 25, 253
    turning off, 202
Automatic Update Layout, 25, 203
Automatic Update Target, 231

B

Bach, "Fugue 16 in G Minor," 189–224
Bach Chorale, 345
backgrounds options, 193
backups, making, 28, 192, 307
Band-in-a-Box Auto-Harmonizing dialog
    box, 276, 285–87
barlines
    altering, 129
    beaming across, 331–32
    breaking between staves, 168–69, 301
    double, 70, 129, 131, 176, 229, 272, 307,
        310
baselines
    for expressions, 138, 237, 327
    for lyrics, 57
batch processing, 261
Beam Angle tool, 204, 206, 210, 212
Beam Break took, 324
Beam Extension tool, 322
Beam Over Barlines plug-in, 331–32
beams
    in 2/8 time, 309
    in 3/8 time, 310
    in 4/8 time, 308–9
    in 5/8 time, 310, 320–21
    across-the-barline, 331–32
    adjusting, 204–12
    breaking, 210–11
    controlling with time signatures, 308–10
    eliminating wedges, 221–22
    separating from stems in tremolos, 322
Beat Duration controls, 320–21
Bend Hat tool, 215
Berkleemusic, 361
big-band score, 267–90
blank document, creating, 358
blank notation, selecting, 208
"Blues for a Hiccup," 225–64, 267–90
braces. *See* brackets
brackets
    adding, 304–5
    displaying on several staves, 130
    multiple ending, 130
    over-text and under-text, 244–46
    repeat, 157
    tuplet, 65
burning CDs, 148

C

Cautionary Accidental Options dialog
    box, 136
CD, archiving on, 336
CD burning software, 148
centering music for viewing, 11
Change Clef dialog box, 7, 107–8, 320
Change Fonts plug-in, 57–58
Change Notehead dialog box, 240
Character Map utility, 227
character sets, 244–46, 249
Check Range plug-in, 151, 286
Chopin Mazurka, 345
choral music, 165–87
Chord Definition dialog box, 247–48, 250,
    253
Chord menu
    Left Align Chords, 253
    Manual Input, 247–48, 250, 251
    MIDI Input, 52
    Position Chords, 53–54
    Show Fretboards, 53
    Type into Score, 40, 53
Chord Suffix Editor dialog box, 250–52
Chord Suffix Selection library, 41, 249, 250
chord symbols
    copying, 281
    deleting, 53, 279, 285
    editing, 41, 249
    entry options, 40, 242, 247–54
    in jazz charts, 227
    Metatools, 247–48
    MIDI entry, 52, 247
    positioning, 53–54, 258
    Rhythm Section Generator and, 288–90
    staff analysis entry, 249
    suffixes for, 41, 248–49, 250–54
    Type into Score entry, 40–41, 53, 247,
        248–49, 250, 275
Chord tool, 40, 52, 53–54, 247, 249, 251,
    253, 258, 275, 279, 285, 289
chords, entering, 31–46, 47–62
    alignment and spacing, 253–54
Classical MIDI Archives, 344, 345
Clear Items dialog box, 92, 184
Clear key, 135
Clef Selection dialog box, 168, 319
Clef tool, 107–8, 149, 319–20
clefs, changing, 7, 107–8, 168, 319–20
Click and Countoff dialog box, 90
Click Assignment dialog box, 180–81, 183

coda
    adding word "Coda" to, 259
    beginning new staff system for, 229
    positioning, 81–82, 257
    signs, 77–78, 230, 259
Component Files folder, 228
composer name
    custom font size for, 220, 258
    entering in Setup Wizard, 18, 32, 64,
        104, 123
composition applications, 353–55
computer crashes, 28
computer internal sound source, 78, 80,
    90
computer numeric keypad, 21
concert pitch, displaying in, 272, 335
contextual menus, 7, 44, 72–73, 83, 87,
        111–12, 116–17, 129, 140, 167, 168,
        176–77, 202, 208, 213, 229, 230,
        242, 244, 249, 262, 272, 277, 299,
        307, 308, 310, 326, 332, 333
contrapuntal music. See layers; voices
copy and paste, 23, 49–51. See also Mass
        Edit Tool
    articulations, chord symbols, and, 71
    between layers, 279–80
    to new file, 271
    to off-screen locations, 67–68, 280
    parts, 172, 175
    selecting specific items, 235–36
    text in Staff Attributes, 300
    as time-saver, 316
copyright
    adding text to, 158, 258
    deleting, 328
    entering in Setup Wizard, 18, 64, 123
copyright symbol, 227
Create Tempo Marking plug-in, 141–43
creativity activities, 356
credits
    deleting, 328
    entering with Text tool, 58, 116
crescendo marks
    editing, 110
    entering, 109–10, 215
Crescendo tool, 109–10, 144, 215, 243
cross-staff notes, 204–7, 211–12
    articulations and, 214–15
    displaying in staff of origin, 205
Cross-Staff plug-in, 204
cue notes
    adding, 148–50, 336
    clearing, 163
    ensemble, 238–39
    reducing size of, 241
cue-sized noteheads, 152
custom exercises, creating, 351
cymbals staff, 301–3

D

Dal Segno. See D.S. al Coda
Dashed Curve tool, 108, 215
Dashed Line tool, 114
D.C. al Coda sign, 76–77, 231–32, 246
D.C. al Fine sign, 111, 113
Decrescendo tool, 110

Delete key, 22, 39
descants, composing, 354
dialog boxes
    closing all, 243
    moving around in, 18
    using, 23
display, turning on or off, 6
Document Options—Beams dialog box,
        222, 239
Document Options—Fonts dialog box,
        247
Document Options—Grace Notes dialog
        box, 66
Document Options—Layers dialog box,
        150, 169–70, 195, 238–39
Document Options—Music Spacing
        dialog box, 253–54
Document Options—Stems dialog box,
        196, 204, 239
Document Options—Time Signatures
        dialog box, 228–29
Document Options—Tuplets dialog box,
        65
Document Setup Wizard. See Setup
        Wizard
Dot tool, 49
dotted notes, entering, 22, 36, 49
double barline, 70, 129, 131, 176, 229,
        272, 307
    multiple, 310
doubling, 276–79
Drum Groove plug-in, 237–38, 241–42
drum set notation. See percussion
        notation
D.S. al Coda sign, 259
DVD, archiving on, 336
dynamic markings. See also crescendo
        marks
    2nd Time Only playback, 282–84
    adding, 41–42, 74, 110–11, 144, 275
    entering and positioning, 138–40
    entering with Expression tool, 217, 244
    piano reductions and, 163
    in playback, 333

E

e-mail tech support, 360
Easy CD Creator, 148
Easy Tremolos plug-in, 321–22
Edit Lyrics window, 179, 184
Edit menu, 5
    Automatic Music Spacing, 12, 25, 202
    Automatic Update Layout, 25
    Copy, 271
    Copy Measure Items, 317
    Replace Entries, 271
    Select All, 44, 80, 83, 92, 98, 116, 136,
        137, 157, 163, 257–58, 313–14,
        316
    Select Partial Measures, 109, 136, 149,
        204, 234, 240, 275, 280, 281,
        286–87, 318, 324
    Select Region, 26, 51, 288, 330
    Special Part Extraction, 159–62
    Undo, 22, 36, 39, 92, 157
    Undo HyperScribe Session, 96

Update Layout, 80, 153, 203, 208, 255,
        329
Edit Page Margins dialog box, 154, 254–
        55, 329
Edit System Margins dialog box, 155–57,
        256, 257, 329–30
editing
    with contextual menus, 7, 44
    with Mass Edit tool, 23
    performance data with MIDI tool, 115
    with Selection tool, 7
    in Simple Entry, 24, 107
    in Speedy Entry, 198–99
Education Templates, 352–53, 358
educational applications, 351–58
Elapsed Time dialog box, 143
Enclosure Designer dialog box, 76
End key, 69
Ending Repeat Bar Assignment dialog
        box, 130
enharmonics, 199, 278
ensemble cues, 238–39
ensemble music, creating, 353–54
"Entertainer, The," 121–64
Entry Items dialog box, 184, 236, 317, 325
Entry Modifications dialog box, 317
"Entry offset" display, 208
EPS files, 348
Eraser tool, 22
erasing music, 92
EVPUs, 125, 154
EWQL Symphonic Orchestra Silver
        Edition, 147
Exercise Wizard, 353
Explode Music dialog box, 274–75, 278–
        79, 280, 286–87
exporting files. See files, exporting
Expression menu
    Adjust Above Staff Baseline, 237
    Adjust Below Staff Baseline, 138
    Metatools: Attach To Note, 141, 217
Expression Selection dialog box, 41–42,
        74, 75, 110, 126–28, 138, 141–43,
        244, 246, 312
Expression tool, 41–42, 74, 75, 110, 114,
        126–28, 138, 139, 141–43, 149, 152,
        215, 217, 236–37, 244, 246, 258,
        259, 272, 275, 281–82, 311–13,
        314–15
    contextual menu, 262, 333
expressions
    adjusting position of, 162, 258, 327
    automatic positioning of, 142–43
    baselines for, 138, 237, 327
    duplicating, 128–29
    entering, 242
    individually positioning, 140
    playback settings, 333
Expressions library, 125, 138, 244
Extract Parts dialog box, 161, 162
extracting parts. See parts, extracting

F

Fast-Forward button, 43
fermata, 38
File menu, 5

Extract Parts, 159–72, 301
Launch Window
   Default Document, 4–5, 86
   Exercise Wizard, 353
   QuickStart Videos, 15
   Setup Wizard, 18–19, 32
   SmartMusic Wizard, 357
Load Library, 146, 178, 217–18
New
   Default Document, 4, 86, 88, 191
   Document From Template, 352
   Document with Setup Wizard, 32,
      104, 123–24, 166, 227, 298
Open, 343, 344, 345
Page Setup, 159, 290
Print, 28, 45, 61, 84, 100, 118, 223
Print Parts, 159–62
Save, 28
Save As, 46, 124, 160, 259, 261, 262–63,
   271, 299, 342, 344
Save Library, 145–46
Save Special
   Save As Audio File, 148
file names, 160
file organization and management, 124,
   298, 307
files, exporting, 341
   Finale files as Standard MIDI files, 342
   Finale files into word processors and
      page layout software, 347–48,
      358
   graphics from Finale to other
      programs, 348–49
   page portions, 349
files, importing, 341
   graphic files into Finale, 347–48
   scanned files, 132–33
files, sharing between Mac and Windows,
   341–42
final barline, 129
Finale book files, 363–64
Finale courses, 361
Finale Installation & Tutorials guide, 3, 4,
   13, 27, 48, 79, 115
Finale mailing lists, 361
Finale NotePad, 336, 356
Finale Performance Assessment, 356–57
Finale print documentation, 13
Finale Quick Reference Card, 66
Finale support, 359–62
Finale upgrades, 359
Finale User Manual, 13–15, 67, 79, 115,
   197, 353
Finale Web Site, 360
FinaleScript, 260–61
FinaleScript Editor dialog box, 260, 261
Fine marking, 112–13
fingering charts, 357
fingerings, entering, 217
Fit Music dialog box, 25, 39, 59–60, 97,
   153, 202–3, 330
Fixed Split Point dialog box, 105
folder options, 192
Font dialog box, 57
fonts, choosing, 57–58, 126, 157–58,
   312–13

foot pedal, controlling tempo with, 89,
   93–95, 106, 107
footers, entering, 220–21
Frame Attributes dialog box, 44, 117, 332

G
Garritan Personal Orchestra, 147
gathered rests. *See* rests, gathered
General MIDI, 79, 90, 114, 145
   exotic instruments and, 304
   Instruments library, 178, 217
   percussion note assignments, 174, 303
Glissando shape, 215
Global Staff Attributes plug-in, 129–30
grace notes
   across the barline, 318–19
   entering, 37, 66
   slashed flags for, 66
graphic files, 347–48
Graphics menu
   Export Pages, 348
   Export Selection, 349
   Place Graphic, 348
Graphics tool, 348, 349
Group Attributes dialog box, 300, 304
grouping measures. *See* measures,
   grouping
groups, creating and editing, 301, 304–5
Guitar Bend shape, 215
guitar fretboards, 53–54
guitar tablature notation, 262–63

H
hairpins. *See* crescendo marks
Hand Grabber tool, 11, 25, 43, 58
Hand Grabber tool (Shape Designer), 313
Handle Positioning dialog box, 326
handles
   accent, 244
   articulation, 38–39, 279–80, 326
   beam, 204
   chord symbol, 279
   crescendo, 110, 144
   expression, 138
   fretboard, 54
   measure, 76
   measure number, 34
   note-mover, 106
   page number, 332
   repeat sign, 112, 130–31
   slur, 144, 216
   staff, 53–54, 97–98, 173, 185, 209, 304,
      306, 331
   system, 257, 259
   text, 44, 45, 58, 158, 220, 257–58
   tuplet, 67
Harmon Mute, 283
harmony, in Simple Entry, 37
headers, entering, 186
Help menu, 5, 13–15, 358, 360
   How To Use the User Manual, 14
   Index, 14
   Jazz Character Map, 244–46, 249
   Keyboard Shortcuts, 24
   QuickStart Videos, 15, 360
   Table of Contents, 14

Home key, 68–69, 70
Home Position, 12, 40
horizontal scroll bar, 11–12, 22
"How Many Measures?" dialog box, 124
"How Many Times?" dialog box, 23, 318
Human Playback
   reverb in, 333–34
   selecting style, 218–19, 232
   turning off, 98–99, 114–15
Human Playback Preferences dialog box,
   27, 333–34
HyperScribe, 85–100
   advantages of, 86
   Auto Save and, 192
   editing performance with MIDI tool,
      115
   entering transposed notes onto
      transposed staves, 133
   limitations of, 96
   tuplets and, 232
   with two hands, 103–19
HyperScribe menu
   Beat Source
      Playback and/or Click, 90–91, 105
      Tap, 93, 105
   HyperScribe Options, 91
   Record Mode
      Record into One Staff, 91
      Split into two Staves, 105
HyperScribe tool, 90, 93, 94, 107

I
Import MIDI File Options dialog box, 343
importing files. *See* files, importing
improvisation, 227
InDesign, 348
Index (online help), 14
installing Finale, 4
Instrument List window, 114, 145–46,
   178–79, 218–19, 239–40, 298–99,
   305, 334, 342
instrument name, adding, 43–45, 58
instrument ranges, checking, 151–52, 286
instrumentation
   choosing, in Setup Wizard, 19, 64, 104,
      123, 166, 193
   choosing, with score template, 297–99
   saving for repeated use, 123
Internet
   Finale online courses, 361
   MIDI files on, 343–44
   tech support, 360–61
iTunes, 148

J
jazz charts, 225–64
Jazz Chord font, 228, 249, 250–52
Jazz Default Fonts, 228
Jazz Font, 227–28
   articulations in, 242–43
Jazz Text font, 228, 249
   expressions in, 244–46
Jump to Measure box, 12, 68, 70, 89, 94
justification setting, 230

K

key commands, 3, 24
  Simple Entry navigation, 36
  Speedy Entry navigation, 197–98
key signature
  changing, 45–46, 87
  choosing, in Setup Wizard, 19, 48, 104, 166
  as guideposts, 131
  minor, 193–94
Key Signature dialog box, 46, 87
Key Signature tool, 45–46, 87
keyboard note entry, 17–29
keyboard terminology, 3–4
Kodaly notation, 352–53

L

landscape-format scores, printing, 290
large ensemble scores, extracting parts for, 162
large ensembles arrangements, creating, 267–90
Launch Window, 4–5
  Exercise Wizard, 353
  Program Options, 191
  Scanning, 132
  Setup Wizard, 18–19, 32, 227–28
  SmartMusic Wizard, 357
  Template, 352
launching Finale, 4
Layer Options dialog box, 318
layers, 169–71
  adding invisible rests in, 207–8
  assigning different voices for, 217–18
  copying music between, 279–80
  cross-staff notes in, 204–7
  cue notes and, 148–50
  disabling playback, 239–40
  entering music by, 198–201
  features and drawbacks of, 194–96
  hiding notes or rests in, 196
  for percussion parts, 173–75
  piano reductions and, 163
  selecting timbres for, 178–79
  setting up, 195
lead sheets, 226, 259
libraries, 145–47, 192, 307, 365–66
  articulation, 217
  building, 246
  chord suffixes, 41, 249, 250, 252–53
  customizable settings in, 215
  Expressions, 125, 138, 244–46
  font, 302
  General MIDI Instruments, 178, 217–18
Line tool (Shape Designer), 316
locked systems, 153, 202–3
  hiding, 26
Lowest Fret dialog box, 262–63
lyrics
  adjusting location of, 185
  baselines for, 57
  changing size of, 57
  cloning, 182–83
  editing, 56, 184
  entering, 47–62, 55–56, 179–82
  entering with Option or Alt key, 181

  erasing, 184
  fonts for, 57–58
  moving location of, 56–57
  using word processors for, 179
Lyrics menu
  Adjust Syllables, 181
  Click Assignment, 180–81, 183, 185
  Clone Lyric, 182–83
  Edit Lyrics, 179
  Specify Current Lyric, 180–81, 182–83, 185
  Type Into Score, 55–56
Lyrics tool, 55, 179, 182, 185

M

Mac OS
  contextual menus in, 7, 44, 341
  key commands for, 3
  launching Finale in, 4
  layer handling in, 170–71
  Message Bar in, 6
  navigation commands, 36
  Plug-ins menu icon, 13
  Print dialog box in, 223
  shortcut command, 32
  shortcut commands, 9, 10, 14, 22, 25, 36, 39, 41, 44, 48, 96, 98, 112, 126, 131, 153, 158, 163, 166, 202, 208, 243, 255, 257, 271
  tool display in, 5
Maestro font, 259
Main Tool Palette, 5–7
  hiding, 6
  moving, 40
  Simple Entry, 20
maintenance upgrades, 359
MakeMusic programs, 356
marcato accent, 137
margin guides, showing, 330–31
margins
  page, 81–82, 152, 154–57, 254–55, 329
  system, 155–57, 203, 256
Mass Edit menu
  Apply SmartFind and Paint, 109
  Change
    Note Size, 241
    Noteheads, 240–41
  Clear Items, 92, 184
  Copy Entry Items, 236, 272, 276, 285, 317, 325
  Copy Everything, 288, 316
  Copy Measure Items, 236, 275, 281
  Fit Music, 25, 39, 153, 202–3, 330
  Lock Systems, 203
  Move/Copy Layers, 279
  Music Spacing
    Apply Note Spacing, 80, 110, 137, 208, 253–54
  Rebeam
    Rebeam to Time Signature, 321
  Retranscribe, 347
  Set SmartFind Source Region, 109
  Transpose, 134, 135, 151, 172, 272, 276, 354–55
  Unlock Systems, 203

Utilities
  Check Elapsed Time, 143
  Explode Music, 274–75
Mass Edit tool, 23, 39, 49–51, 60, 67–68, 80, 92, 97, 109, 130, 134, 135, 136, 137, 143, 148, 151, 153, 163, 172–73, 175, 184, 193, 202, 204, 206, 208, 222, 232, 235–37, 240, 262, 271, 272, 275, 276, 278–81, 285, 286–89, 316, 321, 324, 325, 330, 332, 346, 353, 354
Mass Mover tool, 193
Measure-Attached Expressions, 129, 215
  copying from document to document, 272
  piano reductions and, 163
Measure Attributes dialog box, 176, 229, 310
Measure box, 12
Measure Expression Assignment dialog box, 42, 75, 110–11, 127–28, 139, 140, 244, 259, 262
Measure Items dialog box, 317
Measure menu
  Add, 124, 196, 307
  Delete, 27, 39, 51
  Insert, 284
  Measure Numbers
    Edit Regions, 33, 88–89, 118, 229, 262, 310–11
  Multimeasure Rests
    Create, 81
Measure Number dialog box, 33–34, 88–89, 118, 310
measure numbers
  boxing, 76
  displaying, 33–34, 48, 64, 105, 117–18, 196, 229, 310–11
  multiple sets, 88–89
  positioning, 34, 48
  for repeated measures, 236–37
Measure tool, 26, 33, 39, 45, 48, 64, 70, 76, 81, 88, 105, 110, 118, 124, 176, 196, 207, 210, 262, 284, 310
  contextual menu, 229, 271–72, 307
measurement units, 125, 154, 160–61, 196, 208
measures
  adding, 64–65, 284, 307
  advancing to specific, 68
  deleting extra, 26–27, 39, 51, 97, 176, 288
  grouping, 26, 59–60, 81, 97, 117, 153, 184–85
  making extra space for, 207–8
  moving single, 60, 97
menus, 4, 5. *See also specific menus*
  format for selecting, 51
  shortcut commands in, 8–9
Message Bar, 6–7, 208
  turning off, 191
Metatools
  articulations, 71–73, 137–38, 217, 242–43, 325–26
  chord symbols, 247–48
  clef symbols, 320

Explode Music, 274–75, 278–79, 280, 286–87
expressions, 74, 141
programming, 135–36
staff styles, 233–34, 275
transposition, 151–52, 172–73
types of, 136
meter. *See* time signature
metronome, real-time entry with, 89–92
metronome marks. *See* tempo indications
MiBAC Jazz Rhythm Section Generator plug-in, 288–90
Microsoft Word, 348
MIDI channel assignments, changing, 146, 283
MIDI controllers, 89. *See also* MIDI keyboard
MIDI entry, 47–62, 247
MIDI files, 342–45
sources of, 343–44
transcribing, 345–47
translating and quantizing, 344–45
MIDI keyboard
for chord symbol entry, 52, 249
General MIDI-compatible, 79
multitimbral, 78–80, 90, 146, 334
for percussion entry, 174, 303
real-time entry with, 89–92
setup, 13, 27, 48
MIDI menu, 5, 13
MIDI menu (Mac)
Internal Speaker Playback
SmartMusic SoftSynth Playback, 80
MIDI Setup, 146
MIDI menu (Windows)
MIDI Settings, 147
MIDI note, controlling tempo with, 93–95
MIDI sequencers, 116, 342
MIDI tool, 115
MIDI Tool dialog box, 115
MIDI Tool menu
Key Velocities, 115
Set To, 115
MIDI velocity numbers, 217
mixed-font tempo indications, creating, 311–14
monitor sizes, 9–10, 305
More Quantization Settings dialog box, 96
mouse, 2-button, 4, 7
moving around the score, 11–12
MP3 file format, 148
multimeasure rests. *See* rests, gathered
"Musette," 103–19

N

Native Instruments Kontakt, 147
notation entry options, 20, 48–49, 85–86, 96, 133, 173–74, 316. *See also* HyperScribe; Simple Entry; Speedy Entry
notation software, goal of, 3
Note-Attached Expressions, 138, 141, 149
Note-Attached Shapes, 215
Note Mover menu
Delete After Merge, 106, 280
Note Mover tool, 106, 280

Note Out of Range dialog box, 151, 286
Note Position tool, 208, 209, 210, 211–12, 213–14, 327
note size, changing, 241
noteheads, changing, 240–41, 302–3
Number Repeated Measures plug-in, 236–37

O

octaves
changing, 36
creating instant, 135–36
optimization, 327–31
Options menu, 5, 13
Click and Countoff, 90
Display in Concert Pitch, 272, 277, 285, 335
Document Options, 150, 195, 196, 222, 307
Fonts, 247
Grace Notes, 66
Layers, 169–70, 238–39
Music Spacing, 253–54
Time Signatures, 228–29
Tuplets, 65
Measurement Units, 125
MIDI Setup (Windows), 80
Page Format
Parts, 160
Score, 328
Pickup Measure, 35
Program Options, 28, 191
Quantization Settings, 91, 94, 96, 105, 347
Show Active Layer Only, 206, 240, 321, 332
orchestral music, 291–337
orchestration, changing, 276

P

Page Format for Parts dialog box, 160–61
page layout, 152–54, 254–59
adjusting, 25–27, 80–82, 97, 117, 202–14
optimizing, 327–31
page layout icons, hiding, 26
Page Layout menu
Fit Music, 25, 26, 59–60, 81, 97, 117, 184, 203
Optimize Staff Systems, 330
Page Margins
Edit Page Margins, 154, 254–55, 255, 329
Page Size, 61
Redefine Pages
All Pages, 161, 328–29
Space Systems Evenly, 155, 157, 186, 203, 255, 256–57, 259
Systems
Edit Margins, 155, 256, 257, 329–30
Edit System Margins, 203
page layout software, importing Finale files to, 347–48, 358
Page Layout tool, 25, 39, 59–60, 61, 81–82, 97, 117, 154, 186, 203, 254–55, 259, 328, 329, 330

page margins, editing, 81–82, 152, 154–57, 254–55, 329
page numbers
adding, 116–17, 332
positioning, 258, 332
Page Options dialog box, 161–62
page orientation, choosing, 18, 290
Page Reduction Options (printer), 62
Page Setup dialog box, 159, 290
page size
adjusting with Resize tool, 61–62, 152–53
changing, 61, 184–85, 202
choosing, in Setup Wizard, 18
Page Size dialog box, 61
page turns, 335
Page View, 8–9
adding text elements in, 43–45, 83
adjusting layout in, 25–27, 53, 97–98, 152–54
adjusting repeat markings in, 112
entering notation in, 21
hiding staves in, 304
manual positioning in, 202–14
opening initial layout in, 191
positioning staves in, 328–31
scaling percentages for, 9–11, 58–59
special part extraction in, 159–62
PageMaker, 348
Palettes and Backgrounds options, 193
Palettes dialog box, 193
paper size. *See* page size
parts, extracting, 159–62, 273, 352, 366
groups and, 301
for large or long works, 335–36
two parts from one staff, 336
parts, simplifying, 351
paste. *See* copy and paste; Mass Edit Tool
patch changes, expressions for, 281–83
Patterson Beams, 331–32
Patterson Beams dialog box, 222
Patterson plug-ins, 221–22
Percussion Map Designer dialog box, 175, 303
Percussion Map Selection dialog box, 175, 302
percussion notation, 173–76, 235, 301–3
performance assessment, 356–57
performance time, determining, 143
Petrushka, 291–337
phrase marks, entering, 108, 215
piano part, creating, 103–19
piano part, two-staff, 189–224
piano reductions, 163, 354
pickup measure, creating, 32–33, 35, 167
pickup notes, adjusting position of, 45
PICT files, 348
playback
2nd Time Only, 282–84
adjusting style, 114–15
changing instruments for, 178–79
changing tempos for, 98–99
chord symbols, 251
disabling, 150
disabling a layer's, 239–40
exporting to audio file, 148
expressions and articulations in, 333

for proof listening, 27, 43, 51, 334
repeats and *D.C. al Fine* markings in, 113
setting timbres for, 78–80, 114
using external device for, 146
Playback and/or Click dialog box, 90–91
Playback Controls window, 51
  Human Playback Style, 99, 114–15, 218–19, 232
  moving, 43
  Play, 27, 79, 99
  Save File, 334
  Tempo, 219
playback files, 334
Plug-ins menu, 5, 13
  Expressions
    Create Tempo Markings, 141–43
  Measures
    Number Repeated Measures, 236–37
  Miscellaneous
    Change Fonts, 57–58
    FinaleScript Palette, 260, 261
  New Plug-Ins for 2005
    Apply Human Playback, 232
  Note, Beam, and Rest Editing
    Cautionary Accidentals, 136
    Patterson Plug-ins Lite, 221–22, 331–32
  Scoring and Arranging
    Add Cue Notes, 148
    Band-in-a-Box Auto-Harmonizing, 276, 285–87
    Check Range, 151, 286
    Drum Groove, 238
    Global Staff Attributes, 129–30
    MiBAC Jazz Rhythm Section Generator, 289
    Piano Reduction, 163
  TG Tools, 204, 221
    Cross Staff, 206, 221
    Easy Tremolos, 321–22
    Process Extracted Parts, 273, 336
polyphony. *See* layers; voices
Position Measure Number dialog box, 34, 311
practice exercises, creating, 352
Print dialog box, 223
Printer Page Setup window, 62
Printer Setup dialog box. *See* Page Setup dialog box
printing, 28, 45, 61, 84, 100, 118
  color, 223
  duplex, 335
  landscape-format scores, 290
  multiple copies, 29
  paper size and, 159
PrintMusic, 356
Process Extracted Parts plug-in, 273, 336
Program Options dialog box, 28, 191–94
Program Options menu, 191
  Palettes and Backgrounds, 193
programs, switching between, 14

Q

Quantization level, 91, 105, 344–45
  resetting, 94, 96, 343

Quantization Settings dialog box, 91, 94, 96, 105, 347
QuarkXpress, 348
QuickStart Videos, 15, 353, 360

R

readiness exercises, creating, 352
real-time entry, 86. *See also* HyperScribe
Record Mode, setting, 91
Redraw Screen, 12, 41, 112
Refresh Screen, 91
rehearsal letters and numbers
  boxing, 125–28, 244–45, 311
  as guideposts, 131
reorchestration, 351–52
Repeat menu
  Create First and Second Ending, 112, 129, 177
  Create Forward Repeat Bar, 129, 176
  Create Simple Repeat, 111, 230, 272
Repeat Selection dialog box, 76, 78, 112, 113, 230, 259
repeat signs
  entering, 111–12, 129, 176–77, 230
  as guideposts, 131
  hiding in other staves, 177
Repeat tool, 76–78, 111, 112, 113, 129, 130–31, 176, 230, 272
  contextual menu, 111–12, 176–77
repeats, one-bar, 241–42
Repitch tool, 273–74, 287, 324–25
Resize Notehead dialog box, 152
Resize Page dialog box, 61, 184, 254
Resize tool, 61–62, 152, 153, 162, 184, 254, 329
  contextual menu, 202, 213
Respace Staves dialog box, 125
rests
  adding invisible, 207–8
  adjusting floating, 195, 239
  automatic entry of, 22
  beams and, 239
  chord slashes and, 233
  entering in Simple Entry, 22, 49, 96
  hiding, 196, 200–201, 318–19
  minimizing, 95–96
  repositioning, 195, 206–7, 212, 318, 327
rests, gathered, 81
  breaking for performance-related marks, 126
retranscribing, 346–47
Return/Enter key, Simple Entry with, 34–35
reverb, 333–34
Rewind button, 43
rhythm parts, creating, 352
Rhythm Section Generator, 288–90
rhythm-section sketch, 226–59
Rhythmic Notation, 234, 352
Right Arrow key, nudging notes with, 208–9, 212
rit. on D.C. mark, 114
ritard mark, 114
rulers, 185, 191, 258, 330–31, 332

S

s-curves, 216
sans-serif fonts, 58
Save Library dialog box, 146
saving, 28, 64, 207
  automatically, 28, 192
  copies in different keys, 45–46
  options, 192
Scale View dialog box, 11
scaling view percentage, 9–11, 58–59, 81, 97–98, 112, 131
scanners, 131
scanning, 131–35, 343, 347
  limitations of, 134–35
Score Order popup menu, 166, 299
score size. *See* page size
scripts, creating, 260–61
scroll bars, 11–12. *See also* horizontal scroll bar; vertical scroll bar
Scroll View, 8–9
  advancing to specific measures in, 68
  defining staff sets in, 305
  inputting Smart Shapes in, 144
  for lyrics entry, 55–56
  moving around in, 11–12, 89
  opening initial layout in, 191
  Simple Entry in, 21–22
Secondary Beam Break tool, 324
Select Region dialog box, 27, 288
Selection tool, 7, 41, 53, 67, 71, 110, 149
  contextual menu, 83, 87, 129, 140, 249
  displaying handles with, 39
Selection tool (Shape Designer), 313, 315–16
serif fonts, 58
Setup Wizard, 18–19, 32, 48, 64, 104, 123–24, 145, 157–58, 166, 173, 193–94, 227–28
Shape Designer dialog box, 312–14, 315
Shape Designer menu
  Group, 314, 316
  Select Font, 312–13
  Show
    Grid, 312, 315–16
  Ungroup, 315
Shape Expression Designer dialog box, 312, 314, 315
  Playback tab, 314
Shift-click command, 39
Shift key, Metatools and, 136
shortcut commands, 8–9, 10, 14, 22, 24, 25, 32, 36, 39, 41, 44, 48, 58, 66, 96, 98, 112, 126, 131, 153, 158, 163, 166, 202, 208, 243, 255, 257, 271. *See also* Metatools
shout chorus, 284–87
Simple Entry, 278
  for cleaning up HyperScribe, 92
  compared with HyperScribe, 96
  contextual menu, 72–73, 74
  creating new measures in, 65
  editing in, 24, 346
  entering articulations with, 72–73, 133
  entering harmony in, 37
  hiding notes or rests in, 196
  navigation commands, 36

repositioning rests in, 195
using computer keyboard, 20–24, 34–38, 68
using MIDI keyboard, 48–51
using Return/Enter key, 34–35
Simple Entry caret, 21, 69
Simple Entry Options dialog box, 65
Simple Entry Palette, 20, 24
   Dot tool, 49
   Eraser tool, 22
   note values, 20–21, 22, 24, 34, 50
   Repitch tool, 273–74, 287, 324–25
   Tie tool, 135, 210
   Triplet tool, 35
Simple Entry Rest Palette, 150, 173
Simple Entry tool, 20–24, 21, 48–49, 50, 65, 66, 73, 74, 150, 173
Simple Entry Tuplet Definition dialog box, 67
"Simple Gifts," 165–87
Simple menu
   Simple Edit Commands, 24
      Modify Entry, 66
   Simple Entry Options, 21, 22, 65, 173
   Use MIDI Device for Input, 48
Slash Notation, 227, 232–35, 275, 352
Slur tool, 108, 144, 215, 216, 243
Slur tool (Shape Designer), 313
slurs
   adding with SmartFind and Paste, 109
   entering, 24, 108, 144, 243–44, 275
   manually adjusting, 144
   piano reductions and, 163
small ensemble arrangements, creating, 121–64
Smart Cue Notes plug-in, 336
Smart Page Turns plug-in, 335
Smart Shape palette, 108, 215, 243
   Crescendo tool, 109–10, 144, 215, 243
   Dashed Curve tool, 108, 215
   Dashed Line tool, 114
   Slur tool, 108, 144, 215, 216
Smart Shapes, 157, 163, 242
   expansion/contraction of, 110
   inputting in Scroll View, 144
Smart Shapes (Assigned to Measures), 317
SmartFind and Paint, 109
SmartMusic Accompaniment Wizard, 357
SmartMusic SoftSynth Playback, 80, 145
SmartScore, 131
SmartScore Lite, 131–33
snare and bass drum parts, 173–76
soft accent symbol, 326
SoftSynth Settings dialog box, 147
software synthesizers and samplers, routing to, 146–47
SoundFonts, 145, 148, 217
Space Systems Evenly dialog box, 186, 203, 256, 259
spacing
   applying, 137
   automatic, 12, 25
      turning off, 202
   chord symbols and, 254
   manual, 45, 80–82
Special Tools palette, 204

Beam Angle tool, 204, 206, 210, 212
Beam Break tool, 324
Beam Extension tool, 322
Note Position tool, 208, 209, 210, 211–12, 213–14, 327
Stem Direction tool, 204, 209–10
Specify Current Lyric dialog box, 180
Specify Initial Tempo Marking, 228
Speedy Entry, 197–201, 206–8, 210–14, 275, 316
   dragging notes in, 208
   editing in, 198–99, 346
   hiding notes or rests in, 196, 200–201
   repositioning notes in, 208–10, 327
   repositioning rests in, 195, 212
Speedy Entry menu
   Check for Extra Notes, 318, 319
   Jump To Next Measure, 318
Speedy Entry tool, 197, 322–23
split point, choosing, 105–6, 163
staccato marks, 214–15, 243, 333
Staff Attributes dialog box, 83, 167–68, 169, 175, 177, 228, 299–302, 319
Staff List dialog box, 128, 139–40, 141, 230–31
Staff Lists, copying from document to document, 272
Staff menu, 6
   Add Group and Bracket, 304–5
   Apply Staff Styles, 233–34
   Clear Staff Styles, 288–89
   Define Staff Styles, 241
   Edit Group Attributes, 304
   Edit Staff Attributes, 167, 168, 228, 299–300
   New Staves, 304
   New Staves (with Setup Wizard), 173, 262
   Respace Staves, 125
   Show Staff Style Names, 234
staff names
   General MIDI sounds and, 145
   hiding, 83, 228, 300
Staff Selection Expression dialog box, 75
staff sets, creating, 305–6
Staff Stem Settings dialog box, 302
Staff Style Optimization dialog box, 330
Staff Styles, 208, 246, 275, 352
   copying, 281
   entering with Metatools, 233–34
   Slash Notation, 232–35
   transposition with, 277–78
Staff Styles dialog box, 241, 277
staff systems
   adjusting layout, 155–57, 186, 256–57, 259
   beginning new, 229
   ending brackets on, 130
   fitting on page, 81
   indenting, 81–82, 257
   moving, 82
   optimizing, 328–31
Staff tool, 6, 53, 97, 125, 167–68, 173, 175, 177, 185, 228, 233–34, 236, 241, 259, 275, 288–89, 301, 304, 319, 331

contextual menu, 167, 168, 208, 242, 277, 299
staffs, choosing, in Setup Wizard, 32, 48
Standard MIDI File format, 342
Startup Action menu, 191
staves, multiple
   adding manually, 227–28, 304
   adjusting space of, 185, 330–31
   choosing, in Setup Wizard, 19
   customizing, 167–68
   fitting on one page, 185
   respacing, 125
   saving as separating tracks in MIDI format, 342–43
staves, one-line, 168, 301–2
staves, percussion, 173. See also percussion notation
Stem Direction tool, 204, 209–10
stems
   beam angle and, 206
   changing direction of, 149–50, 209–10, 235, 302
   changing length of, 196, 239
   freezing, 169–70, 173
   separating from beams in tremolos, 322
step entry, 48–51, 86
stick notation, 352–53
Straight Mute, 283
students' uses for Finale, 355–56
submenus, 4
subtitle, adding, 157–58
Suffix Keynumber Offsets, 251
suffixes, chord, 41, 248–49, 250–54
suspended cymbal part, 175–76
sustain pedal. See foot pedal
syllable breaks, entering, 56
system locks, 26, 153, 202–3
system margins, 155–57, 203, 256

T
TAB key, using, 18
TAB Slide shape, 215
tablature, 262–63
Tap Source dialog box, 93, 105
Teachnology Institute for Music Educators, 361
tech support, 360–61
templates, 192, 271, 352–53, 358, 365–66
   checklist for, 306–7
   editing, 306
   locking, 307
   setting up, 298–307
tempo
   changing for playback, 98–99, 219
   controlling in HyperScribe, 89–90, 93–95
Tempo Adjustment dialog box, 99
tempo indications, creating with Expression tool, 141–43, 311–14
Tempo tool (Mac), 99
tenuto mark, 243
text
   alignment, 44
   changing size, 43–44, 57, 83, 116, 157–58

dragging and editing, 7
formatting, 257–58
inserts, 117
page, 157–58
text blocks. *See also specific types*
  centering, 158
  creating and editing, 220–21, 258,
    260–61
  deleting, 328
Text Expression Designer dialog box, 75,
    126–27, 281–83, 311, 314–16
  Measure Positioning tab, 282
  Playback tab, 114, 217, 219, 282, 333
text expressions
  adding, 75, 272
  mixed fonts in, 314–16
  tempo in, 219
Text menu
  Alignment
    Center Horizontally, 158
  Character Settings, 157
  Font, 142
  Frame Attributes, 220–21
  Inserts, 117
  Size, 44, 83, 116, 257, 311
    Fixed Size, 157, 158
    Other, 220
  Style, 116, 126, 311
Text Repeat Assignment dialog box,
    76–77, 113, 230–31
Text tool, 43–45, 58, 83, 98, 116–17, 157,
    186, 220, 257, 258, 315, 328
  contextual menu, 44, 116–17, 332
Text tool (Shape Designer), 312
TG Tools plug-in, 204, 206, 221, 273,
    321–22, 336
theory class assignments, 356
"There Are Tool Many Beats in This
    Measure" dialog box, 198, 318
third party products, 362
"Three Blind Mice," 47–62
Tie tool, 135, 210
ties
  entering across barline, 69–70, 198
  entering in Simple Entry, 24, 36, 38
  entering in Speedy Entry, 198
TIFF files, 131–32, 348
timbre, setting, 78–80
time signature
  beaming and, 308–10, 320–21
  changing, 307–8
  choosing, in Setup Wizard, 19, 32, 48,
    104, 123, 166, 193
  as guideposts, 131
  in Jazz font, 228–29
Time Signature dialog box, 308–10
Time Signature tool, 87, 307–8, 320
  contextual menu, 308, 310
titles
  adding more space for, 256
  custom font size for, 220, 257
  deleting, 328
  entering in Setup Wizard, 18, 32, 64,
    104, 123
  entering with Text tool, 58, 83, 98, 116
  two on one page, 98

Toast, 148
tool palettes, 5–6, 242. *See also specific
    palettes*
tools, 6–7, 13. *See also specific tools*
Tools menu, 5, 13. *See also* Smart Shape
    palette; Special Tools palette
  Advanced Tools
    Graphics Tool, 348, 349
    MIDI tool, 115
    Note Mover, 106
    Special Tools, 204, 208
    Tempo (Windows), 99
  Articulation tool, 38
  Smart Shape, 108
transcribing
  melodies, 355
  MIDI files, 345–47
translating MIDI files, 344–45
Transposition dialog box, 135, 151, 172,
    355
transpositions
  diatonic, 354–55
  with HyperScribe, 133
  with Mass Edit tool, 151–52, 172
  Metatools for, 151–52, 172–73
  scanned documents and, 134
  with Setup Wizard, 124
  with Staff Styles, 277–78
tremolos, entering, 321–22
Triplet tool, 35
triplets. *See also* tuplets
  entering, 35, 96
  quantization settings and, 94
"Trumpet Voluntary," 63–84
Tuplet Definition dialog box, 322–24
Tuplet tool, 65, 323
tuplets
  defining positioning of, 65, 322–24
  entering, 35, 66–67, 96
  moving, 67
  swing playback and, 232

U

Undo command, 36
unisons, Explode Music and, 275
Unknown Chord Suffix dialog box, 249
user manual, 13–15

V

velocity, 115, 217, 281–83, 333
vendor support, 361
vertical scroll bar, 11
View menu, 5, 8–12
  Hide Page Layout Icons, 26
  Home Position, 12, 40, 55–56, 68–69, 70
  Page View, 8–9, 25, 43–45, 58–59, 61–62,
    81, 83, 97, 112, 152, 184, 254,
    348, 349
  Program Staff Sets, 305–6
  Redraw Screen, 12, 41, 112
  Scale View to, 9–11, 25, 81, 97–98, 131,
    271, 305
  Scroll View, 8–9, 11–12, 21–22, 39, 40,
    55–56, 271, 305
  Select Staff Set, 318
    All Staves, 306

shortcut commands in, 9
Show Active Layer Only, 241
Show Grid, 330
Show Margins, 330–31
Show Rulers, 185, 258, 330–31, 332
view percentage, 9–11, 58–59, 81, 97–98,
    112, 131
vocal score with percussion, 165–87
voice tech support, 361
voices, features and drawbacks of, 194–96

W

Waiting for Input box, 73, 74
warm-up exercises, creating, 352
WAV file format, 148
Window menu, 5, 134
  Instrument List, 79, 114, 145, 218, 239,
    305, 334, 342
  Instruments, 178
  Main Tool Palette, 6
  Playback Controls, 27, 99
  Simple Entry Palette, 20
Windows
  contextual menus in, 7, 44, 341
  key commands for, 3
  launching Finale in, 4
  layer handling in, 170–71
  Message Bar in, 6
  navigation commands, 36
  Print dialog box in, 223
  shortcut commands, 9, 10, 14, 22, 25,
    32, 36, 39, 41, 44, 48, 96, 98, 112,
    126, 131, 153, 158, 163, 166, 202,
    208, 243, 255, 257, 271
  tool display in, 5
Windows Metafile, 348
word processors
  for creating lyrics, 179
  importing Finale files to, 347–48, 358
WordPerfect, 348
www.Berkleemusic.com, 361
www.finalebook.com, 363–66
www.finaleforum.com, 362
www.finalemusic.com, 359, 360
www.makemusic.com, 356
www.musicprep.com/coda, 36, 362
www.ti-me.org, 361

Z

Zoom tool, 209, 258, 330